Theodore Dreiser

Theodore Dreiser, May 1938
(from a photograph by Robert H. Elias)

Theodore Dreiser

APOSTLE OF NATURE

EMENDED EDITION WITH
A SURVEY OF RESEARCH AND CRITICISM

ROBERT H. ELIAS

Cornell Paperbacks
CORNELL UNIVERSITY PRESS
ITHACA AND LONDON

To H. P.

Emended edition, 1970
First printing, Cornell Paperbacks, 1970

International Standard Book Number 0-8014-9112-6
Library of Congress Catalog Card Number 70-129563

PRINTED IN THE UNITED STATES OF AMERICA
BY VAIL-BALLOU PRESS, INC.

Introductory Note, 1970

ALMOST since the day on which page proofs of the original edition of this book were returned to the printer, I have wanted to make corrections of errors that had escaped my final check and to rewrite passages that subsequent research by me and others showed to be in need of modification. This new edition has enabled me to do that and thereby, I hope, to strengthen the book's reliability. I have, for example, supplanted Hannah and Hogg's with Chapin and Gore's, delayed Dreiser's arrival in Chicago a whole year, transferred him from a philosophy class at Indiana University to one in "philology," removed Thomas B. Reed temporarily from the Speakership of the House of Representatives, and given Greenwood Lake back to New Jersey. I have also corrected the dates affixed to cases related to the writing of *An American Tragedy*, exchanged Anastas Mikoyan for Georgi Tchicherin among the men Dreiser interviewed in the Soviet Union, and slightly revised the account of Dreiser's hasty departure from Toronto in 1942 and of his church attendance in 1945. Somewhat more extensively, I have rewritten the paragraphs that concern the publication of Dreiser's earliest fiction, both the short stories and *Sister Carrie*, and eliminated inaccuracies in the chronology of his wanderings during 1901 and 1902. Finally, I have restored a few proper names that were deleted at the very last moment to protect the reputations of persons still living. Since the present edition is intended, in part, to make available a work that is referred to by its successors, I have done what I could to maintain the validity of their citations by keeping changes in pagination to an absolute minimum.

Introductory Note

To enhance the usefulness of this book I have, by courtesy of the Duke University Press, provided an appendix containing my survey of research and criticism in Jackson R. Bryer's *Fifteen Modern American Authors: A Survey of Research and Criticism* (Durham, N.C., 1969), slightly enlarged to include publications that reached me too late for discussion in that volume. Although the survey is selective and personal, it should make evident that the amount of important work that scholars and critics have devoted to Dreiser is formidable and that my own contribution is essentially to establish a point of departure for readers who wish to go from primary to secondary sources.

Throughout the past two decades I have benefited from the help of many who knew Dreiser and many who studied or wrote about him. Most of these I have mentioned in my notes and in my introduction to *Letters of Theodore Dreiser* (Philadelphia, 1959). But I would here like specifically to acknowledge the assistance I have received from W. A. Swanberg, Ellen Moers, and Donald Pizer, who have always generously shared their discoveries with me, even before publication, and from Mrs. Neda M. Westlake, curator of the rare-book collection at the University of Pennsylvania, without whose expert knowledge and tireless encouragement work on Dreiser would be seriously handicapped.

ROBERT H. ELIAS

Ithaca, New York
September 1970

From the Preface of 1948

THEODORE DREISER is a challenging figure. Arguing in the role of a determinist on the one hand that men are helpless, and assuming in the role of social reformer on the other hand that men can act and choose, he appears to have been the victim of contradictions that any high-school graduate should know enough to avoid. Yet it is impossible to follow Dreiser's career without realizing that he cannot be so easily dismissed. He cannot be dismissed as a confused genius; he cannot be dismissed as a foggy giant; he cannot be dismissed as a man who, despite a sophomoric philosophy, wrote great novels.

Whether he is a genius or a giant, and whether he wrote great novels, the present book does not attempt to decide. This is neither a study in æsthetics nor a full-length biography of the kind that some day must be written — numerous writings of his are not even mentioned. The interest here is primarily to investigate the apparent contradictions, trace their development, and interpret them in relation to Dreiser's career. How did the sensitive son of an ardently Catholic father come to be the Dreiser who wrote a novel that was labeled as lewd and profane? How did the author of The "Genius" come to be the author of An American Tragedy, or the author of Sister Carrie come to be the author of The Bulwark? How was Dreiser able to say in The Financier and The Titan that living in society is like living in the jungle and scarcely twenty years after insist that society is not and should not be a jungle? These are some of the questions to which the book should suggest an approach. If it succeeds, then perhaps it will serve as a wedge for those who wish to enter the realm of final judgments.

The materials for this study have been contributed largely by Dreiser himself. From 1937, when I was first gathering facts for a master's essay at Columbia University, until October 1945, when I interviewed him in Hollywood for the last time, he liberally gave of his hours to answer my innumerable questions and unhesitatingly granted me unrestricted use of his voluminous files of correspondence and newspaper clippings, dating from 1893, which in 1942 he deposited in the Library of the University of Pennsylvania. Continually encouraging me in what he trusted would become a disinterested consideration of his life and work, he never insisted upon any conditions that would have meant an "authorized" account. For such support — and, I must add, for that of Mrs. Dreiser, who has been unfailingly helpful — the usual expressions of gratitude are entirely inadequate. The book would, of course, have been impossible otherwise.

There are others, however, without whose contributions the story would have remained necessarily incomplete and to whom I am grateful. The names of many of these — some of them friends of Dreiser's, some possessors of valuable materials — appear among the notes; but I should like specifically to acknowledge here my appreciation of invaluable help given me in correspondence, interviews, and documents by Homer Croy, Edward M. Dreiser, Donald B. Elder, T. E. Hanley, Marguerite Tjader Harris, Maude Wood Henry, Arthur Sullivant Hoffman, John F. Huth, Jr., William C. Lengel, A. R. Markle, H. L. Mencken, Fremont Rider, Sarah Field Splint, and Charles Hanson Towne.

I have also received substantial assistance in the collection and use of material from numerous generous persons whom there has been no occasion to cite elsewhere. I wish to thank them all and to mention in particular Harriet Bissell, Louise P. Bohannon, the late Dr. A. A. Brill, Earl Browder, Floyd Dell, Dr. Vera Dreiser, Wharton Esherick, Helen Foote, Leon Gelber, Constance M. Griffin, George H. Healey, Dr. Leonard K. Hirshberg, Karl K. Knecht, Edgar Lee Masters, Edward D. McDonald, Albert Mordell, Burton Rascoe, Benjamin Rothberg, John S. Sumner, Eva Svendsen, Robert van Gelder, and Henry von Sabern. The staff of the Library of the University of Pennsylvania has given me indispensable aid, and I wish to express my gratitude especially to John Alden, Carl L. Anderson, Elisabeth L. Gordon, Edith Hartwell, and Elliott H. Morse. Without the enterprise of Charles W. David, director of the University of Pennsylvania libraries, the Dreiser papers might not have become as accessible as they now are. . . .

I am also indebted to Mrs. Dreiser for permission to quote from Dreiser's books, letters, and manuscripts, and to H. L. Mencken for permission to quote freely from innumerable letters of his.

In the preparation of the manuscript I have enjoyed the continual sympathetic guidance of Professor Sculley Bradley, of the University of Pennsylvania. His critical comments, together with those of his associate Professor Robert E. Spiller, have helped immeasurably to make the book publishable. I have also had the advantage of detailed criticisms of my original draft by my friends George P. Brockway and Edward A. Hoyt, and throughout my work have been influenced by Professor John William Miller, of Williams College, whose philosophic teachings have given my interpretation whatever merit it may have.

Preface

The traditional last sentence of a preface has, I am sure, never been more justly reserved than mine — for my best critic, whose mark is on every page.

R. H. E.

Ithaca, New York
May 1948

Contents

Theodore Dreiser

NOT *till we are lost, in other words, not till we have lost the world, do we begin to find ourselves, and realize where we are and the infinite extent of our relations.*

HENRY DAVID THOREAU

I

Boyhood Dreams

There is a family legend [1] that Theodore Dreiser's coming into the world was presided over by unearthly agents. His father, John Paul Dreiser, and his mother, Sarah, had moved their eight children into a new home on Ninth Street a half-mile south of Chestnut in Terre Haute, Indiana,[2] and had discovered that spirits were ominously striding through the house at night. Since the family had met with such portents before and found reason to regard them seriously, Paul, a zealous Roman Catholic, had summoned Father Gällweiler, the priest at St. Benedict's,[3] to sprinkle holy water about the house. But when on Sunday morning, August 27, 1871, Sarah lay in labor, it was evident that orthodox precautions had been inadequate, for just before the boy was born, three maidens, brightly garbed, with flowers in their hair, danced into Sarah's room and out again, to disappear seemingly into the air; and when afterward the boy himself proved perilously puny and sickly, inimical forces seemed to be in command. In fact, even after his baptism on September 10, when his father moved the family into a larger house at Twelfth and Walnut Streets, one seemingly free of ghosts and similar phenomena, the child so ailed and whimpered that Sarah feared he would die, and it was not until she had secured the help of a mysterious old German woman across the way reported to possess certain supernatural and unhallowed powers that his health was

3

assured. One night when death appeared to be at hand,
Sarah had sent her eldest daughter, Mame, across the
street to summon the old recluse. The woman, knowing
Paul Dreiser's severe religious views, had refused to come,
but she had said: "If your mother wants my help, tell
her to take a string and measure your brother from head
to toe and from finger-tip to finger-tip. If the arms are as
long as the body, bring the string to me." And when the
measurements had proved satisfactory, she had smiled,
sent for Sarah, and announced: "Your child will not die.
But for three nights in succession, you must take him out
in the full of the moon. Leave his head and face uncov-
ered, and stand so that the light will fall slant-wise over
his forehead and eyes. Then say three times: '*Wass ich
hab, nehm ab; wass ich thu, nehm zu!*' " [4] The prescription being faithfully administered, within three months
the boy was well.

Whatever the explanation of this deliverance, it was
appropriate that Theodore's welfare seemed to depend so
completely on forces beyond the jurisdiction of the human will, whether they were supernal or necromantic,
and that he seemed to prosper more under the auspices
of some esoteric arcanum than under the more conventional ministrations of his father's priest; for the course
of his life was to involve him in a persistent scrutiny of
these superhuman forces and an acknowledgment of
their controlling power, and to take him from the shad-
ows of St. Benedict's to ultimate sanctuary at the threshold of the mysterious German woman across the way.

The most important circumstances of Theodore's boyhood were that his family was poor and that his father
was an ardent and ascetic member of the Catholic
Church; but had Theodore's temperament not been what

4

it was, these circumstances might not have been the noteworthy ones. He was, first of all, a serious-minded child, impressing others as always gravely seeking information. Friends of the family noticed that when they came to call, the little, wise-looking boy, then only a few years old, drew up a chair and listened to everything with a knowing air.[5] And his two brothers nearest him in age — Al, who was four years older, and Ed, who was one year younger — found him not long after preferring reading to playing, or, if he associated with anyone, trailing after the brighter boys.[6] In fact, his father, who liked to answer questions, treated him as his favorite and frequently asked him to accompany him on long walks during which the many things that Theodore noticed could be properly explained.[7]

But Theodore was more than intellectually serious. He was emotionally and imaginatively sensitive. When still only young enough to play by crawling about the floor, he showed himself possessed of the capacity for sympathy and tenderness. According to his own account, these feelings came into being the day he first discovered how shabby were his mother's shoes. As he was playing on the floor near her, he came upon her feet and, stopping, began to caress her toes. She looked down at him and said softly: "See poor mother's shoes? See the hole here?" So full of wonder was he, and then, influenced by the tone of her voice, so full of a kind of pity, that he began to examine the shoes and the hole more and more sorrowfully until he felt swollen inside and his pity all welled up into tears.[8] To such a boy the condition of his family and the peculiar religious attitude of his father were bound to be profoundly distressing.

At the time Theodore was born, Paul Dreiser was morose and incapable of the sustained productive effort

5

necessary to maintain the home. Once he had been a vigorous, enterprising man. In 1844, at the age of twenty-three, he had left his native Germany for the United States in order to escape conscription and, by using his skill as a weaver and such mechanical knowledge as he possessed, had earned a livehood in New York and Connecticut, worked his way westward with a friend[9] to reach Dayton, Ohio, and near there met Sarah and so overwhelmed her that she had run away to become his wife against the religious objections of her father, a prospering Moravian farmer who was also a faithful Dunkard or Mennonite. Thereafter, finding work in woolen mills, he had lived with Sarah in Dayton, in Fort Wayne, Indiana, and by 1858[10] in Terre Haute, eventually earning enough to support the eight children that Sarah, after the death of the first three, had borne him between 1858 and 1869. He had filled positions of responsibility, and as recently as 1870 had run a mill that a friend, Chauncey Rose, had financed in Sullivan, Indiana.[11] But lately there had been a series of misfortunes, beginning with destruction of part of the Sullivan mill and of fleece for which farmers had had to be reimbursed[12] and ending with injury, illness, and loss of mortgages through being duped by what the family called "Yankee trickery."[13] Whatever real wealth might have remained had been dissipated, and he now trudged about, a defeated man, without hope of financial reward and with the result that the Dreisers entered upon a period of persistent physical hardship that Theodore was to find closely affecting his daily life until he was almost twenty.

The most immediate effects upon him were that he developed a feeling of insecurity and that he came to resent his economic and social status. From almost the day of his baptism he was part of a family that was on the

move. It was not as though his parents were consumed
with the legendary fire of the pioneer spirit; they moved
simply because a mortgage had been foreclosed or because
the rent had exceeded their means, and they did not move
far. During Theodore's first seven years his father no
longer had any steady employment. In August 1871 Paul
Dreiser worked in a local mill; the next year he was
merely what the city directory called "a laborer"; in 1874
he was a wool-sorter; in 1876 a spinner — and so it went.
If a mill shut down during the winter, he accepted whatever work he could find.[14] Necessarily, the family could
not continue to live in a house as large and expensive as
that on the corner of Twelfth and Walnut. So they
moved to what was, by comparison, a shack and remained
until a friend from New Orleans, in order to escape the yel-
low-fever epidemic then raging, asked if she might come
and live with them awhile, whereupon Paul Dreiser advertised for a ten-room house and Sarah arranged to take in
boarders. There were at least one or two other removals
within Terre Haute afterward, until 1878 or 1879. Then,
the father being out of work entirely, the family split up
in the hope of saving money, and Theodore accompanied
his mother, his sister Tillie, and Ed to a friend's in Vincennes, Indiana. But because Sarah disapproved of the
moral climate of the new home, the four of them went to
Sullivan, Indiana, a few months later. There they passed
three years supported by boarders, laundering, and periodic contributions from Theodore's father, until in 1882
they packed up for Evansville, Indiana. This time it happened to be a move for the better. Young Paul, the oldest
of the children and already — under the name of Paul
Dresser — on his way to being a successful composer, had
returned from wandering to persuade his mistress, one
Annie Brace, who maintained an imposing and profitable

house of prostitution in Evansville, to furnish a comfortable home for the Dreisers. But even this menage did not last for more than two years, for Paul and Annie quarreled and the family had to leave. After they had tried a few weeks in Chicago, they had to entrain for Warsaw, Indiana. The father was out of work again, and his contributions being reduced, they sought lower rents where Sarah had been willed some property. Here Theodore stayed until 1887, but when he left then, it was because *he* was restless. At no time had he been able to strike roots anywhere: at no time could home remain comfortably associated with any one house or city.

Of the full significance of these changes of location Theodore was doubtless unaware. But he could not help being aware of the material want that more than infrequently characterized his existence. In Terre Haute, when the family was living in the cramped quarters that succeeded the house at Twelfth and Walnut, he was often cold and hungry; knew meals consisting of only fried potatoes or fried mush; and learned to pick up coal from between the railroad tracks, even to steal it from the cars, that there might be some warmth at home and some heat to cook what food there was. In Sullivan he, together with Tillie, had to carry the wash his mother was doing to establish her credit with the tradesmen; and one day during the first winter both he and Ed were sent home from school because, the instructor said, it was too cold to be without shoes. When he compared his condition with that of others about him, he saw something of how life might otherwise be.

Indeed, it was the contrast afforded by the lives and circumstances of others that made him dissatisfied with and ashamed of his own, and eventually engendered in him a sense of social and personal inferiority. He became aware of the difference between having less and having more. Many other children had homes in which strangers did not have to be taken in. They did not need to carry wash and coal as he, Tillie, and Ed did. When he and Tillie trudged along back streets in the early dark with a basket of laundry, he was nervous as to who might see them. And when he was stepping across the tracks with Ed to pick up coal, he became terribly worried about what people would say. In fact, for a while before he was seven years old he was afflicted with stuttering, for which his brothers made fun of him,[15] and became so fearful and shy that he was easily bullied by older boys until rescued by his brother Al, whose invincible courage in time of danger Theodore admired and like whom he hoped some day to be.

Other people and their circumstances did more, however, than provide a mere standard of comparison. They suggested a world whose attractions aroused his envy and desire. Part of his consciousness of this world beyond his home must have come from Terre Haute itself, which was energetic with expansion and accomplishment. Standing at the head of Wabash River navigation, the city in the seventies boasted of coal mines, steel mills, foundries, flour mills, distilleries, and a population of more than sixteen thousand. Its workers had become economically class-conscious, the farmers organizing the state's first Grange, while Eugene Debs promoted the consolidation of railroad workmen. And reform and agitation were in the air. Temperance was advocated by the Grangers; natural science was assailed by religious zealots; and the head of the state university argued that prayer might be used to arrest the laws of nature.[16] If any period could be regarded more than another as one of transition, this was such a period. If a community could be affected by the ferment of factory and tavern life, the inhabitants of Terre Haute did not remain immune.

Yet at best the city could provide only a background or setting against which Theodore might project incidents and his experience of individuals. The incidents and individuals themselves were what stirred his imagination and gave this other world shape and meaning, and most of these he found in his own house. There were first of all the boarders. During the days when strangers first occupied some of the rooms in Terre Haute, he was fascinated by a woman who dressed in silks, satins, and laces, who wore huge jewels and heavy perfumes, and who had a little daughter with yellow hair, blue velvet dress, and superior airs that made her seem "a creature out of the skies." [17] Theodore often stood at the threshold of their room marveling at the dresser loaded with silver toilet articles, and longing for such a room and for such a life — the life, apparently, of the comfortable world beyond his own. And later, in Sullivan, when boarders were taken in once more, the marvels multiplied and his longing increased. There was also a book left by a traveling "Professor" clad in cutaway and topper: Thomas Edie Hill's *Manual of Social and Business Forms* — directions on how to get on where it mattered. While Theodore walked weeks without shoes, wore clothes that were old and patched over, and ate cornmeal mush without milk because milk was too expensive, he could, whenever he managed to get the book away from Tillie, read how to write a business letter, how to write a love letter, how to bow to a lady, and how to comport himself among the elegantly dressed at banquet tables whose variety of offerings complicated the problem of dining. [18]

Finally there were the exciting tales of his two oldest

brothers, Rome and Paul. Rome, given to drinking, gambling, and drifting, turned up in Sullivan one day, after two years of wandering, without money but with stories of adventure in a world where there was money. He talked of Chicago, of Mexico, and of the Southwest. He had pictures of wild horses, cowboys, and saloons, and told about ranching and mining and gambling in the high-living West. Listening to such accounts, Theodore wanted at once to be up and away. The trains as they passed near by, even the birds, had more meaningful destinations than he seemed to. And when Paul arrived to take the family from Sullivan to Evansville, the substance of this other world was magnified. Paul came on a snowy day and he came in fur coat and silk hat, with a smart cane — and money for the family's pressing wants, promises of clothes for Theodore and Ed, and assurances of a weekly contribution to make it unnecessary for their mother to continue washing and keeping house for others. His stories were even more appealing to Theodore, for Paul the song-writer was an artist, affectionate and sensitive, and Theodore felt that Paul understood him. He in turn believed he understood Paul — he certainly loved him — and would have liked to spend hour on hour listening to Paul portray the world of wine and women he inhabited. It would, he told himself, be glorious to live as Paul lived. When in Evansville he one day visited Paul in Annie's establishment, the glory was momentarily brought to life. Paul's suite, overlooking the Ohio River, was "rich and wonderful." There were striped awnings, comfortable-looking wicker furniture covered with tan linen, potted plants, a piano strewn with music, and a gleaming bathroom — all bespeaking a marvelous existence, "a kind of fairyland," [19] as he later described it. And a glimpse he had of tumbled bedding and a girl in her chemisette simply made more mysterious and exciting the thoughts to be associated with the money, power, and experiences characterizing Paul's way of life.

In the light of these hints and contrasts it was little wonder that Theodore's fancies should have been aroused. Money came from the outside world. It came from the woman who wore perfume and kept silver-backed brushes on her dresser. It came from Paul and a realm of glamour where doubtless everything was possible. Even while living at Terre Haute and exposed to relatively few suggestions, he had dreams in which colored marbles floated in the air, and bright money lay everywhere on the ground. And one day, when taken to a house in which lay the body of the watchman whom he used to see passing by in the evenings and who often gave him fruit or candy, he stared at the waxy features until he noticed on the eyelids two coins. Then he tried to reach for them.

There was, he came to believe, not much that he could do toward experiencing the better life beyond making such a gesture. As he saw it, his father and the church prevented him. Indeed, as he saw it, poverty and organized religion went hand in hand to bar one from proceeding to the good things of the world. Part of the difficulty could be attributed to the series of accidents that had followed the damage to the Sullivan mill, but much grew out of Paul Dreiser's interpretation of Catholicism. As a victim of financial misfortune he was morose and defeated; but as an adherent of the Catholic Church he was stern and indefatigable, with something of a fanatic's zeal, in his observance of the faith and its ceremonial. He believed that somehow God would provide so long as all the forms of worship were maintained, and as he came more to depend on God, he came less to depend on himself and, instead, bent his efforts to make his family worthy of God's care.

For Theodore, his father's attitude had the force of a great denial. Although at first it touched him mainly through the reactions of the rest of his family, even as indirectly as that Paul Dreiser's view assumed the shape of something disagreeable and hostile to Theodore's happiness. The other children had rebelled against their father's discipline. They would not go to church as he wished; they would not obey the laws of sobriety and virtue. Young Paul was three times in jail for petty crimes. Rome associated with idlers, gamblers, and women of reprehensible morals. The older girls — Mame, Emma, Theresa, and Sylvia — contributed too little to the upkeep of the family, seemed more concerned with spending precious money in selfish, "sinful" pleasures than in practicing the virtues, and behaved "shockingly" with men. Although Paul Dreiser often did not know of each escapade and was sometimes quite innocent of the real source of a daughter's hats and slippers, he so often suspected the worst that his suspicions must now and then have coincided with the facts. And frequently when he happened to find they did, he raged against his wife.

Sarah did not share the strict moral outlook that would maintain the family by Teutonic discipline. Instead of judgment, she gave her children understanding and sympathy and became a refuge for them. Since the burden of the family was almost entirely hers, she viewed their problems in practical terms. When on one occasion young Paul was released from prison after his father had let the law take its course, she covertly arranged to have him sent to a relative's farm. And when the family's financial distress was most acute, her husband being out of work, she allowed a man who had been intimate with

13

one of her daughters to give them aid. Paul charged his wife with allowing the children to go straight to damnation under her lax supervision, but she retorted that he could not make a decent living for them, that he was narrow and hard, and she did not propose to see them governed by theories; let him make a good living first and then talk.

A sensitive temperament like Theodore's must have been painfully tried by these recurrent disputes. To all the children, but especially to him, Sarah was always, as he phrased it in retrospect, "thoughtful, solicitous, wise, and above all, tender and helpful." [20] When troubled and afraid, he turned to her, and when she was criticized, it was surely easy for him to feel the criticism as though it were of himself. At the same time his father presented a pathetic picture. Following the quarrels, he despondently tramped about the house, hands behind his back, talking to himself, or sat in a corner brooding, sometimes saying nothing for days except "yes" and "no" until he burst out in a renewed contest with his wife, only to be again defeated. While Theodore would have been upset because of the tension alone and have regarded his father's dejection with touches of pity, he must also have felt resentment against his father for his part in the quarrel and by association have disliked the ideas his father expressed.

Further impressions of a negative attitude were provided by scenes Theodore witnessed between his father and his sisters. When, for example, the family was living in Warsaw in 1885, the two most wayward of the girls arrived for a visit at about the same time as their father did. Having accustomed themselves to a gay menage in their own city, they proceeded at once to "parade the streets," as the father put it, attracting young men with tainted reputations and hurting the family's social standing. He was shocked by their flashy finery, and exclaimed over shameless spit curls, well-rouged cheeks, patent-leather shoes with white tops, and broad-brimmed hats dancing with ostrich plumes.[21] His opposition was futile, yet it succeeded in impressing on Theodore's mind that his sisters were interested in enjoying themselves and that his father was against it. Pleasure was marked by having things, the opposite to the wants of poverty, and this was declared to be sinful.

It was probably not until he personally experienced restraints, however, and these ultimately upon the freedom of his mind, that his reactions took significant form. Here his father was directly responsible. In order to become worthy of divine providence, the children had to be properly educated; and in order to be properly educated, they had to be educated by the church. Although money might be saved by letting the public schools do the teaching, such savings would be scarcely creditable to pious men. The consequence was that from his seventh year, when he found himself crying and being led by Tillie to St. Benedict's German parochial school, until his fourteenth, when he attended public school in Warsaw, Theodore was subjected to all the terrors and frustrations of the religious training his father believed proper. At the outset he was frightened by the bare schoolroom, the black clothes of the priest and sisters, and the teacher with her flaring hood who presided over the classroom and commanded the children to read mysterious symbols, or to be silent when they were out of order. Later he was frightened by the ritual. He had to attend Mass daily as well as vespers on Sundays. He had to serve as altar boy. He had to prepare for the catechism, and he had to master ceremonies and rites the slightest mistake in which might, it seemed to him, mean nameless but terrible

15

punishments. When during his short stay in Vincennes he one day walked by the county jail and was cursed by one of the inmates who was vainly asking him for a plug of tobacco, he fled with a nightmare feeling that this was probably the sort of physical hell his father was always talking about.[22] As he grew older, his mind became restless, and fears were strengthened by intellectual dislike. In Evansville he began reading romantic narratives in periodicals like the *Fireside Companion* and sometimes joined a few older boys in the shade of a barn to thrill to the exploits recounted by Horatio Alger or Oliver Optic. By contrast the regimen of the school his father had been prompt to locate became repugnant. The nuns were more severe-looking; the priests more grim; the teachers more terrifying. One bewhiskered ogre, a "Herr Professor," [23] was wont to strike disorderly boys across the face or lash them with a whip, and on several occasions Theodore, for laughing or for reading the wrong book, bore welts raised across his hands with a ruler. Once the master pulled his ear so hard he had to cry. When he thought of how he could be spending time with some adventure story, or when, recalling his reading, he closed his eyes and saw himself a young hero triumphantly sweeping across distant continents in crusades against vague but savage menaces, or when he discovered in the attic Gray's "Elegy," Goldsmith's "Deserted Village," Ouida's *Wanda*, and Lytton's *Ernest Maltravers*, then the catechism seemed a pretty pale and joyless rigmarole, representing a heartless interference with the one way the life of having things and being someone was possible. And when he gazed with envy at a dresser sparkling with a silvery hair brush, and pored over chapters on the etiquette of genteel society, and listened to Paul, then the "Praised be Jesus Christ" with which he was supposed to lift his hat to the priests became an affirmation of nothing better than a status whose characteristics were poverty, social inferiority, and compulsion without tangible rewards. His father appeared no longer to lift a finger except to pray — or to wag the prohibitory index. To be good and to be happy seemed incompatible.

Yet if zealous discipline interfered with Theodore's reveries, it also fostered a habit of reverie that was increasingly congenial to his sensibilities. The capacity for appreciation that brought tears to his eyes over the hole in his mother's shoe enabled him to respond to wonders all about him — outside the limits of his physical poverty. In Sullivan, for example, when he awoke early in the morning, he liked to take long walks, accompanied only by his dog, to examine the bejeweled spider webs and the opening morning-glories. Often he stood entranced watching the wrens flit about the house and the swallows swooping low, and on one occasion knelt down and prayed God to let him fly. Sometimes during the days when there was no school he sat on some muddy bank staring raptly at the crawfish as they emerged from their burrows and he wondered about the characteristics of their lives. One evening, beholding an immense comet vividly stretched across the sky, he sensed the existence of mysterious forces. By the time Paul had rehabilitated the family in Evansville, Theodore could lose himself among sights and sounds as though he moved in a dream.

The consequence of his propensity was that when he found himself handicapped by his family's scant resources and restrained by the ascetic denials of his father's morality, he turned to his imagination to find fulfillment. But the consequence of this was, in turn, unfortunate, for it was bound to inhibit the very fulfillments of which he dreamed. Since he was unable to experience the existence

17

he craved, that existence acquired a luster that could be only imagined and was, therefore, likely to become fanciful. And since the teachings of the church impressed him as so negative, any experience beyond his own would seem dangerous, and he would fear the very things he desired most. The forbidden fruit might have bright colors, but it also might be poison.

Just as the tales and fortunes of his brother Paul catered to his romantic imagination, so did it happen that his sisters provided justification for his fears. For after the two most wayward left Warsaw, they both got into the very kind of trouble their father had prophesied they would. One of them, Emma, while supported in Chicago by an architect for whom she had little affection, met the cashier of an eating and drinking establishment of some standing, Chapin and Gore's, and was immediately attracted to him as he was to her. When after some time she discovered he was married, she balked at a plan to run away with him, but he persuaded her anyway and eloped with her to Toronto, explaining that while intoxicated he had stolen thirty-five hundred dollars. He felt remorse shortly after and returned all but eight hundred of it, begging not to be prosecuted and moving with the girl to New York. Although his request was granted, and that was the end of it, the Chicago papers printed lurid accounts of the entire episode. It happened that the Dreisers were not mentioned, for their daughter had been living under an assumed name, but a moral could be read there if one had the bent for it. Once in New York, the couple supported themselves in part by renting rooms to girls of questionable virtue; and not very much later it was to them that the other sister, Sylvia, went, pregnant with the child of a wealthy scion whose mother haughtily explained that he could

autoerotic stimulation found for many years a sexual nirvana where all dreams were true.

Yet even these fulfillments were limited, for he had long ago heard that the thoughts he had were evil, and when he developed a case of pimples, he feared lest his terrible secret be known to all. He brooded morbidly about his practice, suffered dizzy spells, and then dreaded that he had harmed himself for life. But desire continued to overwhelm dread and periodically led him to liberating reveries in which fancy could shape the facts. It was logical, if ironic, that he even began to think regretfully of his younger days in Terre Haute, Evansville, and Sullivan — then childhood was perfect, and, alas, he would never be young again.

A time was bound to come, of course, when he would be impelled to act in behalf of his larger ambitions, and in his sixteenth year, after school ended and he saw other boys leaving to take jobs, he did make the attempt. Now, however, circumstances seemed to conspire against him and alternated with his introspection to thwart his efforts. He secured a job as a farmhand, but at the end of the first full day was so exhausted that he was sent home as too weak for the task. Promptly rationalizing the failure by telling himself he was not meant for a life among people as rough and crude as farmhands, he decided to go to Chicago, where there were certainly all kinds of congenial opportunities. As he entered the city, its bustle and excitement inflamed his imagination. As he attempted to support himself, the concrete realities discouraged him. When he gazed at the factories, the laborers, and the shoppers hurrying through the streets, he felt as though he were beholding a scene from a play; but when he saw "No Help Wanted" signs and was told experience was necessary and could at first get only a job as cleaner of a railway stable, for which after a half-day he was told he was no longer needed, then he reflected upon his lack of strength and training and brooded over his inadequacy.

He soon found a steady job as busboy and dishwasher in a dirty, fly-specked restaurant run by a pudgy Greek named John Paradiso, but he began to think about himself in this particular position and thereupon lost respect for it and, pretending to his brother Al that he was a clerk in Halstead Street, sought something else. This time it was only cleaning stoves for a hardware store, and he was immediately impressed with the unimportance of the work. Although there was some compensation in being able to speculate about the provenance and careers of his various stoves while he polished them, this did not last long. After an hour or two of labor he received his discharge — too weak once again. There followed other brief jobs. But either his temperament or accident terminated them. Hired to clean canvases for a painter friendly to his sister Theresa, he gave his employer so many lectures on art and life that he was no longer wanted and, to his mortification, was superseded by Ed, who had come with the rest of the family to try Chicago again. Subsequently given a job as car-tracer for one of the big railroads, he became fatigued and caught cold after two days and, having to take to his bed, decided not to return. The next job was indoors, with a wholesale hardware company, Hibbard, Spencer, Bartlett & Company.

From these drab frustrations he from time to time found release at the Opera House, where he could drift on surges of music into a realm evoked by pasteboard mountains and girls in tights and see life as it could be — as it must be — as it, in fact, no doubt was, somewhere. Love was exalting and refining. Good and evil were easily detected by their clothes. Truth was ever victorious, and crime did not pay. And amid the complications of romance and temptation were to be witnessed balls, banquets, and grandiose panoramas, such as could be found only in *Ali Baba and the Forty Thieves* or *The Isle of Champagne*, but such as seemed to Theodore within the limits of the attainable.

While this recreation contributed to his romantic fancies, his job with the hardware company indirectly encouraged him to value with increasing seriousness the workings of his mind. For at Hibbard, Spencer, Bartlett & Company he met a man who sympathized with his intellectual interests, an emaciated Dane, Christian Aaberg, who could speak excitingly of Goethe and Ibsen, of Wagner and Grieg, of Napoleon, Danish court-life, the rites of the Parsees, and why Socrates drank the hemlock. The interest of one so young as Theodore in matters of the mind produced in Aaberg the conviction that Theodore would some day succeed at something important, and he liked to share with Theodore what he knew. Theodore, of course, might have been impressed by any knowing patter, but Aaberg's learning was less patter than it was knowing, and his life was one that rubbed against the jagged realities. When he would exclaim on some Monday morning how drunk he had been the night before, or curse women as devils, Theodore could consider whatever Aaberg said as authoritative: he knew life, and he believed in the value of books. "It is a great thing, Dreiser," Aaberg once declared, "just for a few dollars, to be able to live and commune with all the Great through the ages; it is worth the price." [27] Listening to him, Dreiser concluded that mind was what differentiated the classes in society — that mind would make or break him — and his mind proceeded to picture the possibilities.

25

As if designed for him to test himself, a singular opportunity was suddenly afforded him. Almost discharged from his job, afflicted by intestinal disorders, spitting blood because of lungs irritated by dust and excelsior, he had, as the year 1888 proceeded, become deeply depressed. He was making only five dollars a week. How could he buy decent clothing with that? How could he afford a theater ticket? How could he interest girls as others did? And he with the capacities Aaberg was teaching him to believe he had. And then the singular opportunity — to live for at least a little while a life of the mind. For just then his high-school teacher, Mildred Fielding, unaccountably appeared with the proposal that he spend the following year at Indiana University at her expense. He deserved further education, she argued; she had to do this for herself; college would make him think, enable him to find himself; he would be accepted as an individual. In addition, she would arrange to have him admitted despite his not having completed his high-school preparation.

And so it was that during the academic year 1889-90 he studied at Bloomington. If the meaning of his experience there had been confined to what he accomplished in courses, the experience would have meant little. He passed a year of elementary Latin, was conditioned for one term of geometry, passed a course in "philology," and received a "Good" in what was called the Study of Words.[28] He wanted to know a little about everything, but not too much, and to read and be admitted to the realm of pure knowledge. But the meaning of the year at Indiana was in what he gained from association with others his own age who were, like him, curious about life and, unlike him, somewhat versed in it. There was Russell Ratliff, a poet, philosopher, and vegetarian, who

spoke of Darwin, Huxley, Lecky, and Tolstoy and with
whom he read *What Then Must We Do* aloud and discussed the compatibility of Christian doctrine with evolutionary theory. There was his roommate, Bill Yakey,
a football star and popular classmate, who made their
room a social center and put Theodore through setting-
up exercises early every morning out on the lawn to try
to give him strength and a four-inch chest expansion.
There was Howard Hall, an earnest law student who
seemed to Theodore a social equal and liked to plan —
without carrying out — titillating seductions and to go
on the geology department's expeditions among the
amazing caves and underground rivers of the region.
And there was Day Allen Willy, a sophomore and town
dandy, who had a comfortable apartment and introduced Theodore to the girls.

Considered collectively, they whetted his appetite for
life, but they also fostered his introspection in the face
of it. He might be able to discuss Tolstoy, but that would
be of little use when he needed greater chest expansion
to impress the girls. He might lounge in his friend's comfortable living-room, but he felt out of place with his
cheap clothes. When he looked in his mirror, he saw a
homely hobbledehoy, and when during rushing season no
fraternity sent him a bid, he was certain he must be excluded from the company of the socially desirable. He
adored one girl for a few months before he dared hand
her a note; and enticed by another into more intimate
relations, he became so fearful of his probable inadequacy that his fears were realized and he felt even more
inadequate than ever.

Yet he left Indiana with the resolve to be more than
a cog in the commercial machine. He would succeed despite all the persons who had ignored him. Beautiful girls

would be interested in him, and so would society as a whole. And for a while events were promising. He secured a job in a Chicago real-estate office and made such useful, if obvious, suggestions that his employer, Asa Conklin, entrusted him with more responsibilities than he had ever had before. On his business trips about the city he met several women whom, to his surprise, he interested, and he soon discovered he could possess them for the asking. And in the office itself he attracted one tantalizing little Italian girl who gave him every reason to believe in his abilities. But the promise of events was not fulfilled. Where the business was involved, Theodore was scarcely to blame: he was paid three dollars a week and that irregularly because Conklin was too unenterprising to amass profits. In the matter of the women, however, he was still his own enemy. Confronted with those he met on his rounds, he not only was critical of their appearance; he also pondered too precisely upon what were the nature and the extent of his desires and concluded by denying them all. And enticed by the Italian girl into proving himself, he puzzled and brooded over her failure to pay him a second visit, and then felt uncertain of himself all over again.

It was when he was thus becoming simultaneously a more effective person and a victim once again of self-doubt that something happened which took from beneath him what he realized was the little basis of security he had. His mother became ill and had premonitions of death. Through the late summer and early fall of 1890 her health deteriorated, and as Theodore contemplated losing her, he felt helpless. The others of the family who had arrived at her bedside shared his mood and contributed to it, and when the end came on November 14, the fact was fixed forever vividly in his mind, for he was alone with her at the time. She had attempted, with his help, to rise from the bed, and then had slipped weak and gray to the floor, dying before he could summon the others.

The full significance of her death was momentarily lost amid the preparations for the funeral and the behavior of the priest who had been called to bless the body. Theodore's mother had been unable to attend church and go to confession or take communion, and the priest had not been called in at any time. Now the priest doubted whether he could bless her and whether she could even be interred in consecrated ground. Paul Dreiser might plead that she had formerly been devoted, but the clergyman barked in German that the various rites and duties had been slighted and the church reserved its sacraments for those who deserved them. Although eventually she was buried in St. Boniface Cemetery, Theodore would remember that when he had beheld its minister withholding his blessing, he had again seen the Catholic Church in action.

Once the funeral was over, though, the fact of immediate importance to Theodore was that the part of him that was his mother was gone. He still had a father, brothers and sisters, and a place to live; but it was different. He was now attached to no one; he was fundamentally alone —just an "I," "Dreiser" instead of "Theodore." If there had been a time he could venture and then withdraw into his mother's protective understanding, that time was past. Now, wherever he was, he would be abroad in the actual world and have to contend with it. This meant, even though he might not immediately realize it, that reveries would be luxurious indulgence and that he would

29

soon be called upon to reconcile the fancies of his world of dreams with the facts of the world of deeds. And so long as he remained unaware that dreams could never be actualized apart from the acceptance of a world of deeds, he would find the reconciliation a profound and persistently painful problem.

II

Facts versus Fancies

After his emotional ties with his home were cut, Dreiser's physical ties soon frayed and snapped as well. The expenses of his mother's illness and funeral had left debts that required sacrifices of each of the members of his family, but the unifying influence was gone and most of the family objected to sacrifices. His sisters accused each other of shirking responsibilities; his father demanded periodic contributions from all so that a weekly Mass might be said for Sarah Dreiser's soul; his unmarried sisters, jealous of the money his married sisters received from their husbands, insisted their own contributions ought to be smaller. Eventually the tensions became too great, and early in 1891 he, along with Ed, joined Tillie in moving to another apartment, where they remained together for approximately a year, until other quarrels impelled him and Ed to find a single room to themselves. Thus within a few months after his mother had been buried in St. Boniface, Dreiser found himself independent, with no one except himself to whom he need be responsible.

At first his development was toward a clarification of his longings and a more precise definition of his purposes. He had not been paid by Conklin all that was due him and, upon the intervention of his father, who was determined to liquidate the family's debts promptly, had been advised by Conklin to find more remunerative work. This he had soon done, and even before the family had broken up was driving a wagon for the Munger Laundry Company, first in a series of jobs that took him throughout the city. In his trips to pick up laundry, both for Munger's and later for another laundry, Goodhart Brothers, and in subsequent rounds as bill-collector for two household-furnishings companies who sold on the installment plan, he was brought closer to the life he had thitherto been forced to view from a distance. In the wealthier sections of the city, then lying between Washington and Ashland Boulevards, he often beheld at evening men and women in all the accouterments of dress that bespoke a banquet, a dance, a theater party, or an opera. He was sometimes greeted by servants in livery, on occasion spoken to by the aloof inhabitant of some mansion, and now and then admitted to a palatial lounge or boudoir to pick up a bundle and collect money left with impressive nonchalance on the dresser. Many times in the past he had thought how at the end of day in all the nice, comfortable homes pretty women were waiting to embrace their husbands or their lovers, and well-laden tables were being set for feasts, and girls with their young escorts were preparing for an evening of tantalizing pleasures. Now that these thoughts had come to life, he wished to be part of such a world more than ever. He considered the twenty years he had lived, and wondered when he should have money enough in his pocket to leave some on the dresser and when he would feel beautiful warm lips against his own.

His ventures into the poorer sections of Chicago, while arousing his sympathies, served to reaffirm the values of Washington and Ashland Boulevards. He could share something of the desire that plunged impoverished wives and widows into impractical expendi-

tures enabling them to brighten their drab existence
with pink lampshades that accompanied broken lamps
or with superfluous clocks that only echoed others they
already had. And he felt unhappy about making threats
on the doorsteps of homes in which the provider had
died. Yet he, too, wanted money and the power to buy
things, and so, fascinated as he might be by the behavior
and eccentricities of these individuals, he insisted bills
be paid. And when in the most sordid precincts he
picked up laundry from the houses of prostitution or the
haunts of dope addicts, or attempted to collect money
from bleary-eyed families who lived on soggy, unpaved
streets where sour beer, sewer gas from broken mains,
and uric acid befouled the air, then the importance of
money and position was inescapable; then success was
something concrete.

But if his jobs made an objective clear, his lack of experience coupled with his limited training fostered illusions about how the objective might be attained, and in
consequence, whatever his experience might now be, it
would, the more enlightening it proved, become progres-
sively disillusioning. For example, as a result of his early
schooling, he harbored the notion that spiritual integrity
and material well-being were somehow intimately related. Although he could ask himself how then it was
that his father had not prospered, he believed there must
be some point in being good, in abiding by a code of
morals. Were not the good eventually to be rewarded?
And were not wealth and position evident rewards? As
he engaged in the economic struggle, however, facts implied the contrary and made him disturbingly uncertain
of himself. When he was driving the laundry wagon and
one day wrecked it in a collision, he was frightened by
his employers into making false statements that would

enable them to collect the maximum in damages. Although he felt that money was important, he was disgusted by the conniving and convinced one did not acquire riches *that* way. He later came to consider it not entirely right for him to make money as he himself made it, by exacting money from the indigent for the nearly worthless furniture and bric-a-brac they had bought; yet he cheerfully accepted the work lest he be indigent himself.

In a similar way he resented the success with which his employers or their managers seduced attractive girls they had hired. He could not manage as they did and envied them their privileges. Yet he was glad whenever these men were found out by their wives, for it doubtless seemed to reaffirm the moral order which he could not effectively transgress and thus to maintain his equality with those he would emulate. At the same time he wondered why the lovely girls who yielded to them would not yield to him, who deserved them so much more.

He never seemed to suspect that he was sentimentalizing the conduct he witnessed. On his rounds among the run-down districts of the city he was frequently faced with some woman or girl of mood and inclination like his own; but inevitably the moment that he so often idealized produced the repulsion of its facts — unclean bodies, dirty beds, and unintellectual minds — and he would leave somewhat nauseated. When æsthetic distance intervened, however, and he observed his employers or gazed after some lithe stranger in the laundry, he was unable to realize that these girls might come from the same regions as those who disgusted him and that their bodies and minds might be equally unattractive. Indeed, the illusions created by his imagination supported the illusions promoted by his ignorance to keep fulfillments out of reach. He went about for a while with a little Scottish girl who was cashier in Munger's laundry, until his sister Tillie, on Christmas Eve 1891, brought home a friend from where she worked, a fellow clerk named Lois Zahn, who was mild and sweet and, more accomplished than the cashier, played the banjo and guitar. He longed to have such a girl as this and rejoiced when he proved attractive to her. But as soon as she inquired whether *he* liked *her*, he drew back. He liked the idea of having a "girl"; he longed for her until she was his girl; but the moment he was compelled to scrutinize to what extent he wanted her for his girl, then of course he began to measure her against his idealized girls, and she was too real; so he would not commit himself and preferred to think of her as she had been before her inquiry, while his mind, full of thoughts of the wealth and prestige he was seeing, reminded him that his ambitions were yet to be fulfilled.

Something beyond material desires strengthened his hopes, though, and that was his belief that he could be seriously intellectual if he chose. His mind, on which Mildred Fielding had staked money, received renewed stimulation when Ratliff turned up one day and talked of books and ideas, and when Miss Fielding herself invited him to visit her Sundays and urged him to contemplate lofty ideas instead of material pleasures. He found himself craving an insight into the world about him, and while he read Tolstoy's *Death of Ivan Ilyich* and *Kreutzer Sonata* and thought how wonderful it was to be a novelist who could portray life so truly, he listened to lecturers and preachers who might tell him what the truth was. From apostate Methodist ministers to speakers at the Ethical Culture Society, all spoke of social and personal problems in terms free from the glum authoritarianism of his father's church, and implied that one might be good and happy at the same time. Here was something to free the spirit! Dreiser believed that a way to discover the world of the books and operas might now be at hand.

The more intensely he contemplated the ideal world, however, the more aware he became of the material conditions for its realization. As he came to think in terms of the better existence, and of the beautiful girls in it, he believed that if he but had the proper clothes and could afford the proper entertainments, all would be well. As the winter of 1891 approached, he especially desired an overcoat with satin lining; if worn with gloves and cane, it would make him irresistible. Perhaps nothing better exhibited the confusion of his mind and the uncertainty of his values than his attempt to procure the necessary money. In searching for the twenty-five or thirty dollars needed to complete the purchase price, he decided they might be found right in his pocket. He was at the time collecting money for the household furnishings bought on the installment plan, and when some customers settled their bills in full by paying more than the installment due, he had more than his employer expected, and he believed he could withhold the surplus temporarily, accumulating enough for the coat and then repaying it at the rate of thirty-five cents a week, all without being discovered. Within a few weeks he was discovered, however, and the first act of his life that had been intended to realize his dreams rather than simply meet necessity now kept the dreams farther out of reach than before. For although he was not prosecuted, he was discharged, within a week or two of Christmas.

Yet there was some advantage in its being the holiday season, for the *Chicago Herald* annually distributed gifts

among the city's poor and needed young men to help.
Reading their advertisement and noting a possibility of
promotion, Dreiser was clear as to his course of action.
For several months he had been avidly reading Eugene
Field's column, "Sharps and Flats," in the *Daily News,*
and had thought that he too might comment on life in
a humorous and occasionally romantic vein. The more
he saw on his daily rounds, the more he wanted to share
his reactions. If he could make a living expressing the excitement of his mind, what could be more ideal? He had
even sent some jottings off to Field himself. Although
there had been no acknowledgment, journalism had become only more alluring. As he had read of important
people and stirring events, he had speculated on what it
must mean to write of such wonders and believed that
reporters, associating as they did with the wealthy and
the famous, were akin and even equal to the financiers
and statesmen they interviewed. They sat behind desks
in glowing offices whose bustle and name-plates were the
signs and symbols of rank and authority. To aspire to
their distinction took his breath away, but it was a distinction achieved because of a facility of expression and
vigor of mind that he, considering his intellectual bent,
was sure he had. Reading the *Herald's* advertisement, he
thought his turn had come.

There was, of course, no promotion. At the end of the
Christmas season there was only "No vacancies." [1] He
tried other papers with the same luck. Yet he now knew
what he wanted. He even told Lois he was a newspaper
reporter, because that was the role in which he pictured
himself. When one editor advised him to learn newspaper work on a smaller paper, he decided to find such
a paper. To support himself he got his job with the second easy-payment firm, and to prepare himself for his

great career he practiced writing news stories of real or imagined accidents until in April or May 1892 he felt he could haunt the city desks once more. With the National Democratic Convention scheduled to meet in Chicago in June, his determination was strengthened. He had been reading about representative men and heroes in the essays of Emerson and Carlyle and was thinking in terms of nations and their leaders at the very moment when national issues were brought to his city. As a reporter he would be close to the significant events, close to all he had been dreaming. He selected the struggling *Chicago Daily Globe* and concentrated on ingratiating himself with its editor. At his pencil's tip was to be easy glory. At his pencil's tip he was poised for automatic triumph over all the misfortunes he had borne.

He succeeded in securing a position on the *Globe* and holding it for almost six months, but it scarcely marked an entrance into the bright, shiny world he had expected. The *Globe's* offices were plain, cluttered, and commonplace. Its reporters, instead of being the equals of statesmen, turned out to be casual workers who often gained favor by sordid office politics. And its work, for one who expected to be in the midst of historical events, was initially disappointing. At first he spent two weeks doing nothing but becoming acquainted with a copyreader, John Maxwell. Then the editor promised him a tryout only if he would sell at least a hundred and twenty copies of a book the editor had just written. Finally, having sold the books and being given a chance to cover the hotels for political news during the convention, he was not allowed to write the general stories and was told that what he did write was trite.

Nor did reporting appear to mean association with

the enviable and great. He did during the convention speak with a Supreme Court justice and with a United States Senator, but on the whole his faith in the integrity of those he aspired to know was deeply shaken. In fact, the assumption that integrity existed at all was called into question. One day when he wanted to thank Maxwell for encouraging him, he ventured to lay a hand on Maxwell's shoulder. Maxwell frowned. "Cut the gentle con work, Theodore," he said. "I know you. You're just like other newspapermen, or will be: grateful when things are coming your way. If I were out of a job or in your position you'd do just like all the others: pass me up. I know you better than you know yourself. Life is a God-damned stinking, treacherous game, and nine hundred and ninety-nine men out of every thousand are bastards." [2] This was a view others on the paper seemed to share. No man's motives were trustworthy, and no one who had won power or fame was completely honest. On another occasion Maxwell declared: "People make laws for other people to live up to and in order to protect themselves in what they have. They never intend those laws to apply to themselves or to prevent them from doing anything they wish to do." [3] He never seemed surprised by licentious conduct and regarded adultery as commonplace. He himself was married and kept a mistress. Although to Dreiser he appeared to make light of virtue, he simply regarded faithlessness, disloyalty, and vice as part of the order of life. "Read Schopenhauer, Spencer, Voltaire," he advised. "Then you'll get a line on this scheme of things." [4]

The policies of the *Globe* itself could only lead to confirmation of this disturbing outlook. Like other newspapers, the *Globe* was trying to bring its readers to certain conclusions, not to bring merely the truth to its readers.

Profits, through the influence of power or of money, were what mattered, and to gain them editors searched the records of human frailty and evil for usable evidences of corruption. That newspapers should indulge in such ignoble practices in itself shocked Dreiser, but that ignominy and improbity should exist to be so persistently revealed was more shocking, for it made mankind evil beyond his ability to understand it. As he daily made his way from his room on Ogden Street through Madison Street or Washington Boulevard to the river, he gazed at the drooping frame houses and slovenly misery in which the poor subsisted and wondered why it was that some were rich and others poor. He suspected at times that it just happened that way, that it was really no one's fault. Yet some power or force must be responsible. He had been led to believe that God was omnipotent. Why, then, did the Devil seem so often to be in charge? Unable to reconcile his observations with the doctrines that underlay his thinking, he was forced to see some validity in the views of his fellows; but unwilling because of his own assumptions to accept an outlook that would invalidate all his hopes, he retained a vague faith that somehow the traditional moral order would favor him in the end.

This bewilderment when joined with his sensitivity was, however, valuable to him in his work. News stories at that time were written in a discursive vein, and features or specials were designed to read, in all their theatrical details, like the more sentimental passages by Dickens. A bewildered and sensitive mind could regard the turmoil and misery about it without feeling itself too deeply involved. It could regard life as a detached spectacle, and it could therefore comment and speculate in precisely the way demanded by the seekers of "human

40

interest," and with impartiality record details in a dramatic way. Although Dreiser at first knew none of the principles of news-writing, or even what news actually was, he learned quickly under Maxwell's friendly guidance. Maxwell explained the nature and function of lead paragraphs and, as Dreiser stood by his side, blue-penciled Dreiser's sentences until Dreiser had an inkling of how they should have been written. When the Democratic Convention was in progress, Maxwell outlined the political situation, indicating what news was wanted and suggesting which men were likely to supply it. And Dreiser, though confused by the smoky hullabaloo, managed to pick up information presaging Cleveland's nomination. His scoop was the product of mere chance, but it won him praise in the *Globe* offices. Maxwell declared: "You're one of the damnedest crack-brained loons I ever saw, but you seem to know how to get the news just the same, and you're going to be able to write. If I could just keep you under my thumb for four or five weeks I think I could make something out of you." [5] And after the convention Dreiser was retained on the regular staff. At the end of summer Maxwell had told him he knew how to observe and was "cut out to be a writer . . . not just an ordinary newspaper man." [6] And the city editor, John T. McEnnis, called a "slum romance" he had written "a fine piece of writing." Dreiser had promise, he said, and now needed to gain experience on a bigger paper, such as the *St. Louis Globe-Democrat* or New York *Sun.* "You have a future, and I'm going to help you if I can." [7] Meanwhile he gave Dreiser more freedom in his assignments for the *Globe.*

Among these assignments was the covering of fake auction houses that the paper's owner had personal reasons for wishing to expose. Noting the manner in which the mock-auction sharks defrauded the public, fought among themselves, and secured the indifference of the police, he might have come to the conclusion that most men could be labeled either suckers or chiselers. But he did not regard what he reported so seriously. He did not feel implicated and could write with the innocent matter-of-factness of a mild cynic or the lofty humor of one who was at last seeing some justice done.[8] In fact, he was more interested in the impression his reporting made than in what he reported, for the encouragement he had received fostered his hopes of himself.

Even at the moment he was jotting down notes about the fakers, he was writing parables about the value of being acclaimed by his fellow men. Over a nickname Maxwell had given him, "Carl" Dreiser, he occasionally wrote reflective stories or commentaries for the Sunday edition, and in one of these, "The Return of Genius," he speculated about the meaning of fame. A great genius whose younger days are spent in poverty and sorrow wishes aloud for riches, pleasure, and eternal fame. The god of genius hears him and promises him undying glory on the sole condition that the genius shall never hear or see this glory. The genius agrees and prospers in a silver mansion amid idyllic surroundings. But eventually he longs for the world's praise. "What is greatness and glory but to enjoy[?]" he asks. When his god reminds him that if he mingles with the world his fame will die with him, he replies: "I will mingle with men and be of them. They are nearer to me than silver and jewels. . . . I am through with this life. I will again seek mankind." [9] To Dreiser achievement had become meaningless apart from the world of men, no matter what men might be; a dream world failed to provide adequate satisfactions, and though some men might be bad, surely not all were.

Moreover, the achievement he sought presupposed a society whose members were capable of evaluating achievement truly. He now could accept the world of deeds.

When McEnnis, true to his word, enabled Dreiser to receive an offer of a better job working under Joseph B. McCullagh of the *St. Louis Globe-Democrat*, Dreiser was jubilant not only because he was proving himself capable and becoming a somebody, but also because he was now to enter a world that would be what Chicago had not been — the world he had dreamed about.

III

Go East, Young Man . . .

When he stepped off the train in St. Louis on a Sunday evening early in November 1892, he was at once dejected. The air was enervating. The boardwalk approaches to the tracks were shabby compared with Chicago's. The few people about seemed sleepy. The city looked dead. Yet on Monday the Sabbath pall lifted, and he stayed the next year and a quarter to work first on the *Globe-Democrat* and then on the *Republic* and to justify some of McEnnis's faith.

It did not take him long to make a place for himself on the paper. After he showed he could handle the routine news of courts, jails, and hospitals, and proved his capacity to manage interviews with personages such as the city's political boss, Edward Butler, and Terence V. Powderly, leader of the Knights of Labor, he was given an anonymously written column, "Heard in the Corridors," which appeared opposite the editorial page and consisted of five or six curious, wise, or amusing anecdotes allegedly told or "overheard" in the hotels or at the station. For some time it had been written regularly by various hands, W. C. Brann having done it recently, before becoming editor of the *Iconoclast*; but of late it had languished, to appear only when one or another of the staff had bestirred himself to produce a few paragraphs. Dreiser turned to the assignment with some misgivings, for celebrities at the hotels were few and most anecdotes were scarcely worth repeating. Driven, however, to rely primarily on his own resources, he realized he had room to exercise his imagination, and with his interest at least temporarily excited, he wrote a column for almost every weekday issue of the paper until March, when it appeared less regularly.

It was, no doubt, impossible for him to frequent the hotel lobbies in search of either news or suggestions for imaginary interviews without feeling the lure of the atmosphere of wealth. And while his responsibility for the column served to establish him in his own estimation, the experience it occasioned served to sustain his hope that he would become established in the world. But more important, his column helped establish him in the opinion of some others on the paper who contributed to more concrete images of what his future could be.

The two members of the "art department" were the men who made the greatest impression upon him. The first time he had had a story illustrated he had entered their office and upon seeing first the departmental sign on the door and then the wild hair and beard of one of the men, Peter B. McCord, and the flowing tie and pastel-colored shirt of the other, Richard Wood, had imagined himself in the presence of the equals of Rembrandt, or at least Gustave Doré. His desire to be an artist, whatever an artist might be, had been immediately aroused. And when of an evening he had beheld Wood attired in dark blue suit and patent leathers, bedecked with crush hat, scarf pin, and boutonniere, and swinging a cane, he had grieved over his own inferiority, both physical and financial, and decided that art opened the door to social success. He had wanted to know McCord and Wood better, but until he had proved his ability on the paper, he had not earned their social recognition. When he did earn it, however, the artist's life became more definite and even appeared attainable.

The evening following his first "Heard in the Corridors" brought his complete initiation into their company. In Wood's room, surrounded by a collection of Oriental coins, a pile of manuscripts, and engravings of Hamlet and the temptation of Faust, he sat before a fireplace and listened to casual comments about playwriting and the theater which, amid such symbols of the artistic life, led him to suppose he was in an atelier of fabled Bohemia hearing the incisive comments of talented æsthetes. When at one point he said he wished he were in a position to write a play and McCord replied: "Why don't you try? . . . I bet you could write a good one," [1] he glowed with the wonder of possibilities and concluded that in such an atmosphere of genius he could live superior to either poverty or wealth.

Further support for the belief that he might write a play or something of a creative character came from reflecting upon an incident of his experience and the words of another reporter, Robert H. Hazard. A few weeks after his arrival in St. Louis he received a pathetic letter from Lois regretting that things were not as they once had been and wishing that she were dead. Pained with recollection of failures even to write to her, he was soon tortured by dilemma and indecision. He could not afford to marry her, but he had always played the role of the man he wished to be and could not admit the truth to her now. If, on the other hand, he had the money, was she the woman he wanted? He did not like to tell her she was not, and he could not write convincingly that she was. In his tormented bewilderment he found himself writing down words that arranged themselves in the shape of a crude poem. Seeing what he had done, he began at once to revise and perfect the phrases, until he was interrupted by Hazard, who asked: "What are you doing, Dreiser? Writing poetry?"

Dreiser was a little ashamed at being caught doing it, but somewhat pleased at being taken for a poet. When Hazard then told him there was no money in it and he would spend his time better "on a book or a play," [2] he saw himself being treated as a potential dramatist and was thrilled. Moreover, he now learned from Hazard, other newspapermen had become successful writers; Augustus Thomas, Eugene Field, and W. C. Brann were among those Hazard named. Hazard himself had collaborated in writing a novel—as yet unpublished, to be sure—and he promised to let Dreiser read it.

After Hazard walked away, Dreiser contemplated the rewards of talent and felt less grief-stricken about Lois. He was aware of his grief as of something external to him. Now he reread his poem and thought it was good, even beautiful. He could truly be a poet! And, it seemed at the moment, he had found an escape from misery.

Reading Hazard's manuscript after this, he was attracted even more strongly to the idea of writing. Hazard and his collaborator had read their Balzac and their Zola and, setting their story in Paris, depicted sensuality and vice frankly. An actress was the principal character. Her lover was a newspaperman, devoted and unfaithful. The plot included a murder and the lover's arrest for a crime of which he was ignorant. And there were scenes in which the actress spanked another actress with a hairbrush, and a man lost his head to the guillotine. Upon concluding this account of love and transgression, Dreiser felt he had been brought closer to the life he was observing and thought it odd that Hazard should say it could never be published in the United States. He

thought it beautiful and wanted to write something himself now; not a novel or a poem, but a play, for the dramatic technique seemed most congenial. The details of
Hazard's story lingered in his mind — he himself, in fact,
included something similar to the spanking scene in
The Titan more than twenty years later — and creative
writing shaped itself more solidly as an ambition.

Of necessity, however, the ambition remained partially
amorphous, for there was nothing specific he wanted to
present. Life was simply a kaleidoscopic spectacle. His
assignments took him into the orbit of municipal graft
and corruption and exposed him to scenes of brutality,
exploitation, and despair; yet just as merely feelings of
envy were excited by glimpses of the mansions of the
rich, so were merely feelings of sympathy aroused by
sights of the poor. He did not think critically in terms of
systematic remedies for vice and want. "Rights" was a
meaningless term when connected with labor, and workers were, if anything, not quite so "nice" as he was, not
so refined, not so superior in aspiration, and hence not
so deserving of success. What relationship existed between rich and poor was nothing more than colorful
contrast.

He had already noticed that goodness and wealth were
not necessarily associated. The wealthy could do as they
pleased and dictate what was acceptable. But this was
less something to write about than something to make
one wish to be wealthy. Since writing was often profitable, he would be happy if he were a writer. As a prospective writer, though, he was not ready to discover in the
spectacle or the contrast any order that he could transcribe. He could only observe and inquire. In his "Heard
in the Corridors" for February 18, 1893, he attributed to
his brother-in-law, Mame's husband, reflections that were

patently his own. Austin D. Brennan was made to question attempts to reason about "the ethical side of this earthly existence." "The Lord didn't intend that a man should reason out everything," he proclaimed. "At least there are innumerable mysteries which no person has yet been able to comprehend. . . . I may not do exactly right, but if I have faith in a greater benevolent Power, I do believe that I am happier than the man who has only his reason to depend on." [3] The difficulty was that for his faith Dreiser was depending upon his reason to provide, and the great mysteries remained unaccounted for.

Moreover, his attention was continually directed to the unaccountable rather than the accounted for. McCord, for one thing, was wont to argue that nature, not man, could plan, and that nature's forces were inscrutable. Wealth and poverty simply were, and human beings, wriggling in the grip of something they could not comprehend, were as often ridiculous or pathetic as they were magnificent. The fact was that whatever happened was unexpected and unexplainable. McCord delighted in prying into the exotic and unfamiliar, whether it was the customs of the ancient Romans or the worst slums of St. Louis, and he was enthralled by the processes of nature. Often he would contemplate a wasp dragging a grub across a field, or a moth beating itself free from a spider's web, and half-chortle and half-sigh over the cold, seemingly enforced mechanism of it all. [4]

Then there was Annie Besant, the English theosophist, who in January 1893 came to St. Louis to explain the new mysticism. When Dreiser asked her about the problem of poverty, she said: "Poverty is a disease from which both the poor and the rich suffer. There is in this life an element of ether in which and through which

49

this disease thrives and spreads. . . . All nature is out-raged, sinned against by poverty inasmuch as poverty is a crime against nature. The rich being a part of this great nature can not escape the results of the sin . . . and it were best to open their eyes and remove the disease than to endeavor to flee from it."

"You do not recognize, then," Dreiser asked, "a con-trolling principle — a God?"

"No, we do not. If there is a God, the order of this life is then manifestly unjust. Some beings are born with ability and strength, some with dulled senses, with weak-nesses and deformities. . . . Instead of accusing a di-vine being with being partial, we turn to the individual himself and find a solution of the apparent discrepancy in reincarnation." [5]

About the secrets of reincarnation, however, she was not very explicit.

Then there were his own experiences with the spirit world. In August 1893, when Dreiser was working for the *Republic*, J. Alexander McIvor Tyndall, in order to advertise his skill, requested the paper to provide a com-mittee to ride with him in a carriage through the crowded downtown streets while he, blindfolded, fol-lowed the directions that the man seated beside him might be thinking. It fell to Dreiser to do the thinking, and when Tyndall performed the feats decided upon, Dreiser was amazed as only a participant could be. Then that evening Tyndall, having questioned the powers of a rival, Jules Wallace, a medium, was challenged to a contest with Wallace at the opera house. After Wallace had materialized several spirits, promptly recognized by their friends, Tyndall undertook the usual task of find-ing hidden objects. It was when he began hunting a cigar that matters became exciting, for while he sniffed about for thought currents Wallace stepped forward, appeared to go into a trance, and with a demonic glare brought about Tyndall's complete physical collapse. The lights had to be turned out to quell the uproar that ensued — "almost a riot," as Dreiser's article was headlined.[6]

Whether all these accomplishments were genuine, Dreiser could not say. It was sufficient that they could not be explained. And in experiments he and his friends later carried on he was satisfied that mind's power was greater than matter.

There was yet one other mystery to perplex his understanding. That was the mystery of character. The careers of those he met in his work posed the questions of why men behaved as they did and what they lived for anyway. One capable reporter he knew was given to periodic debauches and once, boasting that he took dope, swallowed an overdose of morphine in Dreiser's presence. Another man, with a record more glittering than that of his superiors on the *Republic*, conscientiously proved his ability until he suddenly vanished, to be discovered by Dreiser in the slums, disheveled and dirty, begging a dollar. A third, who could write delightfully of Zola, Poe, or Baudelaire and was a master of epigrams, rejected both material possessions and emotions and drugged himself to death because he could find no pleasure in reality. When on one occasion Dreiser had to interview a wealthy manufacturer who had retired, he was struck by the fact that age and enfeeblement had overtaken a man once influential and strong. Life seemed to go on, sometimes, as though no individual's existence mattered. If one could not adjust oneself to life, that was disregarded. If one could adjust oneself to it, that too was of no importance in the end.[7]

Amid all these uncertainties reporting became colored

with some value, for observation became the form of understanding. To the extent that he could maintain detachment while permitting his feelings to enlist his interest, to that extent Dreiser could function as a useful reporter; and to the extent that the importance of his assignments increased and the facts he observed produced problems of organization, to that extent his reporting could be useful to the clarifying of his own point of view. In describing the layout and workings of a new three-million-dollar pumping plant and a seven-mile conduit being constructed in the northernmost part of the city to anticipate the needs of the rapidly expanding metropolis, he had to manage a vast collection of details that required the control of an ordering mind.[8] In recounting the horror of a train wreck in which a passenger train had crashed into some oil cars and left survivors writhing in blazing oil, he had to write a report in whose mere facts, when properly selected, should be found the terror of what he had witnessed.[9] On such occasions as these, newspaper work approximated self-expression.

But as far as his work for the *Globe-Democrat* was concerned, there were not many such occasions to interrupt the routine and bring out the spectator in him. Indeed, the routine became dreary, and involved situations that tinged his regard for reporting with disappointment. While noting the amoral conduct of successful men of the world, he had somehow assumed that such conduct bore no relationship to the success of newspaper reporters. And although in Chicago he had seen that editors were more interested in persuading readers than in enlightening them, it was not until he worked in St. Louis that he realized the extent to which he was expected to ignore ethics in order to procure news. Then he learned that if a piece of news was the reward, no citizen was entitled to privacy, and no reporter was expected to view anyone's feelings with anything but cold-blooded indifference.

Although this disillusionment contributed to his thoughts of turning to an artist's career, circumstances encouraged him to find new hope where he was. His reporting had brought him praise from McCullagh and a raise in pay, and with the extra money he was able to indulge in clothes that he fancied were Bohemian. At the same time the man who wrote the column entitled "The Theaters" left, and Dreiser, seeing the opportunity to call himself drama editor and to approach the world of art more closely, asked McCullagh for the job and received it. Immediately he considered himself engaged in a great labor and, about to become an important playwright himself, envisaged intimate friendships with actors and beautiful women.

The theatrical fare in St. Louis was varied. The plays ranged from *Ali Baba* and *Robin Hood* to *The Professor's Love Story* and *Aristocracy*, and their actors from Sol Smith Russell and John L. Sullivan to Richard Mansfield and E. H. Sothern. Such an offering could provide a devotee with some practice in evaluation and the formulation of critical standards. But Dreiser was too captivated by the spectacular, romantic idea of the theater to indulge in distinctions, and then, in addition, his column was not designed to provide more than a series of announcements of current attractions, whereby each play received a paragraph of fewer than a dozen sentences outlining the plot, citing the main scene, and listing the cast. At best he tempered conventional opinions with a hint of interested familiarity. *The Man from Boston*, with John L., was "no worse than Gentleman Jack, but . . . certainly no better — a very airy plot interlarded

with specialties." [10] *Paul Kauvar* was "an excellent drama
of high romantic order. . . . Those who are interested
in the exciting times of the great French revolution, with
its streams of blood and mountains of dead bodies, can
get an inkling of the dramatic realism of it all from seeing Paul Kauvar." [11] The closest he came to critical comment was in reviewing Bronson Howard's *Aristocracy*
when he said Howard had learned "there is a chance for
dramatists of the future who will write satires on the
present all-pervading idiocy of the American public in
some things." [12]

Even when he departed from the conventional he remained uncritical, and also unaware of his departure. Attending the recital of a colored singer, Mme Sissieretta
Jones, called by her admirers "the Black Patti" and proclaimed in advance of her arrival as "The Wonder of
19th Century," [13] he was moved to praise her talent. But
it was mainly rhapsody rather than analysis that he provided. "Her singing reminds one of the beauty of nature
and brings back visions of the still, glassy water and
soft swaying branches of some drowsy nook in summer
time," he wrote. Then he explained it very simply: "She
trills the chromatic scale to perfection, and varies it in
a manner too rich to describe. Her last notes sometimes
die away in a long sweet strain." [14] What Dreiser remained unaware of until other editors critized the *Globe-
Democrat* was that in St. Louis one did not praise Negroes, certainly not extravagantly, even if they deserved it.

Rather than try to account for Mme Jones's appeal, he
described visions of nature evoked by her tone. Likewise,
rather than compare what he saw on the stage with what
he saw in daily life, he continued to yield to visions and
supposed that what he witnessed in the theater was what
he could see somewhere in actuality. Love amid velvet

and plush settings; fortune amid gilded salons; exclusiveness amid exclusive people — these were the aspects that defined the realm, and to move in it he needed only to move to it. He would not, to be sure, find it in St. Louis: plays were set in New York, London, Paris, Vienna, or the Orient. To enjoy romance, he would have to go east. Soon he was picturing his life in a New York studio, where he would wear fine clothes and be socially superior, and where if vice and poverty existed they would be, as in the plays, divinely repellent or divinely sad. He would himself be writing plays, of course, dramas of a semi-tragic kind, or emulating the successes of Reginald De Koven with scripts for comic operas.[15]

At that time, in fact, he was jotting down scenes and plots of his own, eventually outlining a comic opera he entitled *Jeremiah I*. Its comic qualities were attested to by the laughter of McCord and Wood, but more significant was the wishful thinking that pervaded the plot. An old Indiana farmer, finding a magical Aztec stone in his field, is enabled to transport himself back to Aztec times just as a religious ceremony is in progress to select a new ruler. He, of course, is selected, and though at first afraid for his life, becomes a despot who sentences some three hundred ex-advisers to be poisoned. Instead of carrying out this mass execution, however, he reforms through the delicious influence of a beautiful maiden who makes his repentance a prerequisite to her accepting his attentions. Because of her he transforms his government into a republic with himself a candidate for president.[16] Thus a cruel tyrant becomes a man of justice and virtue by means of a conversion that costs him none of his power; rather, he is all the more powerful for the fact of his virtue.

Late in May such dreams were ironically dissipated.

One Sunday evening when he was supposed to cover the opening of a new play, he was assigned, in addition, to report a hold-up that had occurred in a distant suburb. Instead of protesting, and thereby allowing another man to be given the theaters, he decided to write his column on the basis of advance notices. Unfortunately, he did not know until he read the papers the next day that rainstorms in neighboring states to the west had caused washouts, halting trains and preventing the opening that he had so glibly reported. Then he did not await a summons from McCullagh, but leaving a note explaining the contretemps, quickly removed his belongings from the offices and slipped away,[17] to start again as an ordinary reporter a week later, on the *Republic*.

Although he was at first humiliated to earn eighteen dollars a week instead of the thirty he had been receiving, and never was satisfied to work for a paper whose prestige was so much less than the *Globe-Democrat's*, as a writer he profited from the experience. Under the influence of the city editor, H. B. Wandell, he became more precise in his use of details and more confident of his ability to handle them. "All the facts you know, just as far as they will carry you," Wandell would say concerning some catastrophe. ". . . Get in all the touches of local color you can. And remember Zola and Balzac, my boy, remember Zola and Balzac. Bare facts are what are needed in cases like this, with lots of color as to the scenery or atmosphere, the room, the other people, the street, and all that. You get me?"[18] And Dreiser would always nod, even though he had never read either Zola or Balzac; but then, the reading was not essential to understanding that facts and a wealth of details were important.

Wandell seemed to gloat most over incidents involving bloodshed and the police, but not all Dreiser's assignments related to brutality or crime. Early in July the *Republic* prepared to raise money for its annual fresh-air fund by sponsoring a baseball game between two fraternal organizations, the Owls and the Elks, consisting respectively of fat men and lean. Dreiser was designated to complete the advance publicity by writing a few humorous prognostications before the game. Although the crude mock-heroics that readers enjoyed demanded but trifling insights, they, as much as a murder, demanded a grasp of detail and a show of confidence in their presentation, and both of these Dreiser exhibited.[19] In fact, he found their writing so easy that he composed them in his room in order that his work should not appear to others to be as easy as it was.

Trivial as such an assignment might be, it gave him the opportunity to impress Wandell, and when the owner of the paper, Charles W. Knapp, and Wandell were both pleased, Dreiser was entrusted with a more important task, for which he was clothed with all the dignity of a special correspondent. The *Republic* had been conducting two state-wide popularity contests for school teachers, the twenty-five most popular of whom were to be given a trip to the Chicago World's Fair of 1893,[20] and he was chosen to accompany the girls and send back news of the trip. This elevation in status provided new occasions for his tireless self-examination and his inclination to romanticize. Worried at the outset about how he should fare among two dozen girls, he was shortly concerned by which of several he should devote himself to. Preferring Sallie White, whom he was eventually to marry, he decided she was so different that he could not bring himself to stroll with her in the evenings and made love to a lusty Irish girl instead. Yet when he was with Sallie in the daytime, he wondered whether he did not really prefer her younger sister Rose, who seemed more sophisticated. In the same way, excited as he was by his return to Chicago and former haunts, he was more excited by recollections of the city in which he had become important and, finding Al and Ed faring poorly, persuaded them to join him in St. Louis later, only to find his own routine there dreary once he had returned from the freedom and wonder of the fair.

It was less his disappointments than his successes, however, that now began to pose problems. Made a traveling correspondent with the privilege of carrying a little card [21] that had "Mr. Theodore Dreiser" and " 'Republic' " printed on it, he saw outlying regions of both Missouri and neighboring states which he would never have seen as an average reporter, and he was exposed to a greater variety of experiences than St. Louis alone could provide. He wrote on Sunday-school conventions [22] and on prize fights,[23] on football games between the merchants and builders,[24] and on life among the water-works laborers; [25] on train robberies, murders,[26] and reforms in the local poorhouse.[27] And as the scope of his obligations was increased, his powers were sharpened. A fluency in humor was evident in his sports stories. Narrative skill was developed in his account of Tyndall's contest with Wallace. In writing about "puddler's row," the camp where the workmen who were constructing the water-works extension lived, he exhibited not only the command of details he had shown in describing the construction itself for the *Globe-Democrat*, but also a sense of character that invested the camp's heterogeneous groups with dramatic interest. And in presenting Gallagher, the boss of the poorhouse, he discovered how to embody his sympathies in the plain recital of facts; by letting events relate their own story, he painted a convincing picture of an honest humanitarian who was being set upon by grafting and callous politicans. But what produced the problem was that the work that had fostered these skills now seemed an unsatisfactory way of exercising them.

The rights and wrongs of matters were not always so obvious to Dreiser as they were in the case of Gallagher. On one occasion he might be engaged in exposing a fraudulent revivalist, only to discover that when he had all the facts, he had to choose between suppressing news and revealing news that would hurt some innocent persons. On another he might find himself aroused by a tale of apparently vicious rape, only to have his sympathies shifted when the accused was lynched in terror and his family left sobbing with grief. A writer could not condemn with certainty — that was certain. Therefore, Dreiser reflected, it was the business of the writer not to indict but to interpret.[28] Yet interpretation itself was so complicated by the presence of mysteries he could not penetrate, like the relationship between morals and success or the importance of an individual's life, that even if he had never been troubled by conflicting emotions he would have been unable to produce an interpretation that went beyond a definition of his perplexity. And newspapers scarcely provided the place for publishing that.

So he became restless in the face of challenges to his curiosity and dissatisfied with journalism as a way of meeting them. Yet at the same time that he longed to question, he longed to be satisfied. Awareness of mystery, the feeling of uncertainty, induced the desire for belief and something he could count on. Consequently, in the moment he was closest to sensing his own mortality, in that moment loneliness became keenest and he craved love.

The satisfaction of this craving was inhibited by the same difficulties as had existed in Chicago when Lois and other girls had been at hand. From the very beginning of his stay in St. Louis he was faced with opportunities for at least physical fulfillment that served only to revive the old dreams of ideal opportunities. The women he confronted most often were his landladies, and they, with a near unanimity that was remarkable, found him an aphrodisiac.[29] The first who endeavored to make a conquest was æsthetically repulsive, and Dreiser was quite shocked at her efforts to seduce him. She usually approached him at breakfast time in a way that was to her doubtless cute, but to him instinctively disgusting. After a week of these jentacular attentions, he quietly packed his suitcase and sneaked out of the house to find safer lodgings elsewhere. But he was not fated to be secure in these matters. Impressed by Dreiser's attempts to dress the Bohemian and, in conformity with his fancied role, to decorate his room with tapestries, Oriental prints, and a plaster nude, the good lady of this next establishment concluded that here was a man of the world, and behaved accordingly. Although the consequences should have had the virtue of convincing Dreiser of powers he had so often doubted, they served at times only as occasions for self-examination and idealization that left him feeling degraded, until he moved again, and again after that, keeping in mind as he hunted rooms that possible romances might ensue and that therefore the landladies had best be acceptable. When he beheld beauty, he was stirred by sex; but when faced with sex alone, he yearned for the beauty that was lacking. Unable to find himself in virtue, he now could not lose himself in vice, and he wondered when his good angel might appear.

It was solely by the chance of his having been assigned to the World's Fair trip that he had met Sallie White, and if he had had doubts and hesitations during the visit in Chicago, he had few doubts in retrospect. When in September 1893 he finally wrote to her and learned she was coming to St. Louis on a visit, he read in her words a delightful simplicity and promptly pictured her walking with him along some leafy lane, or reclining in a boat he was rowing on some stream, and eventually of their both living together, with her pushing a baby carriage and him even accompanying her to church. As he thought of the girl he had known at the fair against the romantic background of his imagining, he was certain this was love of the most exalted character, and was more certain when he discovered himself writing letters thick with emotions and ideals that she seemed to understand. By the time she arrived in St. Louis he was ready to entertain her as a being of her special sphere deserved. As a former drama critic he could get passes to the various theaters and began by taking her to a matinee to hear Chauncey Olcott sing. Thereafter he took her to plays and restaurants; watched the wealthy patrons driving along in carriages and wished he had one to escort her home in; and went with her to the Methodist church. Eventually he was permitted to put his arm around her.

Yet he could not afford to marry right away; he could only think about it. He might have returned to the *Globe-Democrat*, he was led to believe, and there earned more money, but the question of what he really wanted as a career arose and, pondering it, he remained where he was, thus keeping his relationship with Sallie suspended in an aura of ideality. To hold this love, he sought to deserve it; and to deserve it, he arrayed himself in flashy clothes he considered appropriate. The men on the *Republic* thought he was showing "some class" and perhaps "laying it on thick," and Sallie's neighbors considered him "a big silly" who was "going about gawking and mooning." [30] But he was lost in his romance and ecstatic when at last she let him kiss her. He secured a picture of her and hung it on his wall, framed in silver. He purloined one of her ribbons, formally proposed to her, and bought her a diamond ring. But the conflict within him between the longing for her and the longing for the dazzlements of the East was not being resolved to enable her to step out of her frame into his room. The lure of the cities was too strong and their rewards seemed too close to his grasp to allow him to commit himself to something as limited as marriage in St. Louis. Besides, there were people who tried to persuade him he ought to leave, and when he thought about what they were saying, he persuaded himself.

There was the advice of John Maxwell, for one. Maxwell had come to St. Louis looking for another job and, seeing Sallie White's picture, inquired who she was. Upon learning, he urged Dreiser not to tie himself to a wife and settle down at the very moment he was getting a start. Moreover, he shrewdly deduced that Sallie was more than two years older than Dreiser and he suspected that she was a churchgoer and therefore too narrow for him. She would want a home and children, and Dreiser would want freedom to wander and do as he pleased. "Why, man," Maxwell told him, "you don't know your own mind yet." Although Dreiser told himself he rejected this argument, the next time his beloved came to the city he asked her what she would do if he changed. After meditating awhile, she looked at him appealingly and said "But you won't. Let's not think of anything like that any more. We won't, will we?" [31] And then he felt sad and wondered whether she did understand him. He even felt sorry for her at the moment he craved her most.

Then Paul arrived, starring in a melodrama. If his brother's presence enabled Dreiser to boast of his connections to McCord, Wood, and others on the paper, and even to boast of himself to Paul, it also brought compellingly to mind the reality of New York. In a week of breakfasts with Paul, during which Paul insisted the West was too narrow and slow for anyone with the intellectual promise Dreiser had, Dreiser came to feel that only in New York could he hope to realize his ambitions. There Paul had risen to his present position as a song-writer who had organized a publishing company and was in the process of writing a play. There it was McEnnis had originally said he should go, and one newspaperman was wont to say that compared with New York, Chicago was but a way-station. Moreover, Paul assured him, their sister was established there and would be happy to receive him. When in addition Paul was introduced to Sallie and tactfully commented that she was charming but that if he were in his brother's shoes he would not think of marrying just yet, Dreiser needed little more encouragement to pack up his belongings. He felt that he could consider with some confidence making a place for himself almost anywhere now. It was only a question of where to begin.

The answer was suggested by a friend, J. T. Hutchinson, who had been on the *Chicago Daily Globe* and, through Dreiser's influence, now had work in St. Louis.

Unimaginative and unresourceful, he often depended on Dreiser, but seeing no future in St. Louis, talked of their running a country paper near his family's home outside of Grand Rapids, Ohio. He had saved some money and his father would lend them some more. In the country were none of the uncertainties of a city paper, none of the hectic metropolitan chores, none of the filth and noise. In the country one could be independent, and a figure in the community. He began picturing this happy life in December, and by the end of February, Dreiser, with visions of a vine-clad cottage, a job that paid, and a role of importance such as a congressman's or a governor's, temporarily dismissed New York and decided he would go to Ohio. He bade good-by to Sallie, promising all kinds of successes. He rejected a last-minute offer from the *Republic* to increase his wages, telling himself as he did so that they should have made this offer long before.[32] And on Monday evening, March 5, 1894, carrying a letter from Charles W. Knapp that read: "Any favors extended to the bearer[,] Mr. T. H. Dreiser[,] traveling correspondent for the St[.] Louis Republic, will be greatly appreciated by me on behalf of the Republic," [33] he took his bags to the Union Station, eastward bound at last.

Suddenly, however, now that he was really leaving everything he knew, he felt that he was a failure. Successful men did not go about the world in search of a career.

IV

First Principles

Dreiser had only to go to Grand Rapids and neighboring villages to realize the absurdity of the expectations that had taken him there. Although on the train he might revive his self-esteem and on arrival find the Ohio countryside picturesque, the moment he stepped into the scene and became, if only for a few hours, a part of it, that moment he was disabused. The people were unintellectual and narrow. In the lines of their faces he saw the tracings of routine; in the deeper wrinkles he beheld the grooves of custom. Moreover, the financial prospects for the paper itself dispirited him. Hutchinson had discovered that the *Wood County Herald* in the near-by town of Weston was for sale, but when Dreiser accompanied him to inspect it, they found the equipment rundown, the list of subscribers reduced to barely five hundred, and prospective advertisers waiting to be sure the paper conformed to their prejudices before committing themselves.

To Dreiser everything bespoke futility. A visit to a paper in Bowling Green was no more encouraging: the price was too high, and besides, as he looked about and noted forests of derricks driving oil wells, he felt the attraction of all the excitement and tension he had sought to escape. "I'm so used to the noise and bustle of the streets that these fields seem lonely," he told Hutchinson; he would never get used to it.[1] A few days later, after a rest he could enjoy once he had decided to leave, he entrained for the nearest city, Toledo, and began what was destined to be the last stage of his newspaper career, one that was to culminate in a final destruction of his airiest fancies and the development of a way of looking at facts to give them the semblance of order.

He remained in Toledo less than a week and might not have remained even that long had it not been for Arthur Henry, city editor of the *Toledo Blade*.[2] When Dreiser came to the *Blade* asking for a position, Henry offered him a four-day job that included covering a streetcar strike, and Dreiser, because he had found nothing elsewhere and needed money, accepted. He set out for the car barns to observe events on Saturday morning, March 24, 1894, the strike's third day. The company officials, who had precipitated the tie-up by discharging four union men, were then in the process of inducting scabs.[3] But there was little violence, and the self-conscious anxiety of the few persons who risked riding the trolleys afforded Dreiser mainly the opportunity for caricature.[4] Not being blind, however, to more serious implications of the spectacle, he went to the recruiting manager and posed as a St. Louis conductor and union man in order to elicit the information that no union man could be hired.[5] Henry was so pleased with Dreiser's handling of all this that he took the story to the composing-room himself. Then when, in addition, Dreiser wrote one or two brief descriptions of farm life around Toledo and Henry called them beautiful, Dreiser felt he was somehow understood. The two began to talk freely. They had had similar experiences in Chicago; they had mutual acquaintances; they shared almost identical dreams. Henry, a lover of books and author of some poems and fairy tales, wanted to become a poet and novelist;

66

Dreiser, of course, wanted to be a playwright, and was enchanted. By the end of Wednesday, March 28, when Dreiser wrote a last article,[6] the two were intimate friends. A lonely wanderer, craving the affection of women, Dreiser found Henry's understanding rich in meaning. Had Henry been a girl, Dreiser would, he thought, have married him.

Because Henry was fond of Dreiser, in turn,[7] he wanted Dreiser to stay, and Dreiser did try to get a job on a rival paper; but there were still no openings and he knew he must move on. He wondered whether his best chance might not lie west of Chicago or perhaps in Detroit, but Henry suggested that Dreiser canvass Cleveland and Buffalo and be ready to return to Toledo should something develop. Since these cities were so close and, in addition, lay nearer New York, whither Paul would return from his tour during the summer, he decided to follow Henry's advice. Although he still wished for the wealth and artistic atmosphere he had lacked as a reporter, he decided to continue in newspaper work awhile longer; if it did not guarantee success, it at least permitted him to be a looker-on.

The prospects in Cleveland were only discouraging. The papers were well supplied with local men and had little interest in employing outsiders. One editor was willing to let him submit some features for the Sunday edition, but when Dreiser wanted to write of the magnificence of the residential section, or the activity at some new steelworks, the editor rejected these suggestions as trite and let him tell only about a near-by chicken farm. In two weeks the work he was allowed to do earned him barely seven dollars and a half. Eventually, torturing himself as ever by envying the wealthy inhabitants, wondering whether he would succeed or fail, yearning for some beautiful girl to smile at him, he did little else than sit in the lobby of the Hollenden Hotel staring at the passing throng, or wander along Lake Erie, frustrated and sad, thinking about the beauty of nature and his own loneliness, and returning to his room to turn the pages of A *Sentimental Journey*.[8]

Buffalo presented nothing more promising and, though alive with grain elevators, ships, and coal pockets, seemed characterized mainly by slums, filth, and vice. Garbage-littered streets, flickering gaslights, and ragged children were not what he had envisaged when he left St. Louis. In fact, the contrast between wealth and poverty became the more disturbing for its recurrence. More than ever it needed to be accounted for. But then there were other cities, and things might yet be different. Ultimately there would be New York — when his brother returned. Meanwhile Pittsburgh seemed the most likely place. So, buying a ticket at a cut-rate broker's, he was soon gazing from the train at the first mountains he had ever seen, staring at sooty-faced miners and their stocky women, and nearing the place where, it so happened, he would find a justification for the already enjoyable role of spectator and an explanation of the problems that were troubling him.

From the moment he stepped onto the station platform early one mid-April evening, he felt invited to make discoveries. Power and tension seemed to lurk throughout the city which, sparkling with lights, lay crouched among the huge walling hills. As he stood on one of the bridges crossing the Monongahela River, he beheld flames erupting from forty or fifty stacks and heard a titanic pounding and crackling that sounded like echoes from great subterranean anvils. The waters of the river were lit for a mile or more by the glow. To Dreiser all this was the flash and rumbling of a new world, and when he could view his surroundings by daylight he was all the more confirmed. The newspapers reported accidents that he had not encountered before. Men had their hands lacerated while working in a 23-inch mill, or were burned by overturned ladles of hot metal. The names of the injured often suggested ways of life he had met only on occasional wanderings in Chicago. There were Poles, Lithuanians, Hungarians, and Russians in Pittsburgh. And the names where events occurred carried associations: Squirrel Hill, Moon Run, Braddock, and Homestead. Moreover, the city had the attraction of variety. He could stroll in a park or browse in the Carnegie public library. He could watch the streetcars climbing and twisting over the surrounding ridges. He could ascend Mount Washington to the south and find artistically impressive the sight of men below who seemed so small and curious in their activity that they appeared unconnected with him even while he realized that they had created the streets and bridges and factories and that for them the stacks belched fire at night. And he could explore the familiar yet increasingly extreme contrasts between wealth and poverty and investigate the meaning of the success he sought.

April 1894 was a particularly opportune time in Pittsburgh for Dreiser to engage in such exploration and investigation. Early in the month Coxey's Army had been camped in the Allegheny baseball park, and strikes at the Connellsville mines had led to violence. With echoes of the shooting of Henry Clay Frick less than two years before still reverberating along the Monongahela, the plight of the poorer classes was kept vividly before the public. Dreiser's attention was, of course, naturally focused on the problem, but finding the struggle for sur-

vival assuming dramatic form, he was the more affected
by what he discovered. He was greatly shocked, for example, when within a few days of his arrival he visited
Homestead and found the workers' houses grimy with
soot and crammed together along streets of mud, and
saw the yards and alleys cluttered with excrement and
waste. He was depressed by the sullen, defeated expressions of the men, who plodded from dark home to dark
mill and back again without a glimmer of his fascination
before the furnaces, cranes, and cars of molten iron
and without even a particle of his awareness that they
were producing steel for the rails and bridges of the
world. He was heavily oppressed by the discrepancy between their efforts and their perception. When afterward he took his inevitable stroll along the well-paved
streets of the residential sections of the city and admired
the tree-shaded homes with their great lawns, he questioned anew how such disparity of condition should be.
He looked with uncomfortable envy at the expensive carriages attended by servants in livery, and felt resentfully
that the reclining nobles within must be gazing out
with lofty condescension. He wondered whether something could not be done to diminish some of the inequalities. The wealthy might realize that chance sometimes played a part in success and failure. They might
be less arrogant. They might even pay higher wages. Yet
he would have to observe life awhile longer to understand it. He hoped only that he might remain in Pittsburgh to do so.

A job on the *Pittsburgh Dispatch* enabled him to stay,
and although his success in procuring it nourished his
unceasing dream of rising to a position of importance,
his thinking was soon centered on the more specific problems around him. Beginning with ordinary news-report-

ing, he shortly was allowed to prepare feature articles, and eventually, before he left in the early winter, he became a traveling correspondent and unpaid assistant to the dramatics editor. As his experience became further extended, the problems he had to think about became more perplexing. As usual, it was his fellow reporters who exerted the initial influences, in this instance the labor man in particular, a man named Martyn. Martyn helped Dreiser understand something of the nature of industrial strife. He explained the uses of cheap foreign labor, the role of subsidized preachers, and the biased policies of papers subservient to the wealthy interests, then took him on a tour of the city's worst slums, where tenement life was shrouded in smoke and carried on amid the odors and waste of sewage. Dreiser wondered why people submitted to such conditions, why they did not rebel. When he looked at the faces of some, he saw resignation that he realized made thoughts of rebellion absurd, but when he watched others, he beheld a contentment he could not account for. "It must be that just work is happiness," Martyn suggested by way of explanation,[9] and Dreiser accepted that until he began to think of those who did not do what they wanted to do when they worked and those whose living consisted of degrading vice. In Pittsburgh many girls walked the streets and many houses of disrepute flourished under the expensive protection of the police. Surely happiness did not lie there. Yet there must be some answer to the persistence of so much inequality, wretchedness, and frustration.

As he searched for answers, he groped for formulas, but formulas always appeared to ignore the questions and left him, eventually, certain only that life was bewilderingly complex. His father had a formula. The

Catholic Church had a formula. But their formula was of no relevancy to the important, practical matter of living. The existence of poverty among the righteous and of wealth among those devoid of charitable feelings was for Dreiser evidence enough to refute religious doctrine. Similarly, when on one occasion he questioned Thomas B. Reed, recent Speaker of the House of Representatives, about Coxey's Army and heard it likened to "revolution," he found political doctrines unrealistic. "But what about the thing of which they are complaining?" Dreiser asked. "It doesn't matter what their grievance is," Reed retorted. "This is a government of law and prescribed political procedure. Our people must abide by that." [10] The priests and politicians might describe well enough what ought to be, but they certainly seemed to disregard what actually was. As for himself, he had occasion one night in the company of a prostitute to realize his own lack of discernment. Noticing that her arm was spotted with the needle pricks of a dope syringe, he was appalled and proceeded to preach to her and tell her it was not the sort of thing a person like her should be doing; why did she do it — until she wearily said: "Oh, great God[,] why do you talk? What do you know about life, anyhow?" [11]

Dreiser did not actually want to plunge into life and promote reforms. Too aloof and too confused, he was caught up by the currents and carried along while he wondered and speculated about them, observing the baffled gropings of others who were more deeply immersed in the destructive element. He wanted primarily to be superior to those who were sucked down in vortex and undertow; he wanted to be secure and to understand what it was that made life precarious. He wanted to find some recognition somewhere that verbal nostrums were inadequate for man's condition.

It was probably inevitable that he should eventually discover the novels of Balzac and perceive in them the awareness he was looking for. And once he had perceived this, it was certainly inevitable that he should then feel his own views were significant and discern a way to express them. Assigned to cover the news at city hall and police headquarters in Allegheny, he often found so little worth reporting that he had time to spend browsing among the open shelves of the Carnegie Library across the way. One afternoon, noticing a set of the writer whom Wandell had so often invoked, he pulled down a volume entitled *The Wild Ass's Skin*. Within a few pages he was enthralled and sat until dusk reading through the story. It expressed his own moods and ambitions with startling clarity. Like him, Raphael was a seeker of success who brooded about his poverty and his unrecognized greatness and meditated in the presence of nature. Like him, Raphael had worn threadbare clothes, felt awkward and shy, and under the influence of his father looked upon even a café as a disreputable haunt. Like him, Raphael had dreamed of women and was searching for his ideal. And then, unlike him, Raphael, by means of the magic skin, by dint of merely wishing, was able to make all the dreams come true. In the society where Raphael was enabled to experience all delights, Dreiser could see the sophistication of which he had so long wished to partake, and in the unsmirking presentation of revelry and the dispassionate discussions of morality he detected the point of view of a writer who saw that life was amoral. When early in the tale he read of Taillefer's remarkable banquet, he could believe himself in the presence of rare wit and profundity. Men flicked their little fingers at education, raised their eyebrows at world forces, and tossed coins to settle the question of the existence of God. Religion and dogma were placed in a gay tone. Catholicism was criticized without threats of damnation. The Deity was toasted before the serving of coffee. And men and women associated without inhibitions. When Raphael commented that sudden descents into the world from the divine height of scientific meditation were very exhausting, Dreiser surely felt himself comprehended.

The lesson of *The Wild Ass's Skin*, however, he seemed somehow to disregard. Raphael had his wishes, but he also paid his price, slowly killing himself with his desires. Although this raised the question of one's own limits, Dreiser did not pause to ask himself questions. Finding his own feelings transcribed, he failed to inspect their criticism and hungrily reached for another volume, *A Great Man of the Provinces in Paris*, in which he could see himself again represented, this time even more thoroughly than before. Both Dreiser and Lucien de Rubempré desired to be writers, Lucien craving to be a poet and novelist. Both were attracted by displays of wealth and the contrasts between luxury and want. Both envied the well-dressed men and women who walked arm in arm, and both thought about their own inconsequential roles in the glittering welter of the city as they yearned for women grander and more beautiful than those they had known. And both had become journalists. Lucien had done so because he saw no immediate success in the self-denying career of a poet, and then like Dreiser found journalists to be a group of cynical men. In Lucien's world the newspapers were more important than in Dreiser's, but in both worlds the same hypocrisy, exploitation, and cold calculation prevailed. Although Lucien, like Raphael, paid the price of his success, Dreiser was more impressed by the spectacle of the world in which success was possible. The cities he had lived in resembled Paris in all essential respects. As he read two more volumes, he was the more confirmed. What Balzac had said of France might, with some modifications, be said of the United States. Thus, Pittsburgh now, with its rivers and bridges, its poverty and wealth, its huge industries and great financiers, might be regarded as a kind of workaday Paris. And it could be regarded as a spectacle that had meaning because it was a spectacle. Balzac's portrayal seemed to support that. Dreiser liked particularly the way Balzac wove comments and speculations into the narrative and sometimes concluded with an epilogue. The form and content of Balzac's approach to life suited Dreiser's temperament and experience.

Yet he was not entirely satisfied. There was, after all, something distressing in discovering that one was probably right in viewing the world as amoral. He turned away from Balzac for a while and read George Eliot and Bulwer-Lytton. But then he made a study of Fielding, whose *Joseph Andrews* and *Tom Jones* had been favorites of his for some years, and Fielding, of course, like Balzac, presented him with comments on the social spectacle and gave him a further instance of the external and omniscient artistic point of view. The practice of detached observation was in consequence the more solidly founded.

It did not take Dreiser long to embody the Balzacian influence in his work for the *Dispatch*. When shortly after his discovery of *The Wild Ass's Skin* his editor asked him whether he could think up some kind of feature, he invented something that his reading might have

75

suggested. Near the conclusion of *The Wild Ass's Skin*
Balzac had made one of his interpolations, asking:
"Who has not, at some time or other in his life, watched
the comings and goings of an ant, slipped straws into a
yellow slug's one breathing-hole, studied the vagaries of
a slender dragon-fly, pondered admiringly over the countless veins in an oak-leaf . . . ? Who has not looked long
in delight at the effects of sun and rain on a roof of
brown tiles, at the dewdrops, or at the variously shaped
petals of the flower-cups? Who has not sunk into these
idle, absorbing meditations . . . ?"[12] Dreiser, of course,
had sunk into such meditations, and Balzac's words gave
them æsthetic validity. Thus supported, he decided to
write about an ambitious and meditative young fly
which, contemplating the scope of its opportunities in a
world already overcrowded with flies, inspected various
sites where it might alight and finally settled upon a
shiny pate that seemed to offer a polished field of endeavor. The editor liked the piece and told Dreiser to
write others in that vein.

From mid-May through late August Dreiser produced
a column or two every few days.[13] Sometimes, they were
light and whimsical; other times they were melancholy
or serious. Generally they had the tone of the familiar
essay. In subjects they recalled a column that Lucien de
Rubempré, in *A Great Man of the Provinces in Paris,*
wrote early in his career under the title "The Man in the
Street." Lucien's column was devoted to sketches of
Paris life, its oddities, its commonplace events, and its
characters. Dreiser's essays were similarly devoted to
Pittsburgh life. They told how cats became woolly in
cold-storage warehouses and how babies behaved on
streetcars; they set forth the practices of practical jokers
and described the terrors of the weatherman beset by

people who resented his predictions; they expounded the doctrine of the survival of the unfittest, whereby people were shown becoming smaller and meaner, and they portrayed hoboes along the river shore and girls who attempted suicide. Although the majority of these embodied the kind of humor newspaper editors liked, they were not expressive of any witty bent on Dreiser's part. Collectively they reminded readers that one person's smiles were frequently counterbalanced by another's tears, and implied that the world was one which no complacent formula could comprise.

Dreiser's attitude was often best disclosed by the structure of his essays. When he wrote on the blueness of "Blue Monday," he began with reference to the morning's headache, proceeded through the bewildered actions of people throughout the day, and concluded before a pile of the week's laundry, to one side of which was a gloomy little heap of little clothes belonging to a little girl who had just died. When he wrote on music heard on his wanderings about the city, he began with the vender of penny whistles, proceeded to the whistling factory worker, and concluded with the requiem sounding over mourners kneeling before a bier. And when he wrote on men who carried lockets and old letters with them and who stopped during the day's business to gaze at them fondly, he led up to the moment when even the cynic who scorned sentiment was heard to burst out with feeling for his beloved, now dead. Thus from the casual occurrences of daily life Dreiser took his readers to the fact of death and sorrow.

It was the sorrow rather than the death, however, that he liked to emphasize. Even when writing about old Hancock Street and the morgue, he was inclined to wander from the cold slabs to the bethel, where the homeless and hungry might find a rude bed and bowl of soup for a dime. And telling about Potter's Field, he emphasized not that it was a burial ground, but that it was the burial ground of the "nameless" and "friendless" dead, who had "no loving ones to watch over" them.[14] Although he declared: "It's blessed not to be able to feel the desolateness of that mound of the future, which shall be one's own and over which the elements shall sweep in their varying moods, as though we had never been," [15] he could not help returning to the more desolate phases of existence. "Man is not an impartial animal," he explained in a reflective moment. "He cannot regard any struggle between forces with perfect dispassion and disinterestedness." [16] And thus, as though he had to fix his attention on the darker side of life to feel completely the impact of reality, Dreiser was drawn to the unfortunate and the beaten.

At the same time he looked upon distress with the attitude of one who maintained the hope of avoiding it himself. He continued to crave the sophistication Balzac had convinced him was possible, and instead of planning to become a feature-writer in Pittsburgh, dreamed the more, wished he were a Carnegie or a Frick, and encountering New York wherever he turned — in newspapers, in overheard conversations among sportsmen and financiers, in illustrations and society columns of magazines — looked to the east for his salvation.

Now even his relationship with Sallie White contrived to urge him more resolutely to his mecca. Thus, to begin with, reading George Du Maurier's *Trilby*, which ran from January to August in *Harper's New Monthly Magazine*, he transformed Little Billee's predicament to fit his own and began to fear that through poverty rather than trickery he would lose the girl he loved. Then, imagining his future with Sallie in danger, he discarded whatever doubts he had had about her and by the end of August secured a vacation in which to pay her a visit. Finally, visiting her at her home, which was characterized by its idyllic setting and romantic charm, he became so inflamed with desire for her that, when he was restrained from transgressing the ultimate boundary of propriety, he became restless and resolved to find something in New York that would enable them to be truly united. As if timed to prompt him to action, a letter from Paul reached him at the Whites', persuading him to see the city before the summer's end and promising to show him a dozen new worlds.

What he found in New York convinced him that it was there he must live; yet it also convinced him that he was not quite ready to do so. The atmosphere was, on the whole, one of glittering success. There were, to be sure, some poorer sections of Manhattan near the ferry slip, but he soon forgot these and gaped enchanted as Paul guided him through the city. There were huge department stores bustling with shoppers; there were exclusive milliners and jewelers catering to the smartly dressed carriage trade; there were famous theaters where the great actors performed; there were magnificent beach resorts and luxurious hotels where the display of wealth was at its most extravagant. "The people out west don't know yet what's going on," Paul remarked, "but the rich are getting control. . . . A writer like you could make 'em see that." [17] In New York dreams and desires seemed to be fulfilled hourly. Paul himself was palpably tasting the rewards of living here. He spoke familiarly of journalists, actors, and playwrights he knew; he was a partner in the prospering firm of Howley, Haviland & Company, the music publishers; and wherever he stopped he became a center of the knowing gossip and jokes that were going the rounds of the Broadway initiates.

On the other hand, there was for Dreiser a forbidding aspect to New York life. When he sat in his sister's apartment and heard vessels in the harbor some ten miles out, he thought of the huge sea sweeping about the island and of the railroads stretching westward from this one city across a whole continent, and he felt personally small and trivial. He wondered how anyone might hope to become important amid such vastness. When Paul, anxious that his brother should remain innocent of nothing, introduced him to the multifarious haunts of the demimonde, he was aghast at the lavish appointments and, heretofore never having known what "French girls" were, was shocked by the practices. His imagination had not envisaged this kind of life, and the experience now suggested that New York was not to be readily comprehended and hence not readily mastered. When, in addition, he studied the newspapers to discover what working as a reporter in New York might mean, he was overawed by the tone of authority and condescension he detected in their editorials and, reflecting upon his own shortcomings, decided that here was a world without familiar rules where he might easily be overcome and that before attempting to breach it he had better return to Pittsburgh and save enough money to sustain him in case of failure.

In the weeks that followed he resumed a reading of some of the British philosophers he had begun before his trip, turning now from Tyndall and Thomas Huxley to Herbert Spencer and encountering ideas that compelled him to examine his presuppositions concerning his future in terms which made much that had perplexed him clear. Despite his awareness of the unrewarding nature of virtue, he had never been able to dismiss from his thinking the assumption his training had imbued in him that absolute good existed, could be determined, and could be established apart from evil. When he was dissatisfied with the persistence of injustices, he was invoking a conception of what ought to be in terms of this long-ingrained assumption. Even when picturing his own success he proceeded from the same premise. He never considered, for example, that his triumph might involve someone else's frustration or defeat, or that the standards by which his achievement would be recognized might be as suspect as those that prevailed among the grasping materialists of Balzac's Paris. Yet every step into the world of facts led, according to his assumption, into a world of the spiritually lost and thus contributed to a process of continuing disillusionment. If the facts were not misunderstood, then it must be that the assumption was mistaken.

What he found in the books of philosophy was that his assumption was to blame. From reading Huxley's *Science and Hebrew Tradition* and *Science and Christian Tradition* he discovered arguments against accepting the Bible as a revelation from on high and concluded that since the Old and New Testaments were only collections of the experiences of individuals, there was no theoretical justification for judging conduct by Sunday-school standards. Christian doctrine was, then, but one dogma among many. But there remained a need to have some standard to live by, and his heritage was not to be immediately discarded. Here it was that Spencer's *First Principles* affected him. Studying Spencer, especially the first section on the "Unknowable," he could see that he would not have to discard his old outlook so much as to consign it to a sphere that did not affect his daily problems. He learned how religion and science were complementary rather than contradictory and that in the realm of facts religion had no place. It had to do solely with the inscrutable, which it was never permitted to define specifically; it affirmed consciousness of an absolute, but the absolute remained unknowable. Since religion was thus barred from concerning itself with the region of verifiable facts, a region in which Dreiser had found the Catholic Church unrealistic and unreasoning, it had no right to dictate standards of behavior. "Life in its simplest form," Spencer stated, "is the correspondence of certain inner physico-chemical actions with certain outer physico-chemical actions. . . . *Error* . . . is the absence of such correspondence." [18] From assertions such as that Dreiser understood there was no such thing as ethics at all. When in addition he read that the process of life was evolutionary, tending toward a state of quiescent correspondences, a state of equilibrium, and that every man was but one of the myriad agencies through which an Unknown Cause worked to produce this state, then he concluded that mankind was helpless to control its destiny and that whatever one thought or did was natural; nobody could be blamed for anything, and nobody mattered in the total scheme of things. All that was to be done was to stand and watch the workings of the Unknown Cause.

Such a point of view might have meant peace of mind for Dreiser. It explained how the world he had experienced and the one Balzac had pictured came to be. It accounted for the "French girls"; it accounted for apparent injustice; it accounted even for the disturbing behavior of his brothers and sisters. And it relieved him of the obligation to regard human beings as corrupt. Where everything was as it must be, nothing could become what it ought to be. Yet he was only depressed. He had been blown to bits intellectually, according to his own account.[19] Viewing the sorrows about him, he was all the sadder because now they could not be helped. Life, as far as the individual was concerned, seemed to have no point. Since spiritually one arrived nowhere, he could no longer hope to find an absolute good or ultimate reward.

Still an illusion persisted. The trait in him which made accepting the inevitable distressful prevented him from facing all the implications of his discoveries. He began to associate Spencer with Pittsburgh and to imagine that when he reached New York, then he might find some rewarding work and become a person of importance. Materially, perhaps, one might arrive somewhere. What he did not yet see was that this involved effort that his reading had already persuaded him was valueless.

Late in November, spurred by commendation of his talents by a friend on the *Dispatch*, he arrived at his sister's in New York, ready for the great spectacle at last. At once there were difficulties. Paul was away; the man with whom his sister had eloped was out of work; and Dreiser had to assume a large share of the support of that sister and her two children. At the same time he could not penetrate beyond the anterooms of the newspapers to apply for a job. At the *World*, at the *Sun*, at all of them, he was met by apple-gnawing boys who officiously barred his way with "No vacancies" and "You can't go in there." [20] It was not until he had been rebuffed several times and had glumly eyed throngs of Christmas shoppers for more than a week that he became angry and determined enough to burst into the city room and appeal to an editor.

As far as securing a job itself was concerned, he was

successful. Choosing the *World* for his assault, he created sufficient disturbance to attract the sympathetic attention of the managing editor, Arthur Brisbane, who
promptly directed the city editor to give Dreiser an assignment. But with this assignment came the first of several occurrences contributing to disillusionment. Told
to verify an incident in Elizabeth, New Jersey, he asked
his new boss where Elizabeth was and received only a
harsh answer sending him to look it up for himself. Stopping on his way out to announce to the guarding min-
ions that he now belonged, he was informed: "Oh, dat's
all right. We gotta do dat. We gotta keep mosta dese
hams outa here, dough." [21] Harshness was everywhere,
and unless one was on the inside, one was a "ham."
When at the end of the first day he learned that he
would be paid according to "space" and "time," he was
disheartened, for it meant that he would have to be
given opportunities to write lengthy features if he was
to earn anything substantial, and he soon saw that where
long articles were wanted he would be assigned only to
verify facts, which would then be turned over to regular
staff writers.

Amid these frustrating circumstances he made discoveries about the city which wrought a change in his preconceived notions. He learned the details of the Lexow
committee's investigations of municipal graft and heard
how the police profited from their "protection" of the
lowest kinds of brothels. He beheld men lying on the
sidewalk late at night, their pockets turned inside out,
their heads possibly fractured, their assailants never ap-
prehended, and observed the politically fostered corruption at Bellevue Hospital. Throughout his wanderings
he saw greater extremes of poverty and wealth than he

had ever expected. From the destitute men of the parks and lodging houses to the brisk financiers of upper Fifth Avenue, he sensed a terrifying lust for pleasure and riches and a dogged resignation and brutal heartlessness toward misery which tainted the atmosphere and made him feel discouragingly unimportant. As other newspapermen told him how little chance an outsider or beginner had in New York, he began to consider financiers as sharks and tricksters, to regard power and wealth as shameless and cruel, and to wonder whether he might not be a misfit and have to return to some futile routine in the Midwest. Only a stubborn faith in a vague but eventual success sustained him. As the city hummed, buzzed, and roared about him, he stood as if transfixed. New York was the closest he had yet come to the "unknowable" force.

In none of this could he find a solid basis for hope. His work, certainly, failed to compensate for his impressions. Unable to write more than a single article that pleased his editor, unable to extract news from persons who preferred to remain silent, lacking the brash assurance that would have endeared him to the city desk, he soon began to ponder doing different work, writing short stories or magazine articles. Other newspapermen had done so, men such as Kipling, David Graham Phillips, and Richard Harding Davis. But searching *Scribner's*, the *Century*, and *Harper's* for clues as to how he might proceed, he discovered stories about no world he had seen and read of virtues rewarded in no way he had known. There was a dignity and decency to the characters quite foreign to what he had found in the course of his newspaper work. Yet, since these authors were respected and distinguished men, perhaps they knew, and he was wrong; perhaps it was that way in their world. As again he felt the lure of art and the recognition it doubtless assured, writing slipped out of the realm of immediate possibility. In fact, writers so awed him that when one day in the spring of 1895 he encountered Mark Twain standing before a shop window, he could think only that here was the great Mark Twain himself and muffed the attempt to engage him in conversation.[22] A place in the world of Twain, Warner, and Howells seemed hopelessly beyond him, and although he recognized in a novel like Henry Blake Fuller's *With the Procession* familiar elements of the social struggle he was witnessing, the effect of his perusal of the magazines convinced him that if he had anything to say, it did not fall within the province of fiction. It probably belonged in the newspapers, but if so, he was failing there.

Financial difficulties precipitated decisive action. The little he was making on the *World* made it increasingly burdensome to support his sister to the extent he had been doing, and shortly after he got his job, he suggested that she force the father of her children to find employment by separating from him and moving to less expensive lodgings. This she eventually did, and Dreiser took a cheap room elsewhere.[23] At the same time the strain of his precarious and unpromising existence began to tell on him until, one spring afternoon, he found a pretext for a showdown on the paper. Told to turn over to another member of the staff the facts of a story he had just brought in, he complained: "I don't see why I should always have to do this. I'm not a beginner in this game. I wrote stories, and big ones, before ever I came to this paper." The reply was sardonic: "Maybe you did, but we have the feeling that you haven't proved to be of much use to us." [24] There was nothing to reply to that. It was a humiliating comment on his quest for something important to do in New York. He could only resign.

He did, after this, try to get another job, as a reporter, but in vain. Moreover, newspaper work was no longer attractive. So long as it entailed contacts with success and enabled him to view failure from the point of view of the spectator, it was tolerable. So long as he was permitted to take his cue from Balzac and comment on Blue Monday or Potter's Field, then he could feel that life was a spectacle from whose distresses he was personally freed. And if at any moment the work proved distasteful or frustrating, he could accept it so long as there was a New York to look forward to. But now not only was New York discouraging, but newspaper work entailed his participation in the very struggle he had hoped the work would enable him to observe securely, for as soon as he had to fight for the security of observation, the vantage point was contained in what he had hoped to view. Thus he was led at last to see that the position of importance he had longed for required precisely that activity which he had come to regard as futile, and he had to search anew for a career that would consist primarily in observing the careers of others. In this predicament he revived his faint hopes of earning recognition as a writer of fiction; thereby he might externalize society. Having an insight into the nature of the life of which he was a part, he supposed that he could maintain the insight while ignoring the part. Happily for him, the work he did for the next few years was, it so happened, peculiarly appropriate to such a point of view. It enabled him to snipe at the universe.

V

Spectator

It was his relationship to Paul, however, not any talent as a writer of short stories, that earned him his living. In fact, his attempts at fiction only justified his earlier hesitations. Realizing that if stories were to sustain him he would have to sell them to the magazines, but assuming that they then must be modeled after those he read, he sedulously followed plots and locale alien to his experience and sought to envisage equally unfamiliar characters and situations, with results that were naturally rejected by editors. When three or four manuscripts had been returned and his funds had alarmingly diminished to little more than fifty dollars, he went to the offices of Howley, Haviland & Company to look for Paul. But Paul was away and he learned only that Howley and Haviland were talking of starting a magazine. Although he did not realize it at the moment, this talk was to serve him well a few weeks later, before the end of June, when his financial predicament gave it significance. By that time he had tried to live in a room costing a dollar and a half a week, been evicted by a policeman who had informed him the place was in a bedhouse, and lodged at the Mills Hotel, where for a quarter the poor and the jobless purchased a cot for a night in a bare cubicle. He had also accepted a free room from a restaurant-keeper whose daughter had taken a fancy to Dreiser and picked him up, but when he had reflected about his future and remembered Sallie White, or "Jug," as he called her, he had disentangled himself. Now, reminded of the conversations between Paul's partners by magazines he was studiously examining, he went to Howley and Haviland with the proposal that if they made him editor he could produce a magazine better than Ditson's, their rival's. He suggested publishing three or four new songs each month and surrounding them with articles, pictures, and drama criticism. He even suggested the title: *Ev'ry Month.* The partners decided to let Paul's brother try his hand, and paying him ten dollars a week to begin, with a five-dollar raise promised once the magazine was actually under way, they authorized him to collect material for the first issue, which appeared under date of October 1, 1895, with Dreiser's name on the masthead as "The Editor and Arranger." [1]

Although, in keeping with the original plan, three or four songs constituted the core of the magazine, Dreiser's personal interest lay in the more literary pages. In them he possessed an outlet for his own ideas. He could select not only stories like Bret Harte's "A Night in the Divide," which would help the circulation rise to the 65,000 it reached in his two years as editor,[2] but also stories like Stephen Crane's "A Mystery of Heroism," which depicted with a touch of final irony the extent to which human beings were the victims of their emotions and of accidents. He could, in addition, employ discursive cut captions for concise comments, and when he wanted to make more extensive remarks on the spectacle of life, he could include pages dedicated to lengthy editorials entitled "Reflections" or digress in the columns reserved for reviews of current books. He had at last a vehicle in which to define thoroughly what the spectacle meant.

On the whole, the definition was an attempt to reconcile desires directed toward finding some hope for men and facts indicating men were helpless. His "reflections," sometimes appropriately signed "The Prophet," often concerned themselves with questions limited in scope. He supported the social emancipation and quickened activity of women, pointed to the imminence of a war in Europe, forecast bleak failure for the attempt to cure the liquor habit with water, and discussed the possibility of life on Mars. Usually he touched on several independent topics in a single issue. But if he began with a restricted topic, he was likely to expand into universals. Thus, in September 1896, beginning by contemplating the forthcoming elections and exclaiming over graft and human greed, he recommended that voters be vigilant. But if a voter had wondered what criterion to apply, he would have had to look for the answer in the final topic, a recommended reading program that began with light, readable works on astronomy and anthropology and concluded with Herbert Spencer, who would marshal "the whole universe . . . in review before you . . . showing you how certain beautiful laws exist, and how, by these laws, all animate and inanimate things have developed and arranged themselves; how life has gradually become more and more complicated, more and more beautiful. . . ." From the reference to Spencer, it was not difficult for the reader to proceed to a consideration of storms, tidal waves, earthquakes, and even the negligence of other men as illustrating that man was the sport of both nature and his own fellows, and from these illustrations it was easy to follow a transition to the tendency of all things "to equalize and seek a common level." Men no more than mountains were exempt from the disintegrating force of nature. In the face of such "hard, cruel, appalling" facts a vigilant voter would have had little reason to act. Dreiser, however, sought to modify the implications of the facts. "Man is not exactly the sport of the elements in the same sense with rocks, trees and the countless creatures of the air and forest," he wrote. Man had mastered both animate and inanimate nature. Science had subdued the material world. In time man would control the inconsiderate forces: "Nothing can withstand him, for he is working in harmony with great laws which place splendid powers in his hand and assist him to rise. A great maker of stars above is his master, and these, His laws, though cruel in their precision, will do an obedient follower no harm. To-day they sweep the heedless and unthinking from their path, but to-morrow they will aid students and disciples to rise to the highest point of physical and mental power. As a student and disciple of such masterful laws man needs no pity; as a victim of error and misunderstanding regarding them, he deserves none. This is the order of the universe, the plan of irresistable [*sic*] progress, and as an earnest part of it man is safe." Man therefore might be hopeful and trust in an order whose complexity and scope, ranging from the formation of a mustard seed to the regulation of countless sidereal systems, implied universal design and whose design in turn implied "a Being . . . that in His wondrous superiority . . . is not unmindful of the least of his creatures." [3]

Thus man was a superior creature because of the operations of some still higher intelligence whose plan was just beyond understanding. Dreiser's experiences had, at one time, persuaded him that men were not the personal concern of an omnipotent deity, but he could still declare that mankind as a unit was; and if there was a contradiction in the idea of obedience to all-controlling laws, the obedience he demanded was in the form of an awareness of its necessity rather than in the form of a rebellious assertion of will. When Dreiser spoke out, he spoke like those prophets of old who could foresee but could not forfend. The superiority mankind enjoyed occurred within the system of laws from whose workings no one was exempt, and when an individual regarded himself as superior to his fellows, he overlooked that all men were equally subject to external controls. Those persons who labored "to upset this equality" [4] outlawed themselves and doomed themselves or their posterity to destruction by the very law they flouted. Neither wealth nor poverty was evidence of one's intrinsic worth, and no one's intrinsic worth could be absolutely defined. In a characteristic caption for a picture Dreiser commented of the Sultan of Turkey: "This is the gentleman whom Mr. Gladstone calls 'an assassin enthroned' and whom the followers of Islam denominate as 'His Serene Highness' and 'The Sublime Porte.' Between these two are James Gordon Bennett, whose 'Herald' makes excuses for him, and Clara Barton, of the 'Red Cross' legion, who accepts his mark of distinction." Then he added his own opinion: "All this about a sleepy murderer of a twilight kingdom," [5] an indictment whose severity was counterbalanced by its romantic tone. No absolute judgment of the workings and products of the unknown cause was possible; men should realize this, be conscious of their limitations, as mortals, and in this consciousness recognize the equality of all. "Nothing is good that will not benefit the majority; nothing true that will not answer as well for many as for one; nothing just that will not equalize the burdens, the sorrows and the pleasures of life." [6]

That the flouting of the law of equality might itself be the law's product apparently escaped Dreiser. Somehow

— because of how he wished things to be, perhaps — consciousness of the law would modify the consequences of the law, and his own duty consisted, he believed, in arousing among the fortunate a sympathy for the unfortunate that would purge ambition of selfishness and ruthlessness. Once ambition was purified, character would become ennobled; and, he explained, "It is nobility of character alone that will permit of achievement without brutality."[7] Thus awareness would make possible success at nobody's expense. And thus, too, man's hope lay in the knowledge of man's helplessness.

To arouse sympathy and Samaritanize character it was, of course, necessary to emphasize repeatedly the idea of helplessness. In this emphasis Dreiser found that art and literature were fulfilling the same purpose he was. In fact, he derived the same pleasure from the critical inspection of a fine painting as he did from piercing what he called "some of the more irridescent [*sic*] soap bubble illusions" of men. The pleasure was that of discernment rather than of self-satisfaction, however. To understand art one had only to be capable of pity for all helpless creatures, for then one could "sigh in appreciation of the trueness of the lesson taught" by some masterpiece.[8] Yet it was not solely pity that characterized the proper reaction to art or literature. In his book reviews, signed Edward Al, he objected to books in which sordidness was "unrelieved" or in which "the softer traits of character" were "entirely obscured." He preferred stories in which "a sunset glow" softened "the bleakness of the dreary moorland."[9] And, exercising his privileges as editor, he secured from his friend Arthur Henry essays on "The Philosophy of Hope" and "The Good Laugh." For indulgence of a single feeling might be an anodyne instead of a quickener. Sighs were, after all, of many kinds — of pity and compassion, of yearning and relief, of despair, of hope, of love — and it was what they had in common that Dreiser valued; in each was an implied acknowledgment that a situation might be otherwise, that possibility was extensive but individuals had limits, that men were only mortal after all. Once men saw themselves as they were, then they might have the insight of the spectator.

As Dreiser's editing developed he began to feel thwarted by the restrictions of his magazine. There was room for too little of what he liked best; he became restless and by the fall of 1897 felt his abilities were not being adequately appreciated. Arthur Henry was partly responsible for this feeling. Henry had come east to nose about among magazines and publishers, in the hope of making good as a writer outside the newspaper world, and to renew his friendship with Dreiser. Nothing had been lost from their mutual understanding since the Toledo days, and they were soon exchanging confidences as before. Dreiser complained of his frustrations as editor, pointed to green-shaded book-keepers and cashiers and explained that those busy concentrators were "succeeding," and when Henry asked: "And you?" replied he was drawing a good salary, but "From my standpoint, I am not succeeding." [10] Henry opposed Dreiser's solemn contemplation with a gay and stimulating optimism, and urged him to do some writing of his own, even fiction, instead of expending his efforts editing the writings of others. He suggested that Dreiser return with him to Maumee, Ohio, and the House of Four Pillars, which he and his wife, Maude Wood Henry, had bought. He proposed that Dreiser collaborate with him on various articles. He cajoled and talked of possibilities, and before the summer of 1897 was over, Dreiser had seriously considered taking a trip west,[11] been refused an increase in salary and greater freedom in devoloping the magazine, quarreled with Paul, and decided that after he completed work on the September 1897 number, he would do some of the independent writing Henry had suggested.[12] He could, perhaps, have succeeded as a writer of lyrics for Paul's songs if he had wished, for he had composed the first stanza and chorus of "On the Banks of the Wabash," but whenever Paul cited the accomplishment as evidence of ability, Dreiser replied the verses were "slop" and would write nothing further.[13] He was interested in writing that was more speculative.

As a free lance he got at least the equivalent of the increase in salary he wanted, and gained a reputation along with it. His relationship to Paul and his work on *Ev'ry Month* had taken him among men who could be of help to him, with the consequence that between the time he left Howley, Haviland & Company and the end of 1900 he contributed signed articles, essays, and interviews to magazines ranging from *Truth, Success,* and the *New Voice* to the *Cosmopolitan* and *Harper's Monthly* at prices that averaged more than a hundred dollars each,[14] and in addition not only did research and regularly composed anonymous bits for the *Christian Herald,*[15] but also became a consulting editor on *Ainslee's* at a hundred and fifty dollars a month,[16] supplying articles and verse as well as advice and sometimes resorting to the pseudonymous Edward Al and Herman D. White to mask the extent of his monopoly. Within a year of his break with his brother there were rumors that Dodd, Mead & Company were publishing a volume of his poems, for which William Dean Howells had reportedly "expressed a hearty liking." [17] And by the end of 1898 he had sufficient money to marry Jug. There had been intimacies with other women in the year or two preceding, and for a while he had envisaged relationships that would involve no permanent commitments on his part. But when the other women had proved as willful and undesirous of commitments as he,[18] he had emerged from his fantasies long enough to dream the old dream of Jug and recall his engagement, and on December 28 was married to her in Washington, D.C.[19]

Although he thus evinced financial independence, he was not able to evince the intellectual independence that he had enjoyed on *Ev'ry Month*. Indeed, he had less opportunity for expressions as forthright as his "Reflections" had been. He wrote of painters, sculptors, and musicians; he wrote of famous homes and historic haunts; he wrote of successful men and great enterprises, and of defeated men and poverty; and in verse he sometimes speculated about the meaning of what he wrote about in his prose. But if he managed to pursue some of the ideas he had advanced as "The Prophet" and on occasion to suggest generalizations, he could not develop them. In fact, a reader would have grasped their scope only by examining at least a score of unconnected articles in a dozen magazines.

Dreiser wanted to stress the importance of viewing life as a spectacle and the consequent value in art of the associative and the picturesque.[20] Art's function, he believed, was to produce feeling and insight apart from moral judgment, and by the excitation of sense responses to indicate that there was more to life than met the eye or ear. A proper presentation of appearances could convey, somehow, a meaning that transcended appearances. But all this he was able to set forth only in fragments. He would say that one painter possessed "the gift of imparting to subjects realistically treated the poetry of his own nature, thus lifting them above the level of 'faithful transcripts' of nature and life"; [21] another was interested in "beauty alone" with "no craving after purpose of any sort"; [22] a third "wisely tired" of *genre* subjects and painted instead imaginary war scenes, which were, necessarily, more spectacular.[23] He would call a caricaturist "great" who viewed public characters with "an X-ray glance" and drew an appearance more real than photographs presented; [24] and he would remark, when writing of the harp, that it was "the voice of poetry, of sentiment and sorrow." [25]

At the same time he wanted to indicate what the meaning was that art ought to communicate. Men should recognize their limitations, he continued to insist. If men realized how insignificant, commonplace, even petty they were in contrast to the processes that included them, then they might feel their mortality. But he was able to introduce these ideas mainly in his articles on historic sites and homes that the average member of society took for granted, and in occasional articles on civic improvements and natural history, and then he managed to do so only obliquely. Wishing residents of historic regions to appreciate their own traditions and development, he called old landmarks "sacred" and branded as "reprehensible" and "shameless" desires that prompted alterations by indifferent and self-centered contemporaries.[26] Wishing residents of commercial centers to consider how "commonplace" trade was in contrast to the dream-producing beauties of nature they usually disregarded, he rejoiced over municipal plans to preserve the trees and grass along some new city highway and declared that it was in terms of such public works as these that a nation's culture was judged.[27] And wishing all complacent persons to consider the significance of nature and the mysterious laws of development and change, he portrayed sympathetically "the luxury and delight of plain living" that John Burroughs enjoyed in his mountain hut,[28] exclaimed over the inexplicable homing instinct of pigeons in an article devoted to the use of homers on warships,[29] and called attention to Thomas Huxley's evolutionary theory in a discussion of the descent of the horse.[30] Only in this partial way of reclaiming for contemplation subjects a commercial society had become insensitive to could he imply what he had once been able to state so explicitly in connection with Herbert Spencer.

Yet even the implications of these groups of articles left much unexpressed. For in the course of some of his magazine assignments he had been brought gangling and self-consciously taciturn into the presence of successful businessmen and had come to admire as well as envy the active and impersonal efficiency that characterized their lives. As a consequence of his association with editors, he had attracted the attention of Dr. Orison Swett Marden, founder in December 1897 of *Success*, a magazine that Marden edited with the collaboration of George H. Sandison, editor of the *Christian Herald*, and that he dedicated, according to the galaxy of mottoes on its covers, to Education, Enterprise, Enthusiasm, Energy, Economy, Self-respect, Self-reliance, Self-help, Self-culture, Self-control, Work, Sagacity, Honesty, Truth, and Courage. For this publication Marden employed Dreiser to interview contemporary industrialists, and also artists and writers who had "arrived," and to ferret out those secrets of their achievement which would sustain the principles proclaimed on the cover. Beginning with the February 1898 number, Dreiser contributed more than a dozen interviews in a series generically titled "Life

Stories of Successful Men," and these, together with a series of "Studies of Public Characters" he did for *Ainslee's*, led to his meeting individuals who seemed to have a firmer control of destiny than he could ever have.

His subsequent admiration was to be found almost exclusively among the "Life Stories." When he entered the precincts of Philip D. Armour's sanctuary, he was entranced by the "snow storm of white letters [that fell] . . . thickly upon a mass of dark desks" and by the vast "mobilization of energy" solely "to promote the private affairs of one man." [31] When he had interviewed Marshall Field, he wrote: "No more significant story, none more full of stimulus, of encouragement, of brain-inspiring and pulse-thrilling potency has been told in these columns." [32] Yet his admiration was qualified. He might some years later recall sufficient sympathy to write understandingly of a financier in his novels *The Financier* and *The Titan*, but his articles on historic sites and civic improvements made clear that it was not trade as such that he admired. He still hoped for the achievement-without-brutality of which he had spoken in *Ev'ry Month*, and because of the nature of his assignments could indicate the various segments of his attitude only here and there among the series. In telling of Armour and Field he exhibited fascination and envy. In telling of the sculptor Paul Weyland Bartlett he stated a preference for "other gods than money." [33] And several months later, recounting a talk with John H. Patterson, president of the National Cash Register Company, he seemed persuaded by Patterson's paternalistic idea that if one treated workers generously — gave them schools for their children, shops for their hobbies, gymnasiums, lectures, dances, and sermons — they would do better work.[34] A man who possessed Armour's power, Bartlett's ideals,

and Patterson's generosity would, in short, have constituted Dreiser's ideally successful individual.

At the same time he continued to trust in the course
of events rather than in the efforts of individuals to
bring about realization of this ideal, but like his other
ideas this one emerged only in unrelated groups of articles. As he continued to write into 1900 he dealt more
frequently with simple men and unfortunate ones. He
recorded the daily life of the pilots who plied New
York's harbor; he described the shifts of the poor to find
a night's shelter or a meal's crust; he portrayed the victims of the sweatshop and the gaunt, stoop-shouldered
inhabitants of dilapidated tenements. But instead of
finding fault with the system that had produced destitu-
tion, he argued that such conditions were but a measure
of civilization and that rather than pity individuals who
could be no happier than they were anyway, one should
pity "the ignorance and error that cause the distress of
the world." [35] Scattered, incidental observations and occasional verses counseled acceptance of the system. The
pilots might not live glamorous lives, but they possessed
a kind of security, for amid the welter of city life "the
sea seemed safe." [36] The jobless might, like driftwood,
swirl about the fashionable rendezvous on snowy nights
to beg the price of lodging, and thin-bodied men and
women might spend their days in crumbling, odiferous
tenements, but their lot was being gradually ameliorated
by the development of such projects as co-operative villages.[37] Even the nation's large-scale enterprises provided occasions for optimism. Railroads were intent on
helping "the man with energy" and the masses were
wrong in calling them "soulless," for "no corporation is
soulless . . . which helps all others in helping itself." [38]
Shipyards, munitions plants, the packing industry, the

fruit-marketing industry were all so impressively extensive that they directed one's attention to the nation's
vast resources and inspired one's faith in nature. "A
thousand million, dwelling side by side, could not em-
barrass the bounty of nature, which yields a hundred
favors for every blessing asked," Dreiser wrote. "For
every crop growing, ten thousand times its need of
chemicals in the soil! For every ray of sunshine used in
perfecting bloom and fruitage, ten thousand left to pass!
Man shall perfect himself in the wisdom of these things,
and there shall no longer be a cry for food. He shall prepare the estimate of that which is his need, and that
which is asked shall be given." [39] If, as in some of his
poems, he considered the persistence of evil and disaster,
he simply ended by reassuring himself that one must
not despair, for good would prevail. [40] One could safely
depend on the inevitable processes to solve the problems
they had created.

Yet, however completely or incompletely he could
define his attitude toward the spectacle or outline the
obligations of the artist, he had to continue to justify
his own particular role as looker-on. This justification he
embodied in still another article, an account of Israel
Zangwill:

Critic though a man may be — thinking as he may, that
he is sitting apart, . . . still is he bound up in Nature, and
other men rise by the aid of the very wit and wisdom with
which he distinguishes himself. And all his exclusiveness . . .
makes him no less a toiler in the great eventual cause with
[the] . . . man in the street, which uses genius as it uses
stone, to build and build — whereunto we know not, and
neither need we care. [41]

One might, in short, simply hope that nature would use
one well.

As far as his relation to the spectacle was concerned, Dreiser was evidently satisfied, but the fragmentary way in which his various reactions to the spectacle had to take form left him without the necessary feeling of fulfillment. As a consequence, when Arthur Henry continued to exhort him to attempt writing that was completely independent and said more insistently than ever that Dreiser should write short stories, Dreiser was psychologically prepared to be persuaded, and early in the summer of 1899, somewhat secure financially, he acceded to Henry's persistent urgings and with Jug set forth to make the visit to Maumee that he had considered making two years before.

VI

Sister Carrie

Conditions at the Henrys' were ideally suited to foster Dreiser's artistic bent.[1] The village of Maumee, once the head of navigation on the Maumee River, had yielded its trade to Toledo and was now somnolent and picturesque, as though designed for the dreamer. Decaying locks in the canal paralleling the river, weed-grown ruins at the site of the old wharf, fishermen and white-bearded patriarchs who provided business for a handful of shopkeepers, and a few fine old houses gleaming whitely among weather-beaten contemporaries and gay flower gardens created a romantic setting in which one might indulge in reverie without feeling the pressures of the city. And as one of those houses which retained marks of its old-time grandeur, the House of Four Pillars proved a comfortable place for the indulgence. Its Doric columns, two stories tall, supporting a shady portico, bespoke ease, and its fourteen rooms within, most of them spacious and cool, provided it. For several summers guests with artistic interests had gathered here. Here the Henrys had written fairy tales together; here they had assembled a company of actors; and here now, with Maude Henry to keep the house in order, with Jug to do the cooking she liked to do, and with Arthur Henry to supply companionship, Dreiser could relax, completely free of all external concerns, and allow his mind to rove as it pleased, thinking on the spectacle of life.

Of all the influences on Dreiser here, Henry's was probably the most important, for though Dreiser would most likely have given himself to dreaming in such surroundings as these anyway, in Henry's presence his dreams took concrete form and brought him nearer to his artistic goal than he had ever been. From morning, when after a plunge in the river the two, clad in pajamas and bathrobes, repaired to the seclusion of a basement study, until evening, when they fabricated Indian legends for visitors, or sat on the back porch as the moon rose, Dreiser had a congenial friend with whom to share feelings and ideas. He engaged in heated arguments, entered philosophic discussions, and finding Henry always ready for adventure, felt carefree and able to yield to whims. With Henry, Dreiser came to see validity in his own moods, thoughts, and attitudes and to believe they ought to be expressed.

He and Henry had often discussed plans for a novel, and Dreiser had considered using his experiences in the song-publishing business to write about the meaning of success in the career of a writer of popular songs;[2] but he had done little more than dream of the outlines of the plot. Now, however, amid more encouraging circumstances, the discussions were renewed, and Henry urged him to try his hand at least at short stories. He insisted that he saw short stories in Dreiser and was so persistent that Dreiser finally, feeling himself a victim of foolishness, began, working outward from his own situation into his own imagination. "It was a hot day in August," he wrote. "The parching rays of a summer sun had faded the once snappy green leaves of the trees to a dull and dusty hue." His character, Robert McEwen, a man sitting contemplatively in the shade of a fine old beech tree, finds himself observing the ants that are scurrying about the walk. It is a drowsy day and McEwen's dreaming imagination soon takes hold and imperceptibly carries him into the ant colony as a member, suffering through periods of famine and joining the black ants in war against the red. Here, indeed, was an allegory of life, in which the struggle to survive is carried on blindly, uncritically, and in which strength rather than notions of good and evil determines one's fate. Neither strength nor numbers mean security, however; only death or dreams can provide it. McEwen escapes fatal hurt at the last by awakening and relegating the ants' warfare to the realm of dreams, and Dreiser, detached from the struggle, could view McEwen somewhat as McEwen viewed the ants, shaking his head over the vague, sad wonder of it all, but not feeling himself at the moment personally threatened.[3]

When Henry had driven Dreiser to complete the story, "The Shining Slave Makers," and told him it was good, Dreiser thought Henry was only jollying him, but when Henry was firm, had it typed, and sent it on its editorial rounds, eventually to be accepted by *Ainslee's* for seventy-five dollars, Dreiser took his accomplishment seriously. Indeed, Henry's persistence was catalytic; Dreiser wrote four more — "Nigger Jeff," "Butcher Rogaum's Door," "When the Old Century Was New," "The World and the Bubble" — and was to be successful again.[4] Like "The Shining Slave Makers," these stories, because they concerned characters like himself, characters he knew, or incidents out of his personal experience, gave him at last a congenial means of expression. Thus, in one he used a lynching that had occurred in his St. Louis days to demonstrate a reporter's awakening from the assumption that poetic justice ruled the world to the awareness that Dreiser himself had acquired as a reporter. In another he portrayed a conflict between a strict old German father like his own and a rebellious, pleasure-loving daughter like his sisters to show the strength of material attractions in the face of an ascetic religion that refused to acknowledge their appeal. In a third he embodied his own wistful thinking about the past to reconstruct the charms of a society that trade had not yet made commonplace and to suggest a world where ugliness and misery were almost unknown. By the time he returned to New York in September, accompanied by Henry as well as by Jug, he had found fiction so agreeable that he had been persuaded to begin a novel.

He had not proceeded very far with it then, but he and Henry were full of plans. Henry had himself begun a story, *A Princess of Arcady*, and had told Dreiser he needed the moral support that only Dreiser's writing of a novel could give him. Eventually, to please Henry, Dreiser had taken a sheet of yellow paper and, apropos of nothing in particular, had scribbled the title *Sister Carrie*. Then he had begun to wonder what kind of story might be woven about a girl, a Midwestern girl, a dreamer; but it was not until he and Henry were settled in New York that the story assumed shape and direction.[5]

The Midwestern girls whose problems Dreiser knew best were his sisters, and he thought of how they, like himself, had dreamed of the city, where everything would turn out wonderfully. He thought in particular of the one who had been supported by the architect, and then of her preference for the restaurant manager, and his taking of the money and the elopement to New York by way of Canada. For the architect he substituted the traveling salesman Drouet, the kind who had intrigued more than one of his sisters. And for the technique that would enable Drouet to intrigue, he relied to some extent on George Ade's "Fable of the Two Mandolin Players and the Willing Performer." His sister became Carrie, and like one of the women in Bob Hazard's unpublished novel, she developed into an actress. Chapin and Gore's became Fitzgerald and Moy's, and its trusted cashier, L. A. ("Grove") Hopkins, became George Hurstwood, providing facts for the earlier chapters of the story. All the characters moved in regions Dreiser had known, Carrie living in Chicago only a few doors from where Dreiser had lived himself at various times, and Hurstwood participating in a streetcar strike like the one Dreiser had reported in Toledo and mingling among the wretched poor whose shifts to find a night's lodging Dreiser had described in the course of his work for the magazines.

Dreiser wrote with no very definite plan, and proceeded until the middle of October, when he reached the point at which Carrie met Hurstwood. Then he became disgusted. The story seemed dull and inconsequential; it was no good. And neglecting it for almost two months, he turned instead to salable articles about industrial enterprises, sweatshops, and poverty. But Henry renewed the pressure and complained that unless Dreiser resumed, he himself could not write. So, laughing at himself for being a fool, Dreiser wrote for another six weeks, bringing Hurstwood to the point at which he was to steal the money. But Dreiser was puzzled how to have him to do it, for it had to be done in such a way as to leave the problem of guilt or moral wrong ambiguous. Henry had left for a while in the interests of an alluring relationship with Anna T. Mallon, who ran a typing bureau, and Dreiser, annoyed at being deserted, decided

Sister Carrie would never be finished. Yet before the end of February, Henry was back and read what had been done. He insisted it was good and soon Dreiser was writing again, with renewed interest sometimes dropping in on Richard Duffy, one of his friends at *Ainslee's*, to announce the number of words he had written. This time Henry resumed his own book and although Dreiser was worried about the sacrifice of time that might be spent writing articles he could sell, he continued, sometimes in doubt but always driven by Henry, until almost the end of March, when, having dealt with Hurstwood's decline, he was depressed by the recollection of his own hardships during the days on the *World* and did not know how to add another chapter, for there were no other incidents to include.

The book was finished, and yet it seemed uncompleted. He wanted to lead the story to a point — an elevation — where it could be left and still continue into the future. He felt he had not done that. The story had to stop, but the final picture should suggest the continuance of Carrie's destiny along the lines of what had become for Dreiser established truth. When the exact impression persisted in eluding him, he decided to leave the environment of his apartment and see what a change of scene might do. So one afternoon, with notebook and pencil, he took a trip to the Palisades, overlooking the Hudson River, and finding a broad ledge, stretched flat on his back and allowed his thoughts to wander for almost two delightful hours. Suddenly the answer came to him. He reached for his notebook and pencil, and with a Balzacian epilogue, tinged with the dreamer's mood, *Sister Carrie* was done. Some cutting was still necessary, but Henry was ready with suggestions and they would not alter the novel in any radical way. Henry, in fact, had become so interested in the completion of Dreiser's novel that he had neglected A *Princess of Arcady* and now found himself unable to write his own conclusion. He had so often spoken of his plan for it, however, that Dreiser was able to draft it himself and thus bring to completion their two novels almost simultaneously. Dreiser dedicated *Sister Carrie* to Henry, and Henry dedicated A *Princess of Arcady* to Anna Mallon.

Part of Dreiser's difficulty in writing *Carrie* had arisen out of the nature of the tale. On one occasion tentatively entitled *The Flesh and the Spirit*,[6] it was basically the story of Dreiser's own divided heart. On the one hand he regarded all struggle as fundamentally futile; on the other he could not reconcile himself to the prospect of failure. Carrie represents the boyhood Dreiser, who has illusions about the outside world, follows dreams, and never realizes them. Hurstwood, unable to extricate himself from disasters, is the realization of the boyhood Dreiser's fears. Carrie is what Dreiser had been and now saw as sentimentally blind; Hurstwood is what he hoped he might never be. While Carrie's career argues the impossibility of realizing one's dreams, Hurstwood's illustrates the horror of a life in which all dreams have been abandoned. The responsibility for Carrie's and Hurstwood's careers Dreiser attributed to "forces wholly superhuman,"[7] and in matters such as Hurstwood's theft Dreiser remained true to his theory, for whether the decision to take the money is made by Hurstwood or whether it is forced upon him by the accidental clicking of the lock, he carefully left uncertain. Hurstwood is "as a wisp in the wind."[8] Yet Dreiser refused to remain true to the implications of this theory. He shared Carrie's "uncritical upwelling of grief for the weak and the helpless"[9] as though things might be otherwise, and spoke hopefully of an evolution that would bring a "new socialism," a more just understanding of money, and the success of an ideal of good whereby "perfect understanding" would enable free will to replace instinct.[10] In the desire to escape Hurstwood's fate he could, partially aware of what he was doing, yield to Carrie's weakness of dreaming "such happiness as . . . [she might] never feel." [11]

Although Dreiser's attitude involved a contradiction, he was compelled to adopt it if, in denying the possibility of realizing dreams, he still wished to avoid the failure that came when all purpose or focus of activity was gone. Yet the adoption of such an attitude remained possible only so long as he, in viewing the processes of life, was financially secure from their mercilessness. It was a situation similar to the one he had been in during his work for the *World*. If he should become poor, he would have to re-enter the struggle, either joining like McEwen with the black ants or the red ants, or succumbing like Hurstwood. And in that event he would find his attitude challenged. Naturally, therefore, whether he could remain detached depended upon his success in getting the book published, or at least in being persuaded that his efforts would be rewarded.

Despite an initial rejection from Harper & Brothers, to whom he had submitted the manuscript through Henry Mills Alden, editor of *Harper's Monthly*, events gave Dreiser reason for the highest hopes.[12] Alden told Dreiser *Sister Carrie* was a good piece of work and, although he doubted that a publisher would accept such a novel, suggested, after Harper's returned it, that Dreiser next try the younger firm of Doubleday, Page & Company. At the time Dreiser was reading Frank Norris's *McTeague* and felt that if so true a portrayal of

American life as that were publishable, his own novel might also be. Doubleday's in turn encouraged him to think well of his chances. Frank Doubleday himself received the manuscript from Dreiser, promised an early report, and, about to sail for Europe, turned it over to Frank Norris, who was reading for the firm. Norris took it to his cabin on Greenwood Lake in northern New Jersey, exclaimed delightedly over its excellence to his wife, and when Morgan Robertson, the writer of sea stories, wandered into Norris's office one day, declared he had found a masterpiece. Then, when it appeared that Robertson was acquainted with Dreiser, Norris said: "Tell him when you see him what I think of it. I am writing him to call. I hope the house publishes it. It is a wonder."[13] And Robertson hastened to relay the news to Dreiser. On May 28, 1900, Norris confirmed the message Robertson had carried:

My report of *Sister Carrie* has gone astray [he wrote to Dreiser] and I cannot now put my hands on it.

But I remember that I said, and it gives me pleasure to repeat it, that it was the best novel I had read in M.S. since I had been reading for the firm, and that it pleased me as well as any novel I have read in *any* form, published or otherwise.

I have passed it up to Mr. Lanier to read who is now about half way through it, from him it will go to Mr. Page and when *he* is through with it, the three of us will have a pow-wow on it and come to a decision.

You may rest assured I shall do all in my power to see that the decision is for publication. I shall rush it through as fast as may be and possibly you will hear from me by the end of this week.

By June 9 both Henry Lanier, son of the poet and a junior partner, and Walter Hines Page, the senior partner, had read it. Although Lanier had not liked the story, he felt the firm should publish it, and Page, agreeing in the decision, was authorized to tell Dreiser they were "very much pleased with your novel . . . congratulations on so good a piece of work," and to ask him to come and talk it over Monday afternoon, June 11.[14] At that time Page reiterated his congratulations, assured him, as did Lanier, that the book would be well treated, and stated that as soon as Dreiser had made some suggested minor revisions, they would conclude a formal contract. To all intents and purposes *Sister Carrie* had been accepted and — along with A *Princess of Arcady*, it so happened — was soon to appear in print.

Dreiser's head was giddy with prospects of success. His most glittering dreams were about to be realized. He made the necessary revisions in the book, reflected that he had saved up a few hundred dollars, which, now that he was about to become successful, he could begin spending, and decided to follow Jug, who had gone to Missouri for a visit, and to undertake some new writing out there, in an agreeable atmosphere of indolence and — of course — recognition. In fact, his confidence became so strong that although he was beginning to find Jug too conventional and possessive and, in the dreamy Missouri regions, to crave the stimulation of different, younger girls,[15] he was able to ignore his domestic dissatisfactions before the promise of rewards that would make all things possible.

All the hopes and dreams were, however, based on assurances by men who had reckoned without Frank Doubleday — or, perhaps, without the influence of Frank Doubleday's wife. While Dreiser was out of town, the Doubledays returned from abroad, and Doubleday, hearing enthusiastic talk at the office concerning the forthcoming novel, took a set of proofs home to read over the weekend. There his wife also read them, and there their doom was pronounced. Neltje De Graff Doubleday was a social worker and a strong-willed woman who sympathized with the unfortunate, but when it came to literature, she had no evident use for sociology or despair. She was not one to oppose the widely accepted theory that the purpose of a novel was to please or amuse, to represent reality as more agreeable than it was, and, devoting itself to love as the most universally interesting passion, to be so sweet and clean as would enable it to be read aloud in the family circle without bringing a blush to the cheek of even the most innocent schoolgirl. As a matter of fact, she endorsed the theory to the extent that when she read *Sister Carrie* she was horrified at the prospect of its bearing the Doubleday imprint. The book was not merely frank and vulgar, it was immoral. It scorned the accepted idea of love and implied that the wages of sin might easily be success. With a strength of purpose that had been a support to the firm in the past, she impressed her feelings upon her husband, who, already convinced of its commercial impossibility, agreed. The promise to publish could not be kept.

When Arthur Henry in New York, learning the ominous news, wrote Dreiser to inform him, Dreiser professed to be undisturbed; yet, having not only spent money too unhesitatingly but also let word of his impending success reach editors and friends, he was in fact concerned; his good name was at stake, his future was jeopardized. Henry and Norris conferred and recommended that Dreiser insist on the firm's keeping its promise; so, when Page as Doubleday's spokesman asked for a release and offered to help secure a more willing publisher, Dreiser refused. Returning to New York and thinking of his connections with such magazines as the *Christian Herald* and the *New Voice,* he then asked Doubleday whether endorsement by religious magazines would make the book's publication easier. Doubleday assented but defined his final position in words to this effect: "We publish one edition as to contract, but we won't do as we would by a book we liked." [16] Yet Dreiser still assumed that publicity would follow. With faith in the efficacy of documents, on August 20 he signed a formal "Memorandum of Agreement" binding Doubleday, Page & Company "to publish the work at their own expense, and to pay the author, or his legal representative, a royalty of ten per cent." [17] He agreed to a few minor textual revisions that Doubleday wanted — he objected to removing what Doubleday considered profanity but was willing to change the names of real persons — and waited for recognition. His success seemed so nearly within reach that he felt that he had only to heed the advice of his friends and doggedly rely on a contract for all to be well.

It was useless, for there was more than one way to interpret a contract. The Doubleday lawyer, Thomas H. McKee, advised the firm that they had to publish the book, but that they could publish a small edition and put it in the stockroom without attempting to promote it and still would fulfill an agreement that did not mention selling the book. After all, they had warned Dreiser. So they printed a thousand copies, and although Norris sent out more than a hundred for review, they provided no advertising to proclaim its publication on November 8. Those literary editors who depended on advertising to guide them saw no merit in the novel, and book dealers found it dead. Although there were numerous reviews, these were confined mainly to the newspapers, were slow in appearing, and when they did appear, did not all appear at the same time.

Had the reviewers' reception of *Sister Carrie* been unanimously bad, Dreiser might have been able to reconcile himself to the publishers' failure to support it. But the notices were not all unfavorable. If Doubleday's had been inclined, they could have utilized many to the book's advantage. For although a number of the first reviewers expressed reservations, condemning matters of detail and style, they praised the book's power, its characterization, and the author's vision and insight into human nature. If some found the tale unpleasant, they also recognized its importance. Yet the comments would have had to be edited carefully to overcome popular resistance to a novel that was not sentimental or amusing. The *Seattle Post-Intelligencer* defined the situation almost exasperatingly well:

The philosophy of the book is very clear and very interesting. Its incidents, the squalid plane upon which its development takes place, will naturally prevent it from achieving a marked popularity. Even Mr. Dreiser's antiseptic style cannot make it anything but a most unpleasant tale, and you would never dream of recommending [it] to another person to read. Yet the fact remains that as a work of literature and the philosophy of human life it comes within sight of greatness.[18]

Instead of exploiting such tributes as this, though, Doubleday, Page & Company compelled *Sister Carrie* to sell itself, and since most of the New York reviews were completely noncommittal and some others in the West were morally indignant, the publishers actually permitted the derogatory and discouraging remarks to counteract whatever sympathetic criticism appeared. Only six hundred and fifty copies were disposed of, including those given away for review, and since the price of the novel was a dollar and a half, Dreiser's royalties totaled substantially below one hundred dollars. Had he understood the situation, he might have found a way to press Doubleday to fulfill the intent of the contract as well as its letter; but he did not know, and had to content himself with collecting clippings, observing the progress of recognition whose fruits were denied him, and realizing he had written an almost great book that could not be recommended to anyone to read.

There was, to be sure, some work he could still do. He resumed the kind of magazine writing that had proved profitable before *Sister Carrie*, and began two other novels, one of them to be based in part on the lives of two others of his sisters and to be called *The Transgressor* (later *Jennie Gerhardt*); the other to be called *The Rake*.[19] In addition, he received some encouragement in his attempt to continue as a novelist. In December 1900 George P. Brett of Macmillan's wrote that he had read *Sister Carrie*, was favorably impressed, and was ready to discuss new publishing arrangements.[20] Frank Norris, a few weeks later, told him he was "looking forward to news of your next now." [21] And in May the English publisher William Heinemann, seeking *Sister Carrie* for his Dollar Library of American Fiction, whose purpose was to introduce British readers to America's "mercurial genius," [22] offered Dreiser the opportunity of becoming known internationally. Heinemann required only that the first two hundred pages be reduced to eighty, an abridgment that Arthur Henry was eager to undertake in the interests of keeping the novel alive.[23]

The encouragement Dreiser found, however, could only prevent him from immediately realizing the depth of his disappointment. For although some circumstances might favor him, others existed to offset them. When he left a copy of *Carrie* with the Century Company in order that they might consider taking over the plates and reissuing the book, he was given back the volume in a few days by the girl at the reception desk, who said the company did not care even to comment on it. And when he had submitted preliminary chapters of the new novels to McClure, Phillips, & Company, he was apprised by John Phillips that if these represented his approach to literature, he should try his hand at something else; the firm, certainly, wanted none of it.[24] As he sought to elicit interest from among the publishers, he encountered closed doors, or a cold reception that was explained by his supposedly having written a "dirty" book. Once again his detached point of view was confronted with a fundamental challenge, and because his expectations had been naïvely excessive, his immediate failure became magnified, making his efforts seem increasingly futile and obscuring what should have appeared of greater and encouraging significance: that he had at last found an appropriate form of expression in the novel and that his first attempt had earned the support of men like Norris, whose critical judgment was to be respected.

VII

To Live

The consequences of Dreiser's discouragement were almost disastrous. As his prospects vanished, his reflections became infected with recurring thoughts of his apparent failure. His attempts to continue writing fiction served mainly to remind him of himself and came to nothing. And his will to act soon succumbed to neurasthenia and brought him to the verge of suicide. For almost three years he was compelled to struggle with himself, neglect his career, and summon what strength he had to solve the problem of simple, physical survival.

In June 1901, a few weeks after agreeing to Heinemann's offer, he accepted an invitation from Arthur Henry to stay with him for a month or so on a little island Henry had acquired just off the old fishing village of Noank, Connecticut. Jug, still away visiting, would join them later, and Anna Mallon would come up from New York on week-ends. Yet, idyllic as was the setting and congenial as was Henry's temperament, Dreiser found it difficult to accommodate himself to existence on the island. From the very first he was ill at ease in the presence of anything that could even remotely symbolize indigence, as though he saw in the bare walls of Henry's cabin, in its unpainted floor boards, and in dishes moist from the salty air portents of a disaster he had spent his life averting. He insisted the rough floor be scrubbed; he refused to believe the dishes were not greasy; he felt insecure when he perceived that only wire tethers fastened the cabin to the island. Where wild shrubbery grew he wanted a lawn. Where numerous windows admitted the tang of the weather day and night, he wanted protection against draft and dampness. Practical details oppressed him, and before many hours had passed he wished Jug were at hand. "If she were here, I could stay forever," he stated. ". . . She has spoiled me, and I am lost without her." [1]

Even out of doors, amid surroundings he regarded as beautiful, he continued to be different from the companion Henry had known. For example, according to Henry's account, when the two of them went crabbing, Dreiser, picking the crabs from their hiding-places, "cursed them for elusive devils, sighed over their fate, wondered at their intelligence, their trick of assuming the colors of the weeds and pebbles. He held them up to examine them; he watched them eat and fight, and discovered as much in a few moments as I had learned in weeks. But he continued to shake his head dubiously as we dropped them in the bait pail, and when, anchored by the pole buoy, we put them on the hooks and cast them overboard, he seemed to see only the wretched nature of their end. If the fish did not bite, he grew restless; if they did, he hauled them in with a grim zest, and struggled to unhook them, now pitying their state, now damning them for the trouble they made." [2] Later, sitting with Henry overlooking the water as night approached and discussing the beauty of the spectacle and its ultimate purpose, he was inclined to dwell on ideas of his own unimportance. Whereas he had usually subordinated these to a belief that the tendency of life was toward harmony, order, and beauty, and that one must view all events reverently, he now reversed his emphasis and made the subordinate ideas paramount:

119

For my part [he said], I think the universe is an individual very much like McKinley or King Edward. It might be a Bismarck, a Gladstone, a Morgan or a Rockefeller, but I question if it possesses, as a whole, the singleness of purpose and the strength of will of these men. It is certainly not a malicious brute, but it might very well be a John L. Sullivan, good-natured enough when sober, mellowed by a little liquor, made maudlin by more, and ugly by too much. I think, however, it is just an average, rather phlegmatic sort of fellow, preserving a formal, well-balanced poise in mediocrity; or . . . it might be a crab or a leaf or an atom of the air, and man but a minor subdivision in its make-up.[3]

And if he appeared calm and aloof in his reflections, it took only the desperate flopping of a stranded fish to upset him, and only a damp quilt on his bed to plunge him into gloom.

The situation was only temporarily improved when Jug and Anna arrived, for although they relieved him of responsibility for his material comforts, they did not solve his problems. He was, to be sure, now free to row over to Noank during the day, wander idly about its streets, and talk with villagers who could give him an insight into a contented way of life that contrasted agreeably with his own. He was able, for example, to meet men who practiced the Christian ethics they believed rather than preached it, and to discover embodiments of his own ideal of selfless achievement in a few who preferred honesty and integrity to wealth or personal glory and whose only interest in the struggle to survive was to commend those in the community who displayed the virtue of industry.[4] Yet, congenial as he found this atmosphere, by late July he was restless. He resented Anna's claims on Henry's attention and, feeling himself something of an intruder, attributed to Anna a jealousy that was his own magnified by reflection. Despite Henry's urging, he did not want to stay longer, and before the month was over he and Jug returned to New York.

The city, however, posed other problems for him. Since he had very little on which to support a wife there, he had to give up his apartment, comfortably located near Central Park, for less congenial accommodations on East Eighty-second Street, which cost only thirty dollars a month [5] but were located in a neighborhood dreary enough finally to halt his writing. The view overlooking the East River and Blackwells Island, where were housed the sick, the criminal, and the insane, suggested mainly incidents and scenes of despair so real that he was in the end unable to lose himself in sustained narration.

At first it appeared that he might be able actually to re-establish himself. He wrote sketches of distinctive, self-possessed individuals like those he had encountered in Connecticut, and succeeded in selling them to *Harper's Weekly, Success,* and *Ainslee's,*[6] and in eliciting from one editor, John Kendrick Bangs of *Harper's Weekly,* a request for more material.[7] In addition, he began to gain a reputation in England as a consequence of Heinemann's publication of *Sister Carrie* in August. In papers and magazines as diverse as the *Daily Mail, Manchester Guardian, Daily Chronicle, Academy, Spectator,* and *Athenæum,* reviewers agreed in recommending Dreiser's novel. The British exhibited no moralistic predilections, and although some of them might call it "an engrossing and depressing book," [8] or a "grimly-grey story of life," [9] they made clear that their description was a tribute to its power and that the life it depicted was "life near the bone." [10] At least one critic suggested it belonged on the shelf next to Zola's *Nana.*[11] As the fifteen hundred copies of the first printing were being exhausted, Heinemann jubilantly, and without intentional irony or malice, wrote Doubleday a letter that Doubleday forwarded to Dreiser without comment: "I look upon Mr. Dreiser as an author of exceptional merit. . . . I congratulate you very heartily in having discovered him. You should make a great fuss of him. How about his next and future work?" [12]

Dreiser, however, could complete little except short pieces on depressing phases of life. He rewrote his 1899 article on the curious shifts of the poor, provided a different emphasis, and submitted it to *Success* as "a distinct commentary on the social conditions of our day." [13] When *Success* accepted it for March publication, he submitted another, entitled "The Tenement Toilers," in which he presented extreme instances of wretched living in New York's sweatshop districts and exhibited people whose lives had been "warped and distorted in every worthy mental sense by the great fight which they had to make to get their money." [14] When this too was accepted, he doubtless remembered Bangs's request and began to order the impressions that became "Christmas in the Tenements" the following year, describing the pitiful gaiety of those who sought to forget their hardships during the winter holidays and emphasizing the futile, momentary nature of their enjoyment.[15] Dreiser himself, of course, aware of the illusions, could scarcely share them; and unable to share them, could not forget himself. Finally he could not write at all — even of the futility of illusions. If the "next and future work" that Heinemann referred to was to materialize, he would need both assurance of income and a change of scene.

Since he could not depend on selling to magazines and British royalties were ultimately scant, his first hope was to find someone to reissue *Carrie* in the United States. Inasmuch as the established firms had rebuffed him, he submitted *Sister Carrie* and his plans for *The Transgressor* to the newer and smaller firm of J. F. Taylor & Company. But Joseph Taylor, the president, while acknowledging *Carrie's* merits, declared Doubleday had made its revival temporarily impossible. He proposed, however, to take over Doubleday's stock and make Dreiser weekly advances on his next novel if Dreiser would complete the next novel within a year.[16] Although Dreiser had had in mind revising and amplifying the last chapter of *Sister Carrie* in order to make his treatment of Ames less sketchy, he agreed to the proposal and prepared at once to subordinate everything to the writing of the story of Jennie Gerhardt.[17]

The amount that Taylor was willing to advance, fifteen dollars a week, made it possible for Dreiser to leave New York. In November 1901, when he could no longer endure the sights and his reflections, he left with Jug for a town near Roanoke, Virginia, where he had been before his marriage and knew the living was cheaper and the struggle to live less hectic, and where he might complete his novel. Yet, despite his confidence that in sight of the mountains he would experience a new creative drive, the next year provided only further and more substantial support for his most discouraged view of the hopelessness of effort. The town in Virginia was a place in which he could live very cheaply, but his having had to go there was sufficient to occasion further brooding over his career and further questioning of his ability. Such reflections in turn, of course, impaired his writing; and although he was able to forward new material to Taylor, he became dissatisfied with what he did write and regarded Taylor's weekly advances as reproaches for his failure. At Christmas time he went with Jug to visit her family in Missouri and hoped that he could do some writing there. The need now was simply to maintain an objective attitude toward his material. As he explained to a reporter in St. Louis, he believed in "considering every phase of life from a philosophic standpoint. If life is to be made better or more interesting, its conditions must be understood." [18] But the necessary detachment was impossible as he continued to contemplate his own unhappy state. Although he had recently been able to write of Noank's characters, that was doubtless because they were adjusted, quiet people who did not remind him of his own struggles and failures. Jennie, however, a partial portrait of his sisters, was bound to bring his predicament home to him. In addition, when he found Jug insufficiently sympathetic with the kind of writing he was interested in, and at the same time possessive to the point at which he decided she was debilitating him and interfering with his work, he wanted freedom from her and became restless. He traveled with her to the Gulf coast; no recovery followed. Within a few weeks, sometimes meeting her, sometimes alone, he began to walk some ten miles a day through West Virginia, Virginia, and Delaware back into Pennsylvania, and in midsummer 1902 reached Philadelphia during its oppressive humidity and heat to try his luck there. For seven months he declined still further. He recollected predictions of ill fortune by astrologers and palmists, began to see about him omens all freighted with disaster, and worried himself anew.[19] He alternated between moments of extreme exaltation and profound depression, felt ill, imagined he was losing his hair, suffered pains in his fingertips, developed an abnormally large appetite but tried to save money by curtailing the amount he ate, could not sleep when he needed rest, and could not write when he tried to use his mind. Physicians and nerve specialists recommended almost everything from medicines in which he had no faith to diversions that he could not afford. Nothing really helped. For a while he found some palliation in contributing to the Philadelphia *North American's* Sunday supplement four or five anonymous pieces at twenty dollars each,[20] and in writing for the new *Booklover's Magazine* an editorial entitled "True Art speaks Plainly"; [21] but the moment he departed from objective details, he touched on his own problems again. When, for example, he sold the *Era*, another Philadelphia magazine, a sketch entitled "A Mayor and His People" [22] and an article entitled "The Problem of the Soil," [23] both written a year or two before, he was bound to read a personal application into what he had described. In both pieces the situations are those in which efforts are unrewarded: in the one, a humanitarian mayor is discarded by a gullible electorate he has benefited; in the other, an energetic farmer works in vain on poor land while an idler profits on rich. Before the end of January 1903 Dreiser concluded that his his own efforts could only be futile. There was no use remaining in Philadelphia and no use wandering elsewhere. He had made friends with an editor associated with the *Era*, Joseph Hornor Coates, and had let him read *The Transgressor*. But the help and advice of friends was pointless now. He read over *The Rake* and could add nothing beyond the fifteenth chapter.[24] He wrote Taylor that he was giving up *The Transgressor* and would try to repay the advances some day.[25] Then, with thirty-two dollars in his pocket as his weapon for the last phase of his struggle, he returned to New York.

As he looked about him in the city of his former dreams, he felt that whether he rose or fell could no longer matter. All he wanted in his weariness was some rest and peace of mind. His mind, however, had become too much its own helpless victim for him to be able to rescue it. He rented a room in Brooklyn because living was cheaper there than in Manhattan, but he viewed with a melancholy eye everything from the torn wallpaper to the neighborhood tenements that reminded him of the economic level to which he had descended. He continued to toss sleeplessly through the nights, to produce only an unsatisfactory paragraph or two during the day, to return to bed worried about his day's failure, and to fail more dismally the following day for want of sleep the night before. If occasionally he tried to divert himself by visiting a museum or art gallery, he feared some acquaintance might see him and treat him as a pitiable object. If he thought of looking for a job, he told himself he knew no skill other than writing and retained too little strength to attempt unskilled physical labor. Moreover, he did not wish to risk the humiliation of being laughed at, scorned, or simply refused. He jotted down some reflections on being poor, whereby he tried to convince himself that material wants were not important so long as he could enjoy art, literature, and the beauty of nature; [26] and after puzzling to account for his predicament, he decided that his ills were all predestined, that all forms of life were bound up with some power or star under whose jurisdiction they were born, and that he would have to await his patron fate's prosperity before he could expect any of his own.

As his funds diminished he did make some efforts. He approached one publisher and proposed advances on work he could do once he regained his health. He visited newspaper editors. He applied for work in a sugar refinery and with a streetcar company. But these ventures, all of them in vain, only confirmed his hesitations. More often he stood undecided outside shop doors until he felt himself observed; then, certain that he appeared above the work he was ashamed to reveal he was seeking, he walked away. Eventually, unable to earn money, he saved a little by moving into a cell-like room that cost only a dollar and a quarter a week and by restricting himself first to two meals a day, then to one, then to a bottle of milk and a loaf of bread, supplemented by an apple and perhaps some vegetable he could pick up in the streets of the public market and heat on the oil stove that warmed his room.

Under this regimen a crisis was inevitable. A strange half-wakefulness soon came over him during which he wandered about confused and uncertain as to what he actually was. He sometimes regarded himself as two persons, one of whom viewed the struggles of the other with philosophic detachment. Then he experienced hallucinations. At night, frequently, he imagined there was an intruder creeping about the room; often he leaped from his bed to see what hand was touching his pillow. In addition, the pains he had felt in his fingertips when he was in Philadelphia now returned with increasing severity. Fingers and also toes burned and blistered. His eyes began to itch and sting; his left eye became slightly weaker, losing some of its power of accommodation; [27] and wherever he looked, the angles and lines of houses, streets, pictures, newspaper columns appeared crooked. Moreover, whether he was sitting or standing, he found himself strangely compelled to turn around as though he must go in a circle to bring himself into alignment with something. To the extent that he was aware of his difficulties, he became to that extent more inhibited than ever in regard to finding work. His appearance, he was sure, bespoke his fallen state. On one occasion he appealed to a charitable organization for a job, but when he disclosed that he had two sisters, Mame and Emma, and a brother, Paul, in New York, he was told to overlook his pride and go to them and was given only letters of introduction which might lead to temporary work and which, when he saw the charity's name on the letterhead, he destroyed and flung into the gutter. The more he thought about himself, the more sorry for himself he became. He visited Mame and her husband one evening and throughout a sumptuous meal experienced the torture of contrasting their happiness with his despair and of withholding from them the true nature of his affairs. On another evening he dined with a brother-in-law, an officer in the Navy, aboard a battleship and suffered envy and self-pity in contemplating how well nourished and secure young officers were. Finally, when he was reduced to a last dollar and three cents and received an invitation from Paul to come and see him, he made up his mind that because he and Paul had had a quarrel a few years before, Paul should come to him instead, and he ignored the letter. On Friday of the last week for which he had paid rent, he told himself that at the end of the next day he would have no place to sleep. A last-minute round of Brooklyn and Manhattan newspapers, publishers, shops, and factories afforded no encouragement. One street-railway clerk told him to return Monday, but Monday would be too late. When he had returned to his neighborhood that evening and bought what he told himself was his last loaf of bread, he wandered down to the East River and considered ending all his torment and weariness by plunging in; and in fact he might have, had he not been interrupted in his gloomy meditations by an intoxicated Scotsman who danced about him singing, and then been addressed by a canal boatman who offered him a ride to Tonawanda because "I thought you might be running away from your wife." The incongruity of the boatman's idea freed him from his spell, and he laughed.[28] That night he was able actually to sleep awhile.

The crisis was over. Next day after relatively few hours of wandering he remembered that the general passenger agent of the New York Central Railroad was known for his willingness to help writers, and upon applying at the company's offices he was promised a healthful job out of doors if he returned Monday. Then he realized he had a gold watch he could pawn and suddenly found himself with twenty-five dollars. As he hastened to a store to buy a new hat, he encountered Paul, who immediately recognized his plight, tearfully pressed a thick roll of bills into his hand, and made him promise to visit him Monday. With immediate security thus guaranteed, he felt that the threats of misery and want were being permanently put behind. He spent that night at the Mills Hotel, able to view the aged and weary without seeing himself mirrored, and passed Sunday at the Palisades dreaming of future accomplishment.

He was not destined to work for the New York Central at once, however, for by Monday Paul had arranged for him to spend the next six weeks in Westchester County at William Muldoon's famous sanitarium for the wealthy. Although Dreiser argued, Paul fortunately would hear of no alternatives, and Dreiser found himself two days later submitting to the strict discipline of a lithe tiger of a man who was famous as a wrestler and trainer of prizefighters and who was hostile to all self-indulgence and moody introspection. Everyone rose at the same time, wore woolen underwear, changed clothes at stated intervals, ate the same meals, maintained the same hours, engaged in the same exercises. From the six a.m. medicine-ball work-out and the one-minute shower following it to the moment of retiring, all activity was regulated, and all morose speculation was ridiculed. When Dreiser was ordered to ride horseback for the first time in his life and, bouncing uncomfortably, became confused in the attempt to ease himself, Muldoon at once pointed him out to the company, scoffed at him for thinking himself "a philosopher," and called him a "long-legged ignoramus." When on another occasion Dreiser tried to persuade Muldoon that Muldoon like all men was helplessly the sport of chance, Muldoon utterly repudiated the argument and would condone no statement that justified resignation or inaction. If Dreiser sat alone somewhere to meditate, Muldoon was likely to rouse him and say he did not want Dreiser loafing about the house. If, on the other hand, Dreiser strolled off by himself, Muldoon declared he did not want him to wander "without my consent." Under such supervision Dreiser necessarily began to recover. He regained some of the weight he had lost, slept better, and took a renewed interest in the world about him. In addition he became clear as to his purpose, and when his six weeks were ending, wrote to the official he had talked with at the New York Central offices and said he was returning to accept the job he had originally been promised.

From early June to late December 1903 he remained with the railroad on the outskirts of New York City, doing work that helped complete the restoration of his health and enabled him to make his living by writing once more.[29] At first he only swept the carpenter's shop, scooped shavings, or lifted heavy planks, but as daily exhaustion enabled him to sleep soundly again, he was able to think with increasing clarity and to accept responsibilities. He supervised the driving of piles for a freight house, worked out modifications of the time schedule for fellow laborers who wished to persuade the foreman to end work earlier on Saturdays, sought new opportunities on the plumber's staff, and finally became a clerical assistant to the masons' Irish foreman, Mike Burke, whose energy and determination in the face of educational and financial handicaps Dreiser found contagious. As Dreiser's vitality returned, his confidence returned with it, and thus one November afternoon, when he had become morose and written a poem,[30] he decided to cease feeling sorry for himself and to send what he had done to a magazine. Then when the editor mailed him a check, he felt he might become some kind of writer again. On Christmas Eve he bade Burke farewell and went home to begin an account of his collapse and rehabilitation.

After a long battle I am once more the possessor of health [he wrote]. That necessary poise in which the mind and body reflect the pulsations of the infinite is mine. . . . All that is, now passes before me a rich, varied and beautiful procession. I have fought a battle for the right to live and for the present, musing with stilled nerves and a serene gaze, I seem the victor. . . .[31]

Then, communicating with Richard Duffy and other editors he had known, he canvassed opportunities among newspapers and magazines, secured a position as assistant feature-section editor of Frank Munsey's *New York Daily News*, and, not yet disposed to resume attempts at fiction, used his editorial position to provide himself with an outlet for his views.

Now at last he was restored in ability and outlook to where he had been before the disappointment over *Sister*

Carrie. Still insisting that the neglected aspects of life deserved attention, he recounted the love affairs of "Little Italy," [32] told of the fates of Shanghaied sailors,[33] and portrayed pathetic scenes at a foundlings' hospital.[34] Later, when Munsey discontinued the Sunday features, he contributed similar pieces to the *New York Tribune* [35] and *Tom Watson's Magazine,*[36] of which Duffy was an editor. If his thinking had not progressed beyond the contradictions of his novel, it was, at least, no longer darkened by melancholy. The expectations and discouragements that had so deeply affected him were no longer realities, and he could turn to practical problems with determination and zest. Whereas he continued, on the one hand, to deplore the frustrations and spiritual loneliness that the struggle for money made inevitable,[37] and, on the other hand, to dream of "the beauty of wealth" and the rewards of money "properly invested," [38] he was able to detach himself from the problem sufficiently to regard money as simply a force that contributed wonderfully to the excitement of the spectacle. The details of the world invited investigation everywhere. He suddenly wanted to educate himself about everything from the very beginning, and before the end of 1904 began to read books on the history of the world and to immerse himself in the philosophy of such thinkers as Immanuel Kant.[39]

VIII

Editorial Days

It was to be another five years before Dreiser felt again the frustrations of editorial work and acquired enough money to resume the career of disinterested novelist. Meanwhile, however, his point of view proved profitable, for it favored a portrayal of life in all its variety and thereby could benefit magazines willing to pay him a high salary to increase circulation.

His first substantial opportunity to indicate his ability came shortly after the cessation of Munsey's features in July 1904. He had heard from Duffy that Street & Smith, publishers of cheap magazines and nickel romances, needed someone to help Charles Agnew MacLean edit their dime novels, and upon applying to Ormond G. Smith was hired as fiction editor to cut sixty-thousand-word manuscripts in half, a task he allegedly accomplished by writing new endings for the first halves and new beginnings for the second.[1] Then when Smith wanted to launch a new illustrated monthly, he was called upon to edit it and make of it a popular "publication for the home." Paid a salary of thirty-five dollars a week, he let Jug return from Missouri to look after him, repaid Joseph Taylor the advances on The Transgressor, and when he came to know MacLean well, talked confidently of organizing a publishing house and reissuing Sister Carrie, the plates and sheets of which MacLean bought from Taylor in January for five hundred dollars.[2]

Commercially the spectatorial attitude now began to pay.

From almost the first number, in April 1905, *Smith's Magazine* expressed the Dreiserian view. Although it declared at the outset that the role of fiction was, in Hall Caine's words, "to show us that success may be the worst failure and failure the best success," [3] it insisted in June that "*Success* is what counts in the world, and it is little matter how the success is won. . . . No matter how fine our conceptions of art or ethics, we can never see the world as it actually is, until we look this fact in the face and take it into our considerations." [4] And it proceeded — indirectly, to be sure — to help readers "see the world as it actually is." Dreiser promised not only "human" fiction, but also articles on the latest researches in sciences and on the latest advances made by the human mind, photographs of interesting people, and "a hearty advocacy of every sane and reasonable movement that makes for the real betterment of the rank and file of the American people." [5] He promised "something new, fresh and vivid. . . . This is the biggest, newest and most interesting country in the world, and to produce a big, new and interesting magazine we must reflect American manners and customs, thought and feeling." [6] From April 1905 to July 1906 the contents included a serial entitled "Diana's Destiny" and articles on grade-crossings and food adulteration, stories about boys and an account of "The Serious Side of Burlesque," a department devoted to physical culture for women and biographical sketches of Charles M. Schwab and Tom Johnson, humorous stories by Charles Fort and serious ones by George Bronson-Howard. Dreiser himself in one issue contributed a signed essay, "The City of Crowds," in the vein of his comments for the *Daily News* and

Tom Watson's, expressing his fascination with the contrasts of the city and his preoccupation with the weary,
the poor, and the troubled.[7] Although he did not become so pointed here as he did in *Tom Watson's* a few
months later in "A Lesson from the Aquarium," wherein
he likened the behavior of human beings to the behavior
of stort minnows, hermit crabs, shark-suckers, and
sharks,[8] he nevertheless left readers with a picture over
which they must shake their heads. At the same time he
provided compensation, for it was all part of "a wonderful sight," [9] and in the first year of his editorship he
presented sufficient wonder and variety to double the
initial circulation of *Smith's* so that it reached 125,000
readers.[10]

Having succeeded to this extent, he sought something
better for himself, and found it in April 1906 as managing editor of the *Broadway Magazine,* which Benjamin
Bowles Hampton, an advertising agent, had just bought.
Hampton offered Dreiser a starting salary of sixty-five
dollars a week and promised an increase if the circulation rose from its present 12,000 to more than 75,000.
Since Dreiser would now be assured of comfortable security and able not only to move from an apartment in
the Bronx to one on Morningside Heights, but also to
buy back from MacLean for $550 the plates and sheets
of *Sister Carrie,*[11] he set to work at once organizing the
staff, recruiting it in a new building still filled with lum-
ber. His task was to transform a "white light" monthly
that should not be left on the parlor table into a "home"
magazine that presented a mature view of metropolitan
life. His plan was made clear in his first number, in June.
He established an editor's page that took readers into his
confidence. He promised a magazine that would not be
"a drain on your intellectual resources to appreciate,"

for "the heavy is never the effective or the important."
He set forth purposes similar to those that had been effective on *Smith's*. He gave them an explicitly Manhattan orientation, and declared: "We are after novelties;
we are after entertaining features that sparkle; we are
after beauty, and variety, and to obtain these we propose to spare neither labor nor expense." [12] With more
money at his disposal than he had controlled before,
to entice better writers like Channing Pollock, Brian
Hooker, and Rudyard Kipling and to purchase "stories
of life as it is being lived to-day — stories of real men and
women, not fabrications of fancied sentiment and emotion" — stories with "universal appeal; strength and
sweetness; purity and power," [13] he was able to accomplish in little more than a year what the *Standard* in
New York called "the prettiest piece of transformation
work seen in New York for many a day. . . ." [14] Soon
he found himself regarded as a member of the social life
he had for so long had to view from a distance. He was
elected a resident member of the National Arts Club
and invited to participate in the Economic Club of
New York and listen to discussions of the overcapitaliza-
tion of railroads. Even John Phillips of McClure,
Phillips, who had so sharply refused to have anything
to do with his novels, now stopped him on the street to
say he had changed his mind about *Sister Carrie*.[15]

In fact, as he became established as an editor, he
found himself becoming re-established as the author of
Sister Carrie. In March 1907, through the initiative of
Ethel M. Kelley, a writer associated with him on the
Broadway, and the enterprise of Flora Mai Holly, a
literary agent just beginning her career, a publisher
was discovered who was interested in reissuing the book.
Ben W. Dodge, then in the process of organizing

B. W. Dodge & Company, offered to pay Dreiser a ten per cent royalty on the first three thousand copies and to consult him in matters of publicity if Dreiser in turn would give him the plates.[16] Dreiser accepted, and later in the year, reviving the plans he had discussed with MacLean, joined the firm as its editorial director. Meanwhile, on May 18, 1907, he watched the reappearance of his novel.

This time it was effectively advertised. The company circulated leaflets [17] bearing excerpts from the English reviews of 1901, together with comments by such American writers as Brand Whitlock, William Marion Reedy, and Hamlin Garland. They offered "a beautiful poster in color free on application" and represented the first edition as sold out in less than two weeks. Their newspaper announcements set the stage for a triumph as they trumpeted:

The Curtain Raised

on a generally unwritten

Phase of Life.

Startling in reality. Sensational revelations. Masterful in Simplicity. Forceful in genuine art. Theodore Dreiser has written one of the most remarkable novels in literature and everybody is going to read it. The realism of a Zola without the faults.[18]

On the whole, the audience applauded as hoped. Although some reviewers complained of sordid pictures, unwholesome reading, and split infinitives, and almost all reviewers were unanalytical, the weight of opinion was enthusiastic. If Dreiser found occasion to complain of those who called his book both gripping and expendable [19] and ridiculed others who criticized his diction and rhetoric,[20] he was now at least an author who had the opportunity in interviews to reiterate that "the mere living of your daily life" was "drastic drama," that this mere living was "intensely interesting" and appalling, and that he wanted to record "life as it is" without any moral, unless it was the afterthought "that all humanity must stand together and war against and overcome the forces of nature." [21] In addition, his novel was now reaching the people on whom, he told his interviewer, he was relying for understanding. By September 1 there were sold 4,617 copies, earning Dreiser more than eight hundred dollars, and a year later Grosset & Dunlap contracted with Dodge for an edition of 10,000, of which they had sold 5,248 by the end of 1908. In the Midwest, university students who could become excited over Heine, Zola, Ibsen, and Nietzsche, and who delighted in reading books their professors never mentioned, now began to argue about *Sister Carrie* and to regard Dreiser as an American who could at least rank with the Europeans.[22] Soon the novel's enhanced reputation spread farther. An edition was published in Canada, and in Australia a publisher began negotiations for the right to distribute it on that continent.[23]

Although conditions now appeared favorable for submitting a second novel to some publisher, Dreiser's mind continued to be occupied with editorial projects. For a while he considered publishing a daily, four-page penny digest of the news.[24] Later he began to search for alternatives to the *Broadway*. Hampton had begun to interfere with the editing, insisting on the purity of stories as against their power, on the popular appeal of articles as against their novelty, and, for the magazine as a whole, on the newly profitable attitude of the muckraker as

against the disinterested Dreiserian view of the metropolitan microcosm.[25] Consequently, when early in June
1907 George W. Wilder, president of the Butterick Publishing Company, the distributor of Butterick Fashions,
offered Dreiser a beginning salary of seven thousand dollars to direct the *Delineator*, the *Designer*, and *New
Idea Woman's Magazine* — the Butterick "Trio" —
Dreiser naturally accepted unhesitatingly.[26] Asked by an
interviewer shortly thereafter concerning his plans for
another novel, he replied that he was too busy to work
on it.[27] He had, after all, gained the opportunity to go
about as far as anyone could expect to go as an editor
who wished to maintain the point of view of spectatorial
catholicity in respectable magazines published primarily
for profits.

He found, from the very first, that unlike the novelist,
who might at best be smilingly tolerated for his genius
and seized upon as an ornament at receptions, an editor
at Butterick's was a person who would be taken seriously
in the commercial world. The Butterick Building alone
was sufficient to communicate to him some sense of this
power. Standing impressively fifteen stories tall at Spring
and Macdougal Streets in downtown New York, it
looked across Manhattan to the edges of the city's far
boroughs and included within its vista acres of the mist-
covered Jersey flats and the waters of the bay stretching
out past the Statue of Liberty to the dim reaches of the
open sea. From Butterick's upper stories Dreiser could
watch with dreamer's detachment the river and harbor
traffic and the antlike streams of people in the streets
below, while within the building he could awaken to
the stir of two thousand workers who served a printing
plant that boasted of being the largest in the world. To
be in command here meant, as he saw it, to be able to

utter a word and promptly have numerous servitors hurrying to do one's bidding,[28] and when he took up his task of directing the Butterick trio, he was quick to reflect this sense of activity and to infuse the editorial rooms with an immediate energy appropriate to their surroundings. Work schedules and layout were promptly planned for the fall and early winter issues, and even though he was compelled to remain away in July and August because of a sudden appendectomy, his associates were able to proceed as if automatically.

The magazines were primarily suppliers of fashions and patterns, although the *Delineator* had already developed somewhat along literary lines, and it was Dreiser's task to increase their circulation by making them all more readable.[29] Granted a free hand, he began at once to reorganize the editorial boards, giving each its own staff, taking direct charge of the *Delineator* himself, and luring Charles Hanson Towne from the *Smart Set* as fiction editor to secure better stories for the trio. At the same time he began to develop a cautious editorial policy. His story-writers included Ludwig Lewisohn, Mary Stewart Cutting, Zona Gale, Rupert Hughes, Ella Wheeler Wilcox, F. Marion Crawford, and Honoré Willsie, and he took care that nothing should offend the readers. As he explained to a correspondent:

We like sentiment, we like humor, we like realism, but it must be tinged with sufficient idealism to make it all of a truly uplifting character. Our field in this respect is limited by the same limitations which govern the well regulated home. We cannot admit stories which deal with false or immoral relations, or which point a false moral, or which deal with things degrading, such as drunkenness. I am personally opposed in this magazine to stories which have an element of horror in them, or which are disgusting in their realism

and fidelity to life. The finer side of things — the idealistic —
is the answer for us, and we find really splendid material
within these limitations.[30]

In addition, his illustrators were not to draw characters
with cigarettes in their hands, or set wineglasses on a
Thanksgiving table.[31] Literary quality might be thus
maintained without upsetting any moral code.

He desired more than merely to avoid negative reactions, however. He desired to elicit positive responses,
and to this end sought to imbue the magazines with an
informal tone. He urged his staff to stress the human
and personal in their writing, to focus attention less on
institutions than on the individuals who ran them.[32] He
suggested that ordinary third-person generalizations on
such subjects as child care be cast in the second person
and addressed to the mother in order to maintain the illusion of personal contact.[33] He planned a beauty department that would draw some eight or ten thousand
letters a month and established a correspondence department to give each letter the personal consideration that
would make the writers feel the *Delineator* was their
magazine.[34] When problems verged on the serious, he
balanced them with humorous commentary, such as
"The Funny Side of Woman's Suffrage," or with parody,
such as the *Delineator's* "Man's Page," which was supposed to have, according to Dreiser, "a basis of serious
advice with just a slight undertone of josh" [35] and to
which Homer Croy, Franklin P. Adams, and H. L.
Mencken, then only a Baltimore newspaperman, contributed. And when he wanted to approach the readers
himself, he repeated the practice he had employed on
the *Broadway* of setting aside a page for editorial chat-
ting and under the heading "Concerning Us All"
frequently presented sociological and philosophical

problems that readers might feel they were solving with him.

An opportunity to present such problems was, in fact, as important to Dreiser as ever, for his views of the world had not changed and he wanted his magazine to reflect them. If fiction and informality of tone might be used to attract readers, other devices might be used to influence them and make them more conscious of the condition of society. When Dreiser assumed charge of the *Delineator*, there was running in it a series of articles on marital unrest and divorce. As soon as he had instituted his column, in October, he asked readers to write answers to the question of what a man who had progressed in the world owed a wife who had failed to keep pace with him, intellectually or emotionally.[36] Attempting to make the question seem critical by pointing out that men love change and novelty where women are satisfied to rest in the keeping of one man, a situation he called "the primal tragedy of life," he implied that human beings were fundamentally helpless to determine their own fate. On the other hand, the *Delineator* purported to stand for "betterment and Twentieth Century methods in bringing it about," [37] and at the same time that he was suggesting man was helpless, Dreiser prepared for a campaign to help rescue orphans from institutions and uniforms and place them as individuals in private homes. Beginning with an article on "the little human derelicts cast up on the tide of our great cities," [38] he set aside a section of the magazine each month "for the child that needs a home and the home that needs a child," sent out letters calling attention to the campaign, persuaded President Theodore Roosevelt to call a national conference in January 1909, and finally organized a National Child Rescue League, with James E. West as its secretary. While Dreiser was still the observer disturbed by what he beheld, he was now in a better position than he had been before to help ameliorate conditions that grieved him.

His reforms, however, constituted no comprehensive program. During his editorship the *Delineator* printed articles, symposia, or editorial discussions concerning woman suffrage, what factories and railroads could do for the people, what women could do for their towns, what was the matter with the public schools, what was wrong with the churches, what was the fate of prisoners' families, and what might be done "if I were our national Santa Claus." But at best they dealt with specific evils of which the public was perhaps only partially aware. When broader and more radical social issues arose, Dreiser did not acknowledge them. Thus when the typographical union at Butterick's struggled for union recognition, and two writers refused to contribute to the *Delineator* because Butterick's would not accord this recognition, Dreiser suggested only that the granting of an eight-hour day might be the solution.[39] A more positive program would have required a more rigidly defined belief in right and wrong than he could entertain, believing as he did in the inscrutability of life. He preferred as ever to contemplate what he called "The Romance of the Unexplainable" [40] — what was the origin and nature of matter, what was the reason for being alive — to ask readers to consider the unanswerable questions, and printing a series of articles on the ultimate problem, "Are the Dead Alive?" [41] to indicate that there were more things in heaven and earth than were dreamt of in any complacent philosophy. Life remained for Dreiser nearly what it had been at the time of *Sister Carrie's* publication, except that now he had achieved a position of security

143

and a feeling of power by virtue of the same kinds of accidents as daily brought want and defeat to others.

Although the *Delineator* thus lacked the specific purpose that distinguished the crusading magazine, it had the advantage not only of an objectivity that persuaded the public of its reliability, but also of a receptivity to new and original ideas that stimulated the staff. Dreiser was able, on the whole, to make his staff feel that the magazine was moving and that they were a necessary part of it. He selected his writers with care. He personally checked every manuscript that was accepted. He scrutinized the work of every department. And he made decisions quickly and demanded efficiency. If to Sinclair Lewis, fresh out of Yale, he looked "more like a wholesale hardware merchant than a properly hollow-cheeked realist" because he wore "waistcoats, real vescits, and they are well-filled," [42] to others who had never seen a Westerner before he was "different" and even awesome. When writers or prospective editors came to see him, he frequently let them sit before him nervous and trembling, shifting uncomfortably, as he eyed them searchingly, balancing on his nose a pair of eyeglasses from which hung a long black cord, and pleating and unpleating his handkerchief. When he demanded "ideas" from his staff, he made the demand unmistakably serious and let them know their positions depended upon their response, for he was persistent in delving into their minds and compelling them to contribute suggestions. He tested them by their reactions to particular manuscripts, told them they could remain "as long as you have ideas," [43] and compared them with each other at weekly editorial conferences, during which he asked for comments on ideas that had been submitted in writing, a single idea to a page, and studied them as he launched a discussion upon some subject of special interest to himself.[44] In this way he assured the existence of some variety in the contents of the magazine and gave importance to the work of the people he directed.

But what accounted for his success editorially began to undermine his position within the Butterick organization as a whole. Since to him an idea was the most important aspect of a situation, he was prepared, in the interests of some last-minute thought, to change the layout of the forthcoming number whether it meant discarding some dress-designer's advertisement or not. He was also, if a passing feeling moved him, willing to disregard the moral requirements for a story and allow the principal female character to smoke a cigarette, on the ground that "to touch the lives of our readers, we've got to get down to vitals." [45] Inevitably there developed serious tension between him and the business departments — "the God damned hyenas on the eighth floor," as he termed them [46] — and when Butterick's in October 1909 took over ownership of the Ridgway Company, publisher of *Everybody's*, and thereby brought in a budgetary rival, conflicts became more frequent and more serious. Dreiser's allotments were contested. His view of life was counterbalanced by ideas he could see no force to, Erman J. Ridgway establishing a column in the *Delineator* to make statements like: ". . . life is so much sweeter when we can attune our spirits to the Great Spirit; when we can join our fellows in inspiring antiphony with the morning stars singing in glory. . . ." [47] And his editorial policy was criticized by more systematic rivals who could not regard as policy the efforts of a man to push ahead anyone who had an idea.[48] Before long he began to feel insecure and, once again, restless.

Once again, too, he began to search for new security

and more congenial outlets. His salary having now increased to ten thousand dollars a year, he began to in-
vest it. He entered into a contract with Arthur Henry's
brother Alfred in North Yakima, Washington, to amass
profits from some apple orchards; he acquired some land
in Rockland County, New York; and he considered plans
for publishing a series of seventy-five-cent books. At the
same time, with money more of a reality than it ever had
been, he was able to regain sufficient confidence to return to creative writing. He not only wrote down observations in the vein he had for *Tom Watson's*, sketch-
ing the jobless, the Bowery Mission, the waterfront, the
factory, the stockyards, and the flight of pigeons, among
other subjects, for a volume he hoped to publish as *Idylls
of the Poor*, but also wrote character sketches of his
brother Paul, who had died in January 1906, and of
Mike Burke and the men on the railroad, filed away
some poems in irregular, unrhymed verse, and tinkered
with *The Transgressor* — or *Jennie Gerhardt* as it was
to be called — for which the English publisher Grant
Richards had already become encouragingly eager.[49] Still,
it was not to fiction that he yet turned. It was to another magazine.

During the summer of 1909 he secured control of a
monthly entitled the *Bohemian* and planned "to have
some fun with this" while retaining his position at Butterick's.[50] Keeping his connection with the *Bohemian*
secret lest it jeopardize his regular job, he made Fritz
Krog, a friend from Missouri, the nominal editor, and
published the magazine in the name of William Neil
Smith, an architect, who was the president of "The Bohemian Publishing Company," and of Fremont Rider,
a man who was already associated with him on the *Delineator* and in B. W. Dodge & Company, and was the

secretary-treasurer. Editorial support was to come from H. L. Mencken, who had visited Butterick's one day in the spring of 1908 in connection with some articles on child care he was ghost-writing and whom Dreiser had found at once to be an understanding friend,[51] and the contents were to be primarily "clever" or "interesting." As Dreiser explained to Mencken, he did not want "any tainted fiction or cheap sex-struck articles," but did want "a big catholic point of view, a sense of humor, grim or gray, and an apt realistic perception of things as they are."

I want some good interviews with big people, some clever take-offs on current political conditions, some truthful interesting pictures of current day society, and jabs and skits of all sorts. I want bright stuff. I want humor. And above all I want knowledge of life *as it is*[,] broad, simple, good natured.[52]

In the four months in which the *Bohemian* appeared, from September through December, Dreiser fulfilled most of his wants and expressed a characteristic variety of his own views. He had editorials from Mencken with such titles as "In Defense of Profanity," "The Gastronomic Value of the Knife," and "The Psychology of Kissing," as well as a play called "The Artist." He had fiction from writers like Thomas Ybarra, Homer Croy, James L. Ford, and Morgan Robertson. He had features concerning Mme Schumann-Heink's favorite American song, Maude Miner's work as a probation officer, and Hereward Carrington's experiences with present-day mediums. He had a department for skits, to which Homer Croy, Clare Kummer, and O. Henry contributed. And he had his own work, mainly serious, unsigned editorials and brief prose meditations signed either with his own name or, more often, with his pseudonym, Edward Al, in which he could comment on life's disturbing contradictions. He called attention to the grim impersonality of the city, emphasized the need for affection, and urged the Pittsburgh steel barons to provide decent working and living conditions for their laborers. But he also asked whether J. P. Morgan and the poor cobbler down the street could be made any more equal by being ruled by the same principles, and referred to the Chicago stockyards as "an exemplification of the first law of life — the survival of one by the failure and death of another." [53] Thanking Mencken for sending him his *The Philosophy of Friedrich Nietzsche*, he said: "If the outline of Mr. Nietzsche's philosophy in the introduction is correct, he and myself are hale fellows well met." [54] But unable to accept any single formulation of life, and reflecting that there might not be death after all, he pondered on the larger mystery as usual, encouraged spiritualists, and recommended that test seances be held before scientists, college professors, and newspapermen. "If there is anything in it, out with it, and let us all be admitted to the evidence of the fact. Only so the world progresses. And only so can we come to a better understanding of what we ourselves are, of what we are going to be, and what and whence come the things of which we are a part." [55]

When the want of advertising and a drop in circulation forced Dreiser to discontinue the *Bohemian*, he was left with only the *Delineator* as an outlet. And as his relations with the business departments deteriorated, he thought more frequently of *Jennie Gerhardt*. It remained only for a fundamental issue to arise on which there might be a showdown. The showdown when it came, however, did not come because of editorial policy, although his policies had made him his enemies; it came from the failure of his marriage. He had become tired of Jug and begun to feel she was using his talent as a means to her triumph. He felt she did not understand him. She did not care for *Sister Carrie* and did not "understand" when, during his days on the railroad and after, he had had affairs with other women. She pursued his affection, irritated him with her possessiveness, and when presiding at open houses in which he was surrounded by writers and artists, embarrassed him with endearments. For him love was something that arose out of spontaneous desire inflamed by a dreamer's conception of the ideal. But now he knew Jug too well to be able to see her at the distance a desire-inflaming ideal required. The loyalty and devotion to him which were her virtues became barriers to retaining his affections and led him to feel that she was trying to put him under obligation to her. According to evidence that should be reliable, he was unable to beget children, but children would have provided no solution, for John Maxwell's insight in St. Louis fifteen years before was sound: Dreiser and Sallie White had been fundamentally incompatible from the very beginning. He now claimed the freedom to wander and do as he pleased, and when he attempted to establish a liaison with the daughter of a woman in the Butterick organization, produced a crisis both at Butterick's and at home.

Thelma Cudlipp was precisely the person to arouse Dreiser's yearnings. She was young, she was beautiful, and she was artistic. She even set about teaching Dreiser how to dance. But it was largely because of her mother that matters reached the point they did. It was, to begin with, her mother who thought to strengthen her own position at the office and at the same time promote her daugh-

149

ter's career as a painter by gaining Dreiser's interest. It was her mother, too, who often felt obliged to entertain Dreiser and his friends and who consented to Thelma's staying overnight at the Dreiser apartment after parties. Although the girl was an innocent, that fact simply made her more interesting,[56] and except for the rivalry of a friend of Dreiser's, who one day seriously proposed to shoot Dreiser, nothing interrupted the course of the relationship until Jug returned, ill with rheumatic fever. Then Thelma's mother, finding matters had become more serious than she had envisaged, burst into the sickroom, disclosed all she knew, asked whether Jug would give up Dreiser, and when Jug refused, rushed to Erman Ridgway with a threat of public exposure if something were not done at once.

Dreiser could not remain as editor with a scandal racing through the Butterick Building. He had made too many powerful enemies to be able to maintain his part against this new weapon that had been handed to them. Accordingly, on October 10, 1910, he began notifying his friends that as of October 15 his connections with the *Delineator* would be severed. Some friends bewailed his departure, asking what would now happen to the homeless children. Others said it would be a loss for Butterick. Still others congratulated him on the ground that he might now have time to do his own writing. But with his discovery of the final limits of an editor's freedom, he found his own consolation. He explained to Fremont Rider: "I do not consider my resignation in the light of a loss. The big work was done here. We were in smooth waters. I had been fighting interference for sometime & finally stood the whole thing out. There are several things I can do at once, even to editing a newspaper, but I believe I will finish my book. Mrs. Dreiser is getting on slowly but I don't believe she'll be able to keep house this winter. She's not very strong." [57]

Jug, of course, would consider no divorce, and the girl, aloof and noncommittal to the very last, directed by her mother, withdrew from the situation. Dreiser shortly thereafter moved to a furnished room on Riverside Drive, attempted to find a publisher for *Idylls of the Poor*, and, freed of editorial responsibilities and pressing financial cares, returned at last to the completion of *Jennie Gerhardt*.

IX

The Survival of the Fittest

J*ennie Gerhardt* proved to be the first of four new
novels completed within five years of Dreiser's leaving
Butterick's, but based as it was on material and plans
developed some ten years before, it recalled the past
more than it reflected the present and disclosed a Dreiser
who was troubled by poverty and disaster rather than a
Dreiser who had lately relinquished a salary amounting
to ten thousand dollars a year.

In his second novel as in his first, Dreiser exhibited
characters who were the victims of circumstances or
forces beyond their control. Jennie, a member of a pov-
erty-driven family such as was Dreiser's own, is deprived
of social distinction and financial security when a United
States Senator who wants to marry her and has seduced
her dies suddenly and leaves her an unwed mother.
Then, supporting herself and her daughter by working
as a maid, she attracts one of her employer's house
guests, Lester Kane, becomes his mistress, bears his
name, and has almost re-established herself when the
Kane family, threatening Lester with the loss of his inheritance if he does not give up Jennie, brings an end to
the liaison and leaves Jennie with only her daughter to
remind her of any love she has ever known. Finally,
while Lester, eager for social position, marries an alluring sophisticate, Jennie helplessly endures further misfortune as typhoid claims her child. In the end she has

the satisfaction of hearing Lester tell her that his married life has not been happy and that she is the only one
he has ever loved, but his realization comes too late to
matter, for he is on his deathbed and she can look forward only to "Days and days in endless reiteration." [1]

Although Dreiser implied by this story that individuals
as mere human beings were uncertain of fulfilling their
purposes, he also implied even more clearly that individuals like Jennie and Lester were the ones most likely
to fail. For Jennie is "the idealist, the dreamer," [2] and
Lester is good-natured, with "a larger vision of the sub-
tleties that underlie life." [3] And where Jennie lacks
"power to strike and destroy . . . to be able to fall upon
a fellow-being, tearing that which is momentarily desirable from his grasp," [4] Lester lacks "the ruthless,
narrow-minded insistence on his individual superiority
which is a necessary element in almost every great business success." [5] On the other hand, Lester's brother
Robert, less imaginative, sensitive, or scrupulous, is an
individual who succeeds in his undertakings, and an impression remains that it is primarily persons of feeling
and insight who are incapable of successful struggle in
the realm of the material.

Yet for one who had achieved what Dreiser had, the
idea that success must be completely alien to the artistic
temperament was no longer compellingly axiomatic. He
had risen too far since *Sister Carrie* to suppose he was
destined for failure, and if he had recently been forced
to resign his position, he was for that very reason only
the more concerned with the anatomy of achievement
and somewhat more disinterested in his reactions to
other strugglers. Life was still something he could call
"dramatic" and "more thrilling than the most gorgeous
spectacle that man ever planned," [6] but the drama had a

different effect from what it had had. Although *Jennie Gerhardt* had been constructed to exhibit the pathetic consequences of accidents, Dreiser could now tell an interviewer that "these accidents merely serve to make . . . [life] more entrancing." [7] And although he had sympathetically portrayed the jobless in *Sister Carrie* and had energetically sought homes for homeless children during his editorship of the *Delineator,* he now viewed misfortune as merely an exciting part of the great play and stated: "I consider the beggar sitting by the roadside one of the most dramatic things that could be imagined. He has a precarious existence and it depends entirely on chance. It is really thrilling to see the way in which he ekes out a living." [8] The temperament of persons like Jennie no longer interested him.[9] In fact, Lester's not marrying Jennie and the death of Jennie's child were incidents Dreiser had to contrive in revising his novel, to give the story a "poignancy" which the original tone demanded but which he had not been able to maintain.[10] The process of struggle had become more interesting than struggle's ultimate futility, and those individuals capable of the greatest efforts were necessarily more significant than the passive and neglected failures. It was scarcely surprising, therefore, that even before *Jennie Gerhardt* was completed Dreiser had begun other novels and had chosen to explore the careers, not of helpless women, but of forceful men who possessed both artistic propensities and the characteristics required for material success.[11] And it was simply a measure of his new concerns that when *Jennie* was accepted by Harper & Brothers at the end of April 1911, his next novel, *The "Genius,"* was so far advanced that he was able to conclude it only a few months later.

The story of *The "Genius"* was the story of how a sensitive dreamer and artist who disregarded social conventions could fare in a fierce society from which he hoped to remain detached. Originally drafted to concern a St. Louis newspaperman, then changed to concern a painter whose work Dreiser modeled on that of a friend, Everett Shinn,[12] it was in all essential respects an account of Dreiser's own career. Eugene Witla, after a boyhood of romantic daydreaming in the Midwest and yearning for girls he idealizes, lives through a period of disillusionment, reads Spencer, Tyndall, and Huxley, and goes to New York to enjoy the attractions of the city and the blandishments of women. Excited by the insoluble drama about him, he gives his paintings of the spectacle a theatrical appeal and becomes successful enough to marry a Midwestern girl, Angela Blue. There then follow misunderstandings between Eugene and Angela, rebellion by Eugene against Angela's possessiveness, a nervous breakdown, work on a railroad, recovery, and positions first with an advertising company analogous to Street & Smith and second with a publisher of magazines reminiscent of Butterick's. Throughout these events Eugene is the victim of the elements in his character that enable him to succeed. His success as an artist depends on his ability to view the forces of life without being subject to them. But his response to the forces he views is the response of a man moved primarily by the sensuous, and hence of a man repeatedly affected by the sight of lovely eighteen-year-old girls. Continually trying to know the beauty of youth intimately, he is continually disillusioned by its disappointing reality. So long as he can escape disillusionment by new conquests, he can escape melancholy, but so long as he is bound to his wife, who is no longer a mere dream, he cannot escape completely. When finally he encounters a girl, Suzanne

Dale, who represents what he believes to be the realization of all dreams, her mother creates trouble that forces him from his position and temporarily separates him from Suzanne; and Angela conceives a baby to compel him to reinterpret his responsibilities, and dies in giving birth. Shocked, bewildered, driven to reflect on his own role in the catastrophe, Eugene seeks salvation in Christian Science and the thought that everything may be regarded as infinite mind, with spirit representing immortal truth and only matter representing mortal error. Subsequently he feels Francis Thompson's "The Hound of Heaven" applies to him, and meditates on the validity of Alfred Russel Wallace's theory of the universe. At the end, while still puzzled by the mystery of life, he is strengthened in his metaphysical tendencies by reading and is "changed notably": now he is "stronger and broader for what he . . . [has] suffered, seen and endured." [13] Writing Suzanne that he is no longer selfish, that love is not all desire, he brings her to him; they marry; and "brooding over the mutation of time and force," he discovers metaphysics beautiful, life calmer and sweeter than he had ever thought it, and a ruling power immanent and "not malicious." [14]

The question dominating the story was a cogent one for Dreiser. Although he himself had not found ultimate salvation in Christian Science and Jug had not died, and his Suzanne Dale had not returned to him, he had suffered a defeat because of his response to sensuous attractions and needed to find a place for himself in which he could see himself as the stronger for what had happened. Hence when he was writing the final chapters of *The "Genius"* he was writing of life as it might be — as, indeed, it ought to be. At the same time, however, the existence of Jug, who had gone away only to regain her health and whom he was not prepared to desert, and the beginning of a new series of amours, which oppressed him with new claims even while they helped him forget old ones,[15] both argued against his soon enjoying Eugene's solution. The answer for Eugene was certainly, in existing circumstances, no answer for Dreiser, and while Dreiser completed the novel and struggled to find himself again, he began to gather material about a man who apparently had encountered few significant limits in his lifetime, a man who had made a fortune in Philadelphia, been imprisoned for embezzling the city's funds, left prison to make a second fortune, gained control of Chicago's street railways, and having lost a fight for long-term franchises, gone to London to fight J. P. Morgan for control of the London subway system, all the while engaging in affairs with a series of mistresses whom he discarded as whim dictated, until at the moment of triumph he fell ill and died, his fortune to be dissipated in lawsuits and his art gallery and business enterprises to pass into the hands of others. In this man, Charles Tyson Yerkes, Dreiser had a character who could provide another answer to his question, by demonstrating on the one hand how to succeed and on the other hand what success finally meant; and in Yerkes's career he had material for a trilogy of novels he planned to call *The Financier*.

Dreiser's readiness to plunge into this new project so quickly was of course not entirely the consequence of theoretical implications or marital difficulties. He had considered the idea while completing *Jennie Gerhardt* and had written *The "Genius"* because he could no longer contain within himself the troubles that remained so immediate. But once *Jennie* was accepted for publication, Harper's preferences affected his decisions. While friends to whom he showed the manuscript of *Jennie*, among them James Huneker and Mencken, encouraged him with their praises of the novel to continue writing, Harper's, by displaying interest in *The Financier* rather than in *The "Genius"* as a sequel to *Jennie*, impelled him to proceed at once with the story of Yerkes, for Dreiser was, after all, concerned with making a living; ". . . if there is no money in the game," he wrote to Mencken, "I [am] going to run a weekly." [16]

It was, in fact, on royalties rather than on praise and publishers' preferences that Dreiser, never able to forget Doubleday's actions, depended for convincing encouragement. British writers like Frank Harris, W. J. Locke, and Arnold Bennett reminded the public of *Sister Carrie* by calling it a great book.[17] Mencken, reading the proofs of *Jennie Gerhardt* in order to review it for *Smart Set*, wrote to Dreiser: "Let no one convince you to the contrary: you have written the best American novel ever done, with the one exception of *Huckleberry Finn*." [18] Most reviewers, once the book was published in October, echoed Mencken's opinions. And Henry Blake Fuller, to whom Dreiser had sent a copy of *Jennie*, welcomed Dreiser into the school of twentieth-century realists, saying: "By the consistent and persistent employment of the approved latter-day method you have reached, cumulatively, results that are remarkable." [19] Yet Dreiser remained uneasy and skeptical about his career. Although *Jennie*'s sales surpassed *Carrie*'s by totaling almost five thousand during the first month, Dreiser was disappointed and the men at Harper's gave him no reason not to be. The experience of *Sister Carrie* had not been helpful in selling *Jennie Gerhardt*, one of them explained.[20] When Grant Richards, the English publisher, arrived in New York early in November, Dreiser delivered to

Richards's hotel an inscribed copy of *Jennie* with a note saying in part: "I hope if you are interviewed you will say something definite about me & Jennie. It seems almost impossible to make my fellow Americans understand that I am alive. I am thinking of moving to London. Once there I will get at least an equal run with Robert Hichens & Arnold Bennett over here." [21] But actually Dreiser was too dispirited to contemplate any kind of trip. He had written thirty-nine chapters of *The Financier* — more than half the first volume — but now was ready to give up the whole trilogy. To go abroad, to travel, to see what Yerkes had seen, he needed money, and *Jennie*'s sales were bringing him too little.

Since Dreiser's problem was solely a financial one this time, however, it was far more easily solved than his former psychological ones, and when Dreiser called on Richards the following day, Richards, finding that Dreiser had overestimated the costs of a European tour, evolved a solution agreeable to Dreiser. He went to friends of his at the Century Company and proposed they commission Dreiser to write for the *Century Magazine* three articles on Europe which might eventually be expanded into book length, and at the same time he directed Dreiser to ask Harper's for an advance on *The Financier*. The result was that on November 18 Century sent Dreiser a check for a thousand dollars for three articles and the option on any book he might write about his trip,[22] and Harper's, upon his depositing with them the first part of his manuscript, agreed to advance him two thousand dollars on *The Financier* and five hundred dollars against the earnings of *Jennie Gerhardt*.[23] In addition Harper's prepared to reissue *Sister Carrie*. When Richards suggested to Dreiser that even the Nobel Prize was now within his grasp,[24] Dreiser regained his confidence and on November 22 sailed with Richards on the *Mauretania,* explaining to an interviewer before embarking that in his new novel "I'm doing the man as I see him. . . . And when I get through with him he'll stand there, unidealized and uncursed, for you . . . to take and judge according to your own lights and blindnesses and attitudes toward life." [25] In this spirit he was seeking to observe the "color of life." [26]

From the very beginning of the journey he was presented with a series of tableaux. The restless throng milling about the decks of the ship before the gangways were hoisted reminded him of a great New York hotel lobby at dinner time. A Miss X during the voyage suggested to him "our raw American force." [27] The engine room provided a glimpse of a new, fascinating, and baffling world. When he reached England, appearances continued to dominate his impressions, as he persistently sought to externalize them. He picked up a girl of the streets and proceeded to cross-examine her while he attempted to contemplate the very scene of which he was a part, imagining as he spoke to her how he must seem to her speaking in this fashion. He beheld buildings black with soot, their original white showing only where wind and rain had whipped the spots bare, and thought at first: "How wretched," then afterward: "This effect is charming." [28] He visited London's East End, St. Michael's Church in St. Albans, Canterbury, the House of Commons, Manchester, and after observing an English Christmas crossed the Channel to be excited by the Continent in the same way. It was a place of looks, words, gestures, and buildings. Whether it was the age of Rome, the width of Perugia's streets, the Grand Canal of Venice under a glittering moon, or the vainglorious German officers at Potsdam, Europe had mainly the effect of a picture postcard.[29]

But the more Dreiser saw, the more restless he became to return home. He worried about his writing, about his expenses, about himself. When he first arrived in England, he began to think he would be uncomfortable in the cold, raw weather and would not be able to write anything. Two days before Christmas he needed medicines for intestinal difficulties. Shortly after that, as he hastened to Paris, he estimated how much he was spending and began to feel insecure. Richards had written him a letter explaining in detail what to tip everyone at the hotel in London; had sent him tickets for Paris and directed his attention to a certain restaurant whose headwaiter was a character; had sent letters to friends in Paris on Dreiser's behalf; had begun negotiating for various dramatic and publication rights for Dreiser's novels — and then Dreiser had taken stock of his situation. The women were expensive. The places he stopped at seemed dear, and he even considered joining a Cook's tour. Moreover, word reached him from the United States that Ridgway had left Butterick, and he now entertained the notion of returning to the *Delineator*, a notion for which Richards took him severely to task. Finally in March he goaded Richards into writing to him resentfully:

"Handicapped financially" indeed! I wish I had half your complaint. That is where you depress me. "I shall cut Paris after Berlin and sail from some port in England." My God! And then: "No more Europe on the worry basis for me." Heavens, what are you talking about? A nice character but too temperamental. You ought to travel with a doctor and a hypodermic syringe. You really ought. However..........

My dear friend, you have, in the vernacular of your country, put it across; and now, having put it across, you are worrying about the exact degree which you have achieved. Such things not having been done before from your country you have nothing to compare yourself with, but I at least cannot see what you have to complain of. *As long as you are in the meantime doing stuff, or preparing to do stuff that you feel will satisfy your own conscience,* about which I am not, naturally, in a position to dogmatise.[30]

Yet, baseless as Dreiser's worries might be, he could not find convincing the assurance of those who had known only comfort and security throughout their lives, and instead of seeing the benefits to him and to his work of what he had been doing, he saw the dangers in the price he was paying for these benefits. He remembered all the writing that he wished to do, wrote Mencken asking whether he would read the manuscript of *The Financier*,[31] and although Richards tried to persuade him to visit the Hardy country, decided early in April that he must take the first available ship back to America. This ship happened to be the *Titanic*, but since it was on its maiden voyage, Richards thought it might be uncomfortable and preferred to secure Dreiser passage on the *Kroonland*, which arrived in New York at the end of the month, when Dreiser began at once completing *The Financier*.

During his absence Harper's had had a typescript made of his first thirty-nine chapters and now clamored for the rest. But there was further research to do, and Dreiser hunted through the files of the Philadelphia *Public Ledger* for 1870 and 1871 and drew upon the knowledge of his friend Joseph Hornor Coates in Philadelphia to secure full details of Yerkes's first debacle. He had earlier learned from Coates what clubs his character Frank Algernon Cowperwood should belong to, what parties Cowperwood should give, and where he should give them; now he found out about the layout of the stock exchange, the location of Yerkes's office, the history of Drexel's firm, and facts about 1871 court procedure. In addition Coates referred him to Oberholtzer's biography of Jay Cooke and other standard sources. As the first 350 pages were prepared for the printer by July 2, work on the rest of the book went on into August.

Meanwhile problems had arisen concerning which Dreiser needed Mencken's advice. Dreiser wanted to call his whole trilogy *The Financier*, and the first volume simply "Volume One," but Harper's insisted that was commercially inadvisable. Dreiser wanted to shorten his novel so that it would not run to 800 pages, but Harper's was giving him no time to make adequate cuts. Mencken, however, was abroad when Dreiser returned from Europe, and it was not until May 7 that Dreiser could write to him from New York: "Lord[,] I'm glad to know you[']r[e] back. . . . I wish I could talk to you. I have a whole raft of things to discuss not the least of which is the present plan of publishing this book in 3 volumes — 1 volume every 6 months. . . . For heaven sake keep in touch with me by mail for I'm rather lonely & I have to work like the devil." [32] Mencken did keep in touch, and while during the summer Jug returned in what was the final attempt to solve the problem of loneliness, Mencken encouraged him in his work, read galleys, suggested the excision of irrelevant details and the expansion of certain incidents, and assured him: "You have described and accounted for and interpreted Cowperwood almost perfectly. You have made him as real as any man could be. And you have given utter reality to his environment, human and otherwise. No better picture of a political-financial camorra has ever been done. It is wholly accurate and wholly American." [33]

Frank Cowperwood's career is both that of a man who recognizes no restraints or limits and that of a man who illustrates the limitations of all men. In the first volume of the trilogy — finally called simply *The Financier* without reference to other volumes — he is shown up to the time when he leaves Philadelphia for Chicago. Born of a family who regard life "as a business situation or deal, with everybody born as more or less capable machines to take a part in it," [34] Cowperwood early in life proves himself one of the more capable machines; he is a "natural-born leader," [35] licks "Spat" McGlathery, and becomes interested not in books but in politics, economics, and what makes the world run. Daily observing a lobster gradually devour a squid in a tank at the fish market, he decides: "That's the way it has to be, I guess." [36] Lobsters live on squids, men live on lobsters, and men even live on one another. From the very first he knows how to make money, and soon grows to regard the stock exchange as the whole world unmasked:

Here men came down to the basic facts of life — the necessity of self care and protection. There was no talk, or very little there, of honor. . . . So far as he could see, force governed this world — hard, cold force and quickness of brain. If one had force, plenty of it, quickness of wit and sublety, there was no need for anything else. . . . To get what you could and hold it fast, without being too cruel, certainly not to individuals — that was the thing to do, and he genially ignored or secretly pitied those who believed otherwise. [37]

With this attitude and something of an artist's liking for the sensuous, he rises in both the world of finance and the world of women. Only because of the accident of the Chicago fire, which leads to banks' calling in their loans, does Cowperwood, who had been free with the city's funds and has all his resources tied up, come to financial disaster. But even then he is not much disturbed, for his imprisonment is only a nuisance he has to endure because he has been "unfortunate"; and treated as a dignitary during a short term in jail, he is soon pardoned and re-established and is able to profit from the panic of 1873. In the world of women, who along with paintings give him a sense of the color and drama of life, he meets fewer obstacles. He overwhelms one woman, tires of her, makes the daughter of a prominent Philadelphian his mistress, divorces his wife, and eventually marries the girl and leaves a socially impossible environment for Chicago. "Isn't it nice to be finally going?" Aileen Butler, his new wife, says to him. He replies: "It is advantageous, anyhow." [38]

Dreiser, however, thinking of Yerkes's later struggles and of the ironic dissolution of the Yerkes fortune after Yerkes's death, provided an epilogue prophesying "sorrow, sorrow, sorrow" for Cowperwood.[39] No one should think that any one way of living, or any one kind of individual, was to be favored. "We live in a stony universe whose hard, brilliant forces rage fiercely," Dreiser remarked in one place.[40] All individuals were disregarded. Man was but an innocent fly caught in the strands of a horrific spider's web. "His feet are in the trap of circumstance; his eyes are on an illusion." [41] Cowperwood was to become "prince of a world of dreams whose reality was sorrow." [42] At the same time Dreiser was not arguing against effort. He was, rather, emphasizing the elements of life that made its events dramatic for him, and by noting the inevitable tragic irony, reaffirming the value of being sufficiently life's observer to detect illusion.

In other work completed or planned at this time he embodied the same view. "The Lost Phoebe," a short story completed in October 1912, but because of its unhappy ending refused by magazines for almost four years, tells of an old widower who, suddenly believing his wife has returned, searches up hill and down valley until, lured by this will-o'-the-wisp and the memory of a world where love was young, he plunges from a cliff to his death, illustrating that dreams might be futile for the dreamer, but in their futility prove artistic for one who could see through them. *The Bulwark*, a novel he had in mind to follow the trilogy, was to tell ironically of a puritanical Quaker father whose devotion to the Decalogue does not bring success and does result in the disruption of his family.[43] And his account of his trip to Europe, completed in January 1913 and published in November, was written to sweep away the filmy illusions that blurred the vision of mankind. There is "something really improving in a plain, straightforward understanding of life," he wrote in A *Traveler at Forty*. "For myself, I accept now no creeds. I do not know what truth is, what beauty is, what love is, what hope is. I do not believe any one absolutely and I do not doubt any one absolutely. I think people are both evil and well-intentioned."[44] Life is but "an expression of contraries. . . . I know there can be no sense of heat without cold; no fullness without emptiness; no force without resistance; no anything, in short, without its contrary. Consequently, I cannot see how there can be great men without little ones, wealth without poverty. . . ."[45] Nature is to be indicted as "aimless, pointless, unfair, unjust. I see in the whole thing no scheme but an accidental one — no justice save accidental justice."[46] And if he is disturbed by reading of a friend's suicide and seeing in it the manifestation of fate,[47] or moved by a drab English manufacturing town to "feel sorry for ignorant humanity," [48] he is also attracted by the contraries for whose sake the despairing and ignorant exist. He likes "people who take themselves with a grand air," finds Americans "wonderful" with their hopes, dreams, and desires,[49] admires plotting labor leaders, "big, raw, crude, hungry men who are eager for gain — for self-glorification," [50] and is so fascinated by the details of the long-familiar history of the amazingly ambitious Borgias that he records in some six pages of small type the family's "raw practicality" with the air of a discoverer.[51]

His disinterested point of view made it impossible for him, of course, to adopt any theory that presupposed uniformity of idea or custom. He wanted only freedom to report the scene as he beheld it. Early in 1912 he had let some of his friends among the Socialists consider *Idylls of the Poor* for publication, and during the summer they had reprinted in the *New York Call* one sketch concerning the unemployed, "The Men in the Dark," which had appeared in the February *American Magazine.*[52] But Dreiser had no mass reform in mind — at most he accepted the views of William Jennings Bryan.[53] He was concerned with the predicament of individuals as individuals rather than as units in a society. He considered forming a "liberal" publishing house.[54] He criticized the American home as "a fetish," saying: "An orphan asylum can bring up a child better than the average mother," [55] and thereby reversing his *Delineator* policies in the interests of saving the individual from a worse kind of uniformity than he had originally opposed. And he defended feminism in the interests of individualism, telling a reporter:

167

I am an intense individualist, and it seems to me that the beauty and interest of life will be increased in proportion to the growing number of great individuals among women as well as among men. I believe that the feminist movement, taken as a whole, has a distinct tendency to strengthen and enrich the individuality of woman.

He made clear, however, that he was in principle no reformer:

I'm not a propagandist in the feminist cause or in any other cause at present. . . . Reform has a tendency to put all but the biggest temperaments in a cocksure intellectual attitude — and that attitude puts one terribly out of harmony with the great underlying life forces. The gods take their revenge on the cocksure.[56]

To help dispel this mistaken cocksureness he not only returned to the second volume of his trilogy, to be called *The Titan* and to tell of Yerkes in Chicago, but wrote a one-act play, "The Girl in the Coffin," which he sent to Mencken in July 1913 for comment and consideration for the *Smart Set*. Its effect was to suggest by bitter irony that life could not be reduced to rules or formulas. A strike leader, Magnet, whose unmarried daughter lies dead of an abortion, refuses to concern himself with a strike that depends on him because he is too grief-stricken over his daughter's death and interested only in detecting her lover. He is persuaded to participate, however, by the strike organizer, Ferguson, who reveals that he too is grief-stricken by the death of one he loves but that despite that misfortune he is working for the strike. At the end, when a little old lady hands Ferguson the girl's ring, the audience discovers that Ferguson is the lover. The curtain is lowered as he stares into the girl's coffin.

Although this play reaffirmed the extent to which individuals are buffeted by the great underlying life forces, Dreiser was not yet prepared to return to his earlier portrayal of man's weakness. When he beheld individuals seemingly favored by accident or fate, individuals who in addition understood that values and destiny were unrelated, he felt he beheld the forces themselves almost incarnate. And although he perceived that even such strength was accidental and must eventually encounter its limits, he could not rid himself of its fascination until he had followed its career nearer to a logical conclusion. Thus, when he hoped for more "great individuals among women as well as among men," he simply renewed the philosophic sanction for the further study of Yerkes.

Such a renewal of purpose was, moreover, timely, since it now became financially desirable to publish the second volume quickly. Reviewers, except for men like Mencken, were markedly less enthusiastic about *The Financier* than they had been about *Jennie*. They noted its length, called it either dull or forthright and true, and at best treated Dreiser as a recognized realistic reporter of life. The sales, after 8,332 copies sold in the last three months of 1912, dropped to 1,569 copies for the next six months and to 1,727 copies for all of 1913, and if the initial sale was better than that of *Jennie Gerhardt*, the sequel was worse, for *Jennie* had at least sold more than five thousand copies during the first six months of 1912. Now, moreover, *Jennie* too had almost ceased to sell, and *Carrie* in its first year under the Harper imprint sold only a few more than two thousand copies and then dropped to fewer than five hundred for 1913. It began to appear that Dreiser would be able to make scarcely enough to pay Harper's advances. In this situation his principal hope seemed to lie in the possibility of *The Titan's* reviving interest in at least *The Financier*. So from the end of 1912 to the beginning of 1914, supported by friends like William Marion Reedy and Edgar Lee Masters, who had been first attracted to Dreiser through *Sister Carrie*, cheered by an eagerness on Mencken's part to print "The Girl in the Coffin," [57] and financed by another two-thousand-dollar advance from Harper's, Dreiser directed all his efforts toward writing *The Titan*.

This time circumstances contributed to his work. Armed with letters of introduction to people who had known Yerkes when he died in 1905, and relying in part on the advice of Edgar Lee Masters, then a practicing lawyer in Chicago,[58] he went to Chicago in December 1912 to consult editors, businessmen, politicians, and other lawyers and to peruse the files of Chicago newspapers. But he had the help of more than persons and papers. He had the help of mood. At last he had permanently separated from Jug, and although she refused to agree to any kind of divorce and thus prevented him from marrying again until her death in 1942, he was now at least freed from persistent reminders of his obligations. In Chicago he could recall the boyhood romantic dreams he had once experienced there, and as he passed places where he had worked or where he had feared to apply for work, he could feel the force of ancient hopes and the meaning of growth and achievement. Perceiving that Yerkes had been a creator of much that had evoked longings, he could sense the significance of Yerkes's accomplishments and amours. Chicago had, moreover, become a center for painters, writers, actors. He went to Jerome Blum's studio and stood delighted before the exciting, bright canvases. He went to the Cliff Dwellers and talked with Fuller and Hamlin Garland. He went to newspaper offices and met Ben Hecht and Floyd Dell, and with Dell visited Maurice Browne's Little Theater and met some of the actors, among them Kirah Markham, dark and statuesque, who had captivated Dell and whom Dreiser now captivated in turn. In this city where Yerkes had lived with the freedom that Dreiser had long craved, Dreiser now found a woman whose youth, beauty, and artistic sympathies represented a realization of his youthful aspirations, and as he and Miss Markham became drawn to each other, he felt the surge of the adventure and accomplishment that shaped the career of his financier. He told interviewers that "a literal transcript of life as it is" would require of readers a "special kind of guts" [59] and, declaring that such a transcript would show that "most lives are failures," insisted he himself was "not a pessimist": "I am not even sentimentally aroused by suffering. I sympathize with struggling merit more than I do with poverty in general." [60] Art should show, he said, "not only the concentrated filth at the bottom but the wonder and mystery of the ideals at the top." [61] It was, after all, the mind that constructed the schemes that "merit" struggled to carry out.

In his new novel Dreiser made his character increasingly aware of the drama as well as of the amoral nature of living. Cowperwood in *The Titan* wishes not only financial power, but also recognition as a grand, colorful force in the drama. He wants to amass money in order to give him personal advantage. He wants to dominate society in order to live as he pleases. He is faithless to his wife and pursues the wives and daughters of his friends mainly to enjoy the interest of variety and to experience the illusion of beauty and the beauty of illusion. Continuing life in Chicago as he began it in

171

Philadelphia, he snatches land from insignificant and helpless citizens, buys street railways until he has nearly a monopoly, inaugurates an impressive series of liaisons with women who appear more exciting than Aileen, and is on the verge of controlling Chicago's transportation lines when the citizenry opposes his efforts and frustrates his purposes. Having by then alienated Aileen, he is apparently a lonely, defeated man until at the very last Berenice Fleming, daughter of a Louisville madame and a girl he has sought to interest since she was fifteen, comes to him and offers to share his life and he promises to live for her alone. Dreiser then interjects: "How strange are realities as opposed to illusion!" [62] and suggests in an epilogue the final days of Cowperwood, "caught at last by the drug of a personality which he could not gainsay." [63]

Dreiser could no more now than in *The Financier* dramatize the meaningful irony of Cowperwood's promise and hope, since another volume was to follow. But another volume was not necessary to make the irony more specific. "Woe to him who places his faith in illusion — the only reality — and woe to him who does not," Dreiser exclaimed. "In one way lies disillusion with its pain, in the other way regret." [64] What consolation there was existed in regarding everything as an inevitable process within which the titans were what mattered. The implications of *The Financier* simply became explicit:

At the ultimate remove, God or the life force, if anything, is an equation, and at its nearest expression for man — the contract social — it is that also. Its method of expression appears to be that of generating the individual, in all his glittering variety and scope, and through him progressing to the mass with its problems. In the end a balance is invariably struck wherein the mass subdues the individual or the individual the mass — for the time being. For, behold, the sea is ever dancing or raging. . . . But without variation how could the balance be maintained? [65]

And Cowperwood, "rushing like a great comet to the zenith, his path a blazing trail . . . did for the hour illuminate the terrors and wonders of individuality." [66] Dreiser had no use for those who would judge Cowperwood's conduct by some moral code or see in it merely evidence of a man interested in profits. He complained to reporters early in 1914 that Chicago's rich men were now interested only in growing rich, that small-town attitudes were dominating the city and producing censors of literature and art, that the spirit that had created Chicago was dead. [67] "A big city is not a little teacup to be seasoned by old maids," he expostulated. "It is a big city where men must fight and think for themselves, where the weak must go down and the strong remain. Removing all the stumbling stones of life, putting to flight the evils of vice and greed, and all that, makes our little path a monotonous journey. Leave things be; the wilder the better for those who are strong enough to survive and the future of Chicago will then be known by the genius of the great men it bred." [68]

But this attention to strength was only to underscore its limits. Cowperwood would not end life as he began it. The lobster and the squid might illustrate life, but lobsters did not always win. Cowperwood was fated to encounter an opposite force: "for him also the eternal equation — the pathos of the discovery that even giants are but pygmies, and that an ultimate balance must be struck." [69]

This conclusion served once more to reaffirm Dreiser's own role. It was not in the actual struggle or illusion

173

that values lay, nor in the fact of potential equilibrium, but rather in the awareness and appreciation of what struggle, illusion, and equilibrium meant. To only the truly aware could individuality be wonderful and the discovery that giants were but pygmies be pathetic. To only the artist, then, could life be dramatic. Dreiser thus was brought again to the problem of the artist's career, already presented in his unpublished *"Genius"* but now assuming a different importance, and difficulties in publishing *The Titan* only helped redefine the question and gave it immediacy.

Early in March 1914 Harper's, having printed 8,500 sets of sheets to send to the binder and having begun to advertise *The Titan*, suddenly decided to halt publication. Reasons for this singular decision varied. From some of his friends Dreiser heard that Harper's had become fearful of his uncompromising realism; from others, that the treatment of financiers would antagonize men on whom the firm was dependent; from still others, that one of the members of the firm was friendly with Emily Grigsby, the prototype for Berenice Fleming, and disapproved of what Dreiser had revealed. Dreiser himself was ill in a Chicago hotel at the time and had to leave to two of his friends in New York, William C. Lengel and Anna P. Tatum, the problem of rescuing the book. But whatever the reasons for his difficulty with *The Titan*, it soon was evident in what publishers said that Dreiser was being limited by the very codes *The Titan* challenged. George H. Doran considered the book unsalable and Dreiser a very abnormal American. Mitchell Kennerley called the handling of Emily Grigsby cheap, slanderous, and sensational. Men at the Century Company said the story was abnormal and impossible. Only the John Lane Company, a British firm recently established in the United States under the managing directorship of J. Jefferson Jones, was interested and they, within three weeks of the Harper decision, enthusiastically accepted the book, advanced Dreiser one thousand dollars, agreed to pay him a twenty per cent royalty, and sought to take over his other books from Harper's, who, however, at once set a prohibitively high valuation upon them.

If Dreiser was jubilant over the Lane acceptance, he was disgusted with the events that had led to it. A month later in Philadelphia, where Kirah Markham was playing at the Adelphi Theater, he criticized the influence of orthodoxy, called socialism misguided, and advocated an intellectual aristocracy. "The tendency here is to put the pyramid on its apex," he complained, "to discard the opinions of those at the highest point of the intellectual scale for the prejudices and stupidity of the multitude. Everything is for the vast, ruling majority. No wonder that Europe laughs at us. The idea that all men are created equal is one of the fundamental errors of our system of Government. For to the distinguishing mind it is quite apparent that the degree of intellectual endowment with which individuals come into this world varies enormously. But to level down is the cry of mediocrity everywhere." [70] At the end of May, writing about his uncompleted trilogy for the New York *Evening Sun*, he noted that usually only the little or common things could be understood by the average man, but explained that the uncommon story of Cowperwood was important:

A rebellious Lucifer this, glorious in his sombre conception of the value of power. A night-black pool his world will seem to some, played over by the fulgerous gleams of his own individualistic and truly titanic mind. To the illuminate it will have a very different meaning, I am sure, a clear suggestion of the inscrutable forces of life as they shift and play — marring what they do not glorify — pagan, fortuitous, inalienably artistic. . . .[71]

Of course, since the artistic element was to be found in the inscrutability, and the inscrutability became evident only when an individual was the victim of the whim of life's forces, it remained for the artist as artist to appreciate the plight. With the eye of the outsider the artist observed the Lucifers and Michaels of the world and gave their struggle relevance. And although Dreiser was willing to contend that "the mind of the great merchant is conscious of the poetry of his work," [72] it was not the merchant's but the poet's role that troubled him. In the fall of 1913 he had begun with a new perspective to revise *The "Genius,"* and now, with continuing financial necessity — for *The Titan* failed to sell in its first year as many copies as *The Financier* had sold in its first few months — he began to prepare it for publication.

X

The Significance of the Unfit

The final version of The *"Genius"* embodied a significant revision of the original manuscript and in that embodiment reflected the beginning of a revision of Dreiser's attitude. As early as 1913 Witla's triumph had necessarily become meaningless. Witla was not a Cowperwood, and even Cowperwood was eventually to discover that giants were but pygmies. It would have been difficult for Dreiser to assert that life was both calmer and sweeter for anyone. Moreover, in terms of Dreiser's own career, Eugene's reunion with Suzanne had come to represent merely wishful thinking, false to Dreiser's experience and thus false to life. Men were not transformed as Eugene had been. In the revised manuscript Dreiser had therefore begun to develop a conclusion radically different from his first. Where he once had described the notable change in Eugene, he now wrote: "Was he not changed, then? Not much — no. Only hardened intellectually and emotionally — tempered for life and work." [1] So hardened, Eugene is here able to be an artist once more. Although there are other women, there is none able to overwhelm him as Suzanne did, and he lives on, "always wishing . . . defying . . . folding a wraith of beauty to the heart." [2] At the end, left with his child, accepting no single doctrine and finding solace mainly in Herbert Spencer's comments on "the unknowable," he turns away from people toward larger concepts of life, reflecting: "What a sweet welter life is — how rich, how tender,

177

how grim, how like a colorful symphony." As he stands beneath the November stars and views "the sparkling deeps of space," "great art dreams . . . [well] up into his soul," and he thinks: "The sound of the wind — how fine it is tonight." [3]

This was what it meant to be an artist. Dreiser now believed that peace of mind was to be found not among men but among the forces that operated in the "deeps of space," and instead of continuing to be concerned with the terror and wonder of individuality, he became concerned with the terror and wonder of the forces to which all individuals were subservient. This was a logical enough development. As long as Dreiser regarded human equity as an illusion — or at best a dream — the strong man was the man to admire, the man who took what he wanted by simple force. Yet as soon as he inspected the character of this force, he had to insist on qualities that made it dramatic and redeemed it from dullness. Force had to be associated with the imaginative and the picaresque. Since, however, all self-gratification, no matter how grand its method, was at the mercy of something greater and was doomed to discover its limitations, it needed for its justification a consciousness of its own pathetic state, and inasmuch as this consciousness resided in the artistic outlook, Dreiser, who became an artist partly because of the futility of the life he observed, was compelled to bring the characters who illustrated futility to a point where they could become observers like himself. Yet even this could not satisfy his needs, for his own experience was evidence that the very qualities that made an artist a spectator were qualities that produced personal disaster and disillusionment. The appeal of the sensuous could inspire art only as long as the appeal could be resisted. And if the pleasures of detachment compensated for failure to find a place in the world of struggle, they also depended on propensities that entangled the artist in the world he sought only to view. What enabled the artist to escape futility originally, his becoming artist, was his undoing once he had escaped. Since Dreiser could neither divorce himself from sensations nor escape the judgments of society, and since he still wished to observe society rather than participate in its contentions, he, like his own character Eugene Witla, now had to turn to contemplate, sometimes in almost abstract terms, the workings of omnipotent natural law.

Dreiser's part in the revision of *The "Genius"* was completed in the summer of 1914. Between then and September 1915, when the book was published, he relied on Floyd Dell, Kirah Markham, and Frederic Chapman, English reader for the John Lane Company, to make suggestions concerning cuts and the improvement of details [4] and, thus freed of the most onerous editorial tasks, was able by the end of August 1914 to take up what was philosophically more pressing.

Of most immediate concern to him was a group of five one-act plays which he wrote during the late summer of 1914 and sent to Mencken and which, together with "The Girl in the Coffin" and perhaps another play he would do, he wished to publish at once in book form under the title *Plays of the Natural and the Supernatural*. Because of his preoccupations, these five plays were primarily abstract dramas — what he called "reading plays" — dramatizing the supernatural rather than the natural and ironically showing man as either the sport of inscrutable and unconquerable forces or the victim of his own illusions. In "The Blue Sphere" a deformed child, a "monstrosity" who is the despair of his family, continually pursues a blue bubble that floats before his mind's eye and persists in leading him toward the railroad tracks until one day, despite everyone's vigilance, enough doors and gates are left unlocked to permit him to totter in the way of a speeding train, the victim of human accidents determined by superhuman fate. In "Laughing Gas," inspired by an experience of Dreiser's own and for a while regarded by Dreiser as "the best thing I ever did," [5] a prominent physician, sleeping under anesthesia, ponders his inadequate knowledge of the vast mysteries of life, the after-life, and universal order, and learns:

There is a solution, but you will never be able to guess it. . . . Far and above the mysteries here and below are other mysteries — deep, deep. You puzzle over the phenomena of man. In a vain, critical, cynical ambitious way you dream. It will all be wiped out and forgotten. To that which you seek there is no solution. A tool, a machine, you spin and spin on a given course through new worlds and old. Vain, vain! For you there is no great end. [6]

Oppressed with a sense of futility upon awaking, he is finally left wondering whether the revelation was truth or mere hallucination. In "In the Dark" and "The Spring Recital" the implications are reaffirmed. The one questions what the difference is between life and death; the other indicates there is no rest or satisfaction after death, and while "The Spring Recital" suggests that living must be now, neither play asserts that in the present life one could be any wiser than the puzzled physician. In fact, in "The Light in the Window," dramatized in terms of "the natural," human beings possess no more understanding than the impoverished people who gaze at the lighted window of a mansion and believe that happiness is to be found within, where in actuality a wealthy couple are engaged in jealous bickerings that destroy their love. The rich lead barren lives and the poor stand excluded, ignorantly dreaming.

In these allegories of omnipotent forces there were, of course, but the skeletons of characters. For Dreiser was now more interested in his theories than in the characters who illustrated them. Hence, while he was writing his plays he was also completing an essay that was to be part of what he called "a new philosophic interpretation of Earthly life," [7] was continuing to work on *The Bulwark*, dedicated to showing the ironical failure of faith, and, employing himself as an illustration of the truth of his assertions, was beginning the first volume of *A History of Myself* to demonstrate how little an individual had to do with what he became. Although he and his family had supplied evidence before, this was the first time he had made himself the avowed subject, as though he felt that where fiction was read as foolish fantasy, autobiography would be read as compelling fact and his family would be viewed with the scientific detachment that his perceptions should have persuaded him was impossible for those who censured him.

People are so involved with current theories [he wrote], so stricken and controlled by moralistic rules of existence that there is little hope of their contemplating any natural, pagan, chemic condition in the light of the primary laws which govern life. . . . [Yet he complained] that man as a chemic animal has been completely lost sight of. . . . [Man] *is* a chemic animal, reacting constantly quite as chemical and physical bodies do to laws. . . . Life and the individual should be judged on their chemical and physical merits and not on some preconceived metaphysical, religious notion or dogma.[8]

Although he did not explain how chemical and physical merits were to be defined, he did undertake to define the problem for himself and, pondering on what it was that caused thought,[9] applied to the New York Public Library for a special study in which to carry on some investigations in chemistry and physics.[10]

At the same time, he gave what personal support and encouragement he could to others who might in any way be making clearer the nature of the laws to which men reacted and the nature of man the reactor. Thus when he found writers who were fulfilling what he conceived as the function of the artist, "to put things down as they are, not as they ought to be," [11] he endorsed their work. In an introduction to a new edition in English of Lieutenant Bilse's suppressed *Life in a Garrison Town*, he referred to this exposé of corruption and cruelty in the German military system as "a veritable chip of the sacred Caaba of fact." [12] In a review for the *New Republic* he called *Of Human Bondage* "a . . . social transcript of the utmost importance. To begin with it is unmoral. . . ." [13] In letters to Mencken he criticized the *Smart Set* for having become "a light, non-disturbing period[ical] of persiflage and badinage," [14] devoted to "gay trifles." [15] "I like to feel the stern, cool winds of an Odessey [*sic*] now and then," he wrote.[16] Attempting to get the works of hitherto neglected writers published, he called J. Jefferson Jones's attention to the existence of Sherwood Anderson and, together with Floyd Dell, succeeded in persuading Lane's to put Anderson in print. He tried to convince Jones that Lane's should publish *Spoon River Anthology* and sought to persuade Macmillan to put out a volume of Harris Merton Lyon's stories. He even crusaded in behalf of the unorthodox Charles Fort, whose unpublished book X startled Dreiser with its argument that some mysterious something, "X," was giving out rays capable of creating everything from matter to emotions. Dreiser even dreamed of the thing — later recording it in another reading play entitled "The Dream" — and was certain that the data were sufficiently supported to deserve a hearing. Every one of his authors had something new to say about forces and men; therefore they should all be allowed to say it. For Dreiser a new insight was a valid insight, and intuition was sometimes more important than objective verification. As he wrote to Fort concerning X, in July 1915, "My general feeling is that it is a remarkable book — so remarkable as a peice [*sic*] of imaginative articulation that I have not be[en] troubled as to whether it is scientifically durable or not." [17]

He was, at the same time, interested in other than literary outlets for the demonstration of "things . . . as they are," and for a year or two after 1914 considered accepting a directorship in a new moving-picture company with a view to producing pictures "of an educational, scientific[,] religious and even social betterment or socio-revolutionary character." [18] He himself had worked out some scenarios, one of which, "The Born Thief," Pathé Frères had seriously considered, and now during 1915 he appealed to Mencken, Ben Hecht, Richard Le Gallienne, and others for suggestions. But what he meant by revolutionary films was more likely to involve a revolution in outlook or idea than a revolution in politics. He was not inclined to join others in overturning anything except dogmatism and complacency, and that work was primarily the task of individuals rather than of groups. If he did occasionally meet with other writers and artists, it was usually with a group whose dominant characteristic was heterogeneity. Late in 1913 he had been elected to the Liberal Club, which met on the floor above "Polly's," Polly Holliday's restaurant on Macdougal Street. Among the habitués at Polly's were such acquaintances as Lincoln Steffens, Bill Haywood, Susan Glaspell, the Irwins, George Cram Cook, and Hyppolyte Havel, editor of *Mother Earth*. He knew Courtney Lemon, the Socialist, Sinclair Lewis, then beginning his career as novelist, Emma Goldman, who invited him to gatherings at her place. He himself, having acquired a studio on West Tenth Street, gave a party for Edgar Lee Masters when Masters was in New York in August 1915, and while Kirah Markham presided at the punch bowl and Masters read his poems by the light of dim lamps and candles, Lemon, Franklin Booth, the artist, Alex Raab, Hungarian pianist, Willy Pogany, another artist, Floyd Dell, Charles Fort, Berkeley Tobey, and other Village characters sat about him, a group held together mainly by an interest in the new.

Into 1916 Dreiser's convictions remained broad and undirected. He was willing to hear all panaceas. He was sympathetic with misfortune, inevitable as it might be. He went to Isadora Duncan's studio to hear her protest the persecution of an unwed mother. He joined Hamlin Garland and other writers in wiring critics to see Hauptmann's *Weavers*. He visited Poultney Bigelow shortly after war began in Europe and wrote to Mencken: "Personally I think it would be an excellent think [*sic*] for Europe and the world . . . if the despicable British aristocracy — the snobbery of English intellectuality were smashed and a German Vice-Roy sat in London." [19] But as an observer of illusions he could not commit himself to any particular program. Groups tended to become doctrinaire and individuals were necessarily ineffective. When in April 1916 George Gordon Battle's Committee

on Industrial and Social Service for the Unemployed sent
out an appeal for thirty thousand dollars to help unemployed men refit and rehabilitate themselves to secure
other jobs during the period of industrial turnover, Dreiser scribbled across the top of the letter: "This is all very
fine but it is a function of the state and should be performed by the state." [20] Yet the state could be only what
the people made it, and people were simply what they
were, and that could not be helped. To observe the facts
and to record them were what Dreiser was left to do to
promote the equilibrium he had first read about in
Spencer.

There was little compensation for the discouragement
of such a point of view, but there was a kind of escape
from prolonged reflection about it. Dreiser's work on his
autobiography had turned his thoughts back to childhood and the time when he had had illusions of a world
of goodness and achievements, and he wondered how his
impressions now would differ from those he had received
then. It would be interesting to contrast the impressions;
it might make a book, and at the same time it would
give him some insight into himself. Hence when Franklin Booth, a fellow Hoosier whom he had known since
working for Munsey's *Daily News,* came up to him at
the party for Masters and proposed that they drive home
to Indiana, Dreiser agreed at once and promptly planned
a book that Booth might illustrate. On August 11, 1915,
they were on their way, through New Jersey, northern
Pennsylvania, and southern New York, with Dreiser bent
on rediscovering his early illusions.

But the trip solved no problems. The first week in September Dreiser was in New York once more, having sat
in the back of the open car gazing at the towns and people
along the way, watching while Booth made sketches, want-

ing to know what people were thinking, and sometimes asking Booth to ask questions while he looked on.[21] The trip had stirred the roots of old experiences. He had seen roads and houses as they once had been, and he had looked in vain for landmarks now gone. He had knocked at familiar doors and been greeted by strangers, and he had gone to new houses and discovered families he had known, now older and changed. The dreams of youth had become momentarily real, but so had many of the miseries. Old memories, he had reflected, were not so cheerful as they might be; and the contradictions in his ideas had produced contradictions in his emotions.

As he began to embody these reactions in the book about his trip, entitling the volume *A Hoosier Holiday,* he also resumed the numerous projects he had been engaged in before the drive west, carrying his concern with omnipotent forces further in the direction in which he had been developing. He continued with *The Bulwark.* He talked to publishers about unknown writers. He sought further suggestions for the movies. And he wrote another play and sent Mencken more of his writing, this time a few poetic meditations for the *Smart Set.* The play, "Old Ragpicker," was an obviously logical product of his present interests. For the power of the all-powerful forces might well be shown by exhibiting men at their weakest and most helpless. If men were ultimately limited, it was perhaps more effective to show them at their most completely limited than to show them as powerful as Cowperwood; it was too easy to find "reasons" for Cowperwood's downfall. And in this play Dreiser pictured on the "natural" level the horror and hopelessness of the most degrading poverty, in which a man did not struggle at all, did not display even a glimmer of Hurstwood at his most despairing. Old Ragpicker, as he is called, is

the extreme of dirt, hunger, and physical disintegration.
He sells rags to junkmen, eats from garbage pails, and
is a target for boys who enjoy throwing cans and stones
at him, yelling: "Old Ragpicker! Old Ragpicker!" In an
early draft Dreiser had called the old creature "Scaven-
ger" and not had him hit by the boys, but to make his
exhibit more pathetic, he employed a word more likely
to be used by little boys and decided the man must be
hurt by a missile.[22] Ragpicker is at best futilely puzzled
by his tormentors. He wishes only to be let alone, and
when two policemen try to find out his name, he cannot
tell them until he recalls the taunts of the boys and becomes elated at discovering he is "Old Ragpicker." Dreiser's poems — among them, "Woodnote," "Ye Ages, Ye
Tribes," "For a Moment the Wind Died," and "They
Shall Fall as Stripped Garments" — were in a more speculative and wistful mood, pervaded by wonder at the
spectacle of impersonal order and by a compassion for
man's ignorance of its meaning; but they and the play
contained what one might feel if, like Eugene Witla, one
gazed long enough and resignedly enough into the deeps
of space.

Meanwhile Dreiser was finding little understanding of
his point of view. When *The "Genius"* was published,
in September 1915, few reviewers praised it whole-
heartedly, and some men sympathetic to Dreiser, like
Randolph Bourne, Masters, and Mencken,[23] either
digressed concerning Dreiser's work as a whole or belabored the book for its rhetoric. Most of the critics chose
to attack the novel in complaints that ranged from impassioned revelations of patriotism to calm and exhaus-
tive examinations of Dreiserian philosophy. It was not to
the virulent attacks, however, that Dreiser most objected.
If one critic, hearing that *The "Genius"* was to appear

in a German translation, rejoiced because "That's how kindly we feel toward the Germans!" [24] and another, attempting to rebut Dreiser's admirers, would never admit the book was "the American prose-epic . . . until I am ready to see the American flag trailing in the dust dark with the stains of my sons, and the Germans completing their world rule by placing their governor general in the White House," [25] Dreiser found the critics "interesting" because they were "so persistent." [26] Their remarks represented only "the loudest cry of the wounded pro moralist." [27] But where innuendoes concerning his Teutonic ancestry were personally inoffensive to him, Stuart Pratt Sherman's three-page systematic discussion of "The Naturalism of Mr. Dreiser" in the *Nation* [28] aroused him to the point of underlining sentences, making marginal comments, and mailing marked copies to friends. Where Sherman said: "But a realistic novel is a representation based upon a theory of human conduct," Dreiser exclaimed: "Rot," or "Good conduct, of course." Where Sherman said: "A naturalistic novel is a representation based upon a theory of animal behavior," Dreiser noted: "Animal behavior being evil of course." [29] When one of Dreiser's followers wrote a letter to the *Nation* insisting that individuals like Eugene Witla were to be found in real life and that Dreiser had simply written reality, Dreiser considered the letter a good one.[30] Unaware of the direction in which criticism was pushing him, he was beginning to have to defend the idea of inevitability.

Understanding was important to Dreiser, even if the lack of it was simply further evidence that his observations were sound. When letters came from readers who had been touched by his work, readers who were poets, readers who were aspiring writers, readers who had been long-silent admirers or who had been won to him by some resemblance they bore to Eugene Witla in his unhappy marital ties, he was grateful and was sometimes moved to admit that, although he felt the world owed him nothing, he craved sympathy and appreciation.[31] Life was fundamentally lonely for him. While on the one hand he felt himself a part of it, on the other hand he was in outlook, feeling, and understanding apart from it. The recognition of the all-pervading forces of nature that made it impossible to distinguish between human and animal conduct separated him from his fellow human beings at the very moment that it enabled him to define his place among them. The society of his time was one in which he had only the role of an observer, and that was without status. It was not surprising that during the winter of 1915–16 he should feel at home among manifestations of supernatural powers and regard half-seriously communications that he, together with Kirah Markham, John Cowper Powys, Frances and Louis Wilkinson, among others, received when gathered around Ouija boards. While Louis Wilkinson learned that America would remain neutral throughout the war and Kirah Markham discovered that the Kaiser's cook would poison him on the day of victory, designated as February 11, 1918, Dreiser ascertained that there was no evil in the universe, no reason for a person to lead a moral life, no preconceived design or controlling intelligence. Everything was simply a phase of God, and all religions were equally valuable.[32] Apparently, though, it would avail one little to pray.

With his convictions and doubts thus mirrored, he departed late in January 1916 for Savannah, where, joined by Kirah Markham, he worked into February completing *A Hoosier Holiday* and into March continuing *The Bulwark*. All the contradictions in his attitude are disclosed in the account of his trip. In *A Hoosier Holiday* he reveals the conflict between a revived awareness of the joy of illusions and a sharpened perception of their invalidity, between a deeply rooted desire to remain a spectator and a growing desire to criticize the spectacle. In Paterson, New Jersey, he recalls a strike of two years before and, alluding to its "nameless brutalities," asserts he sympathizes with "the working rank and file." Yet he believes "that human nature is much the same at the bottom as at the top." [33] He asks: "Why should the man at the top . . . want more than a reasonable authority?" then on the next page declares that some "avatar" or power is "back of man . . . and man is His medium." [34] He even goes on to castigate Billy Sunday and similar purveyors of salvation for making "slaves" of their following.[35] Similarly, he exclaims: "Life orchestrates itself at times so perfectly," [36] then sighs: "Alas for a dusty world that . . . will never permit any perfect thing to be." [37] He disapproves of the "greed or graft" of Carnegie, Frick, Widener, Dolan, and Elkins [38] and wishes the "big brain" would be more generous to the "little one," but his reason is that Dives would thereby "appear so much more pleasing." [39] In fact, he rhapsodizes about the "great days in the capitalistic struggle for control in America," [40] "that vast, splendid, most lawless and most savage period"; [41] he is willing to forgive John D. Rockefeller "everything" "if he weren't intellectually and artistically so dull"; [42] he justifies human cruelty by the statement that it must be necessary, else "the high councils of nature" would not have permitted it.[43] If on the one hand he wants "to compose an ode in praise of the final enfranchisement of the common soul," [44] on the other hand he complains of the commonplace dullness of the middle class, whom he has been trying to impress with their inevitability. In recalling his trip he writes: "I am never tired of looking at just mills and factories and those long lines of simple streets where just common people . . . dwell." [45] But the city that evokes this statement, Scranton, is one he left as quickly as possible because, he declares, it was "so dull." [46]

Dreiser still depended on some illusions. He liked to help the masses and found it poetic and a pleasant dream to try to, but he knew that nature was cruel and that men were cruel too, unable to help it. He liked the masses from afar, before he entered the town; he liked the capitalists of a bygone day, before the unreality of contemporary dreams. But when it came to dealing with the immediate, he was forced to compare it with the glory of a time that was past. Robbers had their place if they were robber barons. To the extent that he could detach himself from a sense of society, he could look down on "dear, crude, asinine, illusioned Americans" [47] and "poor, dogma-bound humanity." [48] And to the extent that he felt himself caught up in the human predicament, he became restless with the unwelcome awareness.

Oh, to escape endless cogitation! [he exclaims.] To feel that a new centre table or a new lamp or a new pair of shoes in the autumn might add something to my happiness! To believe that mere eating and drinking, the cooking of meals, the prospect of promotion in some small job might take away the misery of life, and so to escape chemistry and physics and the horror of ultimate brutal law! [49]

If there was an escape, it was in something like his return to the scene of his childhood, unhappy though it may have been, for he could at least for the moment remember when he believed in his illusions and hopes. And in concluding A *Hoosier Holiday* he advises: "Dream on.

Believe. Perhaps it is unwise, foolish, childlike, but dream anyhow. Disillusionment is destined to appear. You may vanish as have other great dreams, but even so, what a glorious, an imperishable memory! . . . Of dreams and the memory of them is life compounded." [50]

For Dreiser himself, though, this was useless prescription. In his manuscript he had added as a final sentence: "But now it is no more." He could not, after all, remove his perceptions from his consciousness. Were he even to forget them he would be soon enough disillusioned anew. And since the horror of ultimate brutal law lay in not being able to escape it, in being compelled to yield to it, the only alternative was to fight it, or at least to fight its manifestations. This was of course futile unless one were to doubt the validity of specific manifestations, and, significantly enough, Dreiser had begun to doubt.

The ordinary mortal should not be compelled to moil and delve for a fool [a passage in *A Hoosier Holiday* declares]. I refuse to think that it is either necessary or inevitable that I, or any other man, should work for a few dollars a day, skimping and longing, while another, a dunce, who never did anything but come into the world as the heir of a strong man, should take the heavy profits of my work and stuff them into his pockets. It has always been so, I'll admit, and it seems that there is an actual tendency in nature to continue it; but I would just as lief contend with nature on this subject, if possible, as any other. We are not sure that nature inevitably wills it at that. [51]

Once he had implied that forces in nature could oppose the forces of nature, he was describing a world different from the one he had been writing about. If he followed the logic of his implications, his fiction would eventually have to change its emphasis. He would be unable to avoid suggesting what ought to be, or at least speculating about what nature intended. This did not mean that nature would cease to be his primary subject. It meant only that his approach would have a different orientation. At present, however, there was no occasion to act in a radically different way. As he gathered data for new stories, he continued to work on his autobiography and to collect material for *The Bulwark*, for which Lane's in turn prepared a dummy and sent out publicity concerning its forthcoming publication. In fact, Dreiser began to enjoy some financial reward from the writing he had done. Although the sales of *The "Genius"* through June 1916 had totaled only a little more than 8,500 copies, less than either *The Financier* or *Jennie* had sold, almost two thousand of those had been sold in the first six months of 1916, representing a better continuing sale than the earlier novels had had. With the receipt of a new advance from Lane's, as well as a twenty per cent royalty, and with *Plays of the Natural and the Supernatural* published in February 1916 and *A Hoosier Holiday* scheduled for the fall, he could find substantial reason for looking forward to becoming established and even secure — until suddenly, late in July 1916, a blow fell, promptly laying part of his income under an interdict.

Early in the month, in Cincinnati, aroused by the minister of the Ninth Baptist Church, who had been himself aroused by an unidentified voice on the telephone, the Western Society for the Prevention of Vice had read *The "Genius,"* found it filled with "obscenity and blasphemy," [52] authoritatively designated seventy-five pages as "lewd" and seventeen as "profane," and secured its removal from almost every bookstore in the city. At the same time it had secured a temporary cessation-of-circulation order from Washington and filed a complaint with the New York Society for the Suppression of Vice.

The New York Society's executive secretary, John S. Sumner, already in receipt of a few offending pages torn by a morally indignant citizen from a circulating library's copy of the novel, had, with the Cincinnati index at hand, immediately read the book to verify his worst suspicions and, supported by other readers to whom he submitted it, found there was no alternative to betaking himself on July 25 to the offices of the John Lane Company and telling J. Jefferson Jones that if Lane's did not remove all offending matter from *The "Genius"* or discontinue its sale, advertisement, and publication, the Society would bring criminal charges. On July 28, pending a legal contest that he promised would follow, Jones agreed to withdraw the book, and Dreiser, unless he was willing to be ruled by Sumner's dicta, was to be committed at last to the course of action his doubts had predicated.

XI

"Nature's Way Is Correct . . ."

Sumner's action presented a challenge that Dreiser
could not ignore. Chartered by the state legislature for
the purpose of procuring enforcement of the laws pro-
hibiting the sale, distribution, and production of any
obscene, lewd, lascivious, filthy, indecent, or disgusting
book, magazine, motion picture, etc., the New York Society for the Suppression of Vice was ostensibly an instrument of the social will. But in its power, which had already made impossible the circulation of unexpurgated
editions of *The Wandering Jew, The Three Musketeers,*
and Horace's odes, it had come to control the source of
its own authority, and in its standards, presumably determined by statutes and court decisions, it was fostering
attitudes hostile to the kind of enlightenment Dreiser
sought to provide. "We are looking at this particular
book from the standpoint of its effect on female readers
of immature mind," Sumner declared concerning *The
"Genius."* [1] ". . . . [Although Eugene Witla] reaps the
results of his immoral life . . . through the story there
are very vivid descriptions of the activities of certain
female delinquents who do not, apparently, suffer any
ill consequence from their misconduct but, in the language of the day, 'get away with it.' It is wholly conceivable that the reading of such a book by a young woman
would be very harmful. . . ." [2] Whether women outside
of books ever "got away with it," or whether immature

195

minds might be matured by learning from books, was not Sumner's concern; he was only interpreting the laws of the state. Yet at least in the case of *The "Genius"* his actions, attacking the book at its source, affected the whole country, for Jones, wishing to risk nothing, not only refused to let copies leave the Lane stockrooms, but despite the absense of formal legal proceedings, requested bookstores throughout the United States to return whatever copies remained on their shelves. Moreover, the consequences went well beyond the matter of marketing the book. Even in California, outside the reach of Sumner's shadow, the spirit of moral crusading found a response. In Berkeley a librarian decided the book was "unfitted for a place on the open shelves." [3] In San Francisco the public library, noting that the American Library Association had described the book as one not for indiscriminate circulation, did not purchase the book at all, lest it fall into the hands of some juvenile reader foraging in the reading-room.[4] Father James M. Gillis defined the condition facing Dreiser when, speaking of *The "Genius"* in a talk on freedom of the press, he remarked: ". . . unless I fundamentally misunderstand the American public, it will guard the morals of the people even at the sacrifice of the liberty of the individual. In other words, we do believe in censorship." [5] Ideologically, artistically, and financially Dreiser's position was threatened.

For Dreiser, however, there was to be no compromise of ideas or art. When Jones at first was confronted with the possibility of prosecution, he suggested to Dreiser, as did Mencken two days later, that some concessions might be made. But Dreiser refused, and when Jones decided not to risk arrest and Federal agents who had read the book were reported to be divided as to its admissibility into the mails, Dreiser became adamant. He argued that Jones ought to fight the society and wrote to Mencken: "Am perfectly willing to break the postal laws and go to jail myself. It will save me my living expenses." [6] Although Mencken insisted that Dreiser had no chance of success and that any controversy he involved himself in would arouse considerable anti-German sentiment, Dreiser replied that neither he nor Sumner wanted compromise: "If it were a question of a few changes, I would say fine. But consider. And each one is enough according to Sumner to suppress on. A fight is the only thing & I want Lane to fight. I hope & pray they send me to jail." [7] When Mencken reconsidered the situation and modified his stand, saying he thought a fight might compel Sumner to compromise, Dreiser answered: "I am for a scrap and your letter pleases me much. . . . A pretty storm can be brewed." [8] And when by mid-August Jones decided to take some kind of positive action, Dreiser wrote Mencken: "I wish you would spread the news of this scrap as far and wide as you can. I'm going to win it in the open if I can." [9]

If there were aspects of the situation that recalled the original failure of *Sister Carrie,* there was clearly nothing left of the earlier mood of personal futility. Dreiser now had sufficient faith in the validity of his own view of an amoral world to be able to act upon it and to be willing to take advantage of his ability. He was fighting the opponents of what to him was a logical view of nature. Although on all sides were instances of cruelty and force and jungle "law," yet he noted that those who had benefited by means of such lawlessness refused to allow others to expose it. Those who had profited from a laissez-faire attitude would not themselves countenance the attitude by which they had gained their power. And their very refusal to give others the freedom they had themselves enjoyed seemed to Dreiser but further proof of the non-existence of real ethics. Hence, in a world where there was no ethics, what right had any group of men to dictate to their fellows? Nature obviously had not intended it; nature had made no man better than any other. "Life here, as elsewhere, comes down to the brutal methods of nature itself," he stated in a newspaper article.[10] "The rich strike the poor at every turn; the poor defend themselves and further their lives by all the tricks which stark necessity can conceive. No inalienable right keeps the average cost of living from rising steadily while most of the salaries of our idealistic Americans are stationary. No inalienable right has ever yet prevented the strong from either tricking or browbeating the weak. . . . Personally, my quarrel is with America's quarrel with original thought. It is so painful to me to see one after another of our alleged reformers tilting Don Quixote-like at the giant windmills of fact." One's own view of the facts might, according to Dreiser's logic, be less correct than someone else's, but any restraint placed upon one for such a view would be invalid. To hamper the individual was ultimately to hamper nature.

I look on this interference with myself or any other serious writer as an outrage [he declared], and I fear for the ultimate intelligence of America. A band of wasp-like censors has appeared and is attempting to put the quietus on our literature which is at last showing signs of breaking the bonds of Puritanism under which it has so long struggled in vain. . . . When will we lay aside the swaddling clothes forced on us by the antiquated theories of ignorant moralists and their uneducated followers, and stand up free thinking men and women?

To me, this interference by the Vice Society with serious

letters is the worst and most corrupting form of oppression conceivable to the human mind, plumbing as it does the depths of ignorance and intolerance and checking initiative and inspiration at its source. Life, if it is anything at all, is a thing to be observed, studied, interpreted. . . . It is our great realm of discovery. The artist, if left to himself, may be safely trusted to observe, synchronise and articulate human knowledge in the most palatable and delightful form. . . . A literary reign of terror is being attempted. Where will it end? [11]

The fight Dreiser wanted was soon under way. While he made statements in the press, Mencken, planning positive action, on August 9 wrote to Harold Hersey, an admirer of Dreiser's and assistant to the secretary of the executive committee of the Authors' League of America, Eric Schuler, asking whether the league might not be persuaded to defend Dreiser. "A public protest signed by twenty-five or thirty leading American authors would have a tremendous effect. . . . If the moralists score a victory against a man of his range and attainments, they will undoubtedly run amuck." [12] By the evening of August 24 Mencken and John Cowper Powys had each drafted protests for writers to sign; Jones had written to Lane in London to secure support from English writers; columnists and editorial writers had written in Dreiser's behalf; and a quorum of the executive committee of the Authors' League had met with Dreiser and, saying that The *"Genius"* was not subject to the New York Society for the Suppression of Vice's condemnation, that it was not lewd, licentious, or obscene, and that if the unfair test applied to it were not modified, even many of the classics might not be sold, had publicly urged the league to take action to oppose suppression of the book.[13] Despite complaints from members of the league, ranging from Frank Harris, who resigned because the league would not go beyond the committee's resolution,[14] to Hamlin Garland, who was opposed to the committee's statement and any association with Dreiser's cause in the first place,[15] opposition to the society's decision soon gained impressive support, and as cabled endorsements of the protest came from Arnold Bennett, William J. Locke, E. Temple Thurston, Hugh Walpole, and H. G. Wells in England, Dreiser's cause elicited a sheaf of letters and signatures from sympathizers in the United States whose names constituted a *Who's Who in American Civilization.*

Leaflets protesting suppression of *The "Genius"* were circulated by many editors, writers, and publishers, such as Willard Huntington Wright, Francis Hackett, Alfred A. Knopf, B. W. Huebsch, Louis Wilkinson, and John Cowper Powys. Felix Shay in the *Fra*, Frank Harris in *Pearson's*, Ezra Pound in the *Egoist*, Alexander Harvey in his little weekly, the *Bang*, and a New York lawyer, Elias Rosenthal, in a pamphlet, *Theodore Dreiser's "Genius" Damned*, all sought to give additional help by quoting, ridiculing, or denouncing Sumner in print. But the major work was done by Hersey and Mencken. Hersey, on the whole, had the task of circulating mimeographed and printed leaflets among the hundreds of writers, artists, publishers, and professors who would be likely to sign the protest of their own accord. Mencken had the task of writing personal appeals to the more important, respectable, and conservative authors, of coaxing those who were reluctant to sign or had neglected to do so, and of persuading Dreiser that public statements against American beliefs and the inclusion among his following of a number of "tenth-rate Greenwich geniuses" might alienate valuable potential supporters.[16] If Agnes Repplier, William Dean Howells, and Ellen Glasgow would not lend their names without having read The *"Genius,"* and Joyce Kilmer, Mark Sullivan, and Brander Matthews objected to either the ideas of the protest or the vulgarity of the novel, others like Ellis Parker Butler, Rupert Hughes, and William Rose Benét were willing to disregard their feelings about Dreiser and defend the freedom of writers, and Amy Lowell, Rachel Crothers, and Robert Frost offered their names without reservations. Ultimately the advocates of Dreiser's rights ranged from James Lane Allen and Mary E. Wilkins Freeman to Jack London and Sinclair Lewis, from Edwin Arlington Robinson and Willa Cather to Gelett Burgess and James Oliver Curwood, from Ellery Sedgwick and William Allen White to Max Eastman and John Reed, and included names as various as David Belasco, James Montgomery Flagg, William Gillette, Percy Stickney Grant, Adachi Kinnosuké, and David S. Muzzey.

None of this agitation impressed Sumner, however. Authors might be good judges of the literary merits of a book, but they were not any better equipped to judge that book's effect on manners and morals than were mechanics of ordinary education. Where Sumner's organization based its decision on the decisions of the courts, the signers of the protest represented only the private point of view of a limited group. Moreover, Sumner saw no reason why American letters could not survive without exploiting what he regarded as the vicious side of life and introducing into American life immorality characteristic of the foreign element. "We need to uphold our standards of decency more than ever before in the face of this foreign and imitation foreign invasion," he wrote to Alexander Harvey, "rather than to make those things which are vicious and indecent so familiar as to become common and representative of American life and manners." [17] And so believing, he left Dreiser no choice other than to press his case in the courts.

Had Dreiser wanted conviction, there would have been sufficient discouragement in the legal proceedings to lead him to compromise. For to begin with, there appeared to be no one to sue. Sumner had merely threatened, and that threat had been sufficient to deter Jones from doing anything that might place him in jail. He would not sell the book until he was judicially permitted to. Yet in the absence of an attempt to sell the book, there was no occasion for an indictment, and without an indictment, no opportunity to secure a judicial opinion. Finally, early in 1917, after protracted discussions, Dreiser and Jones agreed that Dreiser should sue to enjoin Lane's from violating their contract and should argue that the book did not violate the law. But when the case was at last considered by the Appellate Division in the spring of 1918, Dreiser received no relief, for the court declared its function was not to render advisory opinions; if the book was improper, action should be taken in the criminal courts, and since Jones's voluntary withdrawal of the book had given Sumner no occasion to take such action, the legal status of the book was not properly before it. Subsequent attempts to elicit declaratory judgments or to compel Lane's to publish were equally futile, and The "Genius" remained in the Lane stockrooms until Horace Liveright ventured to reissue it in 1923.

This impasse meant from the start of it that Dreiser was to face new financial difficulties. With The "Genius" suppressed, there were naturally no royalties from it, and when the company, having made Dreiser an advance of

$1,800 on *The Bulwark*, became uneasy over the course of events and decided to liquidate Dreiser's debt by crediting him with the income from the three books of his they published, there were no royalties for him from *The Titan*, *Plays*, and *A Hoosier Holiday*. The books that Harper's and Century had were gradually repaying advances against their earnings, but the amount received from their sales remained inadequate for a livelihood. Since their dates of publication *Sister Carrie* and *The Financier* had each sold less than 24,000 copies and *Jennie* barely 5,000 more than that. In fact, since 1912 *Carrie* had not even sold 4,000. On June 30, 1917, Dreiser's total earnings from the three novels then under the Harper imprint were $7,170.40. With a few thousand in advances to repay, Dreiser needed several thousand dollars in all.

During the first few months of the fight in behalf of his novel, however, Dreiser had been confident of success and more concerned with reaffirming his point of view than with seeking his thousands. He had expanded the statements he had made to the press on behalf of *The "Genius"* into an essay for the *Seven Arts* entitled "Life, Art, and America," defining the influences and tendencies that had made the censors' tyranny possible in the United States; and when it had appeared in the February 1917 number, he had distributed some five thousand reprints in booklet form to friends and followers. He had written criticisms of the faults of American newspapers and of the weaknesses of the medical profession, urging the injection into the newspaper columns of thoughts more serious than those on sports and other subjects appealing to the average mind [18] and attributing the trouble in professions to "the weak, confused, aspiring, selfish animals" compounded by nature.[19] And he had composed an essay on "American Idealism and German Frightfulness," which compared Germany's liberal domestic legislation with England's practices and so attacked the British that no editor would print it for fear of being charged with giving aid and comfort to the enemy and publishing a plea for violence against the United States Government. After considering printing it himself, Dreiser withdrew it and it remained unpublished. But it was not the first instance of difficulties in connection with his views on the war, for on four pages of *A Hoosier Holiday* there had had to be drastic alterations by Jones after the first printing in reply to a frantic cable from Lane's in London.

Meanwhile, during November and December 1916, Dreiser had been trying to restate his ideas in a four-act play, *The Hand of the Potter*, which took its title from Omar Khayyám's "What! did the Hand then of the Potter shake?" and presented the pathetic picture of a twitching and sexually depraved young man who is the victim of his impulses to show that nature is inscrutable. Attracted first by his sister, next by his niece, Isadore Berchansky mutters: "I know I'll do sompin wrong pretty soon. I feel it. I can't help it." [20] He then attacks and kills an eleven-year-old neighbor, complains: "It ain't my fault. . . . I didn't make myself, did I?" [21] and fearfully fills his lungs with gas. A reporter named Quinn explains to colleagues at the scene of the disaster: "Nature is deeper an' stronger than anything we know." [22] Then he adds: "Sometimes I think we're naht unlike those formulæ they give ye in a chemical laboratory — if ye're made up right, ye work right; if ye're naht, ye don't, an' that's aal there is to it — laa or no laa." [23] And to understand what law really was ("laa is merely somethin' that forces people to do what they

don't waant to do whether they will or no"), one must
study Freud.[24] In a world where everyone was at best
imperfect and ultimately helpless, and where life was
nothing more than the accidental workings of nature-
made machines, abnormality was bound to be typical of
man and of life. All men were formed from the same
clay and by the same hand, and so-called normality was
in principle no different from its opposite. Since its opposite was usually blinked by society, that opposite was
what Dreiser stressed to make the workings of all nature
clear.

But again he had met resistance to his work, this time
unexpectedly from Mencken. On December 13 he had
sent the play to Mencken to have the broken-German
dialect of his characters verified; three days later Mencken
had begun a barrage of letters upbraiding him for a
play that was "hopeless . . . impossible on the stage
. . . lacking in every sort of dramatic effectivenes. . . .
Nothing is more abhorrent to the average man than
sexual perversion. He would roar against it in the theatre. . . . Resisting with justice the imbecilities of the
Comstocks, you unconsciously fly to an extreme, and
demand a degree of freedom that is obviously impossible.
I have no patience with impossibilities." [25] Moreover:
"Fully half of the signers of the Protest, painfully seduced into signing by all sorts of artifices, will demand
that their names be taken off. . . . Its publication
would lose you your own case, forfeit the respect of all intelligent persons, and make every man who has labored on
the protest look like an ass." [26] Finally: ". . . you stand
in serious danger, through this play, of being definitely
labeled as a mere shocker of boobs. . . . One of the
things you have got to realize is that a childish interest
in such things as perversion is one of the most salient

proofs of an essentially moral mind. One step more and you will be writing sex hygiene books for use in nunneries." [27]

Dreiser, however, had found in Mencken's attacks only an occasion to return a barrage in his own defense: "When you . . . tell me what I can or cannot put on the stage, what the artistic or moral limitations of the stage are and what the American people will stand for[,] you may be well within your critical rights but my answer is that I have more respect for my own judgment in this matter than I have for yours. In other words your limitations are not mine. . . . You write as if you thought I were entering on a defense of perversion. . . . If you would look at the title page you would see it is labeled a *tragedy*. What has a tragedy ever illuminated — unless it is the inscrutability of life and its forces and its accidents." [28] "Tragedy is tragedy and I will go where I please for my subject. If I fail ridiculously in the execution let the public and the critics kick me out. They will anyhow. But so long as I have an adequate possession of my senses current convention will not dictate to me where I shall look for art — in tragedy or comedy. My inner instincts and passions and pities are going to instruct me — not a numbskull mass that believes one thing and does another." [29] Dreiser told himself that Mencken had no eye for the "newer vein," represented by The *"Genius,"* "Laughing Gas," "Life, Art, and America," and this play. *Sister Carrie* and *Jennie Gerhardt*, which Mencken admired, were to Dreiser now "really old-line conventional sentiment." [30] As a literary intimate, Mencken began to lose some of his importance.

Mencken's predictions concerning the public's reaction to the play proved, however, partially justified. Although both Arthur Hopkins and the Coburns had contemplated producing *The Hand of the Potter* but abandoned the idea, the Provincetown Players finally staged it in New York during the season of 1921–2 and not only lost fifteen hundred dollars but alienated subscribers, critics, and friends. And although Jones had declined to publish the play and advised Dreiser "it would do you immeasurable harm," [31] Liveright undertook to publish it in the spring of 1919, and while no one sought to suppress it, few troubled to buy it.

Making statements, writing denunciatory articles, and dramatizing abnormality thus reiterated ideas but brought no profits, and by the time the complications of legal procedure began to entangle *The "Genius"* early in 1917, Dreiser had to begin finding ways he might make his ideas support him. He did not cease to protest in the interests of free expression. In fact, throughout 1917 and 1918 he, assisted by Hersey and Frank Harris, sought to form an American Critical Society whose function would be to find publishable manuscripts, to influence publishers, to publish work that could not be placed, to encourage discouraged geniuses, and to improve the artistic taste of the community; and he persisted until the more prominent writers and artists he had invited to join him refused to be enlisted and he feared it would become a crank organization.[32] Later, during 1918 and 1919, he contemplated editing for a similar purpose a magazine to be called the *American Quarterly*, and gave it up only when it was going to interfere with his own writing. But because of necessity he concerned himself now primarily with ways of selling the books he had written and with the writing of pieces that could be quickly printed and sold.

The problem of selling the works already published was on its way to being solved when he found a new publisher. At first he had tried to sell his own books by printing and mailing cards listing them and their publishers and suggesting that the recipients apply to local book dealers, to the publishers, or to "George C. Baker," whose address was simply his own.[33] Later he had arranged with Frank Shay, an author and book dealer who had published Edna St. Vincent's Millay's poetry, to reprint *Sister Carrie*. But it was not until Shay's plan suddenly failed and Shay found a new publisher willing to fulfill the contract that Dreiser could feel hopeful. In July 1917 Horace Liveright, the suave and engaging founder of the new firm of Boni & Liveright, approached him with a plan for taking over all his works and thus at last bringing together for effective promotion under one imprint the volumes then distributed among three American publishers. It was the kind of scheme Dreiser wanted, and final arrangements were concluded in 1923. Meanwhile he had new works to submit. Although he had ceased to work on *The Bulwark*, whose Quaker characters he felt would be misunderstood in wartime, he had completed in a flurry of creative activity at least a dozen short stories, several semi-biographical character sketches, much of a second volume of his autobiography, and two short plays, a sheaf of poems, and a score of essays of a philosophical nature. Liveright could look forward to publishing volumes of short pieces almost at once, as well as *The Hand of the Potter*, upon whose immediate publication Dreiser was insisting.

The short stories Dreiser wrote were partially the answer to his financial need and partially the answer to an ideological one. By selling them to magazines before publishing them in book form he could and did make quick profits. During 1917 and 1918, for example, "Married" (an episode cut from the manuscript of *The*

"Genius"), "The Second Choice," and "Free" brought
him from $600 to $750 each. And by writing short narratives about people and their relationships he could restate, in the form that events most often suggested, his
belief that nature must prevail. Whether it was disappointment in love, incompatibility in marriage, the
mystery of coincidence, or the domination of some passion, the subject of each story served to show that individuals were limited by circumstances or feelings for
which only an inscrutable and indifferent nature appeared to be responsible.[34] Men and women, created in
one image, could not make themselves over in any other,
and if there was a solution to their predicaments, no one
knew it, although the one that Dreiser provided in
"Sanctuary" might have been the logical one. Madeleine
Kinsella, having been prostituted and bruised by fickle
men in a rough world, enters the House of the Good
Shepherd to seek refuge and sobs to the Sister who receives her: "Oh, Mother, don't ever make me go out in
the world again, will you? You won't, will you? I'm so
tired! I'm so tired!" to which the Sister answers sooth-
ingly: "No dear, no, not unless you wish it. And now rest.
You need never go out in the world again unless you
wish." [35]

No such retreat, of course, was possible for Dreiser,
since even its advocacy would deny it, but he could find
the security of conviction in his view of human limitation and in the belief that those who failed to share this
view were blind, while those who sought to conceal it
were dangerous. And if he needed a challenge beyond
the suppression of *The "Genius,"* the attitude of the editors who rejected his stories provided it. His work was
frequently called gripping and powerful, but the magazines persistently demanded something more cheerful or

less heartrending.[36] Ray Long of *Cosmopolitan* found "Sanctuary," for example, "a very exceptional piece of work but I do not believe it is a story we should print," [37] and Burton Kline of the *New York Tribune* called it "the most forcible and crushingly truthful of all [Dreiser's present stories]," but feared for his job if he accepted it.[38] Ironically, Kline lost his job for purchasing another Dreiser story, "Love," later retitled "Chains," which had been highly praised and rejected by Douglas Z. Doty of *Cosmopolitan* ("one of the best things you've done"),[39] by Arthur T. Vance of *Pictorial Review* ("a beautiful sketch"),[40] by T. R. Smith of *Century* ("perhaps . . . the finest piece of short fiction . . . that you have accomplished").[41] Clearly the opposition was of a formidable kind, and Liveright's publication in August 1918 of *Free and Other Stories,* containing some of Dreiser's earliest stories as well as some of the recent ones, could be only a partial answer, even when the book promptly became a Modern Library reprint.

More conclusive of what Dreiser found life to be was *Twelve Men,* sketches of people he had personally known. Published in March 1919, it contained both his early portraits of self-possessed individuals and his recently completed ones, and as a collection presented a picture of an amazingly gay, variegated, and unsuspected world. There were, among others, characters from Noank, a family doctor from Warsaw, Indiana, a New York financier, Jug's father, Peter McCord, William Muldoon, and brother Paul. Now and then Dreiser concealed the names of his prototypes or rearranged facts to strengthen impressions, but throughout, drawing on his own experience, he gave the presentation the force of case history and eyewitness narration which fiction frequently lacked. Here, and even more frankly in the autobiographical vol-

umes then in progress, Dreiser was insistently justi-
fying himself. Originally the earliest sketches had been
of persons who embodied Dreiser's ideal of selfless
achievement among a society of self-seekers. Now, in this
new context among fellows of a somewhat different sort,
they became part of a group whose collective impression
was bound to differ from what any one character might
produce. Dreiser might say of his brother: "Take note,
ye men of satire and spleen. All men are not selfish or
hard." [42] Yet the question of self-seeking when applied
to McCord, Muldoon, and some of the rest verged upon
irrelevance. Seen together with the others, each man was
a distinctive contrast to the average mind's conception
of what people were; each was an exception that suggested the impossibility of applying rules or compelling
conformity. Some day and for the same purpose Dreiser
planned to do a second volume, entitled A *Gallery of
Women.* "God, what a work! if I could do it truly," he
wrote to Mencken at this time. "The ghosts of Puritans
would rise and gibber in the streets." [43]

Following the publication of *Twelve Men* Dreiser compiled in book form a selection of the philosophic plays
and essays he had been writing since *The "Genius,"* some
of them already printed in liberal and Socialist periodicals, others rejected by the best and worst magazines, and
arranged for Liveright to publish them late in 1919 under
the title *Hey Rub-a-Dub-Dub*, a phrase which, if it did
not mean that the truth would be unveiled within, did
mean nothing in itself and hence suggested that life was
without meaning. Subtitled A *Book of the Mystery and
Wonder and Terror of Life*, this volume set forth fully
and explicitly the ideas which Dreiser had been expressing more briefly or more indirectly and which he continued to expound for the next three or four years. Be-

tween 1919 and 1923 he completed an autobiographical volume about his newspaper days, *A Book about Myself,* wrote additional stories [44] and character sketches, including many for his *A Gallery of Women,*[45] provided introductions to books by friends,[46] sold articles on fiction [47] and on Hollywood to magazines,[48] composed a hundred more poems of a philosophical kind,[49] collected earlier local-color sketches in a volume he called *The Color of a Great City,* began work on two or three novels, and protested in private and in public against censorship and uniformity.[50] Throughout he attacked the complacency of moralists and materialists, called attention to the great, mysterious all-controlling force, and argued in behalf of ridding the human mind of all illusions; and whether he was accounting for his own disillusionment, or was endorsing a volume of impressions of Africa and England, or was contrasting the New York he had known in 1904 with the less "poetic" one he now beheld,[51] he continually affirmed that there was no truth or theory upon which one could rely and that all one might do was look among the data of experience for inferences to be drawn in terms of assumptions subject to values undisclosed. "If I were to preach any doctrine to the world," he said in *Hey Rub-a-Dub-Dub,* "it would be love of change, or at least lack of fear of it. . . . There is something controlling, of which we are a part and not a part. . . . What is He or It like? Only by the artistry and the terror and the peace and the change through which it works can we guess. . . ."[52]

Dreiser was, however, now prepared to go further than he had gone in *A Hoosier Holiday* in merely doubting the validity of specific manifestations of nature. Man might, he believed, discover by investigation the direction or character of change and thereby anticipate it. Through science as distinguished from religion man might find a kind of salvation. "My personal feeling about life and education in every form is this," he explained at this time, "that the more we know, *exactly*, about the chemic and biologic and social complexities by which we find ourselves generated, regulated and ended, the better. . . . Man has never progressed either self-defensively or economically via either blind faith or illusion. It is exact knowledge that he needs." [53] By a reverence for facts man could ask about himself; by a search for facts he could even discover the basis for asking questions about the possibility of asking any questions at all.

Dreiser himself plunged into scientific and philosophic reading, devoting little time to contemporary novels, and while he pondered the hypotheses of the eccentric Charles Fort, insisted Liveright publish Fort's *The Book of the Damned*, and spoke of the man as a great thinker whose unpublished books X and Y were as wonderful as Karnak,[54] he sought to learn about the science of human behavior by conversations with Jacques Loeb, whose *The Mechanistic Conception of Life* and *The Organism as a Whole* were systematic formulations of Dreiser's own conclusions. "The contents of life from the cradle to the bier," Loeb had written in 1912, "are wishes and hopes, efforts and struggles, and unfortunately also disappointments and suffering." [55] These "contents" were, according to Loeb, amenable to physico-chemical analysis, and when subjected to scientific experiments, were seen to have their sources in instincts comparable to the light instincts of heliotropic animals. The so-called "will" was explicable in physico-chemical terms. Actions were simply the product of chemical changes in the body, and if ideas might be held responsible for those changes, only external stimuli were held responsible for the production of ideas. Yet none of these conclusions made ethics impossible. In Loeb's elucidation Dreiser had a partial rationale for the idea of the anticipation of change; for as Loeb saw it, "our instincts are the root of our ethics and . . . the instincts are just as hereditary as is the form of our body." The struggle for justice and truth was the result of an instinctive compulsion "to see our fellow beings happy." The way a man worked depended on his instinct for successful workmanship. "Economic, social, and political conditions or ignorance and superstition may warp and inhibit the inherited instincts and thus create a civilization with a faulty or low development of ethics," Loeb explained, but if no "individual mutants" arose, the ethical status of the community would be maintained. "Not only is the mechanistic conception of life compatible with ethics: it seems the only conception of life which can lead to an understanding of the source of ethics." [56]

This scientific attitude naturally appealed to Dreiser as the one with which to approach all problems. "The hour has struck," he asserted on a questionnaire, "when man must divorce himself from religious and philosophic theory and confine himself to deductions from scientific and economic facts [,] by which he must be guided in all his acts and relations[,] emotional and economic. . . ." [57] Early in 1918 Dreiser had written an essay entitled "The Right to Kill," published in the *New York Call*, in which he had declared all truth was "inherently un-Christian" because Christianity's theory was opposed to "free scientific research." Introducing the problem of the defective child, he had then urged society to "become selective" and prevent crime by eliminating criminals ahead of time. Society was overloading itself with the ill, the insane, the criminal. If it were to contend with the rest of

nature for power and place, it must guard and exercise
its right to kill against whatever predatory force there
might be. Such action was found in nature everywhere,
from the jungle to Chicago's slaughterhouses. If nature
produced the defective, nature also provided examples
of how to dispose of him.[58] Although this argument might
have suggested that society was to prey upon the weak,
Dreiser had simply been insisting that the question of
what society should do ought to be discussed not in terms
of religious theories, but in terms of what men really
were — in terms provided by strict attention to so-called
facts. And now it was in such terms that he approached
other questions. Asked by Margaret Sanger to write about
birth control for the *Birth Control Review* in 1921, he
attempted to show that birth control was inherent in the
great scheme of things. Since nature's creatures had fewer
and fewer offspring as they rose in the scale of intelligence
from the fish to the human, thus producing with de-
creasing wastage, he inferred that nature was manifesting
" a tendency to overcome useless waste with intelligent
care" and concluded that the possession of intelligence
would therefore require fewer offspring to perpetuate the
human species.[59] Appealed to for support by advocates
of the single tax, he replied that it was useless to remove
inequality by legislation, whatever the benefits of such
measure to the race or the state, since "such generic aids
are constantly paralleled by that inherent necessity for
difference which exists in nature itself, and . . . it is not
man or his laws but nature itself which set[s] up astound-
ing and pathetic differences between men and things, and
so provides that variety and those contrasts, and therefore impulses, and therefore duties or indifferences, which
so interest, charm, amuse, move or irritate and flagellate
us into action and so more life . . . [and] are essential

to life itself." [60] In fine, he proclaimed, "Nature's way is correct, her impulses sound." [61] And in his defense of nature he proceeded to criticize all interpretations that seemed too restricted, even reproving would-be followers among the new writers for attempting to create the great Russian novel in America. [62]

Such a defense of nature of course continually implied the existence of forces able to thwart nature and hence implied a scheme larger than the nature he had defined, a scheme within which his "nature" and anti-nature contended. But at present he sought to impose no doctrine. He sought only to oppose opposition to nature's way and to advocate freedom to investigate oneself and thereby discover something of what nature might be. Not only did he object to suppression of books, but turning his attention to a variety of specific social questions, he advocated policies designed to lessen restrictions on nonconformers in many realms. If he agreed with Senator Hiram Johnson late in 1918 that the United States should not intervene in Russia, [63] assailed labor unions for not adopting general programs for the whole country, [64] advocating ending private ownership of utilities, [65] and favored the election of Eugene Debs in 1920 [66] and Robert M. La Follette later in 1924, [67] he did so because communism was an independent experiment, union labor confined its efforts to making more money and ignored the plight of the unorganized clerks and salesmen, monopolists compelled ideological conformity in the business world, and Debs and La Follette were opposed to the domination of monopolists. If he believed in the desirability of socializing "many things" [68] and even asserted that there was "but one main problem in life . . . the problem of sane economic relations between individuals, nations, and races," [69] he did not sympathize with any orthodoxy [70] or condone any great subordination of the individual.[71] "I don't care a damn about the masses," he told an interviewer. "It is the individual that concerns me." [72] And when he emphasized the individual, he meant that the individual must be freed to seek objectively the ideas and facts that would illuminate the meaning of life.[73]

Wondering and speculating were thus essential, and it was fortunate for Dreiser that during part of this period, from 1919 into 1922, he had been aided in these activities by circumstances enabling him to detach himself from the distractions of New York. For these three years he had lived in California, partially to recuperate from an automobile accident and the nervous strain of the preceding few years and partially to investigate an offer from a moving-picture company, which had paid him five thousand dollars to make the trip.[74] Here everything from climate to people had contributed to a meditative mood. There had been the soothing semitropical atmosphere of Los Angeles; the congenial poetic temperament of George Sterling, who presided in San Francisco over a Bohemian group that ranged from the incisive critic George Douglas to "shapely Soecubi"; [75] and, most important, a new romantic attachment with a struggling young Hollywood actress, Helen Richardson, whom Dreiser had found "too attractive to be ignored" [76] and who forgot her career to spend the rest of his life with him. Llewelyn Powys, having beheld him so happily ensconced, had written him enviously:

I have hardly yet recovered from the shock of seeing your lady[;] how irresistable [*sic*], how perfectly charming, how divine, how lovely, God! what a rascal you are to have discovered anybody so wonderful[.] Think of it living there in retirement at Los Angeles with so exquisite a companion.

Could any existence be possibly more admirably adjusted? The mere thought of it makes me suffer anguish.[77]

Here, able to concentrate comfortably and to feel financially more secure, Dreiser not only had written a number of his new stories, sketches, and articles and completed *A Book about Myself*, for whose publication in 1922 he received an advance of one thousand dollars, but had begun *An American Tragedy*, then entitled *Mirage*, and *The Stoic*, last of the Cowperwood trilogy. By the time he had returned to New York late in 1922, more than a score of chapters for the *Tragedy* were done, and the implications of his position were in the process of being more completely realized.

XII

Society and Science

Having been led to defend his assertions concerning the limitations of human beings, Dreiser had been drawn as an active participant into the society he had originally sought to observe; and where for a while he had regarded this society primarily as a force contending with nature, he was now, as *An American Tragedy* soon made clear, necessarily coming to view it as a realm within which individuals like himself contended with others. Although nature still enthralled him, it enthralled him more in its mystery than in its power.

Since the beginning of his days as a newspaperman, he had been aware of a certain type of crime seemingly produced by financial and social aspiration, the murder of some poorly placed girl by a young, ambitious lover who was attempting to gain freedom to affiliate himself with another girl more sophisticated and wealthy. The young man was usually one who had first fallen in love with someone of his own station, then had risen in the world and met a second girl surpassing his original sweetheart in glamour and attraction, and finally, trying to break old ties and encountering the complications of the first girl's pregnancy, affection, and determination to retain him, had in bewildered desperation committed murder. Whether the hapless sweetheart was morally right or practically foolish in her determination, Dreiser saw the situation as one which was produced by the very society that condemned the outcome.[1] Money and social

219

position were socially approved goals, and yet to attain them individuals encountered obstacles that — if the goals were right — were unfair and unreasonable. There had been the case of Carlyle Harris, in 1893, who had sent a girl poisoned powders. There had been the case of Roland Molineux, another poisoner, in 1899; of Chester Gillette, who had drowned Grace Brown in Big Moose Lake, New York, in July 1906; of the preacher Clarence Richeson in 1911; of William Orpet, finally acquitted, still later. And in all there was a similar predicament, resolved by murder and yet involving men who were not in the ordinary sense murderers. They had, as Dreiser saw it, simply been victims of a characteristically American social dream.[2] Their stories could well be entitled *Mirage* or *An American Tragedy*.

Because these cases were thus significant and because Gillette's, prosecuted in Herkimer County, New York, in 1906, afforded him full and accessible details, Dreiser had by 1920 decided to base a story mainly on Gillette's career. Shortly after his return from California he completed arrangements with Liveright that enabled him to devote almost all his time to it. As Boni & Liveright brought all his works together under their imprint, reissued *The "Genius"* without opposition or threats, and provided him with a $4,000-a-year drawing account, he rented an office on Union Square, hired a secretary, moved to Brooklyn with Helen for greater seclusion, and after visiting places like those in which his principal character was to live and work and talking with his friend Dr. A. A. Brill about the psychology of murder, finished the novel in time for it to be cut and revised and sent to the printer by July 23, 1925. After that there was a visit to the Sing Sing death cells, as well as an interview with a condemned murderer, to confirm the final chapters,[3] but the writing itself was done, and on December 10, despite Liveright's objections to the title — he preferred *Ewing* or *Warner* [4] — *An American Tragedy* could be published.

From his examination of the evidence Dreiser had concluded that Gillette's actions had, both in their details and in their typicalness, been misunderstood. Gillette had been no killer. Too undeveloped mentally to plot against society and too young, inexperienced, and poorly conditioned, religiously and economically, to understand his own plight, he had been unfairly judged. He had, in fact, been doing what Americans would have accepted as the right and American thing had he not committed murder. He had sought to rise financially and socially; he had found a wealthy girl who would enable him to enter a world more respected than the one he and "Billy" Brown knew; and by associating with the "right" people he had endeavored to attain a position in which such crimes as murders were not to be even contemplated. With the favor of happier circumstances and the endowment of more money or authority, he might have found a doctor to perform the necessary abortion and Grace Brown would have lived, with society none the wiser, and he would have been free and respected. Yet it had been Gillette's fate to be entangled in rules and customs whose consequences in the form of public opinion he had believed it possible to escape by murder, and he had committed murder in order to retain the appearance of respectability which the society condemning him had prized. Thus he had become the victim of those whose values he had affirmed.

In telling this story, with Clyde Griffiths and Roberta Alden representing the two principals, Dreiser hewed close to his sources; but his purposes occasionally led him to depart from the original facts.[5] Not only did he portray Clyde's boyhood as though it were his own, with Clyde, the son of religious poverty-stricken parents in the Midwest, craving for what he has been deprived of; but he modified the circumstances of the actual crime to introduce the element of accident. In Gillette's case, a tennis racket had been the instrument allegedly used to strike the girl before she had been plunged into the lake, and since the presence of a racket in a boat was not readily explained, premeditation could be confidently alleged; but Roberta is struck with a camera, and a camera could have been taken along for many innocent reasons. Then, too, in the original case there had been no indication that the girl had been stunned by a blow from the gunwale of the overturning boat, but in Roberta's case the overturning boat is partially to blame for her quick drowning. Finally, Clyde's not actually drowning Roberta but simply letting her drown after the boat accidentally tips makes the issue one that is not to be clearly defined. In the eyes of the jury, who are aroused by a district attorney exploiting the case for private political purposes rather than for justice's sake, the evidence is of first-degree murder; but in the eyes of the reader, who has actually seen acts and been shown motives, the evidence is of a crime against Christian morals rather than against written law.[6] Clarence Darrow told Dreiser after reading the book that on the basis of the novel it would be impossible to determine Clyde's guilt,[7] and in at least one law school the drowning of Roberta was presented to students as a subtle problem in homicide difficult to solve.[8] The complexity and confusion of the issue was, for Dreiser, the issue itself. Justice was not to be found clearly on one side or the other. It was his purpose, he explained to an interviewer, "to show that the snap judg-

ments of juries are inadequate in those knife-edge cases
. . . where there is a subtler distinction to be made than
one between black and white. . . . There are decisions
which casually chosen juries of men, unused to judge
human motives and actions, are ludicrously unfit to render." [9] By no simple formula could an individual be made
blameworthy, and whoever did apply such a formula was
perhaps the one who ought to be blamed.

The indictment implied by the career of Clyde Griffiths was not of Clyde or of nature but of a society in
which Clydes were so often inevitable. Not only were
obstacles constructed that weaklings could not surmount,
but men and women were brought up in an ignorance
that assured they would remain weaklings. It is the attitude and customs of society that force Clyde to embrace
Roberta secretly, and it is Clyde's "ignorance, youth,
poverty and fear" that render him powerless to deal with
the consequences of his actions.[10] For this failure he is
not to be criticized, inasmuch as its roots are in the lacks
of his boyhood; at the very end his mother, still conducting a mission, thinks she may have restrained him too
much and for his sake gives a grandson a dime with which
to buy ice cream, as though the solution were that simple. Hampered by religion in his youngest days, Clyde is
hampered by society in his later ones. Born into a world
which requires that one possess money to live and which
establishes the acquisition of this money as a goal when
one is without it, Clyde is unable to accept the self-
denying, joy-forsaking, moneyless ways of godliness. And
yet the ascetic severity of the parental discipline that
drives him to search for a better life becomes an obstacle
to his ever learning how to succeed in the materialistic
struggle, and he sets forth in the world destined for failure
because he wants strength enough to be responsible and

has not the capacity to acquire it. There would, of course, be no problem did he not long for money and social position. But these longings have not been his fault. If there is a fault, it is society's for setting the standard of success it has and for imposing restraints that will, as the individual's desires drive him, result in "crime." Thus Dreiser condemned society because by its definition of the desirable it stimulated efforts on the part of those who, in consequence of the very condition that led them to exert themselves, could not hope to attain their goal responsibly.

But society was to be condemned for still another reason. It was to be condemned for invoking the wrong standards. Whether individuals en masse could help themselves any more than isolated individuals was not a problem for Dreiser here. What concerned him was not that society's materialistic cravings might be regarded as the result of natural acquisitive impulses, but that its moral prohibitions could be regarded only as forces opposing the natural activities of individuals. In fact, it was in the conflict of impulse with external restraints that the tragedy lay for Dreiser. And it was a conflict he had been able to make real only by giving reality to both the clashing forces and by not only showing that forces within nature could oppose those of nature, but also implying that nature's forces were as limited as those of any mortal. Although he logically could proceed either to assert a more comprehensive mechanism than nature's or to deny nature's importance, he was not impelled to evaluate his premises. Instead he took advantage of the opportunities *An American Tragedy*'s reception provided to reassert his present theory in other forms.

The novel's reception, both popular and critical, was such as to assure him both of genuine financial security for the first time in his life and of numerous occasions to get a hearing for his views. From the very outset, though published in two volumes for five dollars, *An American Tragedy* outsold his other books. By the end of December 1925, more than thirteen thousand copies had been sold, bringing him almost twelve thousand dollars in royalties, and within five more months the sales were doubled. In January 1926 an expensive limited edition was published, the first of his works to be accorded this peculiar distinction; and reviewers stimulated and justified the general interest. Although there were some complaints about Dreiser's style and some about his transcription of mere court records, most critics saw that a character had been created where Chester Gillette had been forgotten, and while Joseph Wood Krutch called it "the greatest American novel of our generation," [11] Stuart Pratt Sherman, who had so exhaustively belabored the naturalism of *The "Genius,"* declared that it marked "a long stride toward a genuine and adequate realism. . . . I do not know where else in American fiction one can find the situation here presented dealt with so fearlessly, so intelligently, so exhaustively, so veraciously, and *therefore* with such unexceptionable moral effect." [12] Dreiser began to receive appeals for help from persons entangled in adulterous situations, from persons on the brink of suicide, from persons in need of money; he was asked to finance this and that worthy project, to listen to tales that would provide him with at least another novel. One man named a yacht after him. Other men, prisoners in cells from Deer Island, Massachusetts, to San Quentin, California, wrote gratefully that they had been understood, that they — those of them who could expect eventual release — would be able to lead better lives as a consequence of having read the book. Gradually, as the phrase "An American Tragedy" entered the language, Dreiser's reputation grew. The novel was dramatized and produced on Broadway. Jesse Lasky paid him eighty thousand dollars for moving-picture rights. Liveright during the next four years published a collection of his poems, *Moods,* a new collection of his short stories, *Chains,* and *A Gallery of Women,* in both trade and limited editions. One story, "Fine Furniture," rejected by nine magazines since 1923, was now bought by *Household Magazine* and then issued by Random House in a special limited edition. If there followed new demands and misunderstandings, ranging from a financial settlement with Jug to his throwing a cup of coffee in Liveright's face in a quarrel over the movie rights, he was at least now so well established that he moved, early in 1927, into a duplex apartment where he could occasionally assemble his own artistic entourage, bought an estate overlooking Croton Lake in Westchester County, where he could escape from the city, and made two trips to Europe, one in the summer of 1926 to visit Scandinavia, search for his father's birthplace in Germany, talk with his foreign publishers, and collect more material about Yerkes; the other late in 1927, at the invitation of the Russian bureau for cultural relations with foreign countries, to observe communism in the Soviet Union. Meanwhile he was besought by publishers and authors for introductions to neglected books and by magazines and newspapers, in Europe as well as in the United States, for articles, interviews, and statements. By 1929 the cables from abroad had become so numerous that he had to acquire a cable-code address.

During the five years following the completion of *An American Tragedy* his views were, for the most part, reiterations of his objections to middle-class standards, of his hope for improved social conditions, and of his rejection of formulas. Thus where the technics and values of the industrial age were most evident, he complained; where least evident, he felt at ease. Writing a series of articles about Florida,[13] whither he had gone with Helen for a vacation late in 1925, he emphasized the meretriciousness and vulgarity that characterized the notorious exploitation of the state's natural resources by boosters and land sharks, and the pitiable indigence and disappointment of those who "somehow vaguely and meagerly follow, at the heels of prosperity or fame." [14] Traveling in Europe a few months later, he deplored the poverty in the workers' quarters in Berlin,[15] the "hard commercialism" and "jaded vivacity" of a Paris that was no longer that of Du Maurier and George Moore, and the fact that on the Seine, once "the river of dreams," there were in 1926 boats loaded with cement.[16] Dreiser preferred to pause among mementoes in the tiny rooms where Balzac had lived,[17] to visit a "wonderful old castle" in Prague,[18] to stroll in the parks of Hamburg and Berlin,[19] or in the fresh air of Denmark, and to gaze at the fiords and midnight sun of Norway.[20] On his return to the United States after a brief stop in England, he disclosed that the British were "America-mad," forgetting "their own very real superiorities, their more intelligent government, their finer statesmanship, their calm and civilized life"; he criticized America for being a country "curiously indifferent to its fate," with politicians and editors so afraid to discuss "really fundamental issues such as the Catholic question, the Negro question, the money-power question or even the liquor question," that a crisis would occur once the population increased to the subsistence level.[21] When Boston banned *An American Tragedy* in 1927, and the New York *World* dismissed

Heywood Broun for criticizing his paper in 1928, and the Collector of the Port of Philadelphia barred the works of Rabelais in 1929, and Jesse Lasky throughout these years did not dare film the case of Clyde Griffiths, Dreiser's accusation seemed to be confirmed. In 1926 in a story entitled "Typhoon" he had written that the world was too busy and indifferent to understand personal tragedies like those he was depicting,[22] and in a foreword to George Sterling's *Lilith* he had remarked that most persons were "comfortably and even joyously deluded." [23] Thereafter events continually provided dismal proof of a popular reluctance to face facts, and while at times he privately blamed the Catholic Church for promoting "mass stupidity," [24] he publicly criticized Americans as a whole, regretting that in the United States man was not moving "nearer toward an understanding of his strange and at present anomalous relation to nature; or his perhaps futile hope that he may not pass as meaningless dust." [25]

If this criticism implied a basis for such hope, both the hope and the basis remained insubstantial. He endorsed a book describing life in a county poorhouse because it might "arouse some humanity in the breasts of public officials, and . . . cause the public institution of this description and others, to be managed with a little more of the milk of human kindness." [26] He defended a law enabling courts to sentence to life imprisonment a man guilty of four minor felonies, because he felt that the world consisted of those who believed in organized life and those who did not, and that this law tended to keep some people on the organized-life side of the fence. He believed it was possible to find out why some opposed organized life and how the causes of their opposition might be altered.[27] During 1928 and 1929, moreover, he contributed to the American Civil Liberties Union, sought permission for Emma Goldman to return to the United States, supported attempts to secure a pardon for Tom Mooney, lent his name to a petition for better housing and elimination of a smoke nuisance, and sent money to a summer camp for workers' children, an emergency committee for the relief of Southern strikers, and a children's hospital for Russia. But he was, clearly, attracted by no program, and social reforms interested but did not excite him, and politics involved him in no choices. In 1928 he decided it was useless to vote, for Hoover was "little more than a hall boy for American corporate powers" and Smith was "at once head and foot of Tammany Hall and a Catholic." He would reserve his ballot for "a better day" and "an honest and capable thinker who can lead." [28] But when John Dewey proposed to form a kind of American Fabian Society in 1929, to hasten the better day, Dreiser had little enthusiasm: "being alive and not wishing to sit down and fold my hands, I find myself interested in the idea of a third party, however hopeless," he said, but the nature of politics and the gullibility of the public persuaded him that the idea was doomed. [29] And when a moving-picture company wanted him to make an eight-minute short, he declined on the ground that there was "no big issue at hand vitally affecting conditions and regarding which I might speak." [30] He knew he could not use the movies to denounce the enemies of independent thinking, and beyond the defense of the free inquiring mind there was really nothing to engage in. If in an introduction to *Tono-Bungay* he agreed with H. G. Wells that the universe was "an ultimate chaos out of which anything can take its rise," he could not agree that mankind's improvement was what would surely emerge from this chaos:

. . . to assume that man is so intelligently constructive and set toward salvation is too much for me [he wrote]. Nor is he, nor can he be, capable of doing nearly as much thinking and leading as Mr. Wells appears to think. Constructively, as I see him, man is much more led or pushed than he is leading or pushing. And to harangue him so grandiosely as does Wells . . . is to address one who stands at best startled and confused by life.[31]

Dreiser consequently continued to regard particular remedies and answers with suspicion and to advocate the posing of insistent questions. Dissatisfied with conditions about him, dreaming of how much better they might be, he was inhibited in action by the extent of his reverence for the insoluble. There were "little keys" that unlocked the "little doors" to little delights and pleasures, he wrote in a poem; but these little keys would not unlock "the great locks" or "the giant doors." [32] In the face of uncertainty concerning the absolute, certainty concerning the relative was impossible. When the League for the Abolition of Capital Punishment, taking heart from *An American Tragedy*, sought Dreiser's endorsement, he replied that he was "by no means convinced that capital punishment is something that should be done away with." [33] It was, after all, the outlook that invoked the laws, not the laws themselves, that needed to be changed, and this change of outlook required recognition of uncertainties. When Sergei Dinamov, a Soviet writer, inquired what alternative Dreiser wanted to capitalists and capitalism, Dreiser wrote in answer that he had "no theories about life, or the solution of economic and political problems. Life, as I see it, is an organized process about which we can do nothing in the final analysis." [34] Until human nature changed, the "fittest" individuals would be the ones to survive. On his trip to Europe in

1926 he stated he was not a Communist and thought a world brotherhood impossible, for life could not be organized "other than on the initiative of the individual who rules others by his mental and material strength, and therefore has the power." [35] In a later interview he said he did not believe in socialism, "because I'm too intense an individualist," and thought more good could be done for the indigent by men like Heckscher than by any "movement." [36] In picking eleven of the world's "best books," he included such challenges to complacency concerning the existing order as *The Riddle of the Universe, Candide, The Way of All Flesh, Memoirs of My Dead Life,* and *Thaïs.* [37] In speaking of the religion that appealed most to him he selected Elias Hicks's Quaker teachings as constituting "the most reasonable of all religions," one which seemed to Dreiser least binding upon the individual. [38] When early in 1927 he wrote a series of articles for a newspaper syndicate concerning the restlessness and changing customs of Americans, he emphasized the kaleidoscopic variety, the changing morals, the uncontrollable evolution of American life. [39] Wherever he looked he found forces and meanings greater than any theory about the details. If social reforms occurred, they were likely to be accidental. If a new social outlook developed, it was more than he could confidently hope for.

The disposition to reject specific theories that were announced with certainty led Dreiser, however, to entertain new theories as long as they had the tone of hypothesis. Where nothing was certain, anything might be said so long as it was not said dogmatically. Hence, when late in September 1927 he was invited by an official of the U.S.S.R. to visit Russia, he accepted. "Government is a concept. Russia has a dream. . . . Ideals are what I want," he explained to an interviewer in Paris. "That is my view of Russia. I am interested in it, its change, its ideals, its dreams." [40] His only conditions in accepting the invitation were that he should be free to choose his own itinerary, be allowed to ask any questions he wished, be provided with a secretary-interpreter, and be at liberty to write unfavorably of the Soviets, or not write at all, without being considered rude. He went to the Soviet Union almost belligerently skeptical that collectivism could be established, and he wanted to be able to point out its limitations.

Handicapped on his arrival in Moscow by a case of bronchitis he had contracted in Berlin, by a feeling that he was surrounded by spies, and by complications attending the loss of his passport, he was nevertheless soon made to feel secure and enabled to spend eleven weeks in almost unhindered explorations.[41] He was established in Moscow's largest and most expensive hotel; he was counseled by other Americans, among them Walter Duranty, Scott Nearing, Dorothy Thompson, and Anna Louise Strong; and he secured for a secretary and interpreter another compatriot, Mrs. Ruth E. Kennell, who was then employed by the Russians but whom he felt he could trust. Although Soviet officials, honestly worried about his health, among other things, would not let him visit Siberia, and although an "official" secretary was assigned to accompany him on his tour, he traveled where he chose, saw and learned more than any ordinary tourist could, and had many opportunities to test his preconceptions. He was, of course, introduced to writers and artists, dining with the poet Mayakovsky,[42] discussing the Moscow Art Theater with Stanislavsky, and talking about the movies with Eisenstein. He visited Tolstoy's tomb with Tolstoy's daughter; [43] he witnessed the Russian ballet; [44]

but, most important, he met some of the Soviet Union's political leaders.

He had reached Moscow early in November, an opportune moment, for November 7 was the tenth anniversary of the Bolsheviki's seizure of the Kremlin. Although the first Five-Year Plan was not yet under way and some of the country's internal difficulties lay well concealed, there were outbreaks in Red Square during the celebration, and Dreiser was able not only to observe Stalinists and Trotskyites flinging missiles at one another, but also to talk with men sympathetic with each faction, some of whom were to be liquidated, others of whom were to liquidate. He discussed Russian politics with Karl Radek at a time when soldiers barred entrance to Radek's house and Radek had to escape surveillance to meet Dreiser at the hotel. He argued with Nikolai Bukharin and chided him about the great and noble intentions of the Soviets until the secretary of the Third International reddened and, choked with his passionate devotion to the cause, rose from his seat to swear that in ten years they would have a heaven on earth in Russia. He listened to Alexei Rykov, president of the All-Union Council of People's Commissars, and questioned Anastas Mikoyan, the commissar for trade. He talked with officials high and low, and stared at Russians from the lowest peasants up to Stalin.

The trend of his discussions and his interviews was to challenge the reality of a seemingly altruistic economy. When he talked with men like Bukharin, he wanted to know, How did Bukharin personally profit by it? What was the compulsion to support it? He reminded the Russians that he himself was an individualist and would die one and sought to be convinced of an alternative. He argued about the freedom of the press. Bukharin would insist that in Russia people were free to discuss whatever required discussion, unlike in the United States, where all kinds of distractions appeared and private interests were in control. But when Dreiser asked who decided what required discussion in Russia, he was told that officials did, and that left him unsatisfied. Wherever he went he was curious about motives, skeptical about human nature, and impressed by appearances. He questioned local officials and knocked at the doors of private homes. When Mrs. Kennell announced that here was an "American delegate," all doors would be opened. On one occasion he descended into a mine by a wet, dripping elevator to ask the coal-diggers what they thought of the present regime in comparison with that of the Czar. On another, trailed by the villagers, he sought the local priest, who remained cautiously noncommittal on perceiving the official secretary. He visited orthopedic institutes, museums of agronomy, monasteries, children's colonies, collective farms, workers' dwellings. He stopped in Kiev, Kharkov, Donbas, Rostov, Baku, Tiflis, and Odessa. And while the Russians viewed him as a vague humanist whose "lack of a definite focal point" gave his writings "a bourgeois character," [45] he completed his trip having "seen nothing that dissuades me in the least from my earliest perceptions of the necessities of man." [46]

Not until the day of his departure from Russia, January 13, 1928, however, did he attempt to criticize the Soviets publicly. At that time he decided he should not leave the Russians with any illusions about his reactions, and so, lying on the sagging springs of a mattressless bed in an unheated hotel in Odessa, wrapped in fur coat, fur gloves, galoshes, and blankets, a fur hat pulled over his ears, he dictated a farewell message to the Russian people. Although the *Chicago Daily News* was the only place in which it appeared, he imagined at the time that the

Russians would all read it. He declared not only that he remained an individualist, but that he thought communism had not in the least altered the individual's tendency to dream of self-advancement. The individual artisan was being exalted by "the most individualistic political leaders of Europe," and "a shimmering array of material benefits" rather than a selfless ideal was enthralling him. Dreiser doubted whether "the right of the superior brain to the superior directing and ruling positions" had been eliminated; he was sure that in Russia as elsewhere one could find "the sly and the self-interested as well as the kind and the wise slipping into the positions of authority." He praised the idealistic leaders for sweeping away the power of dogmatic religion, for building better schools, hospitals, and living quarters, and for giving "the collective mentality of Russia freedom to expand." But he was outraged by the plight of homeless children, disgusted by the ubiquitous filth, indignant at the completely improper ventilation he had consistenly had to endure. "You live too many in one room and are even lunatic enough to identify it with a communistic spirit," he finally declared. "I rise to complain. And I suggest in this connection that more individualism and less communism would be to the great advantage of this mighty country." [47] Having encountered persistently a nearly dogmatic defense of the Russian system, he was at pains to lay stress upon its inadequacies.

At the same time he was prepared to defend the Russians himself whenever antagonism to them seemed cocksure. On his way home he spent a few days in London, where he talked to Winston Churchill of Russia's social and military importance.[48] On his arrival in New York he told reporters he was no more a Communist now then he had been, but proceeded at once to ask why there should be bread lines in a country with America's resources when in Russia "no one is waiting for a handout. . . . Between the free and uncontrolled grafting we face here daily and a regulated accumulation centered in the Government, I prefer the Russian system." [49] When he was promptly rebuked by editors, American Legion spokesmen, and columnists, he elaborated his statement without significant qualification.[50]

His fundamental position, however, was unchanged, as newspaper articles, magazine articles, and his book *Dreiser Looks at Russia* all demonstrated. He could have made his bias clearer had he chosen to utilize records Mrs. Kennell had kept of his many badgering interviews, but even if, in the interests of not hurting an experiment that required disinterested study, he refrained from expanding his objections, he showed that he was no apologist for the Communist state. He simply approved what seemed to coincide with his view of man's nature and rejected what did not. He liked the fact that Russia distributed the wealth and recognized the possibilities of the human mind freed from dogma. He liked the improved working and living conditions, the social approach to knowledge, the easy rules concerning divorce and marriage, and the feeling that Russia had a plan. He thought he would like to send to Russia "the rankest individualists" [51] of America, England, and France to show them that private rights and privileges maintained by force and exploitation had a worthier substitute. On the other hand, he carefully stated that he had not been converted to Russia's present brand of communism, and objected to its "tyranny" [52] and "dogmatic" theory.[53] Thus he favored those measures which seemed to favor the individual and enable him to act naturally, unhampered by artificial restraints. He applauded the attitude toward sex because the importance of impulse was therein affirmed. But he objected the moment social co-operation required fundamental sacrifices. It was well enough to remove artificial strength from entrenched wealth and greed, but as soon as society extracted obligations from its members and forcibly bound them in a common purpose, then he protested, less because he opposed dictatorship as such than because imposed authority was against nature's law. In an introduction to some short stories by a Russian scientist and acquaintance, a follower of Kerensky's, Dreiser at this time referred to communism as "a wholly lunatic theory in regard to altering the very nature of man." [54] The meaning of freedom and accomplishment was still to be measured in terms of whatever promoted knowledge of the nature of man.

For Dreiser this knowledge continued to be scientific knowledge. He valued the literary and artistic, to be sure. He liked John Cowper Powys's *Wolf Solent* because Powys was always "stalking" the "earthly mystery." [55] He opposed Sumner's attempts to suppress *The Well of Loneliness* because the book's description of the "unnatural" challenged the usual conception of natural processes.[56] He commended the Moscow Art Players' cinematic version of *Crime and Punishment* because it probed psychological moods.[57] But in such instances the artistic became simply a means of extending the realm into which science might penetrate. When Dreiser after his return from Russia sought to organize a group that would sponsor an American tour by the Moscow Grand Opera's Ballet,[58] when he recommended that the Film Arts Guild in New York present a number of Russian-made films,[59] when he gave weekly parties in his studio where some friend might talk on the art of science, some hitherto undiscovered virtuoso play an accordion, some

African dancers exhibit forgotten tribal rites,[60] he was appealing to men and women who were prepared to admit there were no final answers and who could see in novel techniques signs of the exploring intellect and in primitive lore some clue to the meaning of mankind. In writing a prose-and-verse pæan to New York entitled "My City" late in 1928, he spoke of tall towers and lowly slums, of riches and poverty-stricken tenements, of the hoping and despairing as though each were an element in a glorious symphony and at the same time a minute phase of a cosmic mystery demanding solution.[61]

In this frame of mind he found science assuming more and more the functions of religion. Reviewing a book which contended that the proximate causes of crimes were glandular and nervous disorders and that such secondary causes as social accidents were frequently themselves the products of glandular troubles, he feared that the significance of the research would be dismissed as a mere fad. The murderer would continue to ask the forgiveness of God for his sins before he went to his death in the electric chair, whereas, according to Dreiser, "Society should ask forgiveness. Perhaps God also." [62] And spending three weeks of the summer of 1928 at the Woods Hole marine biological laboratory in Massachusetts,[63] where he was exposed to discussions about the biological measurement of X-rays, the biological effects of high-frequency sound waves, the relation of filterable viruses to cellular changes, he persistently questioned the research men as to whether there was a God, and, remarking on the "freer mental or spiritual air" he found at the laboratory, declared that the scientific search for "the secret of . . . [man's] descent and his being" was "beautiful" and spoke of "an elation of spirit such as does not ordinarily befall me." [64]

What he had found was a philosophy of the open mind. But it was for him bound to be a philosophy with little substance. He could make no specific assertions with confidence and could accept no specific assertions made by anyone else as final. When on his return to New York from Woods Hole he was asked by the *Bookman* for his credo, he wrote:

I can make no comment on my work or my life that holds either interest or import for me. Nor can I imagine any explanation or interpretation of any life, my own included, that would be either true — or important, if true. Life is to me too much a welter and play of inscrutable forces to permit, in my case at least, any significant comment. One may paint for one's own entertainment, and that of others — perhaps. As I see him the utterly infinitesimal individual weaves among the mysteries a floss-like and wholly meaningless course — if course it be. In short I catch no meaning from all I have seen, and pass quite as I came, confused and dismayed.[65]

And "ashamed," too, he explained to a critic afterward.[66] The philosophy of the open mind was not quite satisfying, for what Dreiser sought was some absolute that would give shape and clarity to all the mysteries, something that would explain both the how and the why of particulars, something that would explain everything. If that something would eventually rob particulars of their particularity, he did not know it; and if the form of freedom, the system of theories, was the absolute he wanted, he did not perceive it amid the clamor of theories whose contents pretended to define his absolute but actually failed to.

Hence at the moment that he revered science, he began to find fault with scientists. He observed experiments with animals in laboratories, he listened to lectures

on conditioned reflexes in New York medical and research centers, he read books such as Le Dantec's *Nature
and Origin of Life* and D'Arcy Thompson's *On Growth
and Form*, but he found answers only to how matter was
constructed, not to why it was so constructed. In a more
extended statement of his beliefs a year after his reply to
the *Bookman*, he wondered, Why should not the atoms
of which man was composed know something of "the
order and meaning of the structure they erect, and so,
via emotions communicated to the brain, say, suggest
something of the meaning of life to us?" [67] The lure of
pleasure in life was certainly no answer, for suns, planets,
and the various "immensities" were not being evolved for
so trivial a purpose. Moreover, man was simply "an atom
in a greater machine, just as is the cell in the greater
body of which it finds itself a part," and therefore could
have only the meaning or importance that the machine
had. To speak of soul or spirit was to speak "nonsense"
since "science knows nothing of a soul or spirit." [68] What
Dreiser actually wanted, therefore, was for science to
know itself scientifically. He wanted the ultimate to be
susceptible to proof. He believed that the idea of
the provable was itself a provable idea. When knowledge
had somehow known itself, then the meaning of knowledge would be plain and the status of the knower clear.
What "meaning" would *then* mean had not become a
problem. At present, though, he could "testify to the
æsthetic perfection of this thing that I see here and which
we call Life!" [69]

Thus he found beauty in the perfectly formed as well
as in the grotesque, in anachronism as well as in syn-
chronism, the beauty of an order that could comprehend
such diversity, the beauty of the unknown and of the
mind seeking to know. Not to realize the nature of this

beauty was to be not only unknowing, but also unseek-
ing. In a world concerned chiefly with "lust of flesh, food,
show, applause," [70] the significance of being personally
insignificant was being lost. Material values became
momentarily all-engrossing, and real values were ignored. The ignorance Dreiser could tolerate as part of the
inscrutable scheme were it not that the ignorant attempted to impose their views on others and to make
what was really trivial absolute, thereby obstructing the
mind's journey into the unknown and destroying its appreciation of that harmony of all things which constituted the beauty of life. One had, therefore, continually
to defend the futility of defense, continually to assert the
hopelessness of assertion, continually to fight for a right
to question that was granted by questioned authority.
Dreiser was pleased when George Douglas, after reading
his expanded credo, wrote to him: ". . . you are helping
to make the bounds of freedom wider . . . by removing
the restrictions imposed by ignorance." [71] But Dreiser was
being driven to a point at which his certainty of ignorance
could not be made effective by proposing the exclusive
possibility of uncertainty. To attack ignorance it was becoming necessary to say what specifically constituted
knowledge. To uphold the right to question it was becoming necessary to uphold the validity of entertaining
particular questions, and hence, inevitably, the validity of
particular answers, for no question could be raised which
did not imply at least the kind of answer that would be
acceptable. Since for Dreiser the defense of the right to
seek and question had necessarily meant becoming involved in the contentions of society rather than in the
contentions between man and nature, the questions in
metaphysics that his social views implied would have to
be posed within the realm of society itself.

XIII

For the Underdog

Beginning in 1930 Dreiser was for almost a decade driven to commit himself to a series of specific social causes. Throughout 1929 the Soviet press had criticized him for the limitations of his petit-bourgeois outlook. He had, they noted, accepted the values of the order to which he was persistently objecting and lacked the strength to lift himself to a point where he might properly criticize it. His worth lay in his artistic portrayal of the decay of the capitalistic system rather than in a valid affirmation of alternatives. But Dreiser had found as yet no valid alternative. Art knew no classes, and man must be studied objectively. Dreiser was not to be restricted in his specuations by Moscow any more than by Boston. The direction of his thinking was, however, affected by restrictions — by the fact that he was living in a land where the dogmatists were of Bostonian rather than Muscovite bent — and hence some of the people he might have had to defend against oppression in Russia he was compelled to denounce in the United States, and those he might have criticized in Russia now represented causes he espoused.

Shortly after returning from a trip to Havana early in 1930, he was presented with an issue about which he could not remain neutral. Pope Pius XI, the Archbishop of Canterbury, Rabbi Stephen S. Wise, and other religious leaders had been protesting against the Soviet

Union's attitude toward religion, and March 16 had been set as the day on which all churches in New York City would join to pray for the end of Soviet persecution. To the John Reed Club, an organization of writers and artists who sided with workers in the class struggle, this agitation foreshadowed armed intervention in Russia, and they called attention to the ominous situation in a circular letter dated March 4. On March 18 Dreiser released a statement opposing "interference with Russia at this time on any ground yet offered," calling the Soviet Union "an important and constructive economic and political system which now rivals and may presently outrival our Western capitalistic system," and accusing monopolists of attempting either to incite a holy war against Russia or "to becloud our Western mind in regard to some of the ills with which unrestrained capitalism is now threatening us." He was no atheist, he said, but he opposed "dogmatic religionists" who were "now warring against the human mind and its possibilities," and he recommended the study of science and "the mathematical certainties of economics, sociology and law." [1]

In defending Russia's measures curbing the power of the Orthodox Greek Church, he appeared at once to be an apologist for communism and was so quoted in France, Germany, Sweden, and Russia. But he was still concerned primarily with the defense of "the human mind and its possibilities," and the Soviet system represented a valuable scientific experiment. Within two weeks after denouncing the oligarchs and churchmen, he denounced the new humanism for similar reasons, if not with similar vehemence. Irving Babbitt and his colleagues represented in Dreiser's eyes "Traditionalism as opposed to newness. . . . Religion as opposed to science. Peace and quiet as opposed to energy and effort.

243

The shades of Oxford and Cambridge . . . as opposed
to the steel mills of Gary," a faith in "decorum" as opposed to an understanding of "life." [2] In April and May,
traveling through Arizona, New Mexico, and Texas on
his way to California and Oregon, he assailed repeatedly
the moralists, the religionists, and those who worshipped
money.[3] "If anything really valuable today is done for
the defective, the insane, the criminal, the deficient or
others who, for some reason or another, limp in the rear
of the ranks, it is not done by Christians," he declared,
"but by up-to-the-minute, generous-minded, warm-
hearted sociologists and economists, trained in the exact
truths of science, and not in the worn-out and threadbare dogmas of the churches. . . . Close the churches,
and open scientific laboratories that seek to know the
secrets, if not the meaning of life and its creative forces
— and see how much more quickly we shall come by wisdom and beauty; how much more valuable and helpful
our relations with our fellow-beings will be." [4]

As he reached California and talked with friends along
the coast, and as he observed and read about the increasing unemployment, the decline in real wages, the effects
of the concentration of wealth, he found the right
to independent thinking and the prevention of economic catastrophe intertwined, and individuals who were
suppressed soon became individuals who could contribute
valuable solutions. Thus in San Francisco he involved
himself in the continuing efforts to secure Tom Mooney's
pardon, appealing to Governor Young in person; and
early in June, when the John Reed Club addressed him
again, this time concerning the plight of radicals imprisoned for allegedly seditious utterances, he took the
occasion to accuse the "capitalistic or directive world"
of refusing to recognize the need to end "industrial ab-

solutism," and pointed out that whereas in Russia there was some attempt at solving economic inequalities, in the United States there was not even the feeling that a solution was necessary. He proposed the abolition of inheritance and the public ownership of utilities and banking; he noted that "it is not money, but mind, that is the really distinguishing thing in life"; and he concluded that "it is time that the world's creative economic geniuses everywhere now sit down together and take counsel in regard to the new necessities — the new order they imply — some new way of living our economic and social lives." [5] On his return to New York in July he was convinced that conditions in the United States were "in many ways similar to those in Russia before the revolution." [6] With the government controlled by private cliques, education dictated by businessmen or patrioteers, the free markets the property of monopolies, and radically critical publications being suppressed on the charge that they were public nuisances, he feared ultimate frustration for the individual unless there were "a really important stand on the part of the intellectuals." "Men could organize this land so it could support three or four times its population without any misery," he said. "I have never seen a land more beautiful. It is self-sufficient. . . . It could live beautifully." [7] He granted the John Reed Club permission to use his name in collecting money for the defense of political prisoners; he became chairman of the Emergency Committee for Southern Political Prisoners, which defended Negro Communists charged with insurrection and treason for distributing Communist leaflets; [8] by the end of October he was willing to endorse the Communist candidates in the November elections on the ground that only the Communists were actively seeking to solve the unemployment problem and that therefore, whatever their "larger aims," they represented "the only current political value worth supporting." [9] He subscribed to the communistic *Labor Defender*, contributed twenty-five dollars to the Unemployed Councils of the Trade Union Unity League, whose general secretary was the Communist leader William Z. Foster; and, revising and completing *Dawn*, the autobiography of his youth, he inserted a few sentences concerning the hopeful light that Russia had kindled in the east.[10] Before long, as readers came to regard him as a radical reformer, he was engulfed by letters, clippings, prospectuses, and even manuscripts of books proposing one or another way out of the depression; and within a year the International Union of Revolutionary Writers cabled him birthday greetings in which they said: "We are happy we can call you comrade." [11]

Dreiser, however, was scarcely a thoroughgoing Communist, as the American members of the party knew, even though they tried to minimize the fact.[12] If he wrote James D. Mooney, president of General Motors Export Company and co-author of *Onward Industry*, that "my solution for the difficulties of the world, and particularly those in America, is Communism"; [13] if he continued to oppose any interference with the Soviets "as now functioning"; [14] if he endorsed the showing of moving pictures about the class war; [15] and if he suggested to Communist Party leaders that they form a society to instruct the lay mind in Marx's teachings [16] and wrote in an article that the Communists' objective was "not only constitutionally, but humanely, politically, sociologically and in every other way, sound" [17] — he did so for reasons that could not be viewed as Marxian. A few weeks before writing Mooney he had told the editor of a working-class magazine that although "I know the Marxian theory thoroughly, and satisfied myself, by going there, of the experiment in Russia, I do not know the details of the lesser issues which confront the Communists here in America." [18] Shortly before insisting that the Soviets must not be hampered, he had, in a discussion with the Russian playwright Boris Pilnyak, asserted that the belief that communism eradicated individualism was "bunk": "Communism is purely a matter of economics and sociology." [19] The moving pictures he advocated and the Marxian society he proposed were not intended to preach doctrine but to present Marxian principles objectively in terms of American conditions. And when he endorsed the Communists' objective, he linked his endorsement with the statements that he would like to see a strong enough third party in the United States to produce "a range of high-minded contentions on government issues," and that he could not imagine "a better base for the contention necessary to party life than Marx's attacks on the limits of capitalism." [20] What Dreiser believed communism offered was not submergence of the individual, but more freedom for more individuals to express themselves; not a new human being, but equitable conditions for the old human species to flourish.

In fact, throughout 1930 and 1931 Dreiser was trying to forestall rather than promote revolution. He was trying to appeal to the middle class rather than to the proletariat. When, for example, he wrote on civil rights or on unemployment, he preferred sending his articles to papers of liberal instead of radical bent, to the *New Freeman* instead of to the *New Masses*, to the *Progressive* instead of to the *Daily Worker*. And when he discussed the profit system, he did not speak of abolishing profits, but only of distributing profits more justly. He supported Senator George Norris's charges against public utilities,[21] criticized the railroads for being disproportionately wealthy,[22] pleaded for an end to "intellectual unemployment" [23] and for "a new trial and a new deal," whereby everyone would "live on a reasonable wage" and share equally of "the fruits of a great land," [24] all in order to "stir . . . [the middle class] to such action . . . as will stop the lid from blowing off." [25] Finally, during 1931, accepting the chairmanship of an active group that became known as the National Committee for the Defense of Political Prisoners and writing a book on the economic plight of the country, he came to see that his defense of the individual implied a society where individuals were assured of the conditions of a free society.

In his activities he was doubtless made more sensitive to the problems of others because of difficulties of his own. Some of these were mainly financial or legal. He had instituted proceedings against his caretaker in Mount Kisco for allowing the house to burn down. He had been seeking a way to compel his German publishers to account for royalties and pay contracted advances. And he had employed lawyers to aid him in a quarrel with Liveright concerning rights to the dramatized version of *An American Tragedy*. But other difficulties had social implications. Early in January 1931 he signed a contract with Jesse Lasky giving Paramount Publix Corporation the talking-picture rights to the thitherto unfilmed *An American Tragedy*. Because no picture had yet been produced and because a scenario prepared by Sergei Eisenstein had been discarded,[26] Dreiser was wary lest his story be perverted by the Hays office, and he agreed to the contract only after reading the tenth clause, in which Paramount agreed to seek and if possible heed such advice and criticism as he might offer. For several weeks he heard nothing further, until suddenly, when he had departed from New York for a trip through the South the first week in February, Paramount sought to show him the script, failed to locate him immediately, and sent him notice that filming was to begin on February 23 and that he had until the 20th to take advantage of Article 10. At once angry and suspicious, Dreiser questioned Paramount's sincerity, rejected the script that finally reached him as "nothing less than an insult to the book," [27] and refused to talk with Samuel Hoffenstein, who had prepared the script and flown from Hollywood to New Orleans for a conference.[28] The scenario, as Dreiser explained to Lasky, showed Clyde as simply a sex-starved drugstore cowboy and, neglecting Clyde's background, hastened to the drowning so rapidly that it failed completely to show the "inescapable web" or "the planned culmination of a series of inescapable circumstances." [29] The effect of the film would be, Dreiser declared, to give audiences the impression that the book was "nothing short of a cheap, tawdry, tabloid confession story," and he warned that he "would not stand idly by" to permit this "inequitable infringement of a vested property" of his.[30] Eventually Paramount yielded to pressure, and Dreiser flew west with a script-writer of his own to propose changes.[31] But the attitude of the producers strengthened his skepticism. Before returning to New York he told reporters that he would bring suit if the film did not meet his "fullest approval." "I feel, in a way, that I am acting for the thousands of authors who haven't had a square deal, in having their works belittled for screen exploitation." [32] And when the film did not meet his approval, he did seek to enjoin Paramount from showing it. Although he knew his case would not succeed,[33] he impelled the company to make further changes and through publicity attending his fight called attention to what he viewed again as a restraint upon independent thought.

A second difficulty of his related even more directly to his defense of those who propounded unpopular doctrines. At a dinner in honor of Boris Pilnyak in March 1931, Sinclair Lewis rose and in the course of a few welcoming remarks accused Dreiser, who was present, of plagiarizing "three thousand words from my wife's book on Russia," [34] Dorothy Thompson's *The New Russia*. After the dinner was finished, Dreiser invited Lewis into an empty room and demanded that he retract his statement. When Lewis simply repeated his charge, saying: "Theodore, you're a liar and a thief," Dreiser slapped him.[35] For the next few days newspapers from New York to Sydney featured the story. Although the explanation of Lewis's charge was not obscure, it was embarrassing, and Dreiser could not undertake to exonerate himself. There were indeed identical phrases here and there in both books. Dreiser and Dorothy Thompson had been in Russia at the same time. They had exchanged notes. They had had access to the same official documents, bulletins, and leaflets. In addition, Dreiser had felt, upon reading some of Miss Thompson's chapters as articles in the *New York Evening Post*, that he had been responsible for some of her material and was therefore entitled to it.[36] When his book had appeared in November 1928, two months after hers, and her lawyers had written him alleging infringement of her property, he had referred the matter to his lawyers, offering to meet the charges in court, and nothing further had come of it. The books, in fact, except for the isolated passages, bore no resemblance to each other, and only peculiarly husbandly resentment of past relationships could have revived the issue. Yet the effect was to give to all whom Dreiser had been criticizing an argument whereby to discredit whatever criticism Dreiser had made. Lewis's charge had simply dramatized for them the fact that the Soviet Government distributed stereotyped propaganda to all gullible tourists, and that therefore all who sympathized with communism were victims of propaganda. In slapping Lewis, Dreiser had defended the integrity of his work, but he had also exposed its validity to question, and in consequence was shown anew the obstacles in the way of securing objective discussion for ideas regarded as radical.

It was because these obstacles had become greater that in April 1931 he undertook to head the National Committee for the Defense of Political Prisoners. Informed while in Hollywood by a telegram from Joseph Pass of International Labor Defense that the extent of persecution for political ideas demanded immediate action, he invited certain artists and writers, among them Gaston Lachaise, Hugo Gellert, Paul Rosenfeld, Lincoln Steffens, the Edmund Wilsons, Samuel Ornitz, and Malcolm Cowley, to meet at his studio on his return in order to discuss the matter. There he told them that "the time is ripe for American intellectuals to render some service to the American worker," and he proposed to organize a committee that would collaborate with International Labor Defense in opposing political persecution, lynchings, and deportations of labor organizers, in informing the public, and in helping workers to build their own organization.[37] Soon, including the usual roster of the socially concerned, from Franz Boaz to William Zorach, the National Committee for the Defense of Political Prisoners was in existence, with Dreiser its chairman and Lincoln Steffens its treasurer. Although Pass, George Maurer, and other members of International Labor De-

fense were to guide the committee and call its attention
to the right problems, and although International Labor
Defense was both closely allied in ideas and associated in
organization with the victims of persecution, Dreiser was
himself desirous only of establishing equitable individualism. In the first of the N.C.D.P.P.'s cases, the Scottsboro
case, the committee made clear that it was seeking simply
a fair trial for the boys, and Dreiser explained to a Town
Hall audience that his interest was that the boys should
be tried as human beings instead of as Negroes, and that
there should be a "general broadening and humanizing
of the universal treatment and condition of the Negroes,
especially in the South." [38]

In this spirit he continued, both as chairman and as an
independent individual, to protest the harsh treatment
of radicals, whether the occasion was their threatened
deportation from the United States to countries that
would execute them or their being tortured in China or
Poland for producing revolutionary literature. "Why torture Polish writers or anybody for trying to think out a
better way?" he asked on one occasion. "Is not one
needed?" [39] And similarly he continued to insist on the
validity of traditional democratic processes. When in
June 1931, at the instigation of William Z. Foster, Earl
Browder, and Joseph Pass, he visited mines in the Pittsburgh area, then the scene of hardship and brutalities
characteristic of industrial warfare, he advocated the dis-
establishment of the American Federation of Labor for
being graft-ridden, narrow, and selfish in its interests,
hostile to Russia, and friendly to capital. But though in
the ensuing public exchange of letters with William
Green he relied for facts on Browder, Foster, and International Labor Defense, he insisted over their objections that labor unions should seek to restrain corpora-

tions through the courts. When informed that the courts did not stand above classes, he merely repeated that the seeking of injunctions was proper.[40] To the extent that freedom was to be promoted, Dreiser could place faith in the idea of law, and if some judges were not above classes, the principles at least remained unsuborned.

The culmination of his activities at this time was an investigation in November 1931 of conditions in Kentucky's Harlan, Bell, and Knox County coal fields, where for more than six months there had been terrorism and bloodshed attending the struggle of the miners to organize a union.[41] Following a wage cut in February, many miners had decided it was better to strike and starve than to work and starve, and had left the pits. Philip Murray, then international vice-president of the United Mine Workers of America, had addressed a meeting and told some two thousand workers to put their hope in the union. The mine operators then had begun discharging union sympathizers and evicting their families from their homes; the sheriff, friendly with the circuit judge, who was associated with the operators, had sworn in deputies and sanctioned their touring the county in armed cars, bullying and terrorizing the miners. Shots had been fired, men on both sides killed, company property fired or looted; and when the A.F.L. organizers had failed to provide substantial aid, the Communist-led National Miners' Union had arrived, with soup kitchens and other relief supplies, provoking worse violence, as the possession of an N.M.U. membership card or a *Daily Worker* became evidence sufficient to convict the possessor of criminal syndicalism, punishable by twenty years at hard labor. Reporters who attempted to disclose the facts were intimidated or shot. Merchants in Knoxville, Tennessee, were threatened with boycott because a Knoxville paper had dared to print a series of revelatory articles. By the end of October the rights of free assembly and discussion were virtually abrogated.

Appealed to in late October by International Labor Defense, Dreiser as chairman of the N.C.D.P.P. had promptly invited almost a score of prominent citizens, such as Charles Taft, Daniel Willard, Felix Frankfurter, and Senator Norris, to accompany him to Kentucky and hold open hearings. Failing to enlist them, he had called for volunteers from among the N.C.D.P.P., and securing the support of such men as John Dos Passos, Charles Rumford Walker, Samuel Ornitz, and Melvin P. Levy, he had entrained for Pineville, Kentucky, where the group was joined by representatives of International Labor Defense and the *Daily Worker*. The press having been notified of the expedition, and the Governor having guaranteed protection, the members of the committee were not assaulted. But as they took testimony, from the sheriff and the district attorney as well as from miners, they encountered tension, received anonymous threats, and were spied upon; and on the whole they found only melancholy confirmation of the worst they had been led to expect. In hotel lobbies where miners deferentially awaited the opportunity to tell their story, in mountain shacks where the walls were lined with newspapers to keep the wind from freezing the family and the pigs, along streets where hard-looking men walked with guns under their jackets, in the sheriff's office, where the *Daily Worker* was considered matter that could not be legally distributed, the evidence was consistent.

It created a familiar pattern. The miners, underpaid, wanting to improve their status, had taken counsel among themselves only to be thwarted by the power of the operators. Turning then to orthodox union channels and finding these clogged, they had discovered that only the more radical organizers could give them hope and concrete assistance. But as soon as the miners had become a force to contend with, they had aroused an opposing force that had led to violence-producing violence. The illiberal attitude of the mine operators had led to the nullification of constitutional rights and thence to lawless forms of rebellion that could be quelled only by greater force. Miners had read the *Daily Worker*, and because it counseled action and assertion of rights, the operators had seen it to be a threat to order and peace. And indeed it was, for where legitimate discussion and redress were frustrated, all action was bound to seem arbitrary and dangerous. The sheriff had sworn in deputies already employed as guards by the operators, and armed them with warrants that had been sworn out before a judge allied with those same operators. Any citizen who alleged a miner was violating a law could swear out a warrant, and since the mere possession of a copy of the *Daily Worker* or an N.M.U. card had become presumptive evidence of criminal intent, there were many allegations once the National Miners' Union had arrived in Harlan, and many warrants. As the committee could see, the law had become only what the local officials said it was, and these officials said whatever the operators wished them to.

The situation strengthened Dreiser's belief that the individual's plight in America was critical. In an interview with a writer for the *Knoxville News-Sentinel*, one of the few papers not afraid to print the facts about the miners, he arraigned the petty officials, the business interests, the press, charities, and churches for being all "subservient to the money barons" and, pointing out the need for a redistribution of wealth, said that "inspiration must not be found in power, but in equity and a chance to develop the latent power of self-entertainment." He cited the system in the Soviet Union. "With the obsession for power and fabulous wealth removed," he said, "the Russian today finds greater opportunity for individualism and a greater inspiration for helping his fellow man." [42] It was an inspiration that, Dreiser had noted elsewhere, came "with and through communism[,] the sense of national companionship rather than individual loneliness and inadequacy in all struggles[,] heartaches and ambitions."[43]

If the citizens in Harlan and Bell Counties failed to agree with Dreiser and his associates, they reacted in such a way as to secure Dreiser a more widespread hearing than he had enjoyed before. During Dreiser's stay in Pineville a group of anxious local patriots had prowled about the halls of his hotel, and one night at about eleven had allegedly beheld a woman enter his room. Quickly, with the clicking of the latch, they had sprung forward and in triumphant silence leaned a few toothpicks against the door. When a few hours later the toothpicks had been discerned to be still vertical, the loyal watchers had been able to infer only one thing, and on November 9, shortly after Dreiser had left for New York, the Bell County grand jury indicted Dreiser and a woman designated as "Marie Pergain" on charges of adultery, whereupon warrants were issued for their arrest should they chance to re-enter the Commonwealth of Kentucky. A week later, largely on the basis of speeches made by representatives of the *Daily Worker* and International Labor Defense while accompanying the Dreiser committee, Dreiser, Dos Passos, and others were indicted for criminal syndicalism, and rumors spread that Kentucky would seek to extradite Dreiser for trial. But these indictments served only to focus attention on Dreiser. He denied the adultery charge by stating that he was "at this writing" (an ambiguous phrase) "completely and finally impotent," and, assured of consequent publicity, then reiterated some of his charges against the Harlan officials.[44] Moving picture, press, and radio sought him out; he talked for a newsreel about the toothpicks and conditions in the mines, and when his picture appeared in the theaters, he evoked spontaneous applause. Forums wanted him to lecture. *Liberty* bought an article of his on American prudery.[45] Editors took Kentucky and its sex-seekers to task. Strangers wrote letters containing praise as well as physiological cures. When extradition was rumored, Governor Roosevelt indicated he would grant Dreiser an open hearing, and John W. Davis agreed to defend the committee. In Washington, Senator Norris arranged to have a Senate subcommittee inquire into the N.C.D.P.P.'s findings. Although at first Kentuckians told Dreiser's lawyer there would be no trouble if only his agitation ceased, they had too much to lose in publicity by pressing their charges, and on March 1, 1932, dropped them all.

The opportunity Dreiser now had to disseminate his ideas was not, however, only another opportunity to assert that the individual was being frustrated; it was also an opportunity to review the implications of his own thinking and revise conceptions he had upheld in the past. Uncontrolled individualism and its justification in terms of nature's laws or intentions he now repudiated; ". . . you will find," he told an interviewer, ". . . that if you have untrammeled individualism — and I have certainly been an advocate of that . . . — you will come just where you are." One individual more crafty than others "will become a giant," subjecting the people to him, no matter how much he might actually derive his power from their existence.[46] Moreover, Dreiser now repeatedly noted, distributing reprints of some of his remarks,[47] "complete individualism" was not what "we need or want or can endure even, but a limited form of individualism which will guarantee to all, in so far as possible, the right, if there is such a right, to life, liberty, and the pursuit of happiness; also, an equitable share in the economic results of any such organization as the presence and harmony of numerous individuals presupposes and compels." Limitation was now essential to liberty; restraint was now a condition of freedom. Such significance as Frank Cowperwood once had had in *The Financier* and *The Titan* was now inverted. In fact, where Dreiser had once invoked the intention of nature to support his belief that jungle law was the only law, he now invoked those intentions to argue precisely the opposite. He declared that the jungle, "where every individual is for itself," was "the best exemplar" of individualism, and he insisted:

. . . Americans should mentally follow individualism to its ultimate conclusion, for society is not and cannot be a jungle. It should be and is, if it is a social organism worthy of the name, an escape from this drastic individualism which, for some, means all, and for the many, little or nothing. And consciously or unconsciously, it is by Nature and evolution intended as such. For certainly the thousands-of-years-old growth of organized society augurs desire on the part of Nature to avoid the extreme and bloody individualism of the jungle. In proof of which, I submit that organized society throughout history has indulged in more and more rules and laws, each intended to limit, yet not frustrate, the individual in his relations to his fellows.

In fact, the dream of organized society, conscious or unconscious, has been to make it not only possible but necessary for the individual to live with his fellow in reasonable equity, in order that he may enjoy equity himself.[48]

Groping for a label to apply to himself, distinguishing him from the Communists, he said he was "an Equitist," whose program was "just one of a fair break for all." [49]

The book he wrote about the country's economic plight, *Tragic America* — at one time tentatively entitled *A New Deal for America* and completed shortly before his trip to Kentucky — was an attempt to set forth his program in detail. Intended to expose the institutions that were enslaving "the average individual" in America and to describe measures which might bring a new deal to the numerous people who were "wholly confused and defeated," [50] it was written in language at times so angry and strong that, despite passages eloquently and sympathetically appealing to Americans to recapture the promise of their national life and reconstitute their society,[51] it became a source rather for new controversies than for new solutions. Organized charity was a "financial racket"; [52] the church had produced "the uninformed and brainless religionist"; [53] whoever was "loyal to God as opposed to organized society, its necessities and benefits," was "either mentally incompetent or a faker!" [54] But Dreiser simply preferred plain to polite speech, and for all his passion, he did make suggestions presupposing careful distinctions. He wanted business to be "noncompetitive"; [55] he wanted all utilities to be owned by the government, and pointed out that government ownership was "a principle socialistic but in no way communistic and not to be confused with the nationalization of all wealth as well as all industry as advocated by Communism"; [56] and he wished education to be so secularized that all children would "bristle with knowledge of . . . rights as well as . . . the real basis of organized society." [57] Indignantly, desperately, hopefully, he tried to define the conditions of "a surer and more pleasing way of life." Economic and social conditions, "like the constantly moving and shattering and rejoining energy of the universe," were relentlessly changing, he noted, but that was life. "And as life there need be no fear of it. More, it is adventure, and who is so mean as to fear adventure?" [58]

If the public reactions to his pronouncements ranged from that of leftists who stretched out their arms to greet a disciple to that of clerics who would have liked to exclude an apostate from the community of decent men, the reactions in the United States were principally unfavorable. Although Russian critics and editors, acclaiming him as "the great master" who "strikes boldly and devastatingly at bourgeois America," [59] thenceforth deluged him with requests for statements or articles concerning Soviet state holidays, revolutionary anniversaries, writers' birthdays, youth movements, and impending wars, the critics at home, even among the more radical, were less hospitable. While V. F. Calverton in *The Liberation of American Literature* believed Dreiser had found the way out of the crisis and predicted fundamentally transformed novels from Dreiser's pen, Bennett Stevens of *New Masses* accused him of failing to grasp the principles of communism,[60] Norman Thomas, on behalf of the Socialists, regarded the book as inaccurate, unsystematic, and important only because Dreiser wrote it,[61] and Stuart Chase, who told Dreiser he agreed with the Dreiserian thesis, challenged sources, statistics, and conclusions.[62] Yet, even if there was a sufficient number of factual errors or oversights to warrant numerous revisions for the British edition, it was for the remarks about religion and the church that *Tragic America* was most lustily assailed. A librarian in Elkhart, Indiana, returned a copy of the book to the publisher as unsuitable for shelving in the precincts. A public library in Cincinnati declined to buy the book since it would corrupt the minds of the young. Bookstores in Los Angeles mysteriously received information that they would receive no further copies. And the Reverend James M. Gillis, writing in the *Catholic News*, called Dreiser "the most unpleasant kind of fanatic" because Dreiser had rejected religion and become impure in heart. "Snap out of it, Theodore," Father Gillis counseled him. "Look up at the sky. Take a squint at the sun. Go out on the hillside and inhale deeply. Get out of the gutters. Come up from those sewers. Be decent, be clean, and America will not seem so tragic." [63] When a reader of the *Catholic News* wrote Dreiser condemning Father Gillis's assault and did not sign his name for fear of a business boycott,[64] and when a subsequent canvass of numerous papers and magazines of more than 100,000 circulation failed to disclose more than two or three — and among them *Outdoor Life* and *Detective Mysteries* — which would print a paid advertisement containing the Gillis review along with the anonymous letter, Dreiser felt there was an attempt to keep his message from the public; and when sales of *Tragic America* suddenly dwindled, he wondered whether he ought not to adopt some method of distributing the book himself.[65]

At the same time, however, he received letters that indicated he had become a spokesman for oppressed persons of all degrees. Never before had he heard from quite so many persons for whom all time and circumstance were out of joint. There came letters from inmates of insane asylums who alleged they were being unjustly and forcibly kept in confinement; letters from victims of jealous relatives and politicians; letters from women being driven mad by radio waves emanating from sets op-

erated by scheming property-seekers; letters from drafts-
men of the depression, who drew diagrams illustrating the
laws of nature, the paths of life, and the economic cycles.
And besides letters, manuscripts expounding one solution and another. Sometimes Dreiser directed the senders
to certain magazines, newspapers, and publishing houses;
sometimes he himself sent the manuscripts to the appropriate editors. But at all times he was kept aware of the
existence of great numbers of desperate and frustrated
Americans, whose predicament continued to require
vigorous "Equitist" criticism of injustice.

From 1932 through 1937 Dreiser engaged in protests
that ranged in scope from the defense of an acquaintance
discharged by a Southern newspaper for radical sympathies [66] to the support of an international committee
formed to call a world congress against war.[67] So long as
the occasion involved someone's right or attempt to speak
out for social equity, Dreiser was likely to support him. He
protested when California police arrested William Z. Foster, Communist Party candidate for president in 1932.[68]
He protested when the Los Angeles police department's
anti-Red squad broke up Communist meetings.[69] He protested when Mayor Kelly suppressed the play *Tobacco
Road* in Chicago.[70] He protested when the Spanish Government imprisoned the artist Luis Quintanilla for membership in the revolutionary Madrid Young Socialist
Committee.[71] He protested when Japan carried on military activities in China.[72] Whether a leftist union was
fighting the American Federation of Labor or Stalinists
were complaining that Trotskyites were lending themselves to anti-Soviet propaganda,[73] Dreiser could be relied
upon to give some assistance. He wrote introductions to
books about forced labor in the United States [74] and
about men who tramped the country homeless and pen-

niless.[75] He answered questions sent him by *Izvestiya*, *New Masses*, or the *Modern Monthly* and wrote articles for such magazines as *Common Sense* and *Today*, warning of impending fascism and violence,[76] exhorting writers and artists to "join with the mass against the class for a better and more equitable order," [77] labeling profit-makers as "thieves," [78] denouncing "industrial Gorgons" and "the non-national group of money-swine who dominate this country." [79] He participated in renewed efforts to right the injustice to Tom Mooney,[80] supported the Communist Party candidates, William Z. Foster and James W. Ford, in the 1932 elections,[81] and overcoming an ingrained antipathy to the lecture platform, made arrangements with lecture bureaus to address people in town halls and colleges concerning what he regarded as the facts of American life.[82]

At the same time he came no closer than he had been to committing himself to the discipline of any single party or program. In fact, whenever he felt that a group he had joined for some specific purpose was being dominated by a doctrine — usually communism — he withdrew. He resigned his chairmanship of the National Committee for the Defense of Political Prisoners early in 1932, resigned all but an honorary chairmanship of the World Congress against War shortly after, objected to being listed as one in the League of Professional Groups for Foster and Ford, refused to endorse a plan of the Intellectual Workers League to guide writers, all because the controlling interests were Communists. Their doctrinaire attitude meant, he discovered, that if he committed himself to one of their causes he was almost automatically committed to numerous other causes that the Communists viewed as necessarily related, but that he himself might not approve, and it also meant that they were more interested in discussing theory than in adapting a foreign program to the needs and prejudices of the American worker.[83] His communism was, he confided to Evelyn Scott, "a very liberal thing. I am not an exact Marxian by any means. . . ." [84] When in 1935 he was quoted as considering the Jews racially distinct [85] and perturbed editors of *New Masses* visited him to proffer corrective instruction, he denied harboring hatreds, disclaimed sympathy with Hitler, and stated that his interest in communism was "that it will equitably solve the relations of man, and I emphatically repudiate any inference in my writing that will be interpreted as counter to this." But he also remarked: "I am an individual. I have a right to say what I please." [86] In 1936, when he might have voted for Earl Browder or even Norman Thomas, he announced that the more radical parties were "so mismanaged that I cannot support them," and seeing a fundamental difference between Alf Landon and Franklin Roosevelt, declared it to be "of major importance to me" that Roosevelt should be re-elected.[87] The New Deal had at least been educating the public as to its social responsibilities.[88]

He did, to be sure, continue to argue that the Soviet system should be studied,[89] but studied primarily as an object lesson in what he regarded as the techniques for securing the greatest freedom for the greatest number. "I am grateful to the Red Marx and the Red Russia," he said on the Revolution's twentieth anniversary,[90] but it was for the impetus given to social reforms that benefited individuals everywhere else than in Russia that he was grateful. Thus he derided attempts of Marxists to dictate to writers and artists, and insisted that no pressure should be brought against a man even if he were a fascist. "Only the other day," Dreiser wrote to a friend, "some young writer was telling me that a man would write a better book if he had read and understood the Marxian dialectic! Imagine!" [91] Similarly, believing that Soviet totalitarianism was but a temporary expedient required to hasten the freedom he cherished, he stated in a never-to-be-published cable to *Izvestiya*, which had requested his opinion concerning individual liberty in the U.S.S.R., that though the absence of individual liberty might still be necessary in Russia to protect the Communist ideal, "individual liberty in the sense of self-criticism for the whole is valuable. For a society which cannot criticize itself is like a body with deadened nerves, and so unable to warn us of evil. When communism is achieved freedom of opinion should be assured." [92] In fact, his conception of the Russian system was such that the terrorism and purges attending the liquidation of the Trotskyites bewildered him and he began to think that "maybe . . . [the Soviet experiment] won't be any better than anything else." [93]

Dreiser's interests remained too broad to be crammed into any ideological capsule, and the problems that challenged society still eluded the simplification of prescriptions. He wrote H. G. Wells attempting to excite his enthusiasm for the works of Charles Fort, and when Wells considered Fort's works trash, suggested that Wells might base stories on them. [94] He continued to collect material for *The Stoic*, and though realizing that critics might consider the novel "decidedly unsocial and even ridiculous as coming from a man who wants social equity," resolved to write it "just that way." [95] And even as he was supporting Foster for president he associated himself with George Jean Nathan, Ernest Boyd, James Branch Cabell, and Eugene O'Neill in editing the *American Spectator*, a literary newspaper that he considered "an open forum for aesthetic temperaments" [96] and that had "no policy in the common sense of that word," advocated "no panaceas," and offered mainly "an opportunity for the untrammelled expression of individual opinion, ignoring what is accepted and may be taken for granted in favor of the unaccepted and misunderstood." [97] In the *Spectator* Dreiser saw a periodical that might print the colorful, the incisive, the reflective, and the socially informed emancipated from ideological rigidity. His own editorial preoccupations ranged from human-interest sketches that he wanted Sergei Dinamov to write "without Communist dogma being lugged in in any form whatsoever," [98] to articles on the dance that he sought from Angna Enters. He tried to secure some article by Stalin. He succeeded in eliciting from Tom Mooney an account of prison life that Mooney had to have smuggled out of San Quentin. [99] He invited contributions from writers as heterogeneous as Karl Radek, Diego Rivera, George Ade, John Cowper Powys, and Arthur Davison Ficke. From the sum total of insights might come the understanding needed to provide an intelligent solution to the world's ills.

Dreiser remained with the *Spectator* only from 1932 to 1934. The possibility of selling scripts to the movies, the failure of foreign publishers to account for what they owed him, arbitration proceedings following upon the insolvency of the Liveright Publishing Company, all conspired with his other activities to interfere with his editing. But it was primarily disagreement with the other editors, especially Nathan and Boyd, that led to his resignation. The paper had begun to accept advertising. One of the publishers was Catholic. Nathan and Boyd were undisposed to print certain material severely critical of the church. In Dreiser's opinion, the opportunity for untrammeled expression of the unaccepted was no longer possible,[100] and he left to turn his attention to the problem of eliminating factionalism among the leftists and unifying all oppressed groups within some indigenous American party that would include the American Civil Liberties Union, the National Association for the Advancement of Colored People, and other non-Communist exponents of the extension of freedom.[101]

At first he proposed founding an American League for National Equity.[102] Then he sought to organize a group that might purchase the *Modern Monthly* and merge it with *Common Sense*.[103] A few years later he tried to persuade the Technocrats to join forces with Upton Sinclair.[104] But in each instance his purpose was to convene those who were in a position to demand social justice. Let the oppressed come together, discuss their problems, and present society with a collective demand. Somehow Dreiser possessed a curiously sublime faith that if a sufficient number of intelligent minds were in conclave, something just would be produced; and thinking of action in terms of form rather than content, he was more likely to advocate co-operation than to advocate specific measures for whose enactment groups should co-operate. In a moving-picture script Dreiser prepared during 1933–4, entitled *Revolt* or *Tobacco* [105] and dealing with the rebellion of Southern tobacco-growers against the Duke trust during Theodore Roosevelt's presidency, he showed something of the technique and feasibility of revolt; but more important than the details of the technique was the lesson that success could come only through unity. He did not affirm unity for unity's sake, but on the other hand he did not affirm unity for any specific purpose. Men were simply to be united in a determination to preserve freedom of discussion among all in order that all might co-operate toward the establish-lishment of an equitable society, the necessary condition of individuality. When the civil war began in Spain, he attacked the fascists and the restrictive activities of the Catholic Church, recommending economic sanctions and, if necessary, war. But his attack was based largely on feelings that he likened to those of a person who was seeing "three or four Great Danes hopping on a Scottish terrier": he was simply in 1937 — as in 1930 — "for the underdog." [106]

XIV

The Red Dawn

The course and consequences of the Spanish revolution implicated Dreiser to a degree that he could scarcely foresee. At first he regarded the plight of the Loyalists as simply another problem in equity, seeing in Franco's program "a lack of intellectual freedom, a strongly militaristic and repressive social control . . . false religious, racial and economic ideologies, and . . . the enslavement of the great mass of the people." [1] He advocated sending aid to the Loyalists and supported groups asking that the United States arms embargo be lifted. But he concerned himself almost as much with efforts to establish a Federal Bureau of Fine Arts, [2] with disagreements with his publishers, at that time Simon & Schuster, and with the expansion of "The Girl in the Coffin" to a full-length play which would show that social equity made love possible. [3]. In fact, he even was preparing to disengage himself from some of the wearisome involvements of protest and to devote himself mainly to his own writing, pondering metaphysics and resuming *The Bulwark*, so long laid aside, when he was suddenly, in July 1938, delegated by the League of American Writers and the League for Peace and Democracy to attend an international peace conference in Paris sponsored by the *Rassemblement Universal pour la Paix*, among whose leaders were Lord Cecil and Georges Bonnet. But even this trip was insufficient to produce a radical revision of his outlook. In Paris he was impressed by France's and England's seeming indifference to the Loyalist predicament, and when, at the instigation of a group of Loyalists, he had visited Barcelona and gained first-hand knowledge of the sufferings and needs of the Spanish people and the hopelessness of the government cause, he returned home feeling that Spain's troubles were great and immediate.[4] Yet the role he wished the United States to play was primarily a humanitarian one. He conferred with President Roosevelt, attempted at the President's suggestion to form an impartial group of representative citizens of various creeds to collect funds for civilians on both sides in Spain, and lectured in several cities concerning his trip; and when he had failed after several months to enlist a sufficient number of persons who did not fear to be identified with Communists or fascists, and late in December 1938 Roosevelt himself organized a committee, he wrote the President appreciatively:

That you should have applied the mechanism of the plan suggested so accurately and effectively, and particularly in the face of the stalemate that any ordinary citizen was certain to encounter, makes still more clear to me the enormous value of a great executive in the Presidential chair at all times but most particularly in periods of stress and change.

I am deeply grateful to you. You did what I so much would have liked to do for you.[5]

If such a committee was no fundamental solution, Dreiser was nevertheless encouraged, for though he considered conditions in Europe "dark," [6] he did not think war in Europe likely and found political graft at home at least as disturbing.[7]

By mid-February, however, he was compelled to change his views. On January 4 Roosevelt had requested extensive appropriations for national defense. Three weeks later Barcelona had fallen to Franco. A few days after that, Hitler, denouncing defamatory statements made in the United States, had demanded colonies and pledged aid to Italy in the event of war. Hearing frequently from friends such as Evelyn Scott, who wrote that most of the girls she was teaching at Skidmore were "all waiting eagerly to see it happen in 1939 when they will attain the romance that distinguished the pasts of their parents and become lost generations able to say at first hand how dreadful war is," [8] Dreiser had become pessimistic; and when in February he began a lecture tour on the west coast, where since December he had had his permanent home, he was increasingly critical of American policies. While he attacked the Catholic Church and the American Federation of Labor and called Roosevelt the greatest President of the last seventy years, he also disapproved of Roosevelt's foreign policy, scoffed at the idea that England was democratic, saying that Great Britain was full of wage slaves and that Germany had done more for the masses, and urged that Americans not save democracy again until her allegedly democratic friends practiced some of the democracy that was to be saved.[9] On February 19, arriving in Salt Lake City for a series of lectures in Utah, he warned that the wealthy might sell out the country and occasion the rise of a fascist dictator and that war was certain, perhaps as early as April, with the United States pitifully unprepared, its people going to the movies, dancing to swing, and reading the comic strips.[10] "No country can prepare for war in less than ten years," he declared. "The United States hasn't even started to prepare and probably we'll have our throats slit before we have a chance to do it." [11]

But by preparation Dreiser did not mean what Roosevelt did. In fact, as war approached and finally began in Europe, Dreiser's criticism of Roosevelt's policies became transformed into opposition. When England and France had recognized Franco and when Hitler had extended his domination over Czechoslovakia, Dreiser circularized a letter he had written to *International Literature* stating that America should strengthen cultural ties with Russia, and that "a traitor press dominated . . . by a fascist minded financial oligarchy" was preventing the American people from learning the truth.[12] When the United States had followed the British and French in recognizing Franco, and Roosevelt, with King George's visit to this country, had demonstrated close friendship for Great Britain, and when following the Russo-German non-aggression pact Poland had been invaded and war declared, Dreiser complained of Roosevelt's hostility toward Hitler and his sympathy for the allied powers.

I begin to suspect that Hitler is correct [he wrote to Mencken]. The president may be part Jewish. His personal animosity toward Hitler has already resulted in placing America in the Allied Camp — strengthening Britain's attitude and injuring Germany in the eyes of the world. The brass!
But we seem to grow Wilsons on every bush.[13]

Asked by *Common Sense* to write on the current threat to Western civilization, Dreiser replied with an article that he circulated in broadside entitled *The Dawn Is in the East,* in which he stated that the only kind of civilization being threatened was that of the economic and social brutalities he had seen all his life in Europe and the United States. Germany was simply seeking a place in the sun and, once satisfied, would treat the Jews more humanely. Moreover, a weakening of Western dominance would be beneficial, for Russia was doing work that might yet "repay the world for all the horrors it endured between 1914–1919." He praised ancient Oriental culture, called the religious beliefs of China and India lovely, profound, and humane, and implied optimistically that Oriental thought, Marxist economics, and modern science all treated man as a being appropriate to the concept of universal equity.[14] With Russia's security guaranteed by Germany, a war between Germany and the Anglo-French alliance would be ultimately for the best.

It was little wonder, in the light of this thinking, that after Roosevelt assailed the Soviets for bombing Helsinki and after Congress passed more than sixty pieces of defense legislation calculated to end American isolation and assist the British,[15] Dreiser became alarmed lest the United States be used by British sympathizers to bolster England in what would ultimately be an attack on the progressive U.S.S.R. If, in October 1939, in reply to an oblique and speculative rebuttal by the President to *The Dawn Is in the East* he could send to the White House inscribed copies of three of his works,[16] he felt compelled a year later to say bitterly that there was no good in Roosevelt,[17] and to support Earl Browder for president as the only acceptable alternative to candidates whose ideas portended imperialistic war.[18] He questioned the motives of Herbert Hoover and others for being concerned with relief for the Finnish after having been silent about Abyssinians, Chinese, and Spaniards. "American relief for Americans first," he insisted.[19] He repeatedly asserted that Britain wished to see Russia destroyed, and alleged that she not only was failing to fight Germany but was seeking to get "sucker countries" and "enslaved colonies" to fight for her.[20] He charged that bankers, munitions makers, and Englishmen were conspiring to rush the United States into war.[21] And, frequently publishing the statements in leaflet form to be mailed to hundreds of people who might be influenced, he usually wrote and spoke as plainly as he had in *Tragic America*. In a reply to *Editor & Publisher*, which had asked him to contribute to an issue commemorating National Newspaper Week, designed "to bring home to America the blessings of her free press" and to emphasize "America's fortunate position, with respect to a free press in a world of tyranny and censorship," [22] he said: "What between sheer awe of the corporation gall which unquestionably prompts and no doubt finances this industrious labor of yours, and wonder as to how, at this late date, I still come to be on your National Corporation sucker list I am fairly flattened — not flattered." And after alluding to "the criminal doings of our national monopolies which today . . . [are] ponderous with stolen money," and after pointing out the failure of the press to publicize violations of civil liberties or to report activities favorable to labor and to peace, he concluded:

Actually if this were a really liberty protected country — one not ruled and stifled by a heartless and greedy band of profiteers, you and your paper might well be charged with fraud in this instance, and, if you ventured to take a court oath in behalf of your innocence, convicted of perjury.[23]

From the summer of 1940 to the summer of 1941 Dreiser devoted himself energetically to expounding the proposition that the United States must not be bled for imperial Britain. He hastened to compile a book, entitled *America Is Worth Saving*, which in the manner of a harangue urged Anglophobes with save-the-world complexes to realize that England was a hater of democracy, that brutal exploitation by England's ruling class had to end, that financial interests in the United States as well as in Britain had been in collusion with the Nazis, that the country's leaders were trying to evade the immediate problem of establishing equity at home by plunging the nation into war, and that America should find an American solution, returning to the principles of the Declaration of Independence and the Constitution.[24]

At the same time he wrote articles extolling Harry Bridges and Upton Sinclair,[25] spoke on the radio in behalf of Earl Browder,[26] and endorsed the Dean of Canterbury's *The Socialist Sixth of the World*, which sought to demonstrate that the Soviet system was the embodiment of Christian values.[27] Completing his book in October, he hastened east to Washington, D.C., early in November to address a mass meeting sponsored by American Peace Mobilization, of which he, along with Paul Robeson and Vito Marcantonio, was a vice-president, and to repeat his charges against the British and the plutocrats.[28] Then, in March 1941, after a return to California and further oral and written tirades,[29] he undertook a series of talks in New York and Philadelphia, where before audiences gathered by the American Council on Soviet Relations and by American Peace Mobilization he damned the corporations and pleaded for popular government, denied he was a Communist but likened Communists to missionaries or Franciscans and called Lenin's plan "the greatest piece of news since the Sermon on the Mount . . . the salvation of the world."[30] If the United States and the Soviet Union would combine, Hitler — whose attempt to unify Europe sounded "like an American idea" — would have to come to terms. Moreover, freedom would be the gainer, for in Russia there was freedom. There one could be anything from a painter to a sewer rat provided only that "you do a little work on the side." [31] "I'll tell you," Dreiser remarked to an interviewer before leaving New York, "if we don't have a revolution here with America modeling itself on Russia, then Americans aren't Americans any more. I won't know what to think of them." [32] After arriving home in Hollywood he continued to protest, issuing two more leaflets,[33] and on June 6 the Fourth American Writers Congress bestowed on him the Randolph Bourne Memorial Award for the most distinguished service to the cause of culture and peace.

Less than a month later, however, Dreiser had completely reversed his view of America's stake in the war. But there was nothing inconsistent in this reversal, for on June 22 Germany had attacked Russia, and he considered American and Russian interests mutual. If Russia was at peace, the United States should support peace; if Russia was at war, the United States should aid Russia. "Nothing can be as important to liberal democratic America as the success of Russia in its fight against Hitler," he wired a mass meeting in Madison Square Garden. ". . . Russia's cause is true democracy's cause, wherever and however. . . . There is nothing in its constitution that is not in ours and vice versa." [34] Moreover, he was no pacifist. A week before the German offensive he had told an inquiring Japanese newspaper that America had legitimate interests in the west Pacific — "Hawaii, the Philippines, Guam, Wake Island" — and that he wanted "to see America arm itself" so that "the right to trade peaceably with the Asiatic lands, just as all Asiatic lands now trade peaceably with us . . . may never, successfully, be interfered with." [35] And when in July the America First Committee requested permission to reprint a chapter from *America Is Worth Saving*, he refused lest somehow he sabotage American aid to Russia.[36] In fact, his concern for Russia was so great that when he read of German victories and thought of the vast destruction of what it had cost the Soviets so much money and sweat to build, he became sick with the image of the disaster and for several days had to spend a morning or afternoon stretched on his bed or couch.

Deep as was this concern, however, his attitude toward Britain remained constant. He believed that, whatever the Anglo-Russian military alliance might mean, England was probably plotting to betray the Russians. British aid to Russia was apparently verbal, he wrote a correspondent. "And while I am honestly anxious that America should aid Russia at once and swiftly, I will be sorry to see her swung to that duty by British influence. For I mistrust England as much as I mistrust Hitler. It is not a democracy. . . ." [37] There was in Dreiser's mind no idea that aid to England might have helped weaken Russia's potential enemy before hostilities began; there was only the idea that England had had no intention of weakening any potential enemy of Russia's and now had no intention of weakening the actual one. Only Russia could be trusted, and what might appear as self-aggrandizement could be seen as simple self-defense.

This reasoning, which some ten years before had brought reporters to interview him, now prevented reporters from being sent. There were, of course, the usual requests for statements from Soviet publications; but when on so notable an occasion as his seventieth birthday he might have expected to be beset by the press, there was only a vengeful silence. Some reviewers had regarded *America Is Worth Saving* as giving aid and comfort to Hitler.[38] His present opinions scarcely redeemed him. The *Los Angeles Examiner* did not photograph him in the swing beneath his lemon tree; the *New York Times* did not ask his opinions on having lived three-score years and ten. There was recognition from only a faithful few, and from the battlefields of Russia, where a Red Army soldier who had read a cable of Dreiser's to the Russian press was inspired to write a poem.[39] After Pearl Harbor, Dreiser could do little other than hope Russia would be truly aided, and not sacrificed to what he regarded as selfish British interests. The military conduct of the war could not be in civilian hands; strategy could not be evaluated without information; and in any event, with national feeling what it was, social criticism of the industrialists whose factories had to be employed and of the British Government, whose support was really necessary, became only a resented and even futile gesture.

In fact, once the United States was engaged in the fighting Dreiser protested only concerning the delay in opening a western front on the European continent, and when in the fall of 1942 he attempted to state his views to others than the editors of *New Masses*, who could be relied upon to agree that England was refusing to fight until Russia was irreparably crippled,[40] he discovered how futile the protest was. Arriving in Toronto, Canada, to address the Toronto Town Forum, he spoke to reporters off the record and said that if the titled and wealthy class of England brought about Russia's defeat, he hoped Hitler would attack England and abolish that class. Because of a misunderstanding, his remarks were quoted, but only partially, and he was reported as saying only: "I would rather see the Germans in England than those damned aristocratic horse-riding snobs there now. The English have done nothing in this war thus far except borrow money, planes and men from the United States. They stay at home and do nothing. They are lousy." [41] Then he criticized Churchill for sending Canadians to be slaughtered at Dieppe. At once an outraged American official phoned to reprove him; the Attorney General in Ontario secured an order enjoining him from further public utterances; and the Toronto Forum, advised that a breach of the peace might ensue, canceled their meeting. When some of the newspapermen sympathetic to Dreiser in his predicament told him he might be arrested and subjected to ridicule and an admirer, Hazel Godwin, offered to drive him to an out-of-the-way station whence he could entrain for Michigan, he accepted the ride; and, reportedly, though a telegram asking that the train be stopped reached the conductor before the border was crossed, the train was so near the boundary that the conductor, a good-humored official, did not pull the cord, and Dreiser was secure, ready to make a speech and distribute a leaflet clarifying his position, but reluctant to speak of his flight even to his friends.[42]

Thereafter he made few public statements. Having become committed to causes, he now found himself prevented from further arguing in behalf of his commitments. But he was also tired from campaigning and depressed by events, and as even his Russia adopted the ruthless practices of her enemies, he gradually became detached from the agony of the struggle. When early in 1943 he submitted to *Writer's Digest* an article asking for an end of fighting, he was told it was identical with Nazi propaganda.[43] In a letter to Mencken shortly afterward, he wrote: "Personally, I do not know what can save humanity unless it is the amazing Creative force which has brought 'humanity' along with its entire environment into being." Humanity should not be saved for murder and starvation, for if that was what it was being saved for, then I think humanity had better be allowed to pass. For I have pity. And pity suggests that no humanity at all is better than what I have seen here and there, — many fractions of the United States included.

Then he added:

I know you have no use for the common man since he cannot distinguish himself. But I have — just as I have for a dog, a worm, a bird, a louse or any living or creeping thing. The use that I see is *contrast* and so *interest* for you and for me.[44]

There seemed to be little for him to do other than observe the creative force manifesting itself in its mysterious ways. But there remained work for him, and though his attitude recalled an earlier one, it was at the same time different, as the last chapter of his life made clear.

XV

The Creative Force

Issues had become increasingly impersonal for Dreiser. If it was in part that the possibility and occasion for crusading had ended, it was also as he had written Mencken. What indeed could save humanity? Humanity itself had become the issue, and projected against an issue such as that, more limited issues were necessarily matters of indifference. Where relatively personal problems were concerned, for example, disagreements lost their edge. Since 1919 Dreiser had had quarrels of one sort or another with Hollywood and moving-picture producers and as recently as 1937 had been unable to find the Hays office willing to approve *Sister Carrie* with its unfortunate kept-woman theme. But now he was prepared, in an article for *Esquire*, to sweep the past away as of little moment. "I never truly hated Hollywood as a whole," he wrote, "— merely certain aspects of it which ran counter to my own ego, which for one reason and another (the sale of a novel like *An American Tragedy* for one thing) caused me to feel that a percentage of consideration, not always at the fingertips of busy men, was due me." [1] He had been infuriated by the indifference of those in power to those vainly seeking places in the industry; but now there was new blood, courtesy, friendliness. The Hollywood of 1943 was not that of the 1920's. "And so I cannot possibly hate it or the industry," he said. "In truth, I never have." [2] In truth, so consuming a personal feeling as hate was no longer easily experienced.

Yet it was more than a matter of personal feelings. For Dreiser's speculations about nature and the meaning of individuality had also produced an attitude of mellow impersonality that, once he was separated from the clamor of daily protests, could dominate him.

Throughout the thirties, despite his social protests, he had refused to accept the perceiving individual as the ultimate reality. The challenge of the very mystery that had led Dreiser to value the individual had also precluded his being satisfied with what he had valued. The attitude toward existence that had prevented him from taking any dogmatic theory of existence for granted had prevented him from taking himself, his awareness, and all his limitations as a man for granted. Seeking to discover within his limitations what those limitations were, he had failed to see that in order to question he had to regard at least the questioning process as unquestionable. And instead of mystery's being the mark of limitation, something ever to be redefined and therefore the reminder that only the secular world was truly sacred in this life, mystery had remained something to be completely dispelled. Dreiser might recognize that an individual came "to know himself as a unit" by "sensing the presence of others"; yet at the same time he had denied the subjectivity of this unit by writing:

All creative thought, in man or animal or vegetable, can but revert to the one, unoriginal, unindividual, almost commonplace thing, the mystery of our existence, or the unified reality behind it. And since by reason of creation, man is not only made but controlled by nature or creation, his thought is its thought; his reactions its reactions. And, by reason of that, man is not really and truly living and thinking, but, on the contrary, is being lived and thought by that which has produced him. Apart from it . . . he has no existence. . . .[3]

He had already argued in 1929 that man was merely an atom in some greater machine and could therefore have only the importance the machine had. He had continued to note that mind was encompassed by all it sought to comprehend. But instead of being content, he had sought to give dignity to the part by defining the whole and, to distinguish the limitations of perception, had demanded that perceptions account for themselves.

Of course, he had not secured an accounting. But rather than feeling defeated he had felt devout. Inscrutability, once wonderful, had become moving. One day in July 1933 when he had asked Arthur Davison Ficke to read him a certain poem and Ficke had read it, tears had welled up in his eyes and he had said: "It's so God damn beautiful, Arthur. Anything beautiful always makes me cry." And a month later, walking with Ficke in Mount Kisco, he had confessed to a deep feeling of unworthiness, and when Ficke had remarked: "But Theodore, every man has to learn, sooner or later, to *forgive himself*," Dreiser had turned to Ficke, his face contorted with emotion: "My God! What a thing you have said! What a tremendous thought! Why, it's enough to change a man's whole life! Why, you could knock me down with a feather!" And several times later that day he had stared at Ficke and muttered: "A man has got to learn to forgive himself! . . . Well, you could knock me down with a feather!"[4] It had been no accident, therefore, that in 1934 he had revised, rearranged, and added to his volume of poetry, *Moods* — reissued in 1935 — and that, having induced Sulamith Ish-Kishor to write an introduction which would point out that the book was not "lyrical poetry in a non-lyrical form" but "lyrical philosophy," [5] he had decided that the more philosophic poems should be mingled with, rather than separated from, the more romantic, "leaving those philosophically bent to the burden of assembling in their own mind the thoughts meant for them." [6] For in the apparent amorphousness there would be at least the semblance of groping and in the groping an affirmation of mystery and consequently beauty. Editing *The Living Thoughts of Thoreau* for Longmans, Green's "Living Thoughts Library" in 1938, he had chosen for the first selection a passage asserting: "Not till we are lost, in other words, not till we have lost the world, do we begin to find ourselves, and realize where we are and the infinite extent of our relations." [7]

This progressive realization of an awful infinity eventually had transformed speculative detachment into reverential worship. During the Century-of-Progress Exposition in Chicago, Dreiser had suggested that Chicago build some edifice dedicated " 'to the helpful spirit of religion' . . . something which will awaken thought and awe and perhaps reverence in man in regard to the universe as a whole . . . and lift . . . [humanity] nearer the realm of pure æstheticism." [8] At the same time, in an occasional story or essay written between 1933 and 1936, he had exhibited sympathy with religious and soberly moral folk,[9] treated as significant the whisperings of the conscience of a man who had failed to keep a bargain with the Lord,[10] emphasized the "dark and devastating, and at the same time quite tender and sorrowing, meditation on the meaning or absence of it in life" by such a writer as Mark Twain,[11] and stated his love for *The Way of All Flesh*, because it was "such an honest, humble and yet fateful picture of a male Alice, wandering in a true blunderland which most certainly this world is." [12] By 1942 he could consider "The Hand" the most representative of his shorter works.[13]

Dreiser's attitude had not, however, involved any repudiation of science. In fact, science had seemed to be simply the means of disclosing the nature of individuality and therefore a means of making religion fundamentally more religious. By 1934 he had begun to consider "item by item and function by function . . . the unreality and mythology of the individual and even of the race," [14] with the intention of producing a volume of philosophical essays to be entitled *The Formulæ Called Life* and designed in part to show that everything from individuality to death was a myth. Not only was man being lived rather than living,[15] but he was also in death not truly dying. Suicide, for example, was impossible; an individual death was simply part of the life of the universal mind, which was therein expressing itself.[16] "I can find nothing that is not mind," Dreiser had remarked in one of his first essays, "You, the Phantom," [17] and he had been referring to the projections of some transcendent mind that was operating everywhere through particles of electrical energy. In the 1928 edition of *Moods* a poem called "Links" had begun:

> Look
> It is Main Street,
> And she sixteen
> He eighteen.
> It is Main Street
> And the evening parade
> Of those who would be happy —
> (The world-old parade)
> Has begun.

Boys and girls,
Pathetic boys and girls,
The twilight parade of the young. . . .[18]

In the 1935 edition the last five of those lines had been significantly expanded and altered; following "those who would be happy" Dreiser had written:

Atoms,
Electrons,
Protons,
Matter-energy
Disguised
As girls and boys
Pathetic boys and girls
Has begun —
The world-old parade
The twilight parade of the young. . . .[19]

Scientific reading and research had thus led him to the conclusion that the universal mind was a kind of ubiquitous electro-physical force.

If he had had doubts concerning the ubiquity of the force, they had been partially resolved by singular experiences attending an illness he had suffered early in 1935. Not only had he lost weight and succumbed to a period of depression, but, as he had written George Douglas:

In connection with the loss of weight and the general depression, there was a sudden probably glandular development which induced, to me, the most amazing morbid fears, which began to descend for periods of from three to seven seconds, at most a minute in duration, but which were really startling and productive of a reflective depression, which were not an integral part of the seven seconds but were of the consequences of it. Being of an analytical and philosophical turn I have been mentally startled and illuminated by something for which I have no words. Perhaps I might call it a sense of psychic earthquake as though something abysmal and final were first opening under or splitting once and for all. The so-called conscious something which is me. I fancy a man standing on a trap with a noose around his neck might have some such feeling, though I doubt it.[20]

Here were the "ineffability," "noetic quality," "transiency," and "passivity" which William James had marked as the distinguishing characteristics of the mystical experience.[21] But it had been an appropriate enough culmination for thought that had come to regard itself as simply part of the mental operation of a universal mind.

Further investigations had but confirmed Dreiser in his beliefs. He had read about subjects ranging from the life of the cell and the autonomic nervous system to cosmic rays and psychic phenomena; he had conferred with such authorities as Dr. Simon Flexner, Professor Harvey Lemon, and Dr. Irving Langmuir; he had spent the summer of 1935 in California discussing his speculations with George Douglas, who could understand him by some kind of "psychic osmosis"; [22] he had visited the observatory on Mount Wilson, the General Electric laboratory in Schenectady, the Westinghouse plant in Bloomfield, New Jersey; and he had been able to continue asserting that human beings were but outwardly distinct manifestations of one great, common, electrical being. In 1936, after reading George W. Crile's *The Phenomena of Life: A Radio-Electric Interpretation,* which argued that "the phenomena of life must be due to radiant and electrical energy," [23] he had written Crile that the book "has reinforced my own feelings and deductions in regard to nature and man." [24] And a few months later, in an introduction to a special edition of Somerset Maugham's

Of Human Bondage, he had stated that books were written by "Life" working "through one of its creations, or *creatives*," [25] and that this novel was "Life itself bursting through all current human limitations." [26] In fact, Life had seemed to burst through all forms to render distinctions between forms of energy meaningless. One day not long before his trip to Spain, Dreiser had encountered a puff adder back of the house in Mount Kisco and, thinking it poisonous, killed it. Learning later that it was harmless, he had been sorry, and when a few days afterward he had encountered a second adder coiled in the grass, its head raised and puffed, he had attempted to speak to it reassuringly, saying he intended it no harm. As it had lowered its head and begun to slip away, Dreiser had followed after, to observe its movements, whereupon the snake had coiled and puffed out its neck again. Again Dreiser had spoken to it, promising he would not harm it, and having stepped back in token of his word, he had observed the snake then uncoil and come toward him, passing by the toe of his shoe as it had crawled away into the grass. Dreiser had been sure the snake had understood — indeed, Dreiser had soon decided man could talk with animals or birds, perhaps even with the grass and the flowers.[27]

Thus at the moment when Dreiser had been actively defending the rights of individuals, he had been thinking in terms that apparently vitiated individuality. Yet since the creative force or energy was everywhere, it might as well have been nowhere, for in explaining everything, it of course could really explain nothing, and Dreiser's argument had then meant simply that men could not control the universal laws. Within those laws life might proceed *as though* men had power to act and as though there were values. "Life is what it *seems*," he had declared in one of his philosophical essays. The "illusions of value which make up the cycle of our life must be necessary and evidently are functional to some other end, unknown to us." Good and evil existed as necessary opposites, but since a larger conception comprehended them, they did not evince any "inherent dualism or cross-purpose in nature." [28] Hence one could be free and individual on the one hand without supposing one was either free or individual on the other. But it was important to remind oneself about the pervasiveness of the creative force, lest one have illusions about the illusions of value; one had to realize that the individual was a vehicle of the universal energy.

It had therefore remained important to Dreiser to know what the character of this force was. Was it whimsical? Was it blind? Was it evil? Was man being used merely carelessly? Was he being lived "meaningly or meaninglessly"? [29] For many years Dreiser had implied that, whatever might be man's relation to the force, man was the victim of something that was very likely blind. Now, however, he had been led to change his mind. During the summer of 1937 he had spent three months at the Long Island Biological Association laboratories, peering at slides in search of the fundamental units of protoplasm. One afternoon, after several hours in the laboratory, he had come out into the sunshine and seen a cluster of little yellow flowers growing along the border of the path. Stooping to examine them, he had been fascinated to discover that, magnified in contrast to the microscopic objects he had just studied, they exhibited the same beautiful design and detail as he had been viewing all day. These flowers had seemed so unnecessarily beautiful there among the weeds that tears had come to his eyes, and for a moment he had felt that loving care must have been lavished upon every object in nature. The creative force was after all not blind but intelligent, he had decided,[30] although whether it was good or evil he had not then been prepared to say.

Feeling and believing thus, he had been almost ready in 1938 to complete work on *The Bulwark*. Its material was closer to his interests than it had ever been, with the principal character not only a religious man, but a Quaker, a man preoccupied with the inner light, the promptings and impulses of the all-pervasive, intelligent creative force. If his career was to be, as Dreiser had often said, a pathetic one,[31] it would nevertheless have to be the career of a positive character, more like the individuals in *Twelve Men* than like Hurstwood or Clyde Griffiths. But first the Spanish war and then the second World War had intervened and Dreiser had been unable until 1942 to concentrate on the writing, and then, having become dissatisfied with Simon & Schuster and having signed an agreement with Putnam's, who had advanced him a thousand dollars, he had found his life psychologically disturbed and the writing of his novel inhibited by the very philosophy that was essential to its success. At the time he wrote Mencken entrusting humanity to the creative force, his own creative impulse had seemed almost spent after barely a year of effort.

The psychological difficulty was, on the whole, embedded in his habits. In the crowded days of writing *Jennie Gerhardt*, the Cowperwood books, and *The "Genius"* he had carried on several projects at the same time; and in the years that had followed he had always been engaged in more than a single activity, as though the observation of life's color and variety had somehow had to have an analogue in the life of the observer. This distribution of interest had certainly characterized his relations with women, and his need for variety and the stimulus that youth could provide had persisted despite emotional difficulties and the passage of time. While throughout the days with George Sterling, the days in Russia, and the days of agitation, there had been Helen, devoted and loyal, there had also been other girls, who had come and gone as Dreiser had tired of them or had differed with their ideology, but who had satisfied his restless need. Now in 1943 there was the old newness again — and this time one of the women wanted to write moving-picture scripts with him, disturbing his creative mood and involving him in complications and resentments, ruses and inner turmoils, which destroyed concentration. Although he had recently written or rewritten some forty chapters of *The Bulwark* — later reduced to the first twenty-five — and although the middle portions of the novel had been completed, he found it difficult to continue. When Putnam's displayed little liking for the long introductory chapters that he viewed as still tentative but that they insisted on his showing them, he became discouraged and was convinced that his genius had left him. Shortly afterward he repaid the advances.

Philosophically, seeing a universal mind permeating all things, he was at the same time bound to find it difficult to write of particulars as though they possessed the ultimate importance that a novel gave them. He wrote an essay entitled "My Creator" testifying to the genius of a creative force that could design flowers as delicate as those he had seen on Long Island, trees as remarkable as the avocado behind his house, with its well-nigh miraculous cycle of blossoming, fruit-bearing, and renewed growth, and creatures as various as those to be found in all climates and conditions. Had a man created a little yellow flower, what an artistic genius he would have been considered!

And so [Dreiser wrote] . . . I am moved not only to awe but to reverence for the Creator . . . concerning whom — his or its presence in all things from worm to star to thought — I meditate constantly even though it be, as I see it, that my import to this, my Creator, can be but as nothing, or less, if that were possible.

Yet awe I have. And, at long last, profound reverence for so amazing and esthetic and wondrous a process, that may truly have been, and for all that I know, may yet continue to be forever and forever. An esthetic and wondrous process of which I might pray — and do — to remain the infinitesimal part of that same that I now am.[32]

As spectator he valued his role as participant in life, but as participant he could be only the spectator again. He had become concerned less with issues than with the order of issues, less with books than with the image of a world in which books could be written.[33] Amid the unsettling incidents of personal life, he impersonally contemplated life's manifestations, its processes, its creatures, not so much to observe the struggle of the weak against the strong, with pity for one or admiration for the other, but to view with religious awe the infinite variations of the procreant urge of the universe — to commit himself willfully to participate in the world, yet ever recognizing his limitations as human being, the fact that his will derived from his mortality and was itself something to be wondered at, both for its willfulness and for its helplessness. Thus at the very moment when he could feel himself a human being, a person with the power and drive to act, at that very moment he knew himself a mortal, with his powers and drives inherent in him and not initiated by him. He had become a kind of "transparent eyeball." If, then, he were to complete his book, the creative force must accomplish it, coursing through him creatively and "bursting through all current human limitations." But for the moment the psychological blocks interfered with the flow, and until these and the related discouragement were removed, the cause for further discouragement would linger.

The hope prerequisite to action grew out of the events of early 1944. In March the American Academy of Arts and Letters decided, largely at the instigation of some of its younger members, to confer upon Dreiser its Award of Merit, comprising a medal and one thousand dollars. Although nine years before, Dreiser had upon Mencken's sardonic advice and in keeping with his own aversion to commitments declined an invitation to become a member of the Academy's parent body, the National Institute of Arts and Letters, he agreed to go to New York to accept this award. No commitment was involved, and the money would certainly be useful, for except for *Sister Carrie* all his books had gone out of print, income from royalties had virtually ceased, and in New York he might make new publishing arrangements. In addition, he might arrange for the sale of the property in Mount Kisco, which he had deeded to Helen in 1933 and which she now insisted be sold to relieve the increasingly distracting financial pressure. When he arrived in the East for the Academy's ceremonial on May 19, he was consequently hopeful. Two months later he had decided to finish *The Bulwark*.

It was neither the Academy award nor conversations with publishers, however, that had transformed his hope into self-confidence. In fact, if his trip had been rewarded only by those events, he might justifiably have felt crushed. Desiring to deliver a brief speech of acceptance at the Academy, recommending that the august body consider the desirability of including a Secretary of the Arts in the presidential cabinet, he had been told it was too controversial and spoke only two or three sentences of thanks. Sitting through long and wearisome ceremonies, in the course of which S. S. McClure and Willa Cather had received awards, warmly and appreciatively presented by Arthur Train, he finally heard his own citation spoken by Professor Chauncey B. Tinker of Yale in words so carefully distinguishing him as a leader of the naturalistic school that it seemed as though the Academy were attempting to exonerate itself from all possible ideological sympathy with him and were giving him the award as leader of a school of writing whose historical importance could no longer respectably be ignored. Later, seated on the terrace for a reception and tea, where all other recipients were surrounded by well-wishers and Academy dignitaries, Dreiser found himself neglected. Although he had been invited to attend a dinner that evening, given by Walter Damrosch, president of the Academy, he decided he would be out of place and preferred to dine in private with Edgar Lee Masters. When Marguerite Tjader Harris, whom he had known since about 1929 and who was acting as his guide and secretary, phoned Damrosch to explain that Dreiser was tired, Damrosch merely replied through a maid that it would be all right — and Dreiser felt he had not been wanted in the first place. As to publishers, they called on him, shook his hand, smiled, and talked philosophy; but wary of an author who had quarreled with publishers before and uninterested in a novelist who seemed to prefer writing dubious philosophy to producing another novel, they avoided drawing up contracts, and Dreiser, wishing he could finish *The Bulwark*, insisted to friends that he was stuck and that he was no longer able to write novels. Quoting a remark of Kipling's to the effect that on a certain date his genius had deserted him, Dreiser said it was thus with him too.[34]

What sustained Dreiser was a form of recognition that enabled him to feel himself once again an effective member of society. Partially this came from friends who insisted that he still had something to say in the form of the novel and even that his philosophy logically demanded *The Bulwark*. But mostly it came out of the circumstances of the very war that had isolated him. The Office of War Information, indicating to him that his voice and name would carry conviction in Europe, asked him to make recordings for broadcast to occupied countries on D-day and to Germany as her borders were reached assuring the conquered that liberation was at hand and appealing to the Germans to purge themselves of their Nazi leaders. This proved the most satisfying work he did in New York.[35] Accepted once more as an international figure whose opinions had importance, and offered a continent for an audience, he spoke to the conquered peoples optimistically of the vigor, power, and promise of America [36] and, suggesting that the Germans assume democratic leadership in a world where the world's goods would be equitably distributed, urged: "Just as a try-out, let's have a few hundred years of the Brotherhood of Man!" [37] In the role of spokesman for equity once more, he was enabled to suggest an appropriate social embodiment of his concept of the creative force.

If his mood was becoming again affirmative, it was tinged with only the slightest rancor. Writing for *Soviet Russia Today* in commemoration of the third anniversary of the German offensive against Russia, he said very little about financial reactionaries, but in a restrained, hopeful tone denied their significance, for America and the rest of the world were "now gradually beginning to envision a society based on the needs of the individual, and of every individual." Everywhere responsible statesmen were assured of Russia's desire for peace and world stability. "The old slogans of revolution are outmoded in her steady advance over colossal obstacles toward a better society, the lessons and benefits of which she is willing to share with all." [38] Russia was still a lesson, if not a detailed model, but impassioned advocacy no longer seemed necessary. Commenting one day about the disbanding of the Communist International, he remarked that now the American party that he had always wanted would have to be formed; the Russians, he pointed out, had not modeled their government upon any foreign system. [39] Writing to Mme Chiang Kai-shek after he had spoken with her in California, he pressed her to see the value of "some social form of Government, — not necessarily Communism — but something near it, instead of our brand of Capitalism which, in so far as the totality of our people is concerned, is by no means a social success." If he recommended that China align herself with Russia, saying Stalin could be trusted, he also called Roosevelt, who had conferred with Stalin at Teheran, "one of the greatest Americans this country has produced." [40] After reading *One World* and the articles that later constituted *An American Program,* he wrote Wendell Willkie congratulating him for his courage "in bringing into the present political discussion the one great problem which now confronts the world . . . that is, the common man, as Vice-President Wallace has described him, and what is more, his right to share proportionately and justly in the age of plenty which is now

upon us." [41] Even clergymen were now sometimes coun-
tenanced, and when, during his visit in New York, Dreiser attended the funeral of his sister Mame, he found
the minister's service "beautiful" and declared that the
minister himself reminded him of Alyosha Karamazov.[42]

Whether it had been the O.W.I. broadcasts, the encouragement of friends, the stimulation of travel or of
old associations, or the actual sale of the Mount Kisco
property, Dreiser was by early summer in a frame of
mind conducive to resuming *The Bulwark*. Some of the
conversations in New York undoubtedly had had some
effect, for before leaving in June he had told Mrs. Harris
that if she would come west he might finish his work.
She provided, he had assured her, the creative sympathy
he needed for the task. Before the end of July both he
and Helen had urged her to make the trip. Before the
middle of August she had boarded the train. And a few
weeks later the writing was in progress once more. The
obstacles to the creative flow had at last been removed.

The task of completing the novel involved at first selection and excision. There were in existence three drafts
of many of the chapters, not all of them arranged in the
same order; some were in manuscript, some in typescript.
Many portions were repetitious, and two of the versions
— one containing extensive character studies of his pro-
tagonist Solon Barnes's children and the other dealing
with details of banking and financial chicanery in a manner reminiscent of *The Financier* — needed to be pared
to a brevity appropriate to the main theme of the novel.
Indeed, when Dreiser began to reread some of the material that he had shown Putnam's, he occasionally remarked on its clumsiness and the departure of his genius.
Yet, stimulated by the presence of a new feminine temperament and its sympathetic zeal, he persisted, gradually

feeling as he revised old chapters and wrote or dictated new ones that the strange and intangible forces which, according to him, were responsible for his inspiration and work were coursing through him again to do the writing and the dictating. In fact, during the period of completing the book, from fall into spring, he was never more conscious of the creative force. He sometimes refused to plan a day ahead, merely waiting to be moved by this power. Frequently, after finishing several paragraphs, he wandered out on the patio of Mrs. Harris's cottage and gazed at the rolling hills or stooped to examine the roses and geraniums near by, finding a kind of refreshment in the contact with nature. When a certain bluebird repeatedly came and perched near him, Dreiser remarked: "He knows me," and noted the bird was not afraid.[43]

The friendliness of the little bird was symbolic of Dreiser's feeling, for he felt that the unity of the creative force must be good and that there was involved with it a kind of love. The puff adder had understood when he had spoken to it; the little flowers had seemed the product of loving care; the little bird was unafraid and came so often — now and then on Sundays Dreiser even went to church, not always the same church, but some church, whether Christian Science or Congregational, and on occasion took Communion, including Good Friday 1945, when the service left him, in at least the eyes of Mrs. Harris, deeply moved.[44] As during these months he felt his oneness with nature and the love that grew from wonder and awe, he remembered his father and his father's wayward and rebellious children, and he thought that perhaps at last he knew and understood his father's real character. The Solon Barnes who might once have been a harsh portrayal of his father, or even a gently ironic one, now became his father lovingly transformed into the embodiment of Dreiser's own feeling of affection. Dreiser even spoke of dedicating the book to the man he had thus transformed.[45]

Despite this spiritual harmony, however, a harmony necessary to the sympathetic completion of the book, there were inevitable difficulties. Dreiser was physically tired and at times restless. There were days when the words did not come so easily, days when the temperamental stimulation he sought required of others tensions greater than they could maintain; and there were even days of inevitable mental exhaustion when memory or recognition lapsed. Yet even these events contributed to the book, for he was prompted to draw upon some of them to portray Solon Barnes's age and decline; and early in May the story was done.

Although this marked the conclusion of Dreiser's work on the book and he, with Helen, Mrs. Harris, and some friends, was able to take a brief vacation in Mexico, the book itself was not in final form.[46] A typescript was shipped to Philadelphia, where Louise Campbell, who had helped edit *An American Tragedy*, read it and wrote that it marked a decline in Dreiser's work and ought not be printed as it stood. Dreiser, for the moment disheartened after his struggle to write it, thereupon decided to ask James T. Farrell to read it. Farrell, after exchanging views with Mrs. Campbell, then outlined for Dreiser what he thought might be done by way of revision, suggesting that certain characters be objectified rather than described or asserted, but on the whole defending the pace, style, structure, and subject. Thus assured, Dreiser forwarded Farrell's suggestions to Donald B. Elder, associate editor of Doubleday & Company, with whom Dreiser had finally made a contract, and at the same time asked Mrs. Campbell to propose revisions and send them to Elder also. It then became Elder's task to construct the final draft from all these suggestions, which he did after discarding many of Mrs. Campbell's alterations. If reviewers subsequently found some inconsistencies in details, some sketchiness in development, some anachronisms, it was little wonder. When Mrs. Harris had arrived in Hollywood, Dreiser had shifted the time of his story a generation later than it had originally been, in order that in verifying certain details she might provide help from her own experience. This inevitably meant that some older sections of the manuscript would have to be carefully checked. In the complications of editing that followed, however, oversights were hardly to be avoided.

Whatever Mrs. Campbell may actually have felt, *The Bulwark* was the logical æsthetic embodiment of Dreiser's philosophic beliefs. Its subject is the spiritual odyssey of Solon Barnes, a Quaker who progresses from a point of view that interprets the Book of Discipline with an orthodox and determined severity to a point of view that enables him to assert tolerance and love for all created things. At the beginning he merely accepts life and the code of the sect. At the end he questions and, questioning, finds the very life of life revealed. In fact, at the end, following a series of shocks beginning with the arrest of his son Stewart for complicity in a girl's death and culminating with the collapse and death of his wife after Stewart's suicide, Solon undergoes a change in character that transforms him into a person whose attitude clearly reflects Dreiser's own. Having always merely taken for granted the meaning of the Quaker faith, never considering the wonder of creation or the possible insignificance of man, he now concludes that he has not lived sufficiently for the things of the spirit. He has long held a position in a bank, but now he resigns it, believing that he has contributed to a materialistic spirit whose manifestations were the basic causes of his boy's catastrophe. Moreover, he argues that banking should not be conducted for the benefit of a few. Instead of losing faith he now gains a stronger one. He becomes calm and reverent; he notes the beauty of vines and flowers; he talks to a snake that crawls toward him with seeming understanding; he becomes aware of the artistry of the creative force, of design in nature, of a universal mind that expresses itself through variety, beauty, and tragedy. He speaks of "the need of love toward all created things." [47] As he becomes old, weak, and ill, his daughter Etta reads to him from John Woolman's *Journal*, and both he and Etta are deeply stirred by a passage in which Woolman recounts a dream concerning the "death of my own will," [48] disclosing that all men are part of a great whole and not autonomous and unrelated. Eventually Solon transmits to Etta so great a measure of his feeling of love that she is able to overcome all personal disappointments over failure in her own affairs.

In this love and unity with all nature, as she now sensed, there was nothing fitful or changing or disappointing — nothing that glowed one minute and was gone the next. This love was rather as constant as nature itself, everywhere the same, in sunshine or in darkness, the filtered splendor of the dawn, the seeded beauty of the night. It was an intimate relation to the very heart of being.[49]

At the very last, reflecting upon her love-seeking youth, her original failure to understand her father's ideals, her share in all the disasters that had ensued, Etta sobs and, when her brother Orville reproves her, explains: "Oh, I am not crying for myself, or for Father — I am crying for *life*." [50]

That was all one really could do. One had to cry for life, that it produced triumph in defeat, victory in death, beauty amid terror and tragedy. Before infinity one had surely to verge on hysteria. Before the eternal one had to weep in order to crumble in awe of limitation. For to see oneself in one's true relations was to see oneself as both infinite and infinitesimal. It was arrogance for a person to think of himself as a being apart, as a special kind of divine delegate to the universe. Human beings had no absolute distinctness, no distinction in themselves. They were not really individuals at all. Solon, instead of learning to love his family more and the universe less — as the logic of his experience might have dictated — comes to experience a love that transcends all private feelings. Yet if he is therefore less of an individual, he is at the same time more of a being. *Apart from* nature a man and his will were perhaps meaningless; but as *a part of* nature he and his will were tinctured by the æsthetic color and swept up in the universal grandeur of the vast and amazing scheme before the idea of which one could only stand in reverent gratefulness for being alive.[51]

What Dreiser understood this point of view to imply in the realm of society was evident from two pieces he wrote while writing *The Bulwark*. In one, an essay entitled "Interdependence," he urged men to understand one another, not as masses of people, but as nations of individuals, who were to be known as individuals and yet understood because of the great principle and divinity uniting all men. "For to know and to understand," he wrote, "is to love, not to hate." [52] In the second piece, a poem entitled "What To Do," he reflected:

Storm
Storm
Storm

The Creative Force

War
Want
Misery.

And each asking of the other what to do
And so
Groups
Committees
Government.

In the meantime one
A small-town editor writes the truth about profit and
   starvation.

And one knocks at a broken door and when it opens
   hands in a loaf of bread.

And one, step by step, all day long, walks to this laborer
   and that saying united we stand, divided we fall.

And one, the workers' friend, says Vote, Speak, for you
   are the Government, By you your leaders rise or fall.

And one, the educator, says to the child, A.B.C. and to
   the adult, Learn! Know that the world grows
   smaller!

And one, the minister, says to all, Love thy neighbor as
   thyself.

And one, the lover of his fellow man says Take, from
   each according to his ability; Give, to each according to his need.

And so from the heart comes the answer
Of him who does and serves

That by degrees,
A new and better world
May be made.[53]

This was the direction men should follow. As Dreiser thought over his own life, he felt he was now atoning for what seemed like irreverent attacks on God. *The Bulwark* was a kind of tribute to the creative force. "It's funny," he remarked on one occasion after he had completed the book, "how a fellow can go along for years and not get it. . . . And when it's there all the time." [54]

In this frame of mind he found it difficult to undertake another task he had set for himself — the completion of *The Stoic*. He felt he must do it now because he had not much time left,[55] and he gave the appearance of clinging determinedly to life in order to finish the trilogy. After the mood and tone of *The Bulwark* the harsher realities of Cowperwood's career provided resistance. Yet he now knew that the ending would go beyond his original plan, beyond the reflection that all was vanity and that wealth was, at the last, only the tombstone in the cemetery. It would now bring forth a redeeming aspect, something to excuse Cowperwood; it would emphasize his search for beauty and enable Berenice, through immersion in the lore of Yoga, to perceive the meaning in all that had occurred. And thus he proceeded and on December 3 sent Farrell the nearly completed book. He had another chapter and a half to add, but was at the moment too exhausted to add it — a psychological study of Berenice — but his epilogue was there, an essay on good and evil and the eternal balance of things, every aspect of which manifested the creative force in its wonderful performance.[56] Later, shortly before his death, he attempted to complete it, and even worked on it the night he died, but he never successfully resolved the issues, for *The Stoic* had ceased to be the story of Cowperwood and had become the story of Berenice's spiritual awakening, a story scarcely told or completed by her study of Indian philosophy and her founding of a children's hospital in memory of her lover.

Dreiser's own story, however, was appropriately concluded. While he was writing *The Stoic* and was conscious of the numbered days, he thought at times of the fact that after he died he would no longer be able to speak out in behalf of any cause and he felt a need to make a final gesture, something that might help promote equity and love even after his death. His books would embody his advocacy of his spiritual cause, but what would remain of his social view — his long and independent struggle to promote the cause of equity? Two book-length polemics and some leaflets? He discussed the matter with John Howard Lawson and others who were either enrolled or interested in the Communist Party and who hoped Dreiser would formally commit himself to its program. They were now able to point out to him that the party leadership in the United States was undergoing a change. Earl Browder, whom Dreiser regarded as something of a bookworm, was being ousted in favor of William Z. Foster, whom Dreiser had known for many years as a kind of saint, a man of sweet disposition. They could also point out that distinguished European scientists and artists were members, and could suggest that the values he found expressed in the Soviet program could be perpetuated only through the Communist Party. And Dreiser desired to be convinced. Unconcerned with details of policy, factionalism, party bickerings, he regarded adherence to dogma as a trivial detail in the face of the theoretical end of social reform and international unity, the end of the social and political embodiment of the form of nature. Convinced of the spiritual value to mankind of the Russian social program, motivated by a religious rather than by a political belief, he agreed to apply for membership in the party. Some of the party members drew up the letter and he, after some comments and slight revisions, signed it.[57]

If critics complained that Dreiser's act was essentially irresponsible, that general programs were meaningless apart from the details that Dreiser found irrelevant, these critics overlooked the fact that Dreiser was simply making a gesture in behalf of the creative force and its total world. And if these critics also insisted that Dreiser had now denied the kind of individuality he was seeking to affirm, they failed to realize that Dreiser did not think so — that perhaps his disregard of details involved also a different reading of slogans. Not many weeks after his joining he was asked whether he intended to submit to party discipline or whether he was still going to disagree and criticize publicly if he wished. He replied that he would say what he pleased whenever he pleased, and that if the party did not like that, they could throw him out. He did not care. He was interested only in their objective, which seemed to him selfless in a way that proved of greatest advantage to the greatest number of selves. Stalin was a truly spiritual person, he explained; he had wept at Lenin's funeral. So was Foster. The principles of communism were, as the Dean of Canterbury had explained, like the principles of Christ. "What the world needs is more spiritual character," Dreiser said. Then he added: "The true religion is in Matthew." [58]

As Dreiser's days ran out, the last events, objectively regarded, acquired a symbolic quality, tinged with pathos and irony. When Dreiser had consented to let Donald

Elder revise *The Bulwark* along the lines Elder wished, he had also agreed with Marguerite Harris that she should check over the galley proofs with him and make whatever final changes were necessary at that time. But in the months that had followed, emotional difficulties had developed, for not every woman whom Dreiser found stimulating would readily relinquish her role to another. When the proofs finally arrived in December, a distressing feminine quarrel ensued as Dreiser stood by, appalled and helpless, almost unable to speak; and the consequence was that the proofs were checked by Dreiser and Helen at home and returned to Elder on December 22 with scarcely a correction. It was ironical that this restrained tale of peace and resolution and death should have been baptized in a quarrel between women, and it was perhaps fitting, too, for it represented elements of contradiction and consequences of a personal irresponsibility from out of the long past — as though all of his life were somehow to be concentrated in a moment's drama before his eyes.

His death came late in the afternoon of December 28, 1945. It began with his suffering a slight pain in his kidney shortly before midnight of the 27th. A second, severe attack came a few hours later. Placed under an oxygen tent during the morning, he temporarily recovered, but apparently sensed the end was at hand, for though the doctor later told him he was much better, he wanted Helen to remain by him. Then, just before his breathing became more shallow he asked her to kiss him. In a little while he was dead.[59]

The funeral services gave finality to the symbolism. John Howard Lawson spoke about Dreiser's social conscience and faith in human dignity; Charles Chaplin, long a friend of Dreiser's, read "The Road I Came" from

Moods, a tribute to the marvelous mystery of the creative power; and Dr. Allan A. Hunter, a Congregational minister to whom Mrs. Harris had introduced Dreiser and whom Dreiser liked, presided and talked of Dreiser's compassion and the spiritual lesson of *The Bulwark.*[60] In those moments the divergent thoughts and attitudes were united in harmony.

On February 1 Dreiser's will was filed for probate. It was the last gesture. After leaving his entire estate to Helen, he requested that upon her death she should bequeath whatever did not go to designated relatives to some home for Negro orphans.[61]

"Oh, what is this / That knows the road I came?" Charles Chaplin had read.

The road had been a long one, but Dreiser was at last one with the forces that he had so persistently scrutinized. It might, however, have been even more appropriate to have read: "*Wass ich hab, nehm ab; wass ich thu, nehm zu!*" for Dreiser had finally crossed the street.

The Documentation

The citations which follow are primarily for reference. Such textual matter as appears is restricted to brief comments about a few sources.

All letters — indicated below by the form "Dreiser to H. L. Mencken, May 13, 1916" — and all manuscripts, typescripts, and unpublished documents are, except where otherwise noted, among the Dreiser papers in the Library of the University of Pennsylvania in Philadelphia. No attempt has been made in these notes to distinguish originals from photostatic, microfilm, or carbon copies.

All leaflets, except where otherwise noted, are in Cornell University's Dreiser collection; my notes on conversations and lectures are still in my own possession.

Among the periodicals, newspapers are, with very few exceptions, cited simply by title, date, and either location or page. When I have relied upon newspaper and magazine clippings such as those among the Dreiser papers at the University of Pennsylvania, I have indicated the library or collection in which the clipping may be found; otherwise I have given the page of the newspaper, and in the case of magazines the volume number as well. Unsigned newspaper articles ascribed to Dreiser are articles designated as his own either among his papers or in *Newspaper Days*.

Throughout the first four chapters I have depended to a considerable extent upon the facts and chronology in Dreiser's admittedly autobiographical books — *Dawn*, *A Hoosier Holiday*, and *Newspaper Days*. There are, however, specific references only where I have quoted, transcribed, or intentionally embodied in my text phrases that are Dreiser's. I have depended upon the original manuscripts of those three works for the actual names of persons that Dreiser felt the need of disguising during his lifetime, and upon the manuscripts of *Newspaper Days* and *The "Genius"* for evidence of the extent to which I might consider *The "Genius"* autobiographical.

I wish to acknowledge here my indebtedness to Dorothy Dudley's *Forgotten Frontiers,* not only the first extended study of Dreiser's life, but also the first based on an examination of some of the original documents among the Dreiser papers. Dorothy Dudley had the opportunity to confer with Dreiser throughout the course of her work and was able to quote him many times. No biographer of Dreiser can afford to neglect her contribution or fail to be stimulated by her observations. On a number of occasions I have, by an independent process, come to share her conclusions; but wherever she is responsible for my views, I have directed the reader to her book.

Throughout the notes the following abbreviations are used:

Hanley: a collection of Dreiser's letters to George Douglas, originally owned by Mr. T. E. Hanley of Bradford, Pennsylvania; now at the University of Texas.

HD: the collection of materials in Mrs. Dreiser's possession when I consulted them. These items have become, either in their original state or in microfilm copies, part of the University of Pennsylvania's collection.

Pratt: bound uncorrected page-proofs of *A Traveler at Forty* in which letters and postcards from Dreiser to H. L. Mencken are inserted at appropriate pages; shelved in the Enoch Pratt Free Library, Baltimore.

RHE: originally my collection; now Cornell's.

UP: the Dreiser papers, University of Pennsylvania library.

Notes

I

1. Theodore Dreiser: *Dawn* (New York: Horace Liveright; cop. 1931), pp. 6–8. See also Mary Frances Brennan to A. R. Markle, January 13, 1941 (RHE).
2. Markle to Robert H. Elias, July 19, 1946 (RHE).
3. Baptismal record, Church of St. Benedict, September 10, 1871.
4. Dreiser: *Dawn*, p. 8. See also Brennan to Markle, May 26, 1941 (RHE).
5. Carmel O'Neill Haley: "The Dreisers," *Commonweal*, XVIII (July 7, 1933), 267.
6. Evelyn Mary Richey to Dreiser, August 5, 1935; Edward M. Dreiser, conversation with Elias, December 27, 1944.
7. Edward M. Dreiser, loc. cit.
8. Dreiser: *Dawn*, p. 19.
9. Extract from pamphlet, "In the Year of 1850 in the Village of Connersville," Connersville, Indiana, 1922 (copy by A. R. Markle: RHE).
10. A. R. Markle: "Some Light on Paul Dresser; His Anniversary Is This Month," *Terre Haute Sunday Tribune and Terre Haute Sunday Star*, April 14, 1941, p. 10.
11. Brennan to Markle, January 13, 1941 (RHE); *History of Greene and Sullivan Counties* (Chicago: Goodspeed Bros.; 1884), p. 613, and Deed Records, XXXII, 145, XXXIII, 7 (cited in Markle to Elias, November 21, 1946, and July 19, 1947: RHE); advertisement, *Sullivan Democrat*, July 7, 1870 (photostat: RHE).
12. Dreiser: *Dawn*, p. 5; Markle to Elias, November 22, 1946 (RHE).
13. Brennan to Markle, January 13, 1941 (RHE); Dreiser: *Dawn*, p. 5.
14. Markle: "Some Light on Paul Dresser"; Brennan to Markle, January 13, 1941 (RHE).
15. Edward M. Dreiser, loc. cit.

[16] Logan Esarey: *A History of Indiana from 1850 to 1920* (3rd ed., 2 vols.; Fort Wayne, Indiana: Hoosier Press; 1924), II, 870–1, 990–4.

[17] Theodore Dreiser: *A Hoosier Holiday* (New York: John Lane; 1916), p. 405; Dreiser: *Dawn*, p. 21.

[18] See Dixon Wecter: *The Saga of American Society* (New York: Scribner's; 1937), pp. 178–9.

[19] Dreiser: *Dawn*, p. 142.

[20] Ibid., p. 4. See also Brennan to Markle, January 13, 1941 (RHE).

[21] Dreiser: *Dawn*, pp. 227–8.

[22] Dreiser: *Dawn* MS., ch. vi, [p. 13].

[23] Dreiser: *Dawn*, pp. 130–1; Dreiser: *A Hoosier Holiday*, p. 461.

[24] Dreiser: *Dawn* MS., chs. xxx–xxxi, xxxiv–xxxv, xli–xliv; George Steinbrecher, Jr.: "Inaccurate Accounts of *Sister Carrie*," *American Literature*, XXIII (January 1952), 490–3.

[25] Dreiser: *Dawn*, pp. 193, 194; Dreiser: *A Hoosier Holiday*, p. 318.

[26] Dorothy Dudley: *Forgotten Frontiers, Dreiser and the Land of the Free* (New York: Smith & Haas; 1932), pp. 52–3.

[27] Christian Aaberg to Dreiser, October 19, 1921.

[28] Transcript of record, 1889–90, Indiana University (RHE).

II

[1] Theodore Dreiser: *Newspaper Days* (New York: Horace Liveright; cop. 1931), p. 15.

[2] Ibid., p. 59. See also John Maxwell to Dreiser, August 5, 1922, and Maxwell to Boni & Liveright, September 3, 1922.

[3] Dreiser: *Newspaper Days*, p. 70.

[4] Dreiser: *Dawn* MS., ch. cix, [pp. 11–12].

[5] Dreiser: *Newspaper Days*, p. 59.

[6] Ibid., p. 67.

[7] Ibid., p. 74–5.

[8] "Fakes," *Chicago Daily Globe*, October 25, 1892, p. 1. See

also Dreiser: *Newspaper Days*, pp. 76–81.
9 Carl Dreiser: "The Return of Genius," *Chicago Daily Globe*, October 23, 1892, p. 4.

III

1 Dreiser: *Newspaper Days*, p. 136.
2 Ibid., p. 129.
3 *St. Louis Globe-Democrat*, February 18, 1893, p. 5.
4 Dreiser to D. P. McCord, April 14, 1936. See also "Peter" in Theodore Dreiser: *Twelve Men* (New York: Boni & Liveright; 1919).
5 "Theosophy and Spiritualism," *St. Louis Globe-Democrat*, January 20, 1893, p. 12.
6 "Almost a Riot," *St. Louis Republic*, August 11, 1893, pp. 1–2. See also Dreiser: *Newspaper Days*, pp. 268–9.
7 Dreiser: *Newspaper Days*, pp. 222–8; Theodore Dreiser: "Mathewson," *Esquire*, I (May 1934), 20–1, 125, II (June 1934), 24–5, 114; Theodore Dreiser: "Lessons I Learned from an Old Man," *Your Life*, II (January 1938), 6–10.
8 "Water Works Extension," *St. Louis Globe-Democrat*, January 15, 1893, p. 31.
9 "Burned to Death," *St. Louis Globe-Democrat*, January 22, 1893, pp. 1, 2; "Sixteen Dead," ibid., January 23, 1893, p. 10; Dreiser: *Newspaper Days*, pp. 156–68; Arch T. Edmonston to Dreiser, September 27, 1929.
10 *St. Louis Globe-Democrat*, February 27, 1893, p. 10.
11 Ibid., March 6, 1893, p. 3.
12 Ibid., April 13, 1893, p. 3.
13 Ibid., March 26, 1893, p. 7.
14 "The Black Diva's Concert," ibid., April 1, 1893, p. 8. I am unable to confirm Dreiser's story (*Newspaper Days*, pp. 185–8) that other St. Louis papers commented on this article, although editors may have spoken of it.
15 Dreiser: *Newspaper Days*, pp. 179–82; Dreiser to H. L. Mencken, May 13, 1916.

[16] Dreiser: *Newspaper Days,* p. 194.

[17] Ibid., pp. 200–3; confirmed by Edward M. Dreiser (loc. cit.), who remembered hearing of the incident when it happened; but I am unable to find support for Dreiser's assertion that three plays were to open at the time of the washouts or that other papers commented editorially.

[18] Dreiser: *Newspaper Days,* p. 211.

[19] E.g., "No More Monkeying," *St. Louis Republic,* July 1, 1893 (UP); "Portentous Pointers," July 14, 1893, p. 7; "A Presage of Disaster," July 15, 1893, p. 11; "Monday the Day," July 16, 1893, p. 2; "The Great Game To-day," July 17, 1893, p. 2. See also "Pictures from Real Life," July 16, 1893, p. 24.

[20] Ibid., May 28, 1893, p. 4.

[21] UP.

[22] "Election of Officers," *St. Louis Republic,* September 5, 1893, p. 3.

[23] "Fighting Now the Fad," ibid., January 22, 1894, p. 3.

[24] E.g., "Bloodshed May Result," ibid., December 30, 1893, p. 5; "Miltenberger's Scheme," December 31, 1893, p. 8; "That Football Fracas," January 2, 1894, p. 8; "Charity Teams Chosen," January 4, 1894, p. 5; "Armed for the Battle," January 5, 1894, p. 2.

[25] "A Cosmopolitan Camp," ibid., December 17, 1893, pp. 30–1.

[26] Dreiser: *Newspaper Days,* pp. 286–306, and "Nigger Jeff" and "A Story of Stories" in Theodore Dreiser: *Free and Other Stories* (New York: Boni & Liveright; 1918).

[27] "Gallagher," *St. Louis Republic,* August 6, 1893, p. 9.

[28] Dreiser: *Free,* p. 111.

[29] Dreiser: *Newspaper Days* MS., passim.

[30] Dreiser: *Newspaper Days,* pp. 328–9; William C. Lengel: "The 'Genius' Himself," *Esquire,* X (September 1938), 120.

[31] Dreiser: *Newspaper Days,* p. 343.

[32] Ibid., pp. 354–7; Dreiser: *A Hoosier Holiday,* pp. 247–8.

See also J. T. Hutchinson to Dreiser, December 18, 1896, and January 21, 1913.

[33] Charles W. Knapp, March 2, 1894; also April 2, 1894.

IV

[1] Dreiser: *Newspaper Days*, p. 367.

[2] For facts concerning Arthur Henry I am indebted to Mrs. Maude Wood Henry of Toledo, letters to me, March 12, 1945 ff. (RHE).

[3] See in the *Toledo Blade*: "A Garbled Report," March 20, 1894, pp. 1, 7; "Work of Vengeance," March 21, 1894, p. 1; "Strikers Arrested," March 22, 1894, p. 1; "Brown Fell Dead," March 23, 1894, pp. 1, 7.

[4] "The Strike Today," ibid., March 24, 1894, p. 1.

[5] Ibid. (subhead: "No Union Men"), p. 6.

[6] "As If in Old Toledo," ibid., March 28, 1894, p. 7.

[7] Dudley: *Forgotten Frontiers*, p. 104.

[8] Dreiser: *Newspaper Days* MS., ch. lii, [pp. 1–2].

[9] Dreiser: *Newspaper Days*, p. 405.

[10] Ibid., pp. 407–8.

[11] Dreiser: *Newspaper Days* MS., ch. lx, [pp. 29–30].

[12] Honoré de Balzac: *The Wild Ass's Skin* (New York: P. F. Collier; 1900), p. 269.

[13] The following all appear from their style to be by Dreiser, and those preceded by an asterisk (*) are either filed among his papers at the University of Pennsylvania or referred to specifically in *Newspaper Days* as having been written for the *Pittsburgh Dispatch*: "Dying Lips Failed," May 5, 1894, p. 2; * "Hospital Violet Day," May 12, 1894, p. 2; * "And It Was Mighty Blue," May 15, 1894, p. 2; * "After the Rain Storm," May 19, 1894, p. 2; "A Tale about Two Cats," May 20, 1894, p. 2; "Funny Man's Gala Day," May 23, 1894, p. 2; "The Weather Man's Woes," May 31, 1894, p. 2; "A Novelty of Its Kind," June 8, 1894, p. 3; "Wheels Went Round,"

June 13, 1894, p. 2; "Some of Baby's Spheres," June 17, 1894, p. 2; "A Midsummer Mania," June 25, 1894, p. 2; "Along the River Shore," July 2, 1894, p. 9; * "Soldiers of Morganza," July 5, 1894 (UP); * "Reapers in the Fields," July 6, 1894, p. 2; * "Odd Scraps of Melody," July 7, 1894 (UP); "This Girl Is a Puzzle," July 11, 1894, p. 3; "The Spirit of the Spire," July 13, 1894, p. 3; "See the Graphomaniac," July 14, 1894, p. 3; "All Sides of the Story," July 15, 1894, p. 14; "Patrons of the Springs," July 16, 1894, p. 3; "Views the Passing Show," July 17, 1894, p. 3; "In Old Hancock Street," July 18, 1894, p. 3; * "Fenced off the Earth," July 19, 1894, p. 3; "The Cat Became Woolly," July 20, 1894, p. 3; "Science Is Amazed" and "With the Nameless Dead," July 23, 1894, p. 3; "It Was Hoax All Around," July 27, 1894, p. 3; "Confound the Mosquito," July 28, 1894, p. 3; "Sleep during Hot Nights," July 31, 1894, p. 3; "This Settles the Japs," August 1, 1894, p. 3; "Woes of Dog Catchers," August 2, 1894, p. 3; "Isobars and Isotherms," August 3, 1894, p. 3; "Spoiled by a Meek Cow," August 6, 1894, p. 3; "Relics of a Bygone Age," August 7, 1894, p. 3; "Midsummer's Day Dream," August 9, 1894, p. 3; * "Some Dabbling in Books," August 14, 1894, p. 3; "Here's to the Sadder Men," August 16, 1894, p. 3; * "Snap Shots at Pleasure," August 18, 1894, p. 3; "Now the Pill Doctrine," August 20, 1894, p. 3; "Survival of the Unfittest," August 24, 1894, p. 3; * "Where Sympathy Failed," August 25, 1894 (UP); * "Our Fleeting Shekels," August 26, 1894, p. 2; * "General Booth Says Farewell," November 12, 1894, pp. 1–2.

[14] "With the Nameless Dead," *Pittsburgh Dispatch,* July 23, 1894, p. 3.

[15] Ibid.

[16] "Isobars and Isotherms," ibid., August 3, 1894, p. 3.

[17] Dreiser: *Newspaper Days,* p. 449.

[18] Herbert Spencer: *First Principles* (New York: Appleton; 1900), pp. 86–7.

[19] Dreiser: *Newspaper Days*, p. 457.

[20] Ibid., p. 463.

[21] Ibid., p. 472.

[22] Theodore Dreiser: "Mark Twain: Three Contacts," *Esquire*, IV (October 1935), 22, 162. I am indebted to Mr. Bernard DeVoto (letter to me, August 11, 1946: RHE) and to Mrs. N. P. Breed of the Mark Twain Papers at Harvard (letter to me, August 19, 1946: RHE) for enabling me to evaluate the reliability of Dreiser's account.

[23] Dreiser: *Newspaper Days* MS., ch. lxxv, [pp. 14 ff.].

[24] Dreiser: *Newspaper Days*, p. 501.

V

[1] I am indebted to Mr. John F. Huth, Jr., of Cleveland, for the opportunity to examine copies of *Ev'ry Month*. Other sources for the discussion of Dreiser's editorship are: John F. Huth, Jr.: "Theodore Dreiser: 'The Prophet,'" *American Literature*, IX (May 1937), 208–17; Dudley: *Forgotten Frontiers*, p. 141; Dreiser, lecture at Columbia University, November 9, 1938 (notes by Elias); Dreiser, conversation with Elias, June 3, 1944; Dreiser to Elias, August 28, 1944 (RHE).

[2] Dreiser, lecture at Columbia, November 9, 1938.

[3] "Reflections," *Ev'ry Month*, II (September 1896), 2–7.

[4] Ibid., p. 7.

[5] Ibid., III (November 1896), 2, quoted by Huth, op. cit., pp. 212–13.

[6] *Ev'ry Month*, II (September 1896), 7.

[7] Ibid., IV (May 1897), 21.

[8] Ibid., II (September 1896), 3.

[9] Ibid., pp. 22, 23.

[10] Arthur Henry: *Lodgings in Town* (New York: Barnes; 1905), pp. 82–3.

[11] Dreiser to Arthur Henry, May 20, 1897 (RHE).

[12] Dreiser, lecture at Columbia, November 9, 1938.

13 *Morning Telegraph* (New York), December 28, 1919 (UP); Dreiser: *Twelve Men*, pp. 100–1.

14 Dreiser to Elias, April 17, 1937 (RHE); Dudley: *Forgotten Frontiers*, p. 144.

15 Dreiser, conversations with Elias, summer 1941, and September 10, 1945.

16 Richard Duffy, conversation with Elias, November 23, 1944.

17 E. C. Martin: "The Literary Outlook," galley proof of column for McClure Syndicate, August 7, 1898 (UP).

18 Dudley: *Forgotten Frontiers*, p. 147.

19 Clerk's Office (U.S. Courthouse, Washington, D.C.) to Elias, July 1945 (RHE).

20 See also Cyrille Arnavon: "Theodore Dreiser and Painting," *American Literature*, XVII (May 1945), 116.

21 Theodore Dreiser: "Benjamin Eggleston, Painter," *Ainslee's Magazine*, I (April 1898), 45, cited by Arnavon, op. cit., p. 116.

22 Theodore Dreisser [*sic*]: "Art Work of Irving R. Wiles," *Metropolitan Magazine*, VII (April 1898), 359.

23 Theodore Dreiser: "A Painter of Travels," *Ainslee's Magazine*, I (June 1898), 398.

24 Theodore Dreiser: "A Great American Caricaturist," ibid., I (May 1898), 336.

25 Theodore Dreiser: "The Harp," *Cosmopolitan*, XXIV (April 1898), 637.

26 Theodore Dreiser: "Historic Tarrytown," *Ainslee's Magazine*, I (March 1898), 26–8, 31. See also Theodore Dreiser: "On the Field of Brandywine," *Truth*, XVI (November 6, 1897), 10, expanded as "Brandywine the Picturesque, After One Hundred and Twenty Years," *Demorest's Family Magazine*, XXXIV (September 1898), 275.

27 Theodore Dreiser: "The Harlem River Speedway," *Ainslee's Magazine*, II (August 1898), 49, 56. See also Theodore Dreiser: "The Haunts of Bayard Taylor," *Munsey's Magazine*, XVIII (January 1898), 594–7, and "The

Home of William Cullen Bryant," *Munsey's Magazine,* XXI (May 1899), 240.

[28] Theodore Dreiser: "John Burroughs in His Mountain Hut," *New Voice,* XVI (August 19, 1899), 7.

[29] Theodore Dreiser: "Carrier Pigeons in War Time," *Demorest's Family Magazine,* XXXIV (July 1898), 223.

[30] Theodore Dreiser: "The Descent of the Horse," *Everybody's Magazine,* II (June 1900), 543.

[31] Theodore Dreiser: "Life Stories of Successful Men — No. 10," *Success,* I (October 1898), 3.

[32] Theodore Dreiser: "Life Stories of Successful Men — No. 12," ibid., II (December 8, 1898), 7.

[33] Theodore Dreiser: "He Became Famous in a Day," ibid., II (January 28, 1899), 143.

[34] Theodore Dreiser: "It Pays to Treat Workers Generously," ibid., II (September 16, 1899), 691–2.

[35] Theodore Dreiser: "Curious Shifts of the Poor," *Demorest's Family Magazine,* XXXVI (November 1899), 26.

[36] Theodore Dreiser: "The Log of an Ocean Pilot," *Ainslee's Magazine,* III (July 1899), 692.

[37] Theodore Dreiser: "The Transmigration of the Sweat Shop," *Puritan,* VIII (July 1900), 498–502. See also Theodore Dreiser: "Little Clubmen of the Tenements," *Puritan,* VII (February 1900), 665–72.

[38] Theodore Dreiser: "The Railroad and the People," *Harper's Monthly Magazine,* C (February 1900), 479–80.

[39] Theodore Dreiser: "Fruit Growing in America," ibid., CI (November 1900), 868. See also Theodore Dreiser: "Great Problems of Organization. III. The Chicago Packing Industry," *Cosmopolitan,* XXV (October 1898), 615; Theodore Dreiser: "The Chicago Drainage Canal," *Ainslee's Magazine,* III (February 1899), 53; Theodore Dreiser: "The Trade of the Mississippi," *Ainslee's Magazine,* IV (January 1900), 735–43.

[40] Theodore Dreiser: "With Whom Is Shadow of Turning," *Demorest's Family Magazine,* XXXIV (June 1898),

189, and "Through All Adversity," *Demorest's Family Magazine*, XXXIV (November 1898), 334.

⁴¹ Theodore Dreiser: "The Real Zangwill," *Ainslee's Magazine*, II (November 1898), 357.

VI

¹ For the details of Dreiser's life at the House of Four Pillars I am indebted to Mrs. Maude Wood Henry (letters to me, March 12, 1945 ff.: RHE). See also Joe Collier: "Homes With A History," *Toledo News-Bee*, October 27, 1930 (photostat: RHE).

² Richard Duffy: "When They Were Twenty-One," *Bookman*, XXXVIII (January 1914), 524–5.

³ Dreiser: *Free*, pp. 54–75.

⁴ Dreiser to Mencken, May 13, 1916. I have been unable to locate or identify "The World and the Bubble."

⁵ The account of the writing of *Sister Carrie* is based largely upon the following statements by Dreiser himself: Dreiser to Mencken, May 13, 1916, and February 20, 1920; "Rona Murtha" in Theodore Dreiser: *A Gallery of Women* (2 vols.; New York: Horace Liveright; 1929), II; *Dawn MS.*, chs. xxx–xxxi, xxxiv–xxxv, xliv; *Newspaper Days MS.*, ch. lxxv, [pp. 14 ff.]; *St. Louis Post-Dispatch*, January 26, 1902 (UP); *New York Herald*, July 7, 1907 (UP); and conversations with Elias, summer 1941. In addition I have relied upon Dudley: *Forgotten Frontiers*, pp. 159–62; Duffy: "When They Were Twenty-One"; Maude Wood Henry correspondence (RHE); and Blanche Micheliu to Dreiser, May 30, 1929.

⁶ "Memorandum of Agreement [with Doubleday, Page & Co.]," August 20, 1900.

⁷ *Sister Carrie* (New York: Doubleday, Page; 1900), p. 2.

⁸ Ibid., p. 83.

⁹ Ibid., pp. 159–60.

¹⁰ Ibid., pp. 43, 70, 83–4.

11 Ibid., p. 557.
12 Material concerning the publishing difficulties relating to *Sister Carrie* is drawn from the sources cited in the rest of this chapter as well as from the following: Dreiser to Mencken, May 13, 1916, and February 20, 1920; Theodore Dreiser: "The Early Adventures of *Sister Carrie*," *Colophon*, part 5 (cop. 1931), [pp. 23–6]; H. L. Mencken: *A Book of Prefaces* (New York: Knopf; 1917), ch. ii; Grant Richards: *Author Hunting by an Old Literary Sportsman* (New York: Coward-McCann; 1934), pp. 168 ff.; Franklin D. Walker to Dreiser, April 22, 1931; James T. Farrell: "Dreiser's *Sister Carrie*," *The League of Frightened Philistines* (New York: Vanguard; cop. 1930–45), pp. 12–19; *Letters of Theodore Dreiser*, edited by Robert H. Elias (3 vols.; Philadelphia: University of Pennsylvania Press; 1959), I, 50–65; II, 417–21.
13 *Style and American Dressmaker*, July 1907 (UP).
14 Walter H. Page to Dreiser, June 9, 1900.
15 "Rella" in Dreiser: *A Gallery of Women*, II.
16 Dreiser, conversation with Kathryn D. Sayre, October 23, 1929 (Sayre notes: UP).
17 Document, August 20, 1900.
18 January 20, 1901 (UP).
19 Dreiser, conversation with Kathryn D. Sayre, loc. cit.; Dudley: *Forgotten Frontiers*, p. 196.
20 George P. Brett to Dreiser, December 5, 1900.
21 Frank Norris to Dreiser, January 28, 1901.
22 Publisher's foreword in Theodore Dreiser: *Sister Carrie* (London: Heinemann; 1901), [p. ii].
23 Doubleday, Page & Co. to Dreiser, May 6, 1901; Dreiser's inscription in copy of Heinemann edition owned by Mrs. A. Dorian Otvos, Los Angeles; Vrest Orton: *Dreiserana* (New York: Chocorua Bibliographies; 1929), pp. 21–2. See also the *Sister Carrie* MS. (in New York Public Library).
24 *New York Times Book Review*, March 16, 1941, p. 2; Dud-

ley: *Forgotten Frontiers*, pp. 196–7; Dreiser, conversation with Kathryn D. Sayre, loc. cit.

VII

[1] Arthur Henry: *An Island Cabin* (New York: McClure, Phillips; 1902), p. 192. Dreiser, Jug, and Anna are referred to herein as Tom, Ruth, and Nancy, respectively. See also Dreiser's semi-fictional portrait of Anna Mallon: "Rona Murtha," in *A Gallery of Women*, II, for supplementary material concerning the island stay.

[2] Henry: *An Island Cabin*, pp. 162–3.

[3] Ibid., pp. 172–3.

[4] "A Doer of the Word" and "The Village Feudists" in Dreiser: *Twelve Men*; Theodore Dreiser: "A Cripple Whose Energy Gives Inspiration," *Success*, V (February 1902), 72–3.

[5] The account of Dreiser's illness is substantially based upon the unpublished and uncompleted MS. "An Amateur Laborer." Additional information is found in the following: Dreiser to William C. Lengel, March 6, 1924; notes of interview by Richard Montague of *New York Herald*, n.d., with Montague to Dreiser, January 26, 1927; "Culhane, the Solid Man" in Dreiser: *Twelve Men*; Dreiser: "The Irish Section Foreman," pp. 20–1, 118–21. See also passim in the obviously autobiographical *The "Genius"* (New York: John Lane; 1915).

[6] "The Color of Today," *Harper's Weekly*, XLV (December 14, 1901), 1272–3; "A Cripple Whose Energy Gives Inspiration," *Success*, V (February 1902), 72–3; "A Doer of the Word," *Ainslee's Magazine*, IX (June 1902), 453–9. See also "A True Patriarch," *McClure's Magazine*, XVIII (December 1901), 136–44; Ellen Moers: *Two Dreisers* (New York: Viking; 1969), 341.

[7] Francis Hyde Bangs: *John Kendrick Bangs, Humorist of the Nineties* (New York: Knopf; 1941), p. 213.

[8] *Spectator*, August 24, 1901 (UP).

[9] *Daily Chronicle* (London), August 26, 1901 (UP).

[10] Ibid.

[11] Theodore Watts-Dunton in the *Athenæum*, September 7, 1901 (UP).

[12] William Heinemann to Frank Doubleday, September 10, 1901.

[13] Theodore Dreiser: "A Touch of Human Brotherhood," *Success*, V (March 1902), 140.

[14] *Success*, V (April 1902), 232.

[15] *Harper's Weekly*, XLVI (December 6, 1902), 52–3.

[16] Joseph F. Taylor to Dreiser, August 14, 1924; Theodore Dreiser: "The Irish Section Foreman Who Taught Me How to Live," *Hearst's International*, XLVI (August 1924), 20–1.

[17] Ibid. and "Chronicle & Comment," *Bookman*, XV (March 1902), 12.

[18] *St. Louis Post-Dispatch*, January 26, 1902 (UP).

[19] Dreiser: *The "Genius,"* pp. 291–2.

[20] Dreiser to Elias, August 28, 1944 (RHE).

[21] I (February 1903), 129.

[22] XI (June 1903), 578–84.

[23] XII (September 1903), 239–49.

[24] Fifteen chapters cited in undated list of Dreiser MSS. extant in the early twenties. See also Dudley: *Forgotten Frontiers*, p. 200.

[25] Joseph F. Taylor to Dreiser, August 14, 1924; Dreiser: "The Irish Section Foreman."

[26] "On Being Poor" in Theodore Dreiser: *The Color of a Great City* (New York: Boni & Liveright; cop. 1923).

[27] See prescriptions by Dr. Frank D. Skeel for glasses and for eyedrops, February 21, 1903. I am indebted to Dr. Dale B. Pritchard, of Ithaca, N. Y., for assistance in analyzing these prescriptions.

[28] Dreiser, conversations with Elias, June 3, 1944, and September 30, 1945; Dreiser to Mencken, March 27, 1943.

[29] In addition to the material cited in note 5 above, the sources for the account of Dreiser's recovery include R. P. Mills to F. A. Strang, June 13, 1903; A. T. Hardin

to Dreiser, June 16, 1903; Mills to Dreiser, June 22 and August 3, 1903; Dreiser to Strang, n.d. [June–July? 1903]; Dreiser to Mills, July 31, 1903; Mills to M. Burke, August 31 and September 16, 1903; Burke to Dreiser, September 1, 1903; Mills to F. A. Gifford, October 7, 1903; Theodore Dreiser: "The Mighty Burke," *McClure's Magazine*, XXXVII (May 1911), 40–50; "The Cruise of the 'Idlewild' " in Dreiser: *Free*; "The Toil of the Laborer" in Theodore Dreiser: *Hey Rub-a-Dub-Dub* (New York: Boni & Liveright; 1920); Homer Croy: *Country Cured* (New York: Harper; cop. 1943), p. 203.

[30] Dreiser: "The Irish Section Foreman," p. 121.

[31] Dreiser: "An Amateur Laborer" MS., p. 1.

[32] "The Love Affairs of Little Italy," *New York Daily News*, magazine section, April 10, 1904.

[33] "Shanghaied! The fate of the Sailor who will *not* Sail," *New York Daily News*, April 10, 1904 (UP, clipping from Munsey's *Washington Times*).

[34] "The Cradle of Tears," *New York Daily News*, March 27, 1904 (UP). See also "The Story of a Human Nine-Pin," April 3, 1904 (UP) and "Just What Happened when the Waters of the Hudson Broke into the North River Tunnel," January 23, 1904 (UP).

[35] Theodore Dreiser: "Sailors' Snug Harbor," *New York Tribune*, sec. 3 (*Sunday Magazine*), May 22, 1904, pp. 3–5, 19.

[36] E.g., "The Rivers of the Nameless Dead," I (March 1905), 112–13; "The Cradle of Tears," I (May 1905), 349–50; "The Track Walker," I (June 1905), 502–3; "The Silent Worker," II (September 1905), 364; "The Loneliness of the City," II (October 1905), 474–5.

[37] Ibid., II (October 1905), 474–5.

[38] Ibid., II (September 1905), 364.

[39] Richard Duffy, conversation with Elias, November 23, 1944; Dreiser to Mencken, April 11, 1939.

VIII

1 Mencken: A *Book of Prefaces*, pp. 103–4; Dreiser, conversation with Elias, September 30, 1945; Dudley: *Forgotten Frontiers*, pp. 205–6.
2 J. F. Taylor & Co., receipt, January 27, 1905. See also R. B. Jewett to Charles MacLean, January 19, 1905.
3 "The Publishers' Word," *Smith's Magazine*, I (April 1905), [12].
4 "A Word to the Public," ibid., June 1905, [p. ii].
5 Ibid., July 1905, [p. iv].
6 "What the Editor has to say," ibid., August 1905, [pp. i–ii].
7 Ibid., II (October 1905), 97–107.
8 *Tom Watson's Magazine*, III (January 1906), 306–8.
9 *Smith's Magazine*, II (October 1905), 97.
10 Dudley: *Forgotten Frontiers*, p. 205; "What the Editor has to say," *Smith's Magazine*, III (May 1906), [ii].
11 Memorandum of agreement, June 19, 1906.
12 "New York and 'the New Broadway,'" *Broadway Magazine*, XVI (June 1906), [vii–ix]. See also Dreiser: "De Maupassant, Junior," *Twelve Men*, pp. 208–32, and Roy L. McCardell: "Benjamin B. Hampton," *Morning Telegraph* (New York), April 24, 1921 (UP).
13 "$5,000 for Short Stories!" *Broadway Magazine*, XVI (August 1906), [iv].
14 January 2, 1908 (UP), quoted in Dudley: *Forgotten Frontiers*, pp. 206, 209.
15 *New York Times Book Review*, March 16, 1941, p. 2.
16 Flora Mai Holly, conversation with Elias, February 15, 1945; Dreiser, conversation with Elias, September 30, 1945; Flora M. Holly to Dreiser, March 5, 18, and 23, 1907.
17 Advertisement, n.d. (UP).
18 Advertisement, proof, n.d. (UP).
19 Dreiser to the editor of the *Evening Sun*, July 15, 1907, in the *Evening Sun* (New York), July 22, 1907 (UP).

[20] *New York Times: Saturday Review of Books,* June 15, 1907 (UP).

[21] Ibid.

[22] Fred B. Wahr to Dreiser, March 27, 1921.

[23] Clipping enclosed in Katherine Leckie to Dreiser, July 29, 1907.

[24] Charles H. Cochrane to Dreiser, October 11, 1906.

[25] McCardell: "Benjamin B. Hampton"; Dudley: *Forgotten Frontiers,* pp. 212–13; Dreiser: *Twelve Men,* pp. 212 ff.; Dreiser to Francis H. Bangs, January 9, 1933.

[26] G. W. Wilder to Dreiser, June 6, 1907, marks the beginning of negotiations.

[27] *New York Times: Saturday Review of Books,* June 15, 1907 (UP).

[28] See *Delineator,* LXXIII (January 1909), 7; *The "Genius"* MS. (HD) and *The "Genius,"* pp. 418, 466–7, and passim; Dudley: *Forgotten Frontiers,* pp. 219 ff.

[29] The account of Dreiser's work at Butterick's is based on my conversations in 1944 and 1945 with Arthur Sullivant Hoffman, Sarah Field Splint, Homer Croy, H. L. Mencken, William C. Lengel, Charles Hanson Towne, Fremont Rider, and John O'Hara Cosgrave, and on the following: Honoré Willsie Morrow: "Theodore Dreiser as a Ladies' Editor," *Brentano's Book Chat,* January–February [1925] (UP); *Sun* (New York), August 25, 1918 (UP); Frank Luther Mott: *A History of American Magazines* (3 vols.; Cambridge, Mass.: Harvard University Press; 1938), III, 481–90; Charles Hanson Towne: "Some Noted Contributors," *Delineator,* LXXVI (November 1910), pp. 368, 449–50, and *Adventures in Editing* (New York & London: Appleton; 1926), pp. 121–7, 133–40, 158–65; Charlotte C. West: *Ageless Youth* (New York: Crowell; 1929), p. vii.

[30] Dreiser to Charles G. Ross, August 16, 1909.

[31] Towne: *Adventures in Editing,* p. 126.

[32] Clipping, n.d. (UP); Arthur Sullivant Hoffman, conver-

sation with Elias, February 14, 1945; Fremont Rider, conversation with Elias, October 25, 1944.

[33] Dreiser to Mencken, October 19, 1907.

[34] Dreiser to G. W. Wilder, August 23, 1907.

[35] Dreiser to Mencken, March 21, 1910.

[36] "Concerning Us All," *Delineator*, LXX (October 1907), 491.

[37] *Delineator*, LXX (December 1907), 864.

[38] Mabel Potter Daggett: "The Child Without a Home," *Delineator*, LXX (October 1907), 505–10.

[39] Clipping, n.d. (UP); Robert Hunter to Dreiser, December 3 and 15, 1908 (clipping, n.d., UP); Charles Stelzle to Dreiser, September 21, 1908 (contained in leaflet *To Organized Labor*, n.d.: UP).

[40] "Concerning Us All," *Delineator*, LXXII (July 1908), 77. See also "The Humdrum Life," *Delineator*, LXXI (January 1908), 68.

[41] First article by Fremont Rider, *Delineator*, LXXII (October 1908), 539–43, 640–1.

[42] Sinclair Lewis: "The Literary Zoo," *Life*, L (October 10, 1907), 414.

[43] Sarah Field Splint, conversation with Elias, February 13, 1945.

[44] Arthur Sullivant Hoffman, conversation with Elias, February 14, 1945.

[45] Croy: *Country Cured*, p. 145.

[46] Arthur Sullivant Hoffman to Elias, January 19, 1945 (RHE)

[47] *Delineator*, LXXVI (July 1910), 4.

[48] John O'Hara Cosgrave, conversation with Elias, December 28, 1944.

[49] Dudley: *Forgotten Frontiers*, pp. 225–6.

[50] Dreiser to Mencken, July 11, 1909. See also his contributions later to the magazine *1910*: "Six O'Clock," I, no. 4, and "The Factory," I, no. 5. (I am indebted to Mr. C. B. Falls for copies of *1910*, which he edited.)

[51] Isaac Goldberg: *The Man Mencken* (New York: Simon & Schuster; 1925), pp. 378–81.

[52] Dreiser to Mencken, August 8, 1909.

[53] Edward Al: "The Red Slayer," *Bohemian*, XVII (December 1909), 793.

[54] Dreiser to Mencken, December 6, 1909.

[55] "In the Matter of Spiritualism," *Bohemian*, XVII (October 1909), 425.

[56] See "Emanuela" in Dreiser: *A Gallery of Women*, II.

[57] Dreiser to Fremont Rider, October 11, 1910. (I am indebted to Mr. Rider for a copy of this letter; RHE.)

IX

[1] *Jennie Gerhardt* (New York & London: Harper; 1911), p. 431.

[2] Ibid., p. 15.

[3] Ibid., p. 146.

[4] Ibid., p. 432.

[5] Ibid., p. 303.

[6] *Morning Telegraph* (New York), November 12, 1911 (UP).

[7] Ibid.

[8] Ibid.

[9] *New York Times Review of Books*, June 23, 1912, p. 378.

[10] Dreiser to Fremont Rider, January 24, 1911 (copy courtesy of Fremont Rider: RHE); Rider to Dreiser, November 6, 1911; Lillian Rosenthal to Dreiser, January 25, 1911; Dreiser, conversation with Elias, October 10, 1938; Rider, conversation with Elias, October 25, 1944.

[11] See *New York Evening Post*, November 15, 1911 (UP).

[12] [Kathryn D. Sayre], note affixed to letter from B. J. to Dreiser, 1916; Dreiser, conversation with Elias, September 10, 1945.

[13] *The "Genius"* MS. (HD).

[14] Ibid.

[15] See Theodore Dreiser: "This Madness, an Honest Novel about Love," *Hearst's International-Cosmopolitan,* LXXXVI, February–May 1929.

[16] Dreiser to Mencken, April 28, 1911. See also Dreiser to Mencken, August 8, 1911.

[17] Dreiser to Mencken, August 5, 1911; Arnold Bennett to Dreiser, October 21, 1911; Arnold Bennett, quoted in the *New York Times,* October 22, 1911, sec. 5, p. 4.

[18] Mencken to Dreiser, September 20, 1911.

[19] Henry B. Fuller to Dreiser, November 4, 1911.

[20] F. T. Leigh to Dreiser, November 8, 1911.

[21] Dreiser to Crant Richards, November 4, 1911, printed by Richards in his *Author Hunting,* pp. 175–6, 299.

[22] Frank H. Scott to Dreiser, November 18, 1911.

[23] F. A. Duneka to Dreiser, November 14 and 15, 1911; F. T. Leigh to Dreiser, May 3, 1912; Harper & Brothers, royalty statement, April 30, 1912.

[24] Dreiser to Mencken, November 11, 1911 (Pratt).

[25] *Chicago Evening Post,* November 24, 1911 (UP).

[26] *New York Times Review of Books,* November 30, 1913, p. 696.

[27] Theodore Dreiser: *A Traveler at Forty* (New York: Century; 1913), p. 12.

[28] Ibid., p. 59.

[29] Dreiser to Mencken, January 19, February 20 and 28, 1912 (Pratt); Dreiser to Anna Tatum, February 28 and March 21, 1912.

[30] March 14, 1912.

[31] Dreiser to Mencken, March 21, 1912 (Pratt).

[32] Ibid., May 7, 1912.

[33] Mencken to Dreiser, October 6, 1912.

[34] *The Financier* (New York & London: Harper; 1912), p. 2.

[35] Ibid., p. 4.

[36] Ibid., p. 13.

[37] Ibid., pp. 102–3.

[38] Ibid., p. 777.

[39] Ibid., p. 780.

[40] Ibid., p. 409.

[41] Ibid., p. 778.

[42] Ibid., p. 780.

[43] Edgar Lee Masters: *Across Spoon River* (New York: Farrar & Rinehart; cop. 1936), pp. 329–30; Orton: *Dreiserana*, p. 40.

[44] *A Traveler at Forty*, p. 4.

[45] Ibid., p. 34.

[46] Ibid., p. 42.

[47] Ibid., p. 6.

[48] Ibid., p. 43.

[49] Ibid., p. 12.

[50] Ibid., p. 178.

[51] Ibid., pp. 329–35.

[52] *Chicago Evening Post*, October 25, 1912 (UP).

[53] R. T. Hale to Dreiser, April 25, 1914.

[54] Dreiser to Mencken, March 23, 1913.

[55] *Chicago Examiner*, January 13, 1913 (UP).

[56] *Press* (Philadelphia), April 26, 1913 (UP).

[57] Mencken to Dreiser, July 18, 1913.

[58] Masters: *Across Spoon River*, pp. 329–31; Edgar Lee Masters: "Dreiser at Spoon River," *Esquire*, XI (May 1939), 66.

[59] *Evening Sun* (New York), September 28, 1912 (UP).

[60] *Philadelphia Record*, December 7, 1913 (UP).

[61] *Evening Sun* (New York), September 28, 1912 (UP).

[62] *The Titan* (New York: John Lane; 1914), p. 550.

[63] Ibid., p. 552.

[64] Ibid., p. 389.

[65] Ibid., pp. 550–1.

[66] Ibid., p. 551.

[67] *Chicago Daily News*, March 17, 1914 (UP); *Chicago Journal*, March 18 and 20, 1914 (UP).

[68] *Chicago Journal*, March 18, 1914 (UP).

[69] *The Titan*, p. 551.

[70] *Public Ledger* (Philadelphia), April 26, 1914 (UP).

71 *Evening Sun* (New York), May 30, 1914 (UP).
72 *Evening World* (New York), June 18, 1914 (UP).

X

1 *The "Genius,"* p. 734.
2 Ibid., p. 733.
3 Ibid., p. 736.
4 Floyd Dell: *Homecoming* (New York: Farrar & Rinehart; 1933), pp. 268–70; Frederic Chapman to Dreiser, July 15, 1915; Kirah Markham, conversation with Elias, February 1946.
5 Dreiser to Mencken, May 13, 1916.
6 *Plays of the Natural and the Supernatural* (New York: John Lane; 1916), p. 100.
7 Dreiser to Mencken, March 16, 1914.
8 *Dawn* MS., ch. iv.
9 *Evening Sun* (New York), September 28, 1912 (UP).
10 New York Public Library to Dreiser, January 15, 1915.
11 Theodore Dreiser: "Neither Devil nor Angel," *New Republic*, III (July 10, 1915), 262.
12 Lieutenant [Oswald Fritz] Bilse: *Life in a Garrison Town* (10th ed.; New York: John Lane; 1914), p. xiii.
13 Theodore Dreiser: "As a Realist Sees It," *New Republic*, V (December 25, 1915), 202.
14 Dreiser to Mencken, April 20, 1915.
15 Ibid., April 26, 1915.
16 Ibid., April 20, 1915.
17 Dreiser to Charles Fort, July 10, 1915.
18 Dreiser to Harold Hersey, November 30, 1915 (RHE).
19 Dreiser to Mencken, November 10, 1914. See also ibid., May 11, 1916.
20 George Gordon Battle to Dreiser, April 22, 1916.
21 Franklin Booth, conversation with Elias, December 27, 1944.
22 Dreiser to Mencken, November 17, 1915.
23 Randolph Bourne: "Desire as Hero," *New Republic*, V

(November 20, 1915), part 2, pp. 5–6; Edgar Lee Masters in the *Chicago Evening Post,* October 22, 1915 (UP); H. L. Mencken: "A Literary Behemoth," *Smart Set,* XLVII (December 1915), 150–4.

[24] N. P. D[awson] in the *Globe & Commercial Advertiser* (New York), October 30, 1915 (UP).

[25] Elia W. Peattie in the *Chicago Daily Tribune,* December 4, 1915 (UP).

[26] Dreiser to Harold Hersey, November 18, 1915 (RHE).

[27] Ibid., December 19, 1915 (RHE).

[28] CI (December 2, 1915), 648–50.

[29] UP copies. See also Dreiser to Harold Hersey, December 13, 1915 (RHE).

[30] Dreiser to Harold Hersey, December 13, 1915 (RHE).

[31] Ibid., October 9, 1915 (RHE).

[32] Ouija board notes, December 26, 1915, and January 1916.

[33] *A Hoosier Holiday,* p. 27.

[34] Ibid., pp. 27–8.

[35] Ibid., pp. 30–1.

[36] Ibid., p. 38.

[37] Ibid., p. 119.

[38] Ibid., p. 50.

[39] Ibid., p. 60.

[40] Ibid., p. 58.

[41] Ibid., p. 171.

[42] Ibid., p. 223.

[43] Ibid., p. 178.

[44] Ibid., p. 175.

[45] Ibid., p. 65.

[46] Ibid., p. 70.

[47] Ibid., p. 78.

[48] Ibid., p. 297.

[49] Ibid., p. 66.

[50] Ibid., pp. 512–13.

[51] Ibid., p. 181.

[52] *Cincinnati Enquirer,* September 14, 1916 (UP). See also undated leaflet (UP) embodying confidential report of

the Law and Order Committee (John F. Herget, chairman) of the Federation of Churches, Cincinnati, and clippings beginning with August 1916 (UP).

XI

1 John S. Sumner to Felix Shay, November 24, 1916.
2 John S. Sumner to George T. Keating, November 22, 1916.
3 *Oakland Tribune*, September 17, 1916 (UP).
4 *San Francisco Call and Post*, October 12, 1916 (UP).
5 *Chicago Examiner*, January 8, 1917 (UP).
6 Dreiser to Mencken, July 29, 1916.
7 Ibid., August 4, 1916.
8 Ibid., August 8, 1916.
9 Ibid., August 10, 1916.
10 Theodore Dreiser in the *Los Angeles Record*, November 7, 1916 (UP).
11 "Writers Oppose Censorship," press release, n.d. [before September 9, 1916]; quoted in the *Sun* (New York), September 9, 1916 (UP). See also *New York Tribune*, August 20, 1916 (UP).
12 Mencken to Harold Hersey, August 9, 1916 (copy: RHE).
13 Harold Hersey, document, August 24, 1916 (RHE).
14 Frank Harris to Eric Schuler, September 20, 1916 (copied extract); Harris to Harold Hersey, September 20, 1916.
15 Hamlin Garland to Eric Schuler, October 2, 1916 (copied extract).
16 Mencken to Dreiser, September 22 and October 6, 1916.
17 September 19, 1916.
18 Theodore Dreiser: "Our Greatest Writer Tells What's Wrong With Our Newspapers," *Pep*, II (July 1917), 8–9.
19 Theodore Dreiser in "Symposium on the Medical Profession," *Medical Review of Reviews*, XXIII (January 1917), 8–9.

[20] *The Hand of the Potter* (New York: Boni & Liveright; 1918), p. 45.

[21] Ibid., p. 169.

[22] Ibid., p. 197.

[23] Ibid., p. 199.

[24] Ibid., p. 200.

[25] Mencken to Dreiser, December 16, 1916.

[26] Ibid., December 20[?], 1916.

[27] Ibid., December 23, 1916.

[28] Dreiser to Mencken, December 18, 1916.

[29] Ibid., December 21, 1916.

[30] Dreiser to B. W. Huebsch, March 10, 1918.

[31] J. Jefferson Jones to Dreiser, September 14, 1917.

[32] See also *The Intimate Notebooks of George Jean Nathan* (New York: Knopf; 1932), pp. 38–40.

[33] See card (UP).

[34] See particularly "Married," "The Second Choice," "Free," and "Will You Walk into My Parlor?" in Dreiser: *Free;* and "Chains," "St. Columba and the River," "The Hand," "Phantom Gold," and "The Old Neighborhood" in Theodore Dreiser: *Chains, Lesser Novels and Stories* (New York: Boni & Liveright; 1927).

[35] *Chains*, p. 42.

[36] *Saturday Evening Post* to Dreiser, August 28, 1918; *Atlantic Monthly* to Dreiser, September 5 and October 28, 1918.

[37] Ray Long to Dreiser, January 14, 1919.

[38] Burton Kline to Dreiser, April 5, 1919.

[39] Douglas Z. Doty to Dreiser, August 7, 1918.

[40] *Pictorial Review* to Dreiser, August 22, 1918.

[41] T. R. Smith to Dreiser, August 9, 1918.

[42] *Twelve Men*, p. 105.

[43] April 8, 1919.

[44] See especially Theodore Dreiser: *Fine Furniture* (New York: Random House; 1930), and "Convention" and "The 'Mercy' of God" in Dreiser: *Chains.*

⁴⁵ See especially "Reina," "Ida Hauchwout," "Giff," "Esther Norn," and "Olive Brand."

⁴⁶ Odin Gregory [J. G. Robin]: *Caius Gracchus* (New York: Boni & Liveright; cop. 1920); Llewelyn Powys: *Ebony and Ivory* (New York: American Library Service; 1923).

⁴⁷ Theodore Dreiser: "The Scope of Fiction," *New Republic*, XXX (April 12, 1922), part 2, pp. 8–9.

⁴⁸ Theodore Dreiser: "Hollywood Now," *McCall's Magazine*, XLVIII (September 1921), 8, 18, 54; Theodore Dreiser: "Hollywood: Its Morals and Manners," *Shadowland*, V, November 1921–February 1922.

⁴⁹ Included in Theodore Dreiser: *Moods, Cadenced and Declaimed* (New York: Boni & Liveright; ltd. ed., 1926; enlarged trade ed., 1928). See also Dreiser to Mencken, August 8, 1923.

⁵⁰ Dreiser to Barrett H. Clark, February 23, 1920, in *Jurgen and the Censor* (New York: privately printed; 1920), pp. 37, 47; Theodore Dreiser: "Why Attack Books?" *Evening Telegram* (New York), March 4, 1923, reprinted in the *Independent*, CX (March 17, 1923), 191; Dreiser to Charles Boni, Jr., February 14, 1921, printed in the *Globe & Commercial Advertiser* (New York), February 22, 1921 (UP); Dreiser to Thomas Boyd, August 26, 1921 (RHE), printed in the *St. Paul Daily News*, September 18, 1921 (UP). See also Gelett Burgess to Dreiser, March 14, 1923; Dreiser to Burgess, n.d. [June 2?, 1923]; Rex Beach to Dreiser, April 26 and May 8, 1923; Dreiser to Beach, May 5, 1923; various clippings, May 15–17, 19, 1923 (UP), and Dreiser's statement in the *Jersey Journal*, June 6, 1923 (UP).

⁵¹ Dreiser: *The Color of a Great City*, p. v.

⁵² Pp. 19, 22.

⁵³ Theodore Dreiser: "A Word Concerning Birth Control," *Birth Control Review*, V (April 1921), 5.

⁵⁴ Dreiser to Mencken, January 26, 1921.

55 Jacques Loeb: *The Mechanistic Conception of Life* (Chicago: University of Chicago Press; 1912), p. 26.
56 Ibid., p. 31. See also Jacques Loeb to Dreiser, June 13, 1919, September 11, 1920, and January 13, 1923.
57 Dreiser to *Tuz*, n.d. [after September 25, 1922].
58 Magazine section, March 16, 1918, pp. 1, 12–13.
59 "A Word Concerning Birth Control," pp. 5–6.
60 Dreiser to James Bann, n.d. [after September 23, 1920].
61 Theodore Dreiser: *A Book about Myself* (New York: Boni & Liveright; cop. 1922), p. 427.
62 Theodore Dreiser in the *Literary Review of the New York Evening Post*, November 17, 1923, p. 255; *New York Times Book Review*, December 23, 1923, p. 7. See also Dreiser to Bruno Lasker, April 5, 1923, printed as "Applied Religion — Applied Art" in the *Survey*, L (May 1, 1923), 175.
63 Hiram Johnson to Dreiser, January 15, 1919.
64 *Brooklyn Daily Eagle*, October 11, 1919 (UP); Dreiser to M. W. Martin, October 4, 1921.
65 *Huntington Press* (Indiana), June 18, 1919 (UP).
66 Dreiser to David F. Karsner, July 26, 1920 (RHE).
67 Oswald Garrison Villard to Dreiser, September 4, 1924.
68 Dreiser to David F. Karsner, August 9, 1922 (property of Schulte's Bookstore, New York, in 1939).
69 Dreiser to Anker Kirkeby, November 26, 1921.
70 Dreiser to Edward H. Smith, January 10, 1921.
71 Dreiser to David F. Karsner, December 12, 1920 (property of Schulte's Bookstore, New York, in 1939), and August 9, 1922 (see note 68 above).
72 *Los Angeles Times*, September 17, 1922 (UP).
73 Dreiser to M. W. Martin, October 4, 1921.
74 Dreiser, conversation with Elias, summer 1941; Theodore Dreiser: "Myself and the Movies," *Esquire*, XX (July 1943), 50.
75 Dreiser to Mencken, October 25, 1920.
76 Dreiser: "Myself and the Movies," p. 50.
77 Llewelyn Powys to Dreiser, n.d. [1920–2].

XII

[1] Theodore Dreiser: "I Find the Real American Tragedy," *Mystery Magazine*, XI (February 1935), 10–11, 88–9.

[2] See also James T. Farrell in the *New York Times Book Review*, April 29, 1945, pp. 7, 28, and May 6, 1945, pp. 6, 16.

[3] See James D. Smith to Lewis E. Lawes, October 6, 1925; Smith to Dreiser, October 26, 1925; Dreiser correspondence with Mencken, n.d. [before November 14] and November 24–December 4, 1925; Mencken to James M. Cain, November 14, 1925; Lawes to James W. Barrett, November 19, 1925; James Wyman Barrett: *Joseph Pulitzer and His World* (New York: Vanguard; cop. 1941), pp. 382–3; Theodore Dreiser in the *World* (New York), November 30, 1925, pp. 1, 14. I am indebted for additional information to conversations with Mrs. Louise Campbell (December 18, 1944) and Mr. Mencken (November 2, 1944).

[4] Horace B. Liveright to Dreiser, April 23 and May 6, 1924.

[5] See also Emil Greenberg: "A Case Study in the Technique of Realism: Theodore Dreiser's *An American Tragedy*," an unpublished M.A. thesis (New York University, Washington Square; June 1936). See, too, "The Ballad of Grace Brown and Chester Gillette" in Harold Thompson: *Body, Boots & Britches* (Philadelphia: Lippincott; 1939), pp. 444–5.

[6] See Albert Lévitt: *Was Clyde Griffiths Guilty of Murder in the First Degree?* mimeographed November 10, 1926 (RHE), quoted at length in the *Charleston Gazette* (West Virginia), April 10, 1927 (UP).

[7] Dreiser, conversation with Elias, undated [1938–41].

[8] Albert Lévitt to Dreiser, November 18, 1926.

[9] *Denver Post*, November 28, 1926 (UP).

[10] Theodore Dreiser: *An American Tragedy* (2 vols.; New York: Boni & Liveright; 1925), I, 396.

[11] *Nation*, CXXII (February 10, 1926), 152.

¹² Stuart P. Sherman in *New York Herald Tribune Books,* January 3, 1926 (UP).

¹³ Theodore Dreiser: "This Florida Scene," *Vanity Fair,* XXVI, May–July 1926.

¹⁴ Ibid., June, p. 43.

¹⁵ Clipping (German), n.p., August 16, 1926 (UP).

¹⁶ Theodore Dreiser: "Paris — 1926," *Vanity Fair,* XXVII (December 1926), 64, 136, 147–8, 150; *Chicago Tribune* (Paris edition), September 29, 1926 (UP).

¹⁷ Victor Llona: "Dreiser Calls on Hugo and Balzac," *Bulletin of the American Women's Club of Paris,* February 1927 (UP).

¹⁸ *Rozpravy Aventina* (Prague), November 1, 1926 (UP) (translation).

¹⁹ *American News* (Hamburg), August 14, 1926 (UP).

²⁰ *Ekstra Bladet* (Copenhagen), July 31, 1926 (UP). See also *Politiken* (Copenhagen), August 5, 1926 (UP).

²¹ *New York Herald Tribune,* October 23, 1926 (UP).

²² Dreiser: *Chains,* pp. 181–218, printed as "The Wages of Sin," *Hearst's International-Cosmopolitan,* LXXXI (October 1926), 42–5, 175–81.

²³ George Sterling: *Lilith* (New York: Macmillan; 1926), p. xi.

²⁴ Dreiser to Claude G. Bowers, May 27, 1929. See also Dreiser to George T. Bye, June 6, 1928.

²⁵ Theodore Dreiser: "The Rights of a Columnist," *Nation,* CXXVI (May 30, 1928), 608.

²⁶ Theodore Dreiser: introduction to *Poorhouse Sweeney,* by Ed Sweeney (New York: Boni & Liveright; 1927), p. xi.

²⁷ *New York Evening Post,* January 11, 1927 (UP).

²⁸ "Theodore Dreiser on the Elections," *New Masses,* IV (November 1928), 17.

²⁹ *New York Telegram,* September 28, 1929 (UP).

³⁰ Dreiser to Melvin Stokes, January 18, 1929.

³¹ H. G. Wells: *Tono-Bungay* (Sandgate edition; New York: Duffield; 1927), pp. v, ix.

[32] "Little Keys," *Moods* (1926), p. 85.
[33] Quoted in Vivian Pierce to Dreiser, March 8, 1926.
[34] Dreiser to Sergei Dinamov, January 5, 1927.
[35] *Rozpravy Aventina* (Prague), November 1, 1926 (UP) (translation).
[36] *New York Evening Post*, January 11, 1927 (UP).
[37] Dreiser's secretary to E. M. Whitman, April 20, 1927.
[38] *Boston Evening Transcript*, January 29, 1927 (UP).
[39] Syndicated by the Metropolitan Newspaper Service in Hearst papers for six Sundays (e.g., *Dallas Morning News, New York American*, or *San Francisco Examiner*, April 10, May 22, July 31, August 28, 1927, and February 5, March 11, 1928).
[40] *New York Herald* (Paris edition), October 27, 1927 (UP).
[41] For most of the details about Dreiser's Russian activities I have relied upon Mrs. Ruth E. Kennell, of Bridgeport, Connecticut, his interpreter and secretary in Russia (conversation with Elias, February 15, 1945), and upon Dreiser (conversations with Elias, March 14, 1938, and September 10, 1945). Supplementary data in UP files include Dreiser's Russian diary, 1927–8.
[42] Ruth Kennell in *Providence Tribune*, July 27, 1930 (UP).
[43] Clipping, n.d., with dateline of November 22, 1927 (UP).
[44] R. H. Wollstein: "You Know Mr. Dreiser," *Musical America*, XLIX (February 25, 1929), 55–6.
[45] *Zarya Vostoka* (Tiflis), January 3, 1928 (UP) (translation).
[46] Theodore Dreiser, typescript (property of Mrs. Ruth E. Kennell); printed with revisions in the *Chicago Daily News*, February 6, 1928, pp. 1–2.
[47] Ibid.
[48] *New York Herald Tribune*, February 22, 1928 (UP).
[49] *New York Evening Post*, February 21, 1928 (UP).
[50] Dreiser to *New York Times*, in the *New York Times*, March 15, 1928, p. 24.

[51] Theodore Dreiser: *Dreiser Looks at Russia* (New York: Horace Liveright; 1928), p. 74.

[52] Ibid., p. 115.

[53] Ibid., p. 10.

[54] Boris Sokoloff: *The Crime of Dr. Garine* (New York: Covici-Friede; 1928), p. viii.

[55] Dreiser to Simon & Schuster, March 26, 1929.

[56] Dreiser to Covici-Friede, January 16, 1929.

[57] Statement by Dreiser in Fifteenth Program (June 29–July 5, 1929) of Film Guild Cinema (New York, 1929), p. 3.

[58] Louise Campbell, conversation with Elias, December 18, 1944.

[59] Statement by Dreiser in Inaugural Program (January 1929) of Film Guild Cinema (New York, 1929), pp. 6, 9.

[60] See Karl K. Kitchen in the *Evening World* (New York), March 29, 1929, p. 17.

[61] *New York Herald Tribune*, December 23, 1928, sec. 3, p. 1; later printed in book form (New York: Horace Liveright; 1929).

[62] *New York Herald Tribune Books*, June 10, 1928, p. 2.

[63] I am indebted for the facts about Dreiser's stay at Woods Hole to Professor L. V. Heilbrunn, of the University of Pennsylvania (conversation with Elias, January 9, 1945). See also the *Collecting Net* (Woods Hole, Mass.), III, July 14 and 21, 1928.

[64] Theodore Dreiser: "Woods Hole and the Marine Biological Laboratory," *Collecting Net*, III (July 21, 1928), 1–2.

[65] "Statements of Belief," *Bookman*, LXVIII (September 1928), 25.

[66] Max Eastman: *The Literary Mind, Its Place in an Age of Science* (New York & London: Scribner's; 1931), p. 232.

[67] Theodore Dreiser: "What I Believe," *Forum*, LXXXII (November 1929), 318–19.

[68] Ibid., p. 320.

[69] Ibid.

70 Ibid., pp. 317–18.
71 November 1, 1929.

XIII

1 Dreiser to John Reed Club, March 18, 1930.
2 Theodore Dreiser: "The New Humanism," *Thinker*, II (July 1930), 8. See also Dreiser as quoted in the *Dallas Morning News*, May 6, 1930 (UP).
3 See *Tucson Daily Citizen*, April 6, 1930 (UP); *New Mexico State Tribune*, April 19, 1930 (UP); *Albuquerque Journal*, April 19, 1930 (UP); *El Paso Evening Post*, April 26, 1930 (UP).
4 *Tucson Daily Citizen*, April 30, 1930 (UP).
5 Dreiser to John Reed Club, June 10, 1930, printed as leaflet: *John Reed Club Answer*.
6 *New York Herald Tribune*, July 8, 1930, p. 14.
7 Ibid.
8 See Theodore Dreiser: "The Trial of the Negro Communists," typescript, with letter from Dreiser's secretary to Joseph Pass, October 14, 1930.
9 Theodore Dreiser: "On the Communists and Their Platform," typescript, October 1930 (HD). See also Theodore Dreiser: "The American Press and Political Prisoners," *Daily Worker* (New York), May 9, 1931 (UP).
10 *Dawn*, p. 22.
11 In *Literaturnaya Gazeta*, August 25, 1931 (UP) (translation), reprinted in *New Masses*, VII (September 1931), 6.
12 See *New Masses*, VII (September 1931), 6–7.
13 Dreiser to James D. Mooney, March 14, 1931.
14 Dreiser to *Illes*, July 3, 1931.
15 "A Statement by Theodore Dreiser," *Experimental Cinema*, no. 4 (cop. 1932), [p. 3].
16 Dreiser, draft of "A Suggestion for the Communist Party," n.d. [before April 22, 1931]; L. Gibarti to Dreiser, April 22, 1931; C. A. Hathaway to Dreiser, May 5, 1931.

[17] Theodore Dreiser: "America and Her Communists," *Time and Tide,* XII (October 31, 1931), 1248.

[18] Dreiser to Anna North, January 17, 1931.

[19] Joseph Brainen: "Human Nature in a Crucible," *Jewish Standard,* September 30, 1932, pp. 166–7 (UP).

[20] Dreiser: "America and Her Communists," p. 1247.

[21] Dreiser to Paul S. Clapp, June 25, 1931; quoted by the *New York Times,* July 2, 1931, p. 16, and printed in the *Progressive,* July 11, 1931 (UP).

[22] Theodore Dreiser: "Take a Look at Our Railroads," *Liberty,* VIII (November 7, 1931), 24–7.

[23] Theodore Dreiser: "Intellectual Unemployment," *New Freeman,* II (March 11, 1931), 616–17.

[24] Dreiser to *New York Times,* May 9, 1931: "Where Is Labor's Share?" *New York Times,* May 13, 1931, p. 24.

[25] Dreiser to David Algar Bailey, May 18, 1931.

[26] S. M. Eisenstein: "An American Tragedy," *Close Up,* X (June 1933), 109–24; Tom Donnelly in the *Washington Daily News,* July 2, 1946, p. 42.

[27] Dreiser to Samuel Hoffenstein, February 26, 1931.

[28] Dreiser correspondence with Samuel Hoffenstein, February 9–26, 1931; Hoffenstein to Louise Campbell, February 10, 1931; Louis E. Swarts to Dreiser, February 13, 1931; Dreiser's secretary, receipt, to Paramount Publix Corporation, February 14, 1931; Dreiser to Helen R. Dreiser, February 16, 1931.

[29] Dreiser to Jesse L. Lasky, March 10, 1931.

[30] Ibid., March 17, 1931.

[31] H. S. Kraft: "Dreiser's War in Hollywood," *Screen Writer,* I (March 1946), 9–13.

[32] *Los Angeles Examiner,* April 8, 1931 (UP).

[33] Arthur Garfield Hays to Dreiser, July 3, 1931.

[34] *New York Times,* March 21, 1931, p. 11.

[35] Reported by William C. Lengel, conversation with Elias, December 27, 1944.

[36] Dreiser, conversation with Elias, March 14, 1938.

[37] Dreiser's introductory remarks, MS. [April 16, 1931]. See also *New York World-Telegram*, April 18, 1931 (UP).

[38] Theodore Dreiser, typescript of speech delivered at Town Hall, New York, June 5, 1931.

[39] Dreiser to Home Secretary [of Polish Government], September 19, 1931.

[40] See Joseph Pass to Dreiser, June 12, 1931; William Green to Dreiser, July 1 and 23, 1931; Anna Rochester to Dreiser, July 7, 1931; A. Basil Wheeler to Dreiser, July 8, 1931; transcription of conversation between Dreiser and Earl Browder, July 9, 1931; Dreiser's secretary to Browder, July 15, August 3 and 7, 1931; Browder to Dreiser, July 16 and August 4, 1931; William Z. Foster to Dreiser, July 17, 1931; Dreiser to Green, July 17, 1931, and a final [?] rejoinder, n.d.; Dreiser's secretary to Pass, August 6, 1931; clippings in *Pittsburgh Press* and *New York World-Telegram*, June 25–July 20, 1931 (UP). See also Theodore Dreiser: *Tragic America* (New York: Horace Liveright; cop. 1931), p. 181.

[41] National Committee for the Defense of Political Prisoners: *Harlan Miners Speak* (New York: Harcourt, Brace; 1932); American Civil Liberties Union: *The Kentucky Miners Struggle*, pamphlet (New York: American Civil Liberties Union; May 1932); "Harlan County Faces," *Fortune*, V (February 1932), 130–1.

[42] *Knoxville News-Sentinel*, November 9, 1931, p. 2.

[43] Dreiser to Vokn Petroff, October 29, 1931.

[44] Theodore Dreiser: "Judge Jones, the Harlan Miners and Myself," press release, typescript, n.d. [before November 12, 1931].

[45] Theodore Dreiser: "The Seventh Commandment," *Liberty*, IX, April 2 and 9, 1932.

[46] *New York Herald Tribune*, November 22, 1931, sec. 8, p. 2.

[47] Theodore Dreiser: "Individualism and the Jungle," speech before Group Forum, December 15, 1931, printed in

Crawford's Weekly (Norton, Virginia), January 12, 1932 (UP), several hundred copies of which Dreiser distributed; reprinted in *New Masses*, VII (January 1932), 3–4, and in expanded form as the introduction to *Harlan Miners Speak*.

[48] Ibid.

[49] *New York Herald Tribune*, November 22, 1931, sec. 8, p. 2.

[50] *Tragic America*, p. 1.

[51] See, for example, pp. 227, 410, 425–6.

[52] Ibid., p. 277.

[53] Ibid., p. 351.

[54] Ibid., p. 365.

[55] Ibid., p. 380.

[56] Ibid., p. 329.

[57] Ibid., p. 364. See also Theodore Dreiser: "The Child and the School," *American Spectator*, I (April 1933), 2.

[58] *Tragic America*, pp. 425–6.

[59] Sergei Dinamov: "Theodore Dreiser Continues the Struggle," *International Literature*, no. 2–3 (1932), pp. 113–14. See also A. Abramov in *Vechernyaya Moskva*, February 19, 1932 (UP).

[60] Bennett Stevens: "The Gnats and Dreiser," *New Masses*, VII (May 1932), 24.

[61] Norman Thomas: "Dreiser as Economist," *Nation*, CXXXIV (April 6, 1932), 402–3.

[62] Stuart Chase to Dreiser, February 12, 1932; Stuart Chase in *New York Herald Tribune Books*, January 24, 1932, pp. 1–2.

[63] James M. Gillis in the *Catholic News* (New York), February 6, 1932, reprinted in Dreiser's proposed advertisement (UP).

[64] "Catholic News Reader" to Dreiser, February 8, 1932.

[65] Dreiser to Upton Sinclair, April 27, 1932.

[66] Dreiser to Merlin N. Hanson, May 26, 1934; quoted by J[ay] H[arrison]: "The Case of Merlin N. Hanson," *Kosmos*, III (August–September 1934), 25.

[67] Dreiser and Roger Baldwin, circular letter, April 28, 1932; Dreiser to *Vechernyaya*, May 16, 1932.

[68] *New York American*, July 1, 1932 (UP).

[69] Dreiser to Marion F. Wotherspoon, November 22, 1932; Dreiser correspondence with Samuel Ornitz, December 30, 1932–April 29, 1933, and with Esther McCoy, January 27–December 1, 1933.

[70] Dreiser to Arnold Gingrich, October 31, 1935 (HD).

[71] John Dos Passos to Dreiser, November 27, 1934; Dreiser to Dos Passos, December 1, 1934.

[72] Dreiser to Sergei Dinamov, April 13, 1932 (HD).

[73] Dreiser to I. Potash, July 5, 1933; Dreiser to Max Eastman, April 26, 1933; Theodore Dreiser: "Is Leon Trotsky Guilty?" *Modern Monthly*, X (March 1937), 5; *Daily Worker* (New York), February 9, 1937, p. 2.

[74] Walter Wilson: *Forced Labor in the United States* (New York: International Publishers; cop. 1933).

[75] Tom Kromer: *Waiting for Nothing* (London: Constable; 1935).

[76] Theodore Dreiser: "Will Fascism Come to America?" *Modern Monthly*, VIII (September 1934), 459–61. See also Theodore Dreiser: "Keep Moving or Starve," *Today*, I (March 3, 1934), 6–7, 22–3.

[77] Theodore Dreiser: "Challenge to the Creative Man," *Common Sense*, II (November 1933), 7.

[78] Theodore Dreiser: "Flies and Locusts," in Walter Winchell's column of the *Daily Mirror* (New York), August 1, 1933, pp. 19, 31; reprinted as "The Profit-Makers Are Thieves," *Common Sense*, II (December 1933), 20–2. See also Theodore Dreiser: "What Has the Great War Taught Me?" *New Masses*, XII (August 7, 1934), 15.

[79] Theodore Dreiser: "America — And War," *Labor Defender*, VIII (August 1932), 143.

[80] Dreiser to James Rolph, Jr., January 29, 1932; "The Crime of the Century!" press release, n.d. [*ca.* December 1933]; *News* (San Francisco), November 5, 1932 (UP); *Call-Bulletin* (San Francisco), November 7, 1932 (UP);

Orrick Johns: *Time of Our Lives* (New York: Stackpole; cop. 1937), pp. 325–9.

[81] Theodore Dreiser, press release, July 5, 1932.

[82] Dreiser to William E. Bohn, January 29, 1930; Dreiser to Seymour A. Seligson, November 20, 1930; Dreiser correspondence with James B. Pond, July 19, 1932–August 26, 1933, with Ernest Briggs, June 4, 1934–January 10, 1939, and with Clark H. Getts, April 4, 1936–October 22, 1938.

[83] Dreiser to Dallas McKown, June 9, 1932; [Evelyn Light] to Dreiser, [August 1, 1932]; Dreiser to Elliott E. Cohen, August 20, 1932; Dreiser's secretary to Dreiser, memorandum with Dreiser to James Rorty, October 12, 1932; Dreiser to MOPR, March 11, 1933; Dreiser's secretary to Dreiser, memorandum with letter to Dreiser from American Committee for Struggle Against War, May 10, 1933; Evelyn Light to Henrietta Helston, memorandum with letter to Dreiser from Writers' League Against Lynching, June 6, 1934; Dreiser, conversation with Elias, August 1941.

[84] Dreiser to Evelyn Scott, October 28, 1932.

[85] Hutchins Hapgood: "Is Dreiser Anti-Semitic?" *Nation*, CXL (April 17, 1935), 436–8.

[86] "Dreiser Denies He Is Anti-Semitic," *New Masses*, XV (April 30, 1935), 10, 11. See also Eugene Lyons: *The Red Decade* (New York & Indianapolis: Bobbs-Merrill; cop. 1941), pp. 145–7.

[87] "How They Are Voting: II," *New Republic*, LXXXVIII (October 7, 1936), 249.

[88] *New York Times*, August 28, 1933, p. 19.

[89] Dreiser to Ralph Holmes, January 9, 1932.

[90] Theodore Dreiser: "I Am Grateful to Soviet Russia," *Soviet Russia Today*, VI (November 1937), 11.

[91] Dreiser to Evelyn Scott, June 17, 1938 (HD).

[92] Dreiser [to Vladimir Romm, *Izvestiya*], typescript, n.d., reply to Romm to Dreiser of April 21, [1936?] (HD); according to the American Russian Institute, this was

not printed in *Izvestiya*'s issue of May 1, 1936, which contains discussions of the subject.

[93] Theodore Dreiser and John Dos Passos: "A Conversation," *Direction*, I (January 1938), 2.

[94] H. G. Wells to Dreiser, April 9, 1931; Dreiser to Wells, May 23, 1931; Dreiser, interview with Reed Harris, typescript, n.d. [March? 1932] (copy by Elias: UP).

[95] Dreiser to Dorothy Dudley Harvey, April 7, 1932.

[96] Dreiser to George Douglas, September 14, 1932 (Hanley).

[97] Editorial, *American Spectator*, I (November 1932), 1.

[98] Dreiser to Sergei Dinamov, September 22, 1932.

[99] Tom Mooney: "Sixteen Years," *American Spectator*, I (February 1933), 1–2; Dreiser, conversation with Elias, June 3, 1944.

[100] Dreiser to Ernest Boyd, March 31, 1933; Dreiser to Benjamin DeCasseres, November 2, 1933; Dreiser to George Douglas, January 9 and 18, 1934 (Hanley); Dreiser, conversation with Elias, August 1941, and June 3, 1944.

[101] Dreiser to Max Eastman, June 14, 1933; Dreiser to Charles E. Yost, April 6, 1932; Evelyn Light to Kathryn D. Sayre, December 2, 1931; Dreiser to Dallas McKown, June 9, 1932; Dreiser to John Dos Passos, June 14, 1933; Theodore Dreiser: "What Is Americanism?" *Partisan Review and Anvil*, III (April 1936), 3–4.

[102] Dreiser to Charles E. Yost, Bruce Crawford, and Fisher C. Baily, April 6, 1932.

[103] Correspondence among Dreiser, Max Eastman, A. J. Muste, Alfred H. Bingham, Evelyn Light, and V. F. Calverton, January 19–March 2, 1934.

[104] Dreiser to Bruce Crawford, January 15, 1935; Dreiser to Upton Sinclair, November 25, 1935; Sinclair to Dreiser, December 13, 1935; Dreiser to Howard Scott, January 9, 1936; Scott to Dreiser, January 7 and 16, 1936.

[105] Typescript (cop. 1933); outline dated January 9, 1934 (HD).

[106] Notes by Elias, May 25, 1937.

XIV

1 *Writers Take Sides* (New York: League of American Writers; 1938), pp. 20–1.

2 Bureau of Fine Arts Hearings before a Subcommittee of the Committee on Education and Labor, United States Senate, 75th Congress, 3rd session, on S. 3296, a bill to provide for a permanent bureau of fine arts, February 28, March 1 and 2, 1938 (Washington, D.C.: U.S. Government Printing Office; 1938), pp. 29–32.

3 Dreiser to John Golden, February 8, 1938; Dreiser to Gertrude Lawrence, February 24, 1938; typescript of outline, n.d.

4 Dreiser, report to National Council of League of American Writers, August 24, 1938 (copy courtesy of Franklin Folsom: RHE); Theodore Dreiser: "Barcelona in August," *Direction*, I (November–December 1938), 4–5; Theodore Dreiser: "Equity between Nations," *Direction*, I (September–October 1938), 5–6, 11; *Dallas Morning News*, August 14, 1938 (UP); Dreiser to Claude G. Bowers, April 14, 1944; *New York Times*, July 31, 1938, p. 25; Dreiser, speech for American Relief Ship for Spain, September 15, 1938 (copy courtesy of Franklin Folsom: RHE); notes on Dreiser speech by Elias, September 15, 1938.

5 Dreiser to Franklin D. Roosevelt, January 5, 1939 (HD). See also Roosevelt to Dreiser, January 24, 1939 (HD); Richard Duffy, conversation with Elias, November 23, 1944; editorial, *Daily News* (New York), October 11, 1938 (RHE); Marguerite Tjader: "Theodore Dreiser: World Spirit," *Free World*, II (April 1946), 57.

6 Dreiser to Mencken, November 3, 1938.

7 Ibid., January 4, 1939.

8 Evelyn Scott to Dreiser, January 8, 1939.

9 *San Francisco Chronicle*, February 15, 1939 (UP); *Morning Oregonian* (Portland), February 16, 1939 (UP); *News-Telegram* (Portland), February 16, 1939 (UP).

[10] *Salt Lake Tribune,* February 20, 1939 (UP); *Salt Lake Telegram,* February 20, 1939 (UP).

[11] *Salt Lake Tribune,* February 20, 1939 (UP).

[12] Dreiser to *International Literature,* n.d. [between February 21 and March 12, 1939] (RHE).

[13] Dreiser to Mencken, October 3, 1939.

[14] *The Dawn Is in the East,* leaflet, n.d.; printed in *Common Sense,* VIII (December 1939), 6–7.

[15] See Roy F. and Jeannette P. Nichols: *A Short History of American Democracy* (New York & London: Appleton-Century; cop. 1943), pp. 570–8.

[16] Franklin D. Roosevelt to Dreiser, October 5, 1939 (HD); Dreiser to Roosevelt, October 16, 1939 (HD).

[17] Theodore Dreiser: "Upton Sinclair," *Clipper* (Hollywood), I (September 1940), 4.

[18] *Daily Worker* (New York), November 1, 1940, p. 5. See also *New York Times,* October 9, 1940, p. 22.

[19] Dreiser to Fred Smith, January 9, 1940 (HD).

[20] Theodore Dreiser: *Concerning Dives and Larazus [sic],* leaflet, n.d.; printed under "The Soviet-Finnish Treaty and World Peace," *Soviet Russia Today,* VIII (April 1940), 8–9. See also Dreiser to John Haynes Holmes, May 28, 1940; Dreiser to Modern Age Books, October 15, 1940; Dreiser to *Sovietland,* n.d. [February 1940]; Dreiser to *New Masses,* February 23, 1940.

[21] Dreiser to John B. Thompson, August 7, 1940.

[22] Walter E. Schneider to Dreiser, September 9, 1940, in leaflet, *Editor & Publisher* [September 1940].

[23] Dreiser to *Editor & Publisher,* September 18, 1940, in leaflet, *Editor & Publisher* [September 1940].

[24] Theodore Dreiser: *America Is Worth Saving* (New York: Modern Age Books; cop. 1941).

[25] Theodore Dreiser: "The Story of Harry Bridges," *Friday,* I, October 4 and 11, 1940; Dreiser: "Upton Sinclair."

[26] *Daily Worker* (New York), November 1, 1940, p. 5.

[27] Dreiser to Modern Age Books, October 15, 1940.

[28] Theodore Dreiser: *U.S. Must Not be Bled for Imperial*

Britain, leaflet, n.d.; reprinted from *People's World* (San Francisco), November 12, 1940.

29 *Radio Interview with Dreiser* [February 1, 1941], leaflet, n.d.; similar version printed in *People's World* (San Francisco), March 6, 1941, p. 5; Theodore Dreiser: "This Is Churchill's 'Democracy,' " *New Masses,* XXXVIII (February 18, 1941), 35–6 (reprinted as leaflet, *Concerning Our Helping England Again,* n.d.); Agnes Brandenstein to Elias, March 4, 1941 (RHE).

30 Commodore Hotel, New York, March 1, 1941 (notes by Elias); Manhattan Center, New York, March 3, 1941 (notes by Elias): see *Daily Worker* (New York), March 4, 1941, p. 2; Academy of Music, Philadelphia, March 6, 1941 (notes by Elias).

31 Philadelphia, March 6, 1941.

32 *New York Times Book Review,* March 16, 1941, p. 2.

33 Untitled leaflet containing Dreiser to Mrs. Franklin D. Roosevelt, April 25, 1941; *To the Writers' League of America,* May 13, 1941.

34 Dreiser to John A. Kingsbury, June 28, 1941 (HD); printed in *People's World* (San Francisco), July 2, 1941, p. 1.

35 Dreiser to Takatika Hosokawa, June 16, 1941 (HD).

36 Helen Richardson to America First Committee, Women's Division, August 1, 1941.

37 Dreiser to Otis Dixon Phillips, July 17, 1941; *Indianapolis Star,* November 22, 1941, p. 7.

38 See R. L. Duffus in the *New York Times Book Review,* February 9, 1941, p. 22.

39 August 6, 1941, enclosed in Mich. Apletin to Dreiser, September 1941.

40 Dreiser to Joseph North, July 24, 1942.

41 *Toronto Evening Telegram,* September 21, 1942, quoted in the *Boston Daily Globe,* September 22, 1942, pp. 1, 4. See also *New York Herald Tribune,* September 22, 1942, p. 1; *New York Times,* September 22, 1942, p. 5; Dreiser,

leaflet, an open letter to editors, October 6, 1942; Dreiser, conversation with Elias, September 30, 1945.

42 Dreiser, conversation with Elias, September 30, 1945; Homer Croy, conversation with Elias, December 29, 1944; *Indianapolis Star*, October 5, 1942 (RHE); Hazel Godwin to Elias, October 5, 1950 (RHE).
43 A. M. Mathieu to Dreiser, February 22, 1943.
44 Dreiser to Mencken, March 27, 1943.

XV

1 Dreiser: "Myself and the Movies," p. 50.
2 Ibid., p. 159.
3 Theodore Dreiser: "The Myth of Individuality," *American Mercury*, XXXI (March 1934), 341.
4 Recorded by Arthur Davison Ficke, and quoted in Ficke to Elias, February 5, 1945 (RHE). Printed here by the kind permission of Mr. Ficke.
5 Dreiser to Richard L. Simon, February 14, 1935.
6 Dreiser to Sulamith Ish-Kishor, March 5, 1935.
7 *The Living Thoughts of Thoreau* (New York & Toronto: Longmans, Green; 1939), p. 35.
8 Theodore Dreiser: "An Address to Caliban," *Esquire*, II (September 1934), 158D.
9 Theodore Dreiser: "Solution," *Woman's Home Companion*, LX (November 1933), 135.
10 Theodore Dreiser: "The Tithe of the Lord," *Esquire*, X (July 1938), 36–7, 150, 155, 157–8.
11 Theodore Dreiser: "Mark the Double Twain," *English Journal*, XXIV (October 1935), 616.
12 Samuel Butler: *The Way of All Flesh*, introduction by Theodore Dreiser (2 vols.; New York: Limited Editions Club; 1936), I, xxx.
13 *This Is My Best*, edited by Whit Burnett (New York: Dial Press; 1942), p. 3.
14 Dreiser to George Douglas, December 15, 1934.
15 Dreiser: "The Myth of Individuality," pp. 337–8; Theo-

dore Dreiser: "You, the Phantom," *Esquire*, II (November 1934), 25–6.

[16] Theodore Dreiser: "Kismet," *Esquire*, III (January 1935), 29, 175–6.

[17] P. 25.

[18] Pp. 382–3.

[19] *Moods, Philosophic and Emotional, Cadenced and Declaimed* (New York: Simon & Schuster; 1935), p. 82. See also Theodore Dreiser: "Overland Journey," *Esquire*, IV (September 1935), 97.

[20] Dreiser to George Douglas, March 16, 1935.

[21] William James: *The Varieties of Religious Experience* (New York: Modern Library; cop. 1902), pp. 371–2.

[22] Dreiser to George Douglas, January 11, 1935 (RHE).

[23] Edited by Amy Rowland (New York: Norton; cop. 1936), p. 17.

[24] Dreiser to George Crile, August 7, 1936.

[25] W. Somerset Maugham: *Of Human Bondage* (2 vols.; New Haven: Limited Editions Club; 1938), I, iv–v.

[26] Ibid., vi. See also May Cameron of the *New York Post* to Dreiser, January 27, 1938, typescript revised by Dreiser; Theodore Dreiser: "If Man Is Free, So Is All Matter," *Forum*, XCVIII (December 1937), 301.

[27] Dreiser, conversation with Elias, August 26, 1941. See also Theodore Dreiser: *The Bulwark* (Garden City, N. Y.: Doubleday; 1946), p. 318.

[28] *I Believe*, edited by Clifton Fadiman (New York: Simon & Schuster; 1939), pp. 361–2. See also Theodore Dreiser: "Good and Evil," *North American Review*, CCXLVI (Autumn 1938), 86.

[29] Dreiser: "You, the Phantom," p. 26.

[30] Marguerite Tjader: "Dreiser's Last Visit to New York," *Twice A Year*, XIV–XV (Fall–Winter 1946–7), 217–18; Dreiser, conversation with Elias, September 21, 1945; Marguerite Tjader Harris, conversation with Elias, October 2, 1945.

[31] *Dallas Morning News*, August 14, 1938 (UP).

[32] Typescript, n.d. [November 1943] (HD). See also Dreiser to Dorothy Payne Davis, July 18, 1940.

[33] I am assisted and supported in my conclusions by John Cowper Powys in a letter to me, December 29, 1944 (RHE).

[34] Dreiser, conversation with Elias, May 20, 1944. See also Tjader: "Dreiser's Last Visit to New York," pp. 217–18, 224. I am indebted to Professor Tinker for a copy of his Academy citation.

[35] Tjader: "Dreiser's Last Visit to New York," p. 220.

[36] Typescript, copy courtesy of Marguerite Tjader Harris; printed as "Broadcast by Theodore Dreiser," *Direction*, VII (Summer 1944), 4.

[37] Typescript, copy courtesy of Marguerite Tjader Harris; quoted in Tjader: "Dreiser's Last Visit to New York," p. 220.

[38] Theodore Dreiser: "The Russian Advance," *Soviet Russia Today*, XIII (July 1944), 9.

[39] Dreiser, conversation with Elias, June 3, 1944.

[40] Dreiser to Mme Chiang Kai-shek, July 3, 1944 (HD).

[41] Dreiser to Wendell L. Willkie, June 23, 1944 (HD).

[42] Tjader: "Dreiser's Last Visit to New York," p. 227.

[43] Marguerite Tjader Harris, conversation with Elias, October 2, 1945. See also Harris, conversation with Elias, August 27, 1945; Marguerite Tjader: "Dreiser's Last Year . . . 'The Bulwark' in the Making," *Book Find News*, II (March 1946), 6–7; Helen R. Dreiser to Elias, February 19, 1946 (RHE).

[44] Marguerite Tjader Harris, conversation with Elias, August 27, 1945; Helen R. Dreiser to Louise Campbell, March 8, 1949. See also Marguerite Tjader: *Theodore Dreiser: A New Dimension* (Norwalk, Conn.: Silvermine Publishers; cop. 1965), pp. 166–7, 176–8.

[45] Marguerite Tjader Harris, conversation with Elias, August 27, 1945.

[46] The account of the revising of *The Bulwark* is based on Dreiser to James T. Farrell, June 20, 1945; Farrell to

Dreiser, June 25, 1945; Dreiser to Donald B. Elder, August 10 and December 22, 1945; Elder to Louise Campbell, September 4, 1945; Elder to Dreiser, September 20, 1945; Farrell to Elder, October 9, 1945; Elder to Farrell, October 11, 1945; my conversations with Elder and Farrell, October 19, 1945; and Helen R. Dreiser to Elias, June 16 and 22, 1948 (RHE). (For copies of the Elder correspondence [RHE] I am indebted to the kindness of Mr. Elder and of Mr. Walter I. Bradbury, of Doubleday & Co.)

⁴⁷ *The Bulwark*, p. 319.

⁴⁸ Ibid., p. 330.

⁴⁹ Ibid., p. 331.

⁵⁰ Ibid., p. 337.

⁵¹ See also Robert Elias: "Theodore Dreiser: or, The World Well Lost," *Book Find News*, II (March 1946), 22.

⁵² *Free World*, X (September 1945), 70.

⁵³ Ibid., IX (March 1945), 10.

⁵⁴ Dreiser, conversation with Elias, September 21, 1945.

⁵⁵ Helen R. Dreiser: "Meet the Author," broadcast over Station KFI (Los Angeles), script, p. 4 (RHE).

⁵⁶ Dreiser to Donald B. Elder, December 22, 1945 (copy courtesy of Doubleday & Co.: RHE); Dreiser to James T. Farrell, October 24, December 3, 14, 24, 1945; James T. Farrell in the *Sunday Bulletin Book Review* (Philadelphia), November 9, 1947, pp. 1, 7; Farrell, conversation with Elias, December 27, 1945.

⁵⁷ Helen R. Dreiser to Elias, September 3, 1946 (RHE); Dreiser to William Z. Foster, July 20, 1945, printed in *Daily Worker* (New York), July 30, 1945, p. 5.

⁵⁸ Dreiser, conversation with Elias, September 10, 1945.

⁵⁹ Helen R. Dreiser to Elias, February 7, 1946 (RHE), and July 26, 1948 (RHE).

⁶⁰ Transcript of services, January 3, 1946 (RHE).

⁶¹ *New York Herald Tribune*, February 3, 1946, sec. 1, p. 46.

A Survey of Research
and Criticism

BIBLIOGRAPHY

No comprehensive bibliography of Dreiser's works exists, nor is there any wholly adequate checklist of books and articles about him. Edward D. McDonald's *A Bibliography of the Writings of Theodore Dreiser* (Philadelphia, 1928) and Vrest Orton's *Dreiserana: A Book about His Books* (New York, 1929) attempt to combine the interests of the scholar with those of the collector, but although each does the collector a service in identifying first issues and first editions, neither can be called complete even for 1928 and 1929, and in the light of evidence gathered during the past forty years concerning Dreiser's contributions to periodicals, neither does more than provide a beginning for the recovery of his uncollected writings. Valuable supplementary information is embodied in John F. Huth, Jr.'s "Theodore Dreiser: Success Monger" (*Colophon*, Winter 1938) and "Dreiser and Success: An Additional Note" (*Colophon*, Summer 1938); in *Merle Johnson's American First Edition* (rev. Jacob Blanck, New York, 1942); in Ralph N. Miller's *A Preliminary Checklist of Books and Articles on Theodore Dreiser* (mimeographed by the Western Michigan College Library, Autumn 1947); in J. H. Birss's "Record of Theodore Dreiser: A Bibliographical Note" (*Notes and Queries*, September 30, 1933); in *The Stature of Theodore Dreiser* (ed. Alfred Kazin and Charles Shapiro, Bloomington, Ind., 1955; hereinafter referred to as K & S); and in Hugh C. Atkinson's *The Merrill Checklist of Theodore Dreiser* (Columbus, Ohio, 1969). A more complete compilation should be found in Atkinson's *Theodore Dreiser: A Checklist* (Kent, Ohio, scheduled 1970). Numerous rare or obscure magazines and newspapers remain unexplored, however; Dreiser's contributions under pseudonyms and writings by others under Dreiser's name are unaccounted for, and, except for Birss, no one has yet attempted to list any of his appearances on the screen or the transcriptions of his voice on the radio. Perhaps the *Dreiser Newsletter*, which the English Department of Indiana State University, Terre Haute, has undertaken to publish semi-annually, beginning in the spring of 1970, will include information such as this.

EDITIONS

Although as early as the twenties Dreiser was hoping for a standard or uniform edition of his complete works, and a few years before his death was still trying to arrange for publication of such a set, no such edition has yet been published, and little care has been devoted to producing reliable texts for even the major works that are kept in print. Claude M. Simpson, Jr., in the Riverside edition of *Sister Carrie* (Boston, 1959), points to one arithmetic error by Dreiser and identifies a few significant manuscript revisions. Jack Salzman, in "Dreiser and Ade: A Note on the Text of *Sister Carrie*" (*American Literature*, January 1969), calls attention to changes Dreiser made for the 1907 reissue (the text till recently for all reprints) to mask his plagiarism from George Ade's *Fables in Slang*—perhaps the most important variant that Salzman lists in his annotated edition of the novel (Indianapolis, 1969). René Rapin ("Dreiser's *Jennie Gerhardt*, Chapter LXII," *Explicator*, May 1956) explains that the lack of clarity in part of the final scene of Dreiser's second novel is the result of a typist's or printer's failure to read Dreiser's handwriting carefully. Robert Palmer Saalbach, editor of *Selected Poems (from Moods) by Theodore Dreiser* (New York, 1969), furnishes publication data and variants for the poetry he reprints. And that is the textual attention that Dreiser has received, even though some of the editorial questions are relatively simple (concerning, for example, the placement of *Sister Carrie's* chapter titles, the retention of *Jennie Gerhardt's* Epilogue, the choice between the 1912 and the

1927 *The Financier*, the identification of the corrected edition of *Tragic America*) and the different published forms of many of Dreiser's shorter works are accessible and easy to collate. A definitive, scholarly edition of Dreiser's writings was projected in 1969 with the University of Pennsylvania as sponsor, but unhappily could not at that time proceed beyond the initial discussions for want of funds. It is worth noting that the first attempt to collect some of Dreiser's uncollected writings has been made in the Soviet Union: Dreiser's *Essays and Articles* (Moscow, 1951) includes (in English) chapters from *Tragic America* and *America Is Worth Saving*, together with five articles or public statements culled from *New Masses, International Literature, Soviet Russia Today,* and the *Daily Worker.*

MANUSCRIPTS AND LETTERS

The major repository for Dreiser's papers is the Charles Patterson Van Pelt Library of the University of Pennsylvania. Notes, various manuscript drafts, and the galley and page proofs of almost all the published works are housed there, as well as a number of unpublished and unfinished works, diaries and journals, notes for projects, photographs, Dreiser's own library, a vast collection of first editions and translations of his writings, files of his contributions to periodicals, folders of clippings and reviews, thousands of letters by or to him, memorabilia—and photocopies of material in other libraries. Although no other library can lay claim to possessing any unusually large collection of Dreiserana, Cornell University, the Enoch Pratt Free Library in Baltimore, Indiana University, and the New York Public Library have a number of manuscripts, valuable documents, and rare editions.

The scope and character of the University of Pennsylvania collection has been briefly described in Robert H. Elias, "The Library's Dreiser Collection" (*Library Chronicle* [University of Pennsylvania] Fall 1950); in the American Philosophical Society's *Yearbook 1953* (Philadelphia, 1954);

and in Neda M. Westlake, "Theodore Dreiser's 'Notes on Life'" (*Library Chronicle,* Summer 1954) and "Theodore Dreiser Collection—Addenda" (*Library Chronicle,* Winter 1959); and in R. N. Mookerjee, "An Embarrassment of Riches: Dreiser Research: Materials and Problems" (*Indian Journal of American Studies,* July 1969).

Of such manuscript materials, thus far only selections of Dreiser's letters have reached print in book form. Robert H. Elias has edited a three-volume *Letters of Theodore Dreiser* (Philadelphia, 1959), and Louise Campbell has edited *Letters to Louise: Theodore Dreiser's Letters to Louise Campbell* (Philadelphia, 1959). *Letters of Theodore Dreiser* makes generally accessible some letters that illuminate Dreiser the writer. The emphasis is on his literary interests, his attitudes toward his work and the work of contemporaries, his relationship to other writers, especially H. L. Mencken, his conception of the social or public role of the literary artist, the point of view that, in short, shaped his books. A few letters to women with whom Dreiser was intimate are included, but these are limited to documents that relate directly to his writing. With very few exceptions, the letters are printed in their entirety, and the standardization of form has been kept to a minimum. There are numerous explanatory notes, full of bibliographical as well as biographical information. The effect is, on the whole, to clarify the relation of the man to his books.

Mrs. Campbell's volume of 117 letters serves as a useful complement. From 1917 to 1945 she was one of Dreiser's confidantes and literary assistants, and his letters to her show the extent to which he relied on others to "fix up" his manuscripts for publication. In these labors she shares honors with Arthur Henry, H. L. Mencken, Floyd Dell, and Horace Liveright. Although Mrs. Campbell consented to the prior publication of more than a quarter of these letters in the three-volume selection, their presentation here as a unified group, accompanied by her commentaries, increases their biographical value. Unfortunately, her text is not always reliable. Dreiser's handwriting is sometimes misread; phrases, sentences, and even postscripts are on occasion silently omitted; one letter exhibits a radical disarrangement of the order of the pages of the original document—and there is no index.

Some scholars have lamented the omission of genuine love letters from the two selections. Dreiser's emotional attachments were never wholly separate from his literary career, and indeed, some of his work can be accounted for only if one has some knowledge of his private life. In 1959, however, the editors could draw upon but two or three bundles, which illuminated only the most ephemeral of affairs, and in an incredibly tiresome fashion. Since then, however, more important and representative letters have reached the libraries, including many to Dreiser's first wife, "Jug," and any new selection of Dreiser's letters will certainly have to include them along with other recently discovered material that can fill in the gaps in the story of Dreiser's early years. Richard W. Dowell's " 'You will not like me, I'm sure': Dreiser to Miss Emma Rector, November 28, 1893, to April 4, 1894" (*American Literary Realism, 1870–1910*, Summer 1970) and William White's "Dreiser on Hardy, Henley, and Whitman: An Unpublished Letter [1902]" (*English Language Notes*, December 1968) are likely to be only among the first of numerous contributions to this category.

A few letters by Dreiser have from time to time appeared in memoirs or articles written by Dreiser's correspondents. Although almost all the significant ones are included in the three-volume *Letters*, the correspondents often provide a commentary that enlarges the meaning of the documents; so they, too, should be consulted. Four in particular are worth listing: Grant Richards, *Author Hunting by an Old Literary Sportsman* (London, 1934); Albert Mordell, *My Relations with Theodore Dreiser* (Girard, Kan., 1951); "Dreiser Discusses *Sister Carrie*" (*Masses & Mainstream*, December 1955); James T. Farrell, "Some Correspondence with Theodore Dreiser" (*General Magazine and Historical*

A Survey of Research and Criticism

Chronicle [University of Pennsylvania], Summer 1951; reprinted in K & S and in Farrell's *Reflections at Fifty*, New
York, 1954); and Bruce Crawford, "Theodore Dreiser,
Letter-Writing Citizen" (*South Atlantic Quarterly*, April
1954).

BIOGRAPHY

H. L. Mencken is Dreiser's first biographer. Even though
A Book of Prefaces (New York, 1917) is essentially a volume of critical essays (one is reprinted in K & S), his treatment of Dreiser includes an account of Dreiser's career that,
based as it is largely on what Dreiser himself told Mencken,
remained for many years the standard account. Dreiser's
Indiana origins, his journalistic experiences, his first stories,
the writing and publication of *Sister Carrie*, the ensuing
period of want, the editorial work that culminated in his
position at Butterick's, the rapid publication of numerous
books thereafter, the controversy over *The "Genius"*—all is
there, to be merely embellished or brought up to date in
minor ways by others for almost a decade and a half. Burton
Rascoe's *Theodore Dreiser* (New York, 1925), a slim book,
is valuable because it stresses Dreiser's capacity to respond
to "the epical quality . . . of American life" and to suggest
specific ways in which further studies of Dreiser might proceed, but it adds nothing except a few titles to Mencken's
account.

It is in 1932, with Dorothy Dudley's *Forgotten Frontiers:
Dreiser and the Land of the Free* (New York; reprinted as
Dreiser and the Land of the Free, New York, 1946) that
serious, full-length treatment of Dreiser begins. Miss Dudley, drawing on close acquaintance with Dreiser, on her experience in editing some of the sketches in *Twelve Men*,
and on selected but important sheafs of Dreiser's own papers, insists with verve and passion upon Dreiser's literary
dominance and modernity. Miss Dudley's association with
members of a large literary and artistic coterie enables her
to describe with some acuteness Dreiser's personal and artis-

tic relations with his contemporaries. In fact, her purpose is primarily to relate Dreiser to his country and his time, to portray a large figure amid events. *Forgotten Frontiers* is impressionistic rather than analytic, declarative rather than systematic—a drawer full of likely treasures. Miss Dudley quotes from letters, reprints excerpts from newspapers, reports what Dreiser says concerning his career. She is not always accurate, sometimes gullible or misled, seldom interested in documentation, but usually worth verifying. And she must bear credit for having shown the wealth and complexity of material available and for having, more excitingly than any predecessor, pointed, if only by implication, to what would have to be done by future scholars.

Robert H. Elias's *Theodore Dreiser: Apostle of Nature* (New York, 1949), an earlier edition of the present book, is more systematic than Miss Dudley's book, narrower in scope, yet in some ways more complete. Elias is concerned with the career of Dreiser's attitude toward the individual and with how an understanding of that career can clarify the meaning of Dreiser's writings. He shows how Dreiser's boyhood, education, and newspaper experiences prepare him to react as he does when he encounters the works of Balzac and of Herbert Spencer, how his various writings embody and define his central philosophical concerns, and how his social views and political commitments are related to his literary accomplishments. Elias was acquainted with Dreiser during the last eight years of Dreiser's life, and had the benefit of unhampered access to most of Dreiser's papers after his death—although some major documents remained not only inaccessible but unknown. In addition, since his book was also to meet the requirements for a doctoral dissertation, it had to satisfy the usual scholarly criteria. It is, therefore, a carefully documented biography, sharply focused, and full of useful and new source material, with the advantage over *Forgotten Frontiers* of being able to consider Dreiser's complete career. Yet it relates only part of the story. As its most hostile critic (Irving Howe, "Dreiser Undone," *Nation*, February 5, 1949) points out, there is in it no full account of Dreiser's relation to his society and times, or of the extent to which his ideas resemble those of Social Darwinism, or of how he might be considered an intellectual crank. Nor are his novels evaluated and analyzed in primarily aesthetic terms. Nonetheless, insofar as the pattern of Dreiser's life is defined and its ironies are disclosed, judgments are made.

In the nine books about Dreiser that have appeared since 1949, biographical and critical purposes have, for the most part, been kept distinct. On the one hand, a memoir by Dreiser's second wife, Helen Dreiser's *My Life with Dreiser* (Cleveland, 1951), simply tells, from the point of view of a frequent, intimate participant, about Dreiser's activities—the places he went, the people he knew, the causes he advocated—between 1919 and his death. The intention is to recall some of Dreiser's milieu, and, near the conclusion, to clarify the record concerning the completion and publication of *The Bulwark*. The value of such an account is obvious. More important as a contribution to an understanding of Dreiser the writer is Mrs. Dreiser's frank account of his cruel varietism and the way it stimulated his creative work.

F. O. Matthiessen's *Theodore Dreiser* (New York, 1951), on the other hand, is primarily a work of criticism, for he makes no attempt to contribute anything original in the way of facts. Matthiessen's intention is to give Dreiser the sort of full critical consideration that he previously gave the American Renaissance and Henry James. His critical sensibility and liberal sympathies join to enable him to argue that Dreiser's writing, despite some weaknesses, can stand a careful, analytic approach. He finds positive values in Dreiser's use of details: they provide perspective and the weight of historical record to produce the effects that numerous critics have noted but never adequately accounted for. He describes the artistic virtues of Dreiser's images of social insecurity, his symbols, and even his language. Matthiessen establishes his position in his analysis of *Sister Carrie*, but he makes clear that his response to Dreiser is not simple adulation, and goes on to show that *The Titan's* range is limited and that *The "Genius"* wants adequate perspective. It is *An American Tragedy* that provides the critical climax. In the chapter devoted to that novel (reprinted in K & S) Matthiessen distinguishes between Dreiser's tragic sense and traditional tragedy, and although he concedes that Clyde is "below" tragedy and "so exclusively . . . the overwhelmed victim that we feel hardly any of the crisis of moral guilt that is also at the heart of the tragic experience," he treats Dreiser with a respect and devotion that only the important writers can earn.

Charles Shapiro, in *Theodore Dreiser: Our Bitter Patriot* (Carbondale, Ill., 1962), like Matthiessen, does not concern himself with adding to factual knowledge, but also like Matthiessen, attempts to give meaning to Dreiser's literary development. Where Matthiessen is interested in defining Dreiser's life in terms of increasing artistic control, Shapiro is interested in interpreting it in terms of a sequence of "underlying themes" in the novels. *Sister Carrie* is "a close study of the individual"; *Jennie Gerhardt* concerns "the American family"; the Cowperwood trilogy treats business, *The "Genius"* the artist, *The Bulwark* religion; and *An American Tragedy* is "the story of all America." So schematized an account is difficult to accept. Dreiser's shifting concerns were less for specific institutions or aspects of American life than for new ways of exploring the changing fortunes of individuals. Nonetheless, insofar as Shapiro gives attention to details and their functions in his discussions of the novels, and is familiar with the whole canon, his readings, all of them careful, are in themselves illuminating.

A balanced summary of Dreiser's career, combining the factual with the critical, is Philip L. Gerber's *Theodore Dreiser* (New York, 1964). Gerber is primarily interested in emphasizing the events in Dreiser's life that bear most directly on the writings and the extent to which the novels in particular embody Dreiser's ideas. He does little to uncover new material. At the same time, he pays more attention to the relationship between Frank Cowperwood and Charles T. Yerkes than has been paid before, makes more use of secondary sources than Matthiessen or Shapiro does, is rarely inaccurate, and is the first biographer to have before him the published letters. Gerber's tone is generally dispassionate; he is aware of all the arguments bearing on Dreiser's style and absorbs them; his favorable judgment of Dreiser accordingly seems a completely objective one.

The closest to a definitive life that is likely to appear for some years is W. A. Swanberg's *Dreiser* (New York, 1965). Swanberg makes no attempt to account for Dreiser as artist, and he eschews consistently the role of literary critic. But he brings together such a mass of materials, and cites so many sources, that he makes available to the literary critic almost all that a biographer can. From memoirs and earlier biographical studies, from unpublished documents only lately accessible, from interviews with innumerable men and women who knew Dreiser and were willing to talk when approached by a diplomat armed with a tape recorder, Swanberg has produced a rich story. He has documented Dreiser's activities for periods hitherto left relatively empty; he has looked into gossip and rumors; he has placed in proper order the bewildering welter of financial, passional, political, and artistic enterprises that made Dreiser both an involved and an isolated figure in American letters. Diaries are quoted; Dreiser's free use of other writers' phrases is clarified; his association with the minor Bohemians as well as with major literary contemporaries is recounted with insight and understanding. On occasion, Swanberg relies too heavily on Dreiser's autobiographies, which are not always trustworthy, or on those portions of *Forgotten Frontiers* and of the earlier edition of Elias's study that in a few instances neglected to verify Dreiser's oral testimony. And in some minor matters he has been inaccurate (see Elias's review in *American Literature,* November 1966). On the whole, however, although his story may need to be added to here and there, it is unlikely soon to be superseded.

One book that serves to complement Swanberg's is Marguerite Tjader's *Theodore Dreiser: A New Dimension* (Norwalk, Conn., 1965). Comparable to Helen Dreiser's memoir in its personal approach, it is both narrower in scope and more valuable to the scholar and critic. Marguerite Tjader—Mrs. Harris—first met Dreiser in 1928, played a minor part in his literary life in the early thirties, and had a major role as amanuensis in the writing of *The Bulwark.* In referring to matters like the price of the moving-picture rights to *An American Tragedy* or the date of the reprinting of *Forgotten Frontiers,* she is inaccurate; but in larger matters—in portraying Dreiser's friends, gatherings, personal relationships generally—she is a fine observer, and in quoting from Dreiser's notes and early drafts to reveal how Dreiser shaped and completed the final version of *The Bulwark,* she presents Dreiser the writer more authentically than any one else yet has.

A second book that adds to Swanberg's portrait is Ruth Epperson Kennell's *Theodore Dreiser and the Soviet Union, 1927–1945: A First-Hand Chronicle* (New York, 1969). As Dreiser's private secretary, chosen interpreter, guide, and keeper of his diary, she was in a position to accompany him on the tour that colored the last eighteen years of his life, to participate in most of the social gatherings he attended, and to transcribe with careful attention to gestures and settings the numerous interviews he had with artists, journalists, political figures, and just ordinary workers. Since the original diary, many pages of which are in Dreiser's own hand, is in the University of Pennsylvania's collection, it was already used by Swanberg. But Mrs. Kennell does more than merely corroborate what has been told; from her own carbon copy she records the most important interviews in full and then goes on, in the last part of the book, to show that the meaning of Dreiser's experience is ultimately in the commitment to social causes, especially the support of the Soviet Union, that occupied him to the last. Although there is nothing in her summary of these activities that is new, she quotes from enough of the personal, affectionate letters he wrote her through the years that followed his trip to communicate a genuine sense of the man his intimates knew.

John J. McAleer's *Theodore Dreiser: An Introduction and Interpretation* (New York, 1968) is still another book-length study that attempts to be complementary, in this instance by filling in "voids in Dreiser scholarship" through a brief reinterpretation of published evidence rather than through a presentation of new facts. McAleer's intention is to clarify the relationship between Dreiser's experience and his art, as well as to assess his technique, in order to give new significance to Dreiser's career and accomplishment. As a biographer, McAleer is, unfortunately, insufficiently systematic or rigorous in developing parallels and connections between ideas and events to provide a new view of either Dreiser the man or Dreiser the thinker; one has the impression of two separate books arbitrarily joined. On the other hand, as a literary analyst, McAleer is more acute: he clearly grasps Dreiser's concern with and rendering of the conflict between "Nature" and "the American Dream" and is able to provide both a persuasive, fresh reading of the major works and a suggestion of how to see Dreiser's fiction whole. Although his notion that Dreiser's rocking chair and some other props are sexual surrogates seems occasionally imposed on the materials, he is so consistently successful in demonstrating harmony between theme, structure, and style that he makes a valuable contribution to the understanding of the Dreiser Mrs. Harris presents—the writer who is off stage in Swanberg's book.

It is Dreiser the writer who now most needs to be investigated and understood, and it is this Dreiser who constitutes the subject of two major studies, both recent: Ellen Moers,

Two Dreisers (New York, 1969), and Richard Lehan, *Theodore Dreiser: His World and His Novels* (Carbondale, Ill., 1969). Miss Moers, writing what is essentially a "biography" of *Sister Carrie* and *An American Tragedy*, helps fill in the few remaining gaps in Swanberg's chronicle, gives Dreiser increased historical significance, and offers new light on Dreiser's literary methods. Placing Dreiser in the company of such spokesmen of the modern mind as Yeats, Joyce, Shaw, Proust, Stravinsky, and Picasso, she also sees, and shows, that Dreiser is no "sport." With the support of recently collected material, and of old material often too hastily scrutinized by her predecessors, she documents the pre-*Carrie* years to demonstrate the many points of contact between Dreiser and his contemporaries. The long "classified" letters to Jug, Dreiser's first wife (which Miss Moers was permitted to read but not quote), numerous articles in a variety of elusive magazines, correspondence with biologists, psychologists, and psychiatrists, all help document persuasively the origins of Dreiser's ideas, the course of his reactions to them, and the artistic influence of the Ash-Can painters, photographers such as Stieglitz, and writers such as George Ade and Stephen Crane. Miss Moers spells out in detail Dreiser's neglected interest in the work of his Wundtian friend, Elmer Gates; she establishes beyond challenge Dreiser's extensive verbal indebtedness to Stephen Crane; she traces the development of the Dreiser-Howells relationship and quotes in full a long letter from Dreiser to Howells that is among the most arresting and touching Dreiser ever wrote; she demonstrates how the Bowery themes of the naturalists (writers and painters alike) and the Gay Nineties atmosphere in which Paul moved affect the character of *Sister Carrie*. She also shows the extent to which Dreiser draws on his sister Emma's affair with L. A. Hopkins to form and develop George Hurstwood, the use he makes of the theater not only in dramatizing Carrie's career but also in giving a symbolic dimension to his theme, the way his ambivalent relationship with Paul and Rome influences some of his characterization, how a fear of drowning during his boyhood reverberates in Roberta Alden's death in *An American Tragedy*, and the contribution that Greenwich Village Freudianism and Dr. A. A. Brill make, more generally, to *An American Tragedy*'s imagery and metaphors. She studies the revisions in the *Sister Carrie* manuscript; she examines Dreiser's interest in the work of Jacques Loeb; she establishes more precisely than others have done the dates of composition of some of the early sketches, most notably those later gathered in *Twelve Men*; she even finds the source of "chemism." Biography and criticism thus strengthen each other and open a new path to Dreiser.

Lehan shares some of Miss Moers's interests but is both less and more comprehensive. Focusing on "the genesis and evolution of the novels, their pattern, and their meaning," he narrows his consideration of influences to those that "most shaped Dreiser's imagination"—his family, the city, writing for the newspapers and magazines, books, and political and scientific ideas. At the same time, Lehan extends his discussion to all Dreiser's novels and attempts to define the achievement that they constitute individually and collectively. The biographical information he provides contains only a little that is new, and some of the details of Dreiser's life in the Village and later relations with the Communists lack a clear thematic function. Moreover, as Philip L. Gerber has pointed out (*Dreiser Newsletter*, Spring 1970), there are a number of factual errors, particularly with reference to Charles T. Yerkes's career and the reading of some of Dreiser's handwritten notations. Yet, such defects remain relatively minor in a book that for the first time attempts a systematic examination of Dreiser's notes, files of clippings, holograph versions of the autobiographies and the novels, together with the revisions, to show how he used his personal experiences and his research to create the char-

acters and effects that have given those novels their significance. The scrutiny that Lehan devotes to this material enables him to clarify what is distinctive about each of the
novels, but for all that clarification he is more committed
to demonstrating similarities and recurrences. He believes
that Dreiser's literary preoccupations and emphases were
fixed by 1912; romantic emotion and mechanistic idea would
always contend, leading to the development of characters
whose yearnings would inexorably bring them into encounters with material limits. The relation of chance to the characters' predetermined response to it, the sense of a life beneath the surface of civilization's clichés, the displacement
consequent upon the hero's attempt to reconcile natural and
social contexts—these Lehan finds in each story like variations of a constant. It is their manifestations and not their
author's ideas or fundamental attitudes that evolve. In fact,
according to Lehan, Dreiser's own evolution is primarily in
terms of artistic competence; the concerns may shift in response to a changing world, but the pattern is unchanged.
In *The Bulwark* and *The Stoic*, therefore, Lehan finds the
embodiment of the early Dreiser; the conflicts and contradictions are simply transferred to a larger realm, where self-
fulfillment and greed become the self-fulfillment and greed
of forces. Such transference might, though, be regarded as
evidence of an author's evolution.

Although most of the important published source material has been embodied in large biographical contexts,
some articles offer new evidence for the record and others
remain of interest in themselves. Joseph Katz, in "Theodore
Dreiser at Indiana University" (*Notes and Queries*, March
1966), examines the university's publications not only to
find out what courses Dreiser took and what grades he received, but also to discover that in November 1889 he was
a member of the Philomathean, the major literary society,
and its elected secretary for the winter trimester. Edward D.
McDonald, in "Dreiser Before *Sister Carrie*" (*Bookman*,

June 1928), enumerates and classifies Dreiser's free-lance contributions to the magazines during 1895–1906; his survey is in no sense complete, but it is a pioneering one and suggests projects that have yet to be undertaken in a thoroughgoing way. John F. Huth, Jr., in three articles adds details to McDonald's account: "Theodore Dreiser: Prophet" (*American Literature*, May 1937); "Theodore Dreiser: Success Monger" (*Colophon*, Winter 1938); and "Dreiser and Success: An Additional Note" (*Colophon*, Summer 1938). In the first he analyzes and quotes from Dreiser's editorial contributions to *Ev'ry Month*, a partial file of which came into Huth's possession, and shows Dreiser's early sympathy with Spencer, his interest in the deprived, and his concern with the living conditions in cities. In the other two pieces he demonstrates how numerous interviews that Dreiser wrote for *Success* were published in book form by the editor, Orison Swett Marden, without being credited to Dreiser. Myrta Lockett Avary supplements Huth's articles in "Success—and Dreiser" (*Colophon*, Autumn 1938), telling about some of the individuals who worked with her for *Success* and the *Christian Herald* and briefly mentioning a meeting with Dreiser, "the ugliest man I ever knew and one of the most interesting." Few details are known about Dreiser's editing of dime novels for Street & Smith in 1905, but Kenneth W. Scott, in "Did Dreiser Cut Up Jack Harkaway?" (*Markham Review*, May 1968), conjectures that it was Dreiser who skillfully re-edited Bracebridge Hemyng's series and updated the political references. Although Scott relies on circumstantial evidence rather than on the usual documentary proofs, what he says is plausible.

Dreiser's relations with literary contemporaries are treated in special articles and in books about other writers. Van Wyck Brooks, in *Howells, His Life and World* (New York, 1959), quoting from a 1902 letter Dreiser wrote Howells, establishes Dreiser's "spiritual affection" for Howells and his interest in Hardy and Tolstoy, and notes that Howells in turn praised the "plain poetry" of "The Lost Phoebe." This relationship is one that Miss Moers explores in greater depth and more detail. Lars Åhnebrink, in "Garland and Dreiser: An Abortive Friendship" (*Midwest Journal*, Winter 1955–6), shows that although Garland admired *Sister Carrie* in 1902 and was friendly to Dreiser when they met ten years later, his loyalty to Robert Underwood Johnson, who resigned the editorship of the *Century* because of its publication of *A Traveler at Forty* and was a member of the National Institute of Arts and Letters, led Garland to feel increasingly cool toward Dreiser, to refuse help in the fight against the suppression of *The "Genius,"* and ultimately to view Dreiser with disgust and repulsion. Dreiser's association with other midwesterners is described fully in Dale Kramer's *Chicago Renaissance: The Literary Life in the Midwest, 1900–1930* (New York, 1966). Here, in addition to Garland, are the Dells, Edgar Lee Masters, Henry Blake Fuller, Maurice Browne and his Little Theatre entourage, including Kirah Markham, and William Marion Reedy. Reedy's early encouragement of Dreiser and their joint plan to promote the work of Harris Merton Lyon ("De Maupassant, Jr.") is of particular interest and occupies two chapters of Max Putzel's careful and perceptive *The Man in the Mirror: William Marion Reedy and His Magazine* (Cambridge, Mass., 1963).

Dreiser's most important relationship was with H. L. Mencken. This is usually seen as one in which the critic Mencken champions the rebel Dreiser. Donald R. Stoddard outlines a less familiar part of the story. In "Mencken and Dreiser: An Exchange of Roles" (*Library Chronicle*, Spring 1966), he shows how Dreiser, while editor of the *Delineator*, served as Mencken's counselor and critic and how Dreiser not only helped him secure a book-reviewing job on the *Smart Set* but also set him an example of editorial counseling and energy that Mencken was later to emulate. A similarly unfamiliar account of Dreiser's relations with Sinclair Lewis is provided by Yoshinobu Hakutani, in "Sinclair Lewis and Dreiser: A Study in Continuity and Development" (*Discourse*, Summer 1964). The usual emphasis on the competition for the Nobel Prize and Lewis's charge that Dreiser was a plagiarist yields to Hakutani's interest in the development of the two men as writers, and their opinion of each other, beginning with Lewis's note in *Life* in 1907 and concluding with Lewis's composition of the citation to accompany the American Academy of Letters award to Dreiser in 1944. Dreiser did not have a high opinion of *Main Street*; Lewis always regarded Dreiser's writing with respect.

A number of Dreiser's friends and contemporaries have written memoirs and mentioned Dreiser in them. Scarcely one of them fails to show Dreiser as a hulking, inarticulate peasant, brooding, humorless, solitary, and socially awkward, seated in his rocking chair while, folding and unfolding a handkerchief, he fixes his visitor with a hard glance out of asymmetrically set eyes. There almost invariably follow anecdotes, and the author usually relates how he took Dreiser somewhere and showed him something (a place, a person, a condition) that Dreiser had never seen before, with the effect of making the great man wiser, sadder, or more thoughtful—and leaving the guide a bit triumphant and far more self-satisfied than Vergil ever felt after taking Dante on the rounds. Most of the important memoirs have been drawn upon by the biographers—especially Swanberg —and many have thus served their purpose for Dreiserians. Several, though, even when they have been used as source material, are worth citing, either because their point of view is fresh or because the context they provide has itself value.

Among the reminiscences there is little about the years before 1907. Carmel O'Neill Haley, in "The Dreisers" (*Commonweal*, July 7, 1933), remembers Dreiser's father, his brother Paul, and his sister Mary, but offers few details. Arthur Henry, in *Lodgings in Town* (New York, 1905), provides a glimpse of Dreiser (whom he does not name) during his editorship of *Ev'ry Month* and, in *An Island Cabin* (New York, 1902), tells of the weeks spent, during the summer of 1901, on the island off Noank with Dreiser, Jug, and Anna Mallon, to each of whom he gives a fictitious name. His accounts have the merit, however, of being almost contemporaneous with the facts.

Many writers have recalled Dreiser during the period of his editorship of the Butterick publications. Ludwig Lewisohn (*Cities and Men*, New York, 1927; reprinted in K & S) remembers Dreiser's connection with B. W. Dodge & Company, which first reissued *Sister Carrie*, as well as Dreiser's life in the Village during the First World War. Charles Hanson Towne (*Adventures in Editing*, New York, 1926), Homer Croy (*Country Cured*, New York, 1943), and William C. Lengel ("The 'Genius' Himself," *Esquire*, September 1938) provide portraits of Dreiser at work from the point of view of editorial associates. Lengel, in addition, first hired by Dreiser to be his secretary, then promoted to be his assistant, and ultimately, when an editor in his own right, also one of Dreiser's literary agents, knew Dreiser intimately and tells of reading Dreiser's work in progress—the sketches later gathered in *The Color of a Great City*, poems, and *Jennie Gerhardt*, first shown to Lengel under the title of *The Transgressor*. Lengel also provides, in introductions to reprints of *Twelve Men* and *A Gallery of Women* (Greenwich, Conn., 1962), notes on some of the prototypes for Dreiser's semifictional sketches.

Dreiser as European traveler in 1911–12 is described by Grant Richards in *Author Hunting by an Old Literary Sportsman*, in which the Barfleur of *A Traveler at Forty* not only reprints correspondence cited above, but also presents his side of the falling-out between them. Richards thus helps correct the impression left by Dorothy Dudley's *Forgotten Frontiers*.

Dreiser's visit to Chicago during the period in which he

was doing research for *The Titan* is mentioned by Edgar Lee Masters in *Across Spoon River* (New York, 1936). Masters reports that Dreiser spoke not only about the Cowperwood trilogy but also about his plan for *The Bulwark*, which Masters very briefly summarizes. In 1914 Masters took Dreiser to visit John Armstrong, son of Abe Lincoln's friend and landlady and brother of the man whom Lincoln defended with an almanac. The reaction of the two men to each other is effectively recounted in "Dreiser at Spoon River" (*Esquire*, May 1939).

Of the various accounts by writers who knew Dreiser immediately preceding World War I and during the war years and their aftermath, those most worth reading are those that either quote Dreiser or include details to document their impressions. Konrad Bercovici, in "Romantic Realist" (*Mentor*, May 1930), records how Dreiser could rhapsodize concerning New York, even while arguing that Glendale, California, was the place to live. H. L. Mencken, in "That Was New York: The Life of an Artist" (*New Yorker*, April 17, 1948), contrasts Dreiser's "strictly bourgeois" prewar life with his existence in the Village, where he was victimized by "Little Red Riding Hoods," boozers, lady poets, and cranks. Ford Madox Ford, who first met Dreiser in 1914, describes in *Portraits from Life* (Boston, 1937; reprinted in K & S) the impact that Dreiser's arguments could have and credits Dreiser with knowing all about literary style. Frank Harris, in *Contemporary Portraits, Second Series* (New York, 1919), quoting Dreiser extensively, attributes most of what he says about Dreiser's career and opinions to Dreiser himself. What he gives Dreiser to say rings true enough to give authenticity to the discussion of Dreiser's plans for a third volume about Yerkes. Of dubious critical importance, but of some biographical use, is a collection of primarily personal reactions, in prose, poetry, and caricature, published by the John Lane Company in a Pamphlet, *Theodore Dreiser: America's Foremost Novelist* (New York,

1916–17). Harris Merton Lyon, John Cowper Powys, Edgar Lee Masters, Peter B. McCord, and Arthur Davison Ficke are represented, and *The Bulwark* is advertised.

Dreiser in the twenties is seen from only restricted points of view. Claude Bowers, in *My Life: The Memoirs of Claude Bowers* (New York, 1962), dwells on Dreiser's interest in politics "and his abysmal ignorance of it"—and only sketchily portrays his life in the West 57th Street studio and at Iroki. George Jean Nathan, in *The Intimate Notebooks of George Jean Nathan* (New York, 1932), restricts himself mainly to the Dreiser who wished to encourage struggling artists ("neglected geniuses"), who was surprised by what everyone else found familiar, and who was too easily attracted to causes that urbane sophisticates like Nathan patiently disdained. The same account with a few sentences added about the *American Spectator* is included in Nathan's "Memories of Fitzgerald, Lewis, and Dreiser" (*Esquire*, October 1958). Donald Friede, in *The Mechanical Angel: His Adventures and Enterprises in the Glittering 1920's* (New York, 1948), reports Dreiser's reactions to a performance of Patrick Kearney's dramatization of *An American Tragedy* and explains his own participation in the defense of *An American Tragedy* in Boston. Michael Gold, in "The Dreiser I Knew," collected by Samuel Sillen in *The Mike Gold Reader* (New York, 1954), tells about showing Dreiser the East Side and taking him to meet Gold's mother at about the time Dreiser was writing *The Hand of the Potter*.

The Dreiser of the thirties is remembered as primarily a political figure. Orrick Johns, in *Time of Our Lives* (New York, 1937), speaks about the activities of the National Committee for the Defense of Political Prisoners and Dreiser's visit to Tom Mooney at San Quentin. Lester Cohen, in "Theodore Dreiser: A Personal Memoir," *Discovery 4* (New York, 1954), and Bruce Crawford, "Theodore Dreiser, Letter-Writing Citizen" (*South Atlantic Quarterly,*

April 1954), both make Dreiser's investigation of the Harlan County coal mines the center of interest. Hutchins Hapgood, in *A Victorian in the Modern World* (New York, 1939), was acquainted with Dreiser when Dreiser lived in the Village and was instrumental in having *The Hand of the Potter* staged; but the most valuable part of his recollection relates to his controversy with Dreiser over anti-Semitism, arising out of an *American Spectator* editorial symposium and concluding with an exchange of letters published in the *Nation*. *Sherwood Anderson's Memoirs* (New York, 1942) constitutes the single important exception to the political emphasis. Dreiser's parties in the twenties, including one at which F. Scott Fitzgerald appeared, Dreiser's conversations with friends such as Arthur Davison Ficke, who told Dreiser a man must learn to forgive himself, Dreiser's visit to an orphan asylum, provide the substance of some of Anderson's typical anecdotes. Anderson is so notoriously unreliable in his rendering of details, however, that no one can safely turn to his autobiographies for anything more objective than artistic reactions. James T. Farrell, in "Some Correspondence with Theodore Dreiser," cited earlier, documents the origin and course of Dreiser's final literary relationship.

A suggestive commentary on the whole of Dreiser's career with particular reference to his relations with other people is embodied in Anthony West's review of *Letters of Theodore Dreiser*, "Man Overboard" (*New Yorker*, April 25, 1959). West finds Dreiser increasingly concerned with his own status, full of self-regard, and limited by simplicity of mind.

Although interviewers are not usually considered biographers, four must be cited for their contribution to an interpretation of Dreiser's character and work. Edward H. Smith, a friend of Dreiser's, in "Dreiser—After 20 Years" (*Bookman*, March 1921), provides an accurate close-up of Dreiser the individual together with an extensive statement of

Dreiser's opinions about American literature. The accuracy of Smith's quotations can be verified by consulting the *Letters*: Dreiser was a collaborator. Rose C. Feld, in the *New York Times Book Review* (December 23, 1923), quotes at length Dreiser's views on realism and his condemnation of those younger writers who dwell on the dark and ugly aspects of American life. It is a significant and authentic document. Karl Sebestyén, in "Persons and Personages: Theodore Dreiser at Home" (*Living Age*, December 1930; translated from *Pester Lloyd*), offers a sensible interpretation of Dreiser the leftward-bound writer who also believes that the artist cannot be restricted by political doctrine. Finally, Robert Van Gelder, in "An Interview with Theodore Dreiser" (*New York Times Book Review*, March 16, 1941; collected in Van Gelder's *Writers and Writing*, New York, 1946), discloses the Dreiser of the closing years: pro-Soviet, anti-British and French, remembering his own critical struggles in the early 1900's. The rendering of Dreiser's tone of voice and speech patterns is singularly successful.

CRITICISM

General Commentaries

The only published account of Dreiser's critical reception in the United States is Stephen Stepanchev's *Dreiser Among The Critics: A Study of American Reactions to the Work of A Literary Naturalist, 1900–1949* (New York, 1950), an eight-page abridgment of his doctoral dissertation. It attempts to outline the career of Dreiser's reputation generally and of that of some of the individual works in particular. Stepanchev notes that the topics most often commented upon are Dreiser's philosophy, the drabness of his naturalism, his style, his characterization, and the way his works disclose his mind and personality. Stepanchev calls attention to the role of the New Humanists, the interest of well-known critics during the second decade of the century, and the extent to which Dreiser disappeared as a live issue from 1930 to 1941, only to regain some prominence by 1949. His account suggests that social, personal, economic, political, and philosophical considerations explain the fluctuations in Dreiser's reputation and concludes that the high regard in which Dreiser is held (in 1950) constitutes an American success story.

Some of the most significant documents in that story are collected by Alfred Kazin and Charles Shapiro in their anthology, *The Stature of Theodore Dreiser*, cited above. Their volume brings together articles and essays that range from personal reminiscences to special studies and includes statements representative of the most important points of view in the critical battle over naturalism. Sherwood Anderson, Mencken, Stuart Pratt Sherman, Sinclair Lewis, Randolph Bourne, Lionel Trilling, and James T. Farrell are among the better-known critics to be found here; but others of equal value are also included. Kazin's introduction is itself a significant illumination of Dreiser's importance; for it defines the effects of Dreiser's work, reviews the history of his reputation, and examines his total accomplishment in a way that places the essays that follow in clear perspective. Kazin concludes: "Dreiser hurts because he is always looking to the source; to that which broke off into the mysterious halves of man's existence; to that which is behind language and sustains it; to that which is not ourselves but gives life to our words." A list of selected biography and criticism is provided, usually sufficiently complete and accurate in the form of its citations to be useful and, in any event, the most complete checklist yet available.

H. L. Mencken is clearly the first to undertake a serious estimate of Dreiser's accomplishment, and is thus not only his first biographer but also his first critic. Earlier commentary is generally confined to the anonymous or impressionistic notices that once passed for book reviews. Mencken's public efforts in Dreiser's behalf, though beginning with a

378

review of *Jennie Gerhardt* in 1911, are best viewed in *A Book of Prefaces* (New York, 1917; an excerpt reprinted in K & S), for there he brings together in a single essay all his important comments of the preceding six years. Regarding American literature as too inclined to cater to the typical American who "seeks escape from the insoluble by pretending that it is solved," Mencken praises Dreiser by linking him with Hardy and Conrad as writers who bring to literature a "profound sense of wonder." Mencken makes clear that Dreiser is not a follower of Frank Norris or Émile Zola, and he carefully shows that although there are parallels between *Tess* and *Jennie*, the importance to Dreiser of Hardy, as of Balzac, was in conveying "a sense of the scope and dignity of the novel" and "the drama of the commonplace." Mencken understands how Dreiser's boyhood reading in Hawthorne and Irving could affect him, precisely how important was the impact of Thomas Huxley and Herbert Spencer, and how Dreiser finally simply adopted what was most congenial from the fiction and philosophy he read. For Mencken, the closest literary parallel is Conrad: "Both novelists see human existence as a seeking without a finding; both reject the prevailing interpretations of its meaning and mechanism; both take refuge in 'I do not know.'" The greatest of Dreiser's novels, for Mencken in 1917, are *Jennie Gerhardt*, which portrays a Chicago that epitomizes America, and *The Titan*, which dramatizes the struggle between idealist and naturalist, or spirit and flesh, that constitutes Dreiser's major theme. Dreiser's naturalism, Mencken concludes, is not French but "stems directly from the Greeks."

Contemporary with Mencken's advocacy is the attack by Stuart Pratt Sherman that has become the classic statement for all who disapprove of Dreiser's point of view: "The Naturalism of Mr. Theodore Dreiser" (*Nation*, December 2, 1915; reprinted in his *On Contemporary Literature*, New York, 1917, and in K & S). Sherman finds Dreiser no more courageous than John Bunyan; it is only a matter of what facts are reported. Dreiser's facts are colored; the situations he describes—the want of remorse in Jennie, for example—are improbable. Sherman shows awareness of the contemporary mood, with its opposition to the timorous elders and their illusions, and he acknowledges that the realists have compelled the critic to ask of the artist not "whether . . . [he] has created beauty but whether he has told the truth." Dreiser, however, by treating man as an animal "has deliberately rejected the novelist's supreme task—understanding and presenting the development of character." According to Sherman, "a realistic novel is a representation based upon a theory of human conduct. . . . A naturalistic novel is a representation based upon a theory of animal behavior." Sherman ultimately, in a review of *An American Tragedy*, would argue for Dreiser's greatness, but his assumptions would remain unchanged. An account of his debate with Mencken is provided by Robert Bloom in "Past Indefinite: The Sherman-Mencken Debate on an American Tradition" (*Western Humanities Review*, Winter 1961).

The principal consequence of Sherman's articles was to stimulate controversy and on the whole to lead Dreiser's defenders to strengthen their arguments. No other critic sympathetic with Sherman goes beyond him. At best there is only a scholarly echo, with ethical overtones, in Arthur Hobson Quinn's *American Fiction* (New York, 1936), which takes Dreiser to task for the abnormality of some of his characters, for the excessive dramatization of sexual experiences, for Carrie's having only material aspirations, and for confused moral values. Only *Jennie Gerhardt* is acceptable—because of the "imaginative nature of the heroine and her quiet self-sacrifice."

Most of the critics and literary historians whom one can still read without embarrassment have shared Mencken's assumptions and dwelt on Dreiser's success in using literature to capture life. The differences among them have been differences of emphasis rather than of principle or approach.

Sherwood Anderson, in "Dreiser" (*Little Review*, April 1916; reprinted in his introduction to his *Horses and Men*, New York, 1923, and in his introduction to the Modern Library edition of Dreiser's *Free and Other Stories*, New York, 1925), anticipating Sinclair Lewis's Nobel Prize speech of 1930 (reprinted in K & S), pays tribute to Dreiser as a pioneer for all who would portray life truly, a brave man, "full of respect" for his work and his characters. Randolph Bourne, in "The Novels of Theodore Dreiser" (*New Republic*, April 17, 1915), finds "the stuff of life" in Dreiser's fiction, "a Continental quality," and "a more universal psychology" than American novels contain; and in "Desire as Hero" (*New Republic*, November 20, 1915), occasioned by the publication of *The "Genius,"* he refers to Dreiser as "our only novelist who tries to plumb far below . . . [the] conventional superstructure." Waldo Frank, in a chapter on Chicago in *Our America* (New York, 1919), regards Dreiser's novels as providing "the most majestic monument" of the transition to an industrial civilization; but he also sees that in a character such as Cowperwood there is a "sense of Emptiness"; Dreiser, like Edgar Lee Masters, attacks the past because it is still "emotionally real" and holds Dreiser back "from full bestowal upon the Present." Martin Mac-Collough, in *Letters on Contemporary American Authors* (Boston, 1921), explicitly declares his general agreement with Mencken and, though criticizing Dreiser's deficiencies as craftsman and stylist, considers him "a first-rate artist" because "he has got into every one of his novels, to some degree at least, the two philosophical rhythms that are the distinguishing marks of all great narrative fiction"—the sense of man as a helpless plaything of forces and the reflection that man's lifelong search for self-gratification is "ever unrewarded."

Greater precision, detachment, and breadth of view distinguish Carl Van Doren's "Theodore Dreiser" (*Nation*, March 16, 1921), which dwells on Dreiser's "true peasant simplicity of outlook," his "large tolerance," and his ability to present characters "without malice or excuses." With literary history in mind, Van Doren expands his discussion later, in *The American Novel, 1789–1939* (rev. ed., New York, 1940), noting that Dreiser's attitude was "almost wholly strange to the native tradition," that "Dreiser was the first important American writer who rose from the immigrants of the nineteenth century, as distinguished from those of the seventeenth or eighteenth," and that Dreiser comprehended the new codes. The obscure people of Dreiser's novels, Van Doren states, "take on a dignity from his contemplation of them."

A focus on Dreiser as both a historical figure and something of a historian characterizes Lewis Mumford's *The Golden Day* (New York, 1926), Gorham B. Munson's *Destinations: A Canvas of American Literature since 1900* (New York, 1928), T. K. Whipple's *Spokesmen: Modern Writers and American Life* (New York, 1928; reprinted in K & S), and two essays by British critics, Milton Waldman's "Contemporary American Authors: VII—Theodore Dreiser" (*London Mercury*, July 1926) and G. R. Stirling Taylor's "The United States as Seen by an American Writer" (*Nineteenth Century*, December 1926). Mumford acknowledges Dreiser's "power and reach," describes his characters as wandering about "like dinosaurs in the ooze of industrialism," and finds in the novels evidence of "the total evaporation of values in the modern industrial environment." Munson prizes Dreiser's novels as social documents and sees Dreiser as typifying American youth, motivated by a wish for self-importance and an awareness that the struggle must be ruthless. Whipple, disturbed by stylistic failures, considers the importance of Dreiser's work largely that of social history. Dreiser's observation is what matters. Yet Dreiser's view of his world is, Whipple insists, too one-sided to permit its values to be called into question within the framework of the novels. Waldman finds that Dreiser illuminates the

United States's limitations and the dark avenues of escape; Taylor regards Dreiser's works not as novels but as volumes that belong in the category of *The Origin of Species* and *The Descent of Man*, contemplating Darwin: where Darwin looks for origins, Dreiser looks for the outcome. F. L. Pattee, in *The New American Literature, 1890–1930* (New York, 1930), defines Dreiser's search for this outcome as that of a romantic.

Some of the special preoccupations of the intellectuals between the two world wars are reflected in commentaries published in the thirties. Vernon L. Parrington's "Theodore Dreiser: Chief of American Naturalists," rescued from his lecture notes, in *The Beginnings of Critical Realism in America, 1860–1920* (*Main Currents in American Thought*, III, New York, 1930), declares that Dreiser's significance lies in his having "broken with the group" and sat "in judgment on the group sanctions." Parrington considers Dreiser an agnostic but imbued with "a profound morality—the morality of truth and pity and mercy." Clifton Fadiman, in "Dreiser and the American Dream" (*Nation*, October 19, 1932), traces perceptively the genesis and development of Dreiser's "romantic materialism" and shows how Dreiser's brooding mind is able to transform his observations into "a kind of wild poetry." Better than most, Fadiman understands precisely what change in point of view is represented by *An American Tragedy*, the extent to which Clyde's tragedy is a class tragedy, and the way "the ruin of the victim and the guilt of the victor are seen as the obverse and reverse of the same process." Ludwig Lewisohn, in *Expression in America* (New York, 1932), attributes Dreiser's eminence "to his dealing with sex" and believes that what Dreiser most needs as an artist is to be sustained by "criticism both cordial and severe." V. F. Calverton, in *The Liberation of American Literature* (New York, 1932), like Parrington, praises Dreiser's opposition to middle-class codes, but goes on to say that Dreiser was handicapped by petit bourgeois ideologies unitl he discovered the way out in communism as elucidated in *Tragic America*. A more sensitive Marxist, Granville Hicks, in *The Great Tradition* (rev. ed., New York, 1935), primarily restates Parrington's position; and Herbert J. Muller, in *Modern Fiction: A Study in Values* (New York, 1937), objects to Dreiser's obtrusive moralizing, although he concludes that Dreiser sees life as a magnificent drama and establishes man as an actor worthy of his role in it. It remains for Alfred Kazin, in "The Lady and the Tiger: Edith Wharton and Theodore Dreiser" (*Virginia Quarterly Review*, Winter 1941; reprinted in Kazin's *On Native Grounds*, New York, 1942; and in K & S), to renew Van Doren's description of Dreiser as a peasant and use it to invert Calverton's judgment. Dreiser's circumstances, Kazin argues, enabled Dreiser to learn that "men on different levels of belief and custom were bound together in a single community of desire," and so restricted his experience that "he lavished his whole spirit on the spectacle of the present," finding like "the great peasant novelists . . . Hamsun and Maxim Gorky . . . in the boundless freedom and unparalleled range of naturalism the only approximation of a life that is essentially brutal and disorderly." For Kazin, Dreiser is "one of the great folk writers," one who has given "voice to the Manifest Destiny of the spirit."

Dreiser's death provided the occasion for reconsideration of his position and for briefly renewed debate. Supported in his account of American life by Richard Hofstadter's *Social Darwinism in American Thought, 1860–1915* (Philadelphia, 1944), James T. Farrell sought to establish Dreiser's importance by showing in general essays as well as in analyses of individual novels (cited below) how both biological and social determinism shaped Dreiser's outlook. His general ones, "Theodore Dreiser: In Memoriam" (*Saturday Review of Literature*, January 12, 1946; collected in Farrell's *Literature and Morality*, New York, 1947), "Social Themes in American Realism" (*English Journal*, June 1946; reprinted in Farrell's *Selected Essays*, ed. Luna Wolf, New

York, 1964), and "Theodore Dreiser" (*Chicago Review*, Summer 1946; also reprinted in *Selected Essays*), all relate Dreiser to the cultural and intellectual ferment of the Midwest during the period of capitalist growth and present Dreiser as one who, understanding "the pitilessness and the hierarchical character of capitalist society," could share and dramatize without sentimentalizing the American struggle to fulfill the dream of success or power.

Lionel Trilling, on the other hand, reacting against what he considered uncritical acceptance of Dreiser by a group of contributors to the *Book Find News* (March 1946), issued by the Book Find Club in conjunction with its choice of *The Bulwark* as its March selection, launched a major attack on Parrington and all his intellectual heirs. In "Dreiser and the Liberal Mind" (*Nation*, April 20, 1946; revised and embodied in a larger context in Trilling's *The Liberal Imagination*, New York, 1950; reprinted in K & S), Trilling challenges Parrington's belief that reality and mind are opposed and require enlistment in the "party of reality." Trilling accuses liberals of failure in their doctrinaire acceptance of Dreiser, and contrasts the unsparing liberal criticism of Henry James for his political vices with the liberal translation of Dreiser's literary faults into "social and political virtues." According to Trilling, the equation of peasant qualities with democratic virtues is simply an instance of the American "fear of intellect." What the liberal critics should question is the usefulness of Dreiser's moral preoccupations "in confronting the disasters that threaten us" and the extent to which Dreiser transcends the limits of his time, class, and experience. Dreiser's "nihilism" is simply "showy." Trilling further argues, in "Dreiser, Anderson, Lewis and the Riddle of Society" (*Reporter*, November 13, 1951), that Dreiser resembles Henry Adams in that his "interest in society arises from his self-pity over his exclusion from power; and like Adams, Dreiser transcends his interests in social power . . . to put himself into relation first with cosmic and then with divine power." Dreiser and Sherwood Anderson remain interesting as "late and deteriorated modes of a continuous tendency in American writing, exemplars of the sensitive, demanding, self-justifying modern soul."

Bernard Rosenberg, in "Mr. Trilling, Theodore Dreiser (and Life in the U.S.)" (*Dissent*, Spring 1955), attempts to show that Dreiser's fiction fulfills the requirements for fiction that Trilling exacts of Cervantes and Flaubert. Dreiser understands the cultural realities and explores the implications of "what it means to live in the country of the dollar." Rosenberg might have added that Trilling could affirm the value of intellect and the priority of art the more easily for Dreiser's having labored to make expression freer.

Other recent estimates worth citing have been judicious rather than polemical in tone. Van Wyck Brooks, devoting a chapter of *The Confident Years: 1885–1915* (New York, 1952) to the subject, writes a sympathetic summary of Dreiser's development. He praises Dreiser for his "delight in the banal" that makes *A Hoosier Holiday* "so human and so winning"; he states that Dreiser has "a wonderful ear for the idiom of the people"; he calls attention to Dreiser's "sense of wonder"—and he understands fully the contradictions, paradoxes, and religious themes in Dreiser's life, and precisely how the final days of Dreiser's life should be interpreted. The account is in contrast to Brooks's earlier judgment in *Letters and Leadership* (New York, 1918), in which he complains that Dreiser's characters tell "only of the vacuity of life." Edward Wagenknecht, in *Cavalcade of the American Novel* (New York, 1952), proposes no new theory, but in calling Dreiser a "mystic naturalist" points to a central biographical problem, and is aware of the danger of imposing too schematic a pattern on Dreiser's development. Robert E. Spiller, in a chapter ("Theodore Dreiser") indebted to Farrell in *Literary History of the United States* (New York, 1948), in *The Cycle of American Literature* (New York, 1955), and in "The Alchemy of Literature," *The Third Dimension* (New York, 1965), brings the knowledge and point of view of literary history to enlarge the context of Dreiser's work. Like Farrell, he considers Dreiser's tragedies social tragedies, and like Matthiessen, he treats Dreiser as an organic artist. In addition, he sees Dreiser as the center of the second American Renaissance, the writer who brings the naturalistic movement to a focus in America, and the novelist who discovers in economic and biological necessity "the modern stage on which the eternal battle between man's will and his destiny could be disclosed and understood." Dreiser's works mark "the beginning of a new process of symbolization of actual life." His failure is in lack of aesthetic perspective only. In "the escape from the petty," however, Dreiser produces catharsis.

Concerned with the same issues as those discussed by Spiller, Kenneth S. Lynn, in *The Dream of Success: A Study of the Modern American Imagination* (Boston, 1955), finds that Dreiser's career provides the basic pattern for showing how such writers as Frank Norris, David Graham Phillips, Jack London, and Robert Herrick were molded by the society that believed in the Alger dream of success and accepted the values inherent in that dream, with the result that their critiques of their society entrapped them. Dreiser, dwelling on the struggle to succeed, cannot envisage any outcome but boredom for Carrie, death for Lester Kane, interminable conquests for Cowperwood. Lynn's argument is attractive; yet, even though Dreiser returns to the theme of success in story after story, that fact alone is not the proof of Dreiser's values. After all, Dreiser consistently calls into question the finality of material achievement and seeks a standard by which to condemn it.

What Lynn overlooks Charles Child Walcutt sees: the role of the dialectic in Dreiser's development. In *American Literary Naturalism: A Divided Stream* (Minneapolis, 1956), Walcutt traces the movement of Dreiser's point of view through three stages of naturalism and a fourth stage that is not "naturalism" to show that Dreiser struggles between antithetical premises, inherited from transcendentalism, until he manages to find an affirmation that, because it puts an end to tensions, vitiates his final work. A more favorable view of the process—described in terms of a dialectic between what Dreiser's father and mother represent—is advanced by Kenneth Bernard in "The Flight of Dreiser" (*University of Kansas City Review,* Summer 1960). Here *The Bulwark* is seen as a successful reconciliation: the mother's joyful mysticism and the father's bitter view of fate are harmonized, and Dreiser's end returns to his beginning.

The most penetrating of recent general estimates is Maxwell Geismar's "Theodore Dreiser: The Double Soul," in his *Rebels and Ancestors: The American Novel, 1890–1915* (Boston, 1953). He notes how Dreiser is at once a critic of social institutions and, as artist, a revealer rather than judge of lfe. He understands in precisely what respects Dreiser is both "the last Victorian" and a modern. He indicates the ways in which the "poetry of nature" softens the logic of the philosophers and how Dreiser's philosophy becomes Dreiser's fiction. Like Mencken and Farrell, he admires Dreiser's handling of the economic man—especially in *The Financier*—and calls the achievement "that of a world beyond irony." He believes *The "Genius"* leads into the art novels of the twenties. He gives attention to the minor works—short stories and *Moods*—as well as the major. He relates Dreiser to "the modern symbolists of frustration" and points to a significant ambivalence in Dreiser's subjecting the most defiant characters to the greatest suffering. He concludes, nonetheless, that "the polar contrasts in . . . [Dreiser's] view of experience . . . [give] to his work a sort of marvelous ambiguity," and that "Dreiser can illuminate the vital center in the most obscure or mediocre souls."

Studies of Special Topics

Special topical studies range from examinations of Dreiser's ideas to analyses of his style. All assume that Dreiser is of major importance generally and the most important of American naturalists in particular. Concerning what his naturalism is, however, there is disagreement. Parrington, in "The Development of Realism," in *The Reinterpretation of American Literature*, edited by Norman Foerster (New York, 1928), places Dreiser's naturalism in a category with Zola's and says that it gives expression to the impact of the industrial and scientific revolutions. He considers Dreiser "objective, detached, amoral, never concerned with reform." Oscar Cargill, discussing "The Naturalists" in *Intellectual America* (New York, 1941), goes further and calls Dreiser a nihilist. And Randall Stewart, in "Dreiser and the Naturalistic Heresy" (*Virginia Quarterly Review*, Winter 1958), acknowledging the "vigor" of American naturalism, the "exciting impact of *An American Tragedy*," and Dreiser's power to move the reader, agrees with those who insist that Dreiser should be classed with Zola and Stephen Crane in depriving the individual of all responsibility and subscribing to the materialism of his characters. Stewart, it turns out, does not believe that Dreiser's compassion requires naturalistic premises; he prefers the literary leaders of the South, who have never lost sight of the doctrine of Original Sin.

Others subject Dreiser's naturalism to more discriminating consideration. George Wilbur Meyer, in "The Original Social Purpose of the Naturalistic Novel" (*Sewanee Review*, October–December 1942), sharply distinguishes between Zola's optimistic attempt to improve society and Dreiser's pessimistic fatalism. Malcolm Cowley, in " 'Not Men': A Natural History of Naturalism" (*Kenyon Review*, Spring 1947; reprinted in *Evolutionary Thought in America*, ed. Stow Persons, New Haven, Conn., 1950), points out that the naturalists were not simply observers but also rebels against particular moral codes, and that their objectivity was qualified by their own conflicts and obsessions. Robert W. Schneider, in *Five Novelists of the Progressive Era* (New York, 1965), both explains how the Progressives were caught between the values of the past and the scientific faith in the future and describes how Dreiser, having rejected the notion that man was sufficiently free and creative to make industrialism serve progress, could succumb to his sympathies and voice rebellion. And Donald Pizer, in *Realism and Naturalism in Nineteenth-Century American Literature* (Carbondale, Ill., 1966), likewise emphazing the complexities of naturalism, restates Walcutt's position and goes beyond it to describe two sets of tensions—between the middle-class subjects and the heroic concept of man, and between the role of environment or circumstance and the humanistic value of self-affirmation—which render reductive theories of naturalism simplistic.

Further explications of Dreiser's point of view are found in Edward J. Drummond, S.J., "Theodore Dreiser: Shifting Naturalism," in *Fifty Years of the American Novel*, edited by Harold C. Gardiner, S.J. (New York, 1951); David Brion Davis, "Dreiser and Naturalism Revisited," K & S; Joseph J. Kwiat, "Theodore Dreiser: The Writer and Early Twentieth-Century American Society," *Sprache und Literatur Englands und Amerikas: Lehrgansvorträge der Akademie Coburg*, 1956; Eliseo Vivas, "Dreiser, an Inconsistent Mechanist" (*Ethics*, July 1938); Woodburn O. Ross, "Concerning Dreiser's Mind" (*American Literature*, November 1946); Gerald Willen, "Dreiser's Moral Seriousness" (*University of Kansas City Review*, Spring 1957); J. D. Thomas, "The Natural Supernaturalism of Dreiser's Novels" (*Rice Institute Pamphlets*, April 1957), "The Supernatural Naturalism of Dreiser's Novels" (*Rice Institute Pamphlets*, April 1959), and "Epimetheus Bound: Theodore Dreiser and the Novel of Thought" (*Southern Humanities Review*, Fall 1969); David W. Noble, "Dreiser and Veblen and the Literature of Cultural Change" (*Social Research*, Autumn 1957; reprinted in *Studies in American Culture*, ed. Joseph J. Kwiat and Mary C. Turpie, Minneapolis, 1960); Roger Asselineau, "Theodore Dreiser's Transcendentalism," in *English Studies Today*, edited by G. A. Bonnard (Bern, 1961); H. Alan Wycherley, "Mechanism and Vitalism in Dreiser's Nonfiction" (*Texas Studies in Literature and Language*, Summer 1969); and

Ernest G. Griffin, "Sympathetic Materialism: A Re-reading of Theodore Dreiser" (*Humanities Association Bulletin,* Winter 1969). Davis in particular is helpful in distinguishing between the naturalism of Dreiser and the materialism often attributed to him. Connections between the experiences of Whitman, John Sloan, and Dreiser in their encounter with the turbulent life of the city serve to point up Dreiser's meditative concern, the appeal of the spectacle, his contemplation of misery, and a pietistic love of Being. Both Davis and Vivas understand exactly the sort of will Dreiser affirms in his characters and the way the struggle for harmony between the individual and the cosmos constitutes the substance of Dreiser's vision. Willen's contribution is to relate that struggle to Dreiser's moral preoccupations. Noble's is to suggest that, compared with Veblen, Dreiser is the modern critic; for Veblen accepts Spencer's "belief in an inevitable and controlled progress," whereas Dreiser exposes "the disintegrating social effects of the new industrial order." Griffin, concurring with Davis's definitions and sharing Noble's sense of Dreiser's modernity, provides a perspective that differs from each of theirs. He finds in the novels "something of the new synthesis of evolution and religion . . . which characterizes the work of Teilhard de Chardin" and in their plots and characters significant foreshadowings of the social philosophy of Norman O. Brown and Herbert Marcuse. It is not the "thing-oriented person" whom Dreiser favors but "the one [Frank Cowperwood serves as the principal example] who has a vision of life beyond the material." Dreiser's materialism involves "the feeling and movement of sympathy" that within evolutionary naturalism "allows for the continuity of self."

Dreiser's political views are treated in a variety of ways. Their development is traced in Daniel Aaron's *Writers on the Left: Episodes in American Literary Communism* (New York, 1961). Their relation to his fiction is considered by George J. Becker in "Theodore Dreiser: The Realist as Social Critic" (*Twentieth Century Literature,* October 1955), which examines the record to establish that Dreiser's work was not for him an instrument of social action. Their lack of conformity with orthodox Marxist doctrine is described in the Communists' criticism of Dreiser for his lack of understanding of the rationale and requirements of social commitment: Floyd Dell's "Talks with Live Authors: Theodore Dreiser" (*Masses*, August 1916); Max Eastman's *The Literary Mind: Its Place in an Age of Science* (New York, 1931); Bennett Stevens's "The Gnats and Dreiser" (*New Masses*, May 1932); and Samuel Sillen's "Dreiser's 'J'accuse'" (*New Masses*, January 28, 1941).

Dreiser's dramatization of the role of money, of the idea of success, and of the impact of the city—touched on by Kenneth Lynn and James T. Farrell in the context of their general estimates and surveys of Dreiser's career (see above) —is viewed in a number of useful studies: Blanche H. Gelfant, *The American City Novel* (Norman, Okla., 1954); Walter Blackstock, "Dreiser's Dramatizations of American Success" (*Florida State University Studies No. 14: History and Literature*, 1954), and "Dreiser's Dramatizations of Art, the Artist, and the Beautiful in American Life" (*Southern Quarterly*, October 1962), which is valuable for showing how money and beauty are related in Dreiser's novels; David R. Weimer, "Heathen Catacombs," in his *The City as Metaphor* (New York, 1966); John T. Flanagan, "Theodore Dreiser's Chicago" (*Revue des Langues Vivantes*, Winter 1966), which considers not only Dreiser's attitude but also how factual data were embodied in the fiction; and Jay Martin, *Harvests of Change: American Literature, 1865–1914* (New York, 1967).

Among other special topics, Dreiser's attitude toward the Jews is often alluded to but has never been fully examined. A brief account appears in Sol Liptzin's *The Jew in American Literature* (New York, 1966). More important is Dreiser's use of the seduction theme in his fiction. The moral implications are part of the general criticism advanced by Stuart Pratt Sherman and Arthur Hobson Quinn (indicated above), but the relation of Dreiser's attitude toward it and its meaning for his fiction is considered nowhere so fully as in Leslie Fiedler's *Love and Death in the American Novel* (New York, 1960). Fiedler points out that Dreiser was able to revive the theme for serious literature because, having been nourished by Laura Jean Libby and Ouida, he took it seriously himself. It is the deflowering of the heroines that starts the girls toward alienation; his working girls are the traditionally seduced ones. *Sister Carrie* is "a Portrait of the Artist as a Girl Gone Wrong," and Roberta Alden in *An American Tragedy* is a Clarissa who is prey not to Lovelace but to Horatio Alger. Dreiser, according to Fiedler, was brought up on the kind of book that "made it impossible for him to write convincingly about the act of love." Dreiser's novels, therefore, do not deal with passion.

The issue of Dreiser's style has been mentioned by most of the critics since 1900. Mencken, Matthiessen, Moers, Gerber, Kazin, and Lehan among others already cited, all consider its strengths and weaknesses. Some writers, however, have made it the subject of special study, and of these the following deserve mention: Cyrille Arnavon, "Theodore Dreiser and Painting" (*American Literature*, May 1945), which relates Dreiser's views of specific painters to his artistic aims; Alexander Kern, "Dreiser's Difficult Beauty" (*Western Review*, Winter 1952; reprinted in K & S), which distinguishes style from characterization and the handling of details and states that, despite Dreiser's insensitivity to "sound," his style "often succeeds"; Joseph J. Kwiat, "Dreiser and the Graphic Artist" (*American Quarterly*, Summer 1951), which describes Dreiser's relationship with the members of the Ash-Can school, the extent to which he admired the painters' use of "detail," their "brusqueness and power," their "raw and undecorated masses," and their "solidity of effect," and the way he developed into a portrayer of the spectacle of the city; and "The Newspaper Experience: Crane, Norris, and Dreiser" (*Nineteenth-Century Fiction*,

September 1953), which shows how Dreiser's newspaper assignments brought him into contact with finance and politics and helped him develop from a simple reporter to a writer of feature stories with the focus on human interest; and William L. Phillips, "The Imagery of Dreiser's Novels" (*PMLA*, December 1963), which analyzes complex patterns of imagery found in five of Dreiser's novels and shows how they function to produce rich effects and which also suggests, without imposing a rigid scheme, how Dreiser's shift from the use of sea images to animals and from animals to fairyland reflects his movement from a questioning of nature to acceptance. Neil Leonard's "Theodore Dreiser and the Film" (*Film Heritage*, Fall 1966), examining the development and character of Dreiser's interest in movies as a medium for realistic expression, introduces a new perspective on Dreiser's stylistic preoccupations generally. And Richard Poirier, in *A World Elsewhere: The Place of Style in American Literature* (New York, 1966), concerned with the struggle of American writers since Cooper "to create through language an environment in which the inner consciousness of the hero-poet can freely express itself," shows the extent to which Dreiser "derive[s] his creative energy from a kind of fascinated surrender to the mysterious forces that in the City destroy freedom and even any consciousness of its loss" and the way in which his language defines the significance of that surrender and of the surrender of his characters, who sustain a more meaningful relation "to the scenery of urban energy" than to each other.

Discussions of Individual Works

Sister Carrie, both because of its place in Dreiser's career and because of its merits, is one of the two books of his to have received any substantial attention beyond what is said in the book-length studies about him or the general estimates of his work, and is the first to become the subject of a "study guide," John C. Broderick's *Theodore Dreiser's "Sister Carrie"* (Bound Brook, N.J., 1963). Discussions of its relationship to the works of other writers or to literary movements generally confirm the views of the biographers and critics already cited. Lars Ahnebrink's "Dreiser's *Sister Carrie* and Balzac" (*Symposium*, November 1953), for example, documents an acknowledged influence with details that establish parallels in theme, in spirit, in the rendering of city contrasts and liaisons, in awareness of the limitations of wealth, in some of the characterization, and in the use of reflective passages. Malcolm Cowley, in "Sister Carrie's Brother" and "The Slow Triumph of *Sister Carrie*" (*New Republic*, May 26 and June 23, 1947; reprinted in K & S), views the book's failure in 1900 as "part of a general disaster that involved the whole literary movement of the 1890's," many of whose representative writers he names. And Yoshinobu Hakutani, in "*Sister Carrie* and the Problem of Literary Naturalism" (*Twentieth Century Literature*, April 1967), closely examines the setting, the tone, and the handling of such incidents as Hurstwood's theft to show that Dreiser's mechanism was only halfhearted and that his sensibility was romantic, an interpretation in keeping with Donald Pizer's more general analysis mentioned above. Yet, a different historical classification is possible, and Charles Child Walcutt, in "*Sister Carrie*: Naturalism or Novel of Manners" (*Genre*, January 1968), becomes something of a revisionist in proposing that *Sister Carrie*, although not in the tradition of the well-made novel about the intellectually and ethically trained, actually should be regarded as a novel of manners. He argues that the characters embody the values of their society, that "their problems are typical," that Dreiser does not "challenge the Victorian sexual code" so much as he "describes, and accepts, a very different social order," that finally the book's naturalism "is far more incidental and superficial than its quality as a novel of manners."

The story of Doubleday's so-called suppression of the novel, originally told by Mencken on Dreiser's authority, repeated by Dreiser himself in "The Early Adventures of *Sister Carrie*" (*Colophon*, February 1931; reprinted in the

Modern Library edition of the novel, New York, 1932), and subsequently accepted by all the biographers as reliable, is challenged in Jack Salzman's "The Publication of *Sister Carrie*: Fact and Fiction" (*Library Chronicle*, Spring 1967). Salzman questions whether Mrs. Doubleday shared any responsibility for the firm's decision, and doubts that Frank Norris was the ardent champion of legend—in addition, he proves that no legal contract to publish the book was drawn up until more than a month after the publishers had sought to persuade Dreiser to take the manuscript elsewhere. The questions he poses are reasonable, but refutation of Dreiser and the biographers falls short of conclusive proof. Salzman is more persuasive when, in "The Critical Recognition of *Sister Carrie*: 1900–1907" (*Journal of American Studies*, July 1969), he argues that the critical reaction to the novel was more favorable than what Dreiser recalled and that the British reception to the Heinemann edition provided the lead for American acceptance when Carrie was reprinted in 1907.

Dreiser's sources have also been examined with care. George Steinbrecher, Jr., in "Inaccurate Accounts of *Sister Carrie*" (*American Literature*, January 1952), refers to the original newspaper stories about the events on which Hurstwood's safe robbery is based to show that Elias and Matthiessen are wrong about details and to illustrate how Dreiser's modification of the source material illuminates his methods. Sally L. Tippetts, in "The Theatre in Dreiser's *Sister Carrie*" (*Notes and Queries*, March 1966), establishes that all but two of the sentimental melodramas mentioned in the novel were actually staged and are accurately described and explains why Dreiser's two fabrications are necessary for the plot and the irony.

The evaluation of *Sister Carrie* has been partly in terms of its themes. James T. Farrell, in "James T. Farrell Revalues Dreiser's *Sister Carrie*" (*New York Times Book Review*, July 4, 1943; reprinted in Farrell's *The League of Frightened Philistines*, New York, 1945, and in K & S), emphasizes the importance of its subject, its identification of social forces and correlation of them with human destiny, its recreation of "a sense of an epoch." For Farrell the novel is no "mere document," however; it is "a powerful and tragic story," in which "the role of money" and "the social processes of evil" are displayed. In Dreiser, "evil is social," and "his realism is the realism of social structures." Claude M. Simpson, Jr., in *"Sister Carrie* Reconsidered" (*Southwest Review,* Winter 1959; reprinted with added footnotes as an introduction to the Riverside edition of the novel), after summarizing the familiar story of its publication, points out how Dreiser's preoccupation with documentary detail and his penetration of the "psychology of the derelict" lead to "a documentation of the life of instinct and emotion." Simpson also analyzes the way "the diurnal round and the rhythm of the seasons define the nature of temporal reality" and concentrates on three pivotal scenes to indicate how the chraacters' moral choices reflect Dreiser's own "moral ambiguities." In the reprinted version of the article, the footnotes record some of the manuscript changes made by Dreiser to emphasize these ambiguities. Sheldon N. Grebstein, in "Dreiser's Victorian Vamp" (*Midcontinent American Studies Journal,* Spring 1963), examines the novel as "both the apogee of Victorian prudery and, simultaneously, the beginning of the modern American novel." Carrie is, for him, a Victorian stereotype who "operates within the sphere of naturalistic and iconoclastic pragmatism." He finds Dreiser reticent about sex, bedroom scenes, seductions, and the female form —even about the workings of the forces asserted to be dominant. Like Fiedler, Grebstein is aware that Dreiser requires Carrie to be morally blameless. And James E. Mulqueen, in *"Sister Carrie:* A Modern *Pilgrim's Progress"* (*CEA Critic,* March 1969), sees in the story an ironic inversion of John Bunyan's values. The pilgrimage to the city of wealth, described with occasional military metaphors suggesting the medieval romance, in chapters whose titles are Biblically allusive, gains in significance because of the tension that is created with the accepted Christian point of view, a tension that puts *Carrie* as much in the tradtition of Hawthorne and Melville as in the tradition of Zola.

Julian Markels, William A. Freedman, and Ellen Moers emphasize the artistry of Dreiser's structure, or form, rather than the cogency of his ideas or values. Markels, in "Dreiser and the Plotting of Inarticulate Experience" (*Massachusetts Review*, Spring 1961), argues with considerable success that the real "source of . . . [Dreiser's] power and his meaning for us lies . . . in his method of arranging the episodes of his plots in order to dramatize with perfect coherence that absence of preordained purpose in the universe, and its corollary, the hegemony of chance, of which he speaks so awkwardly in his 'philosophical' writings." Dreiser sees human experience as an unfolding process; the characters adjust to "what is"; Dreiser's structure constitutes his strength. It is only when Dreiser tries to define purpose or dramatize the emergence of consciousness that he fails; hence the failure to make Ames significant: Carrie cannot take up the challenge. Freedman, in "A Look at Dreiser as an Artist: The Motif of Circularity in *Sister Carrie*" (*Modern Fiction Studies*, Winter 1962–3), finds significance in ubiquitous circular patterns: the uses of the rocking chair, the periodic returns of Carrie and Hurstwood, the futile and circular quest by Carrie for happiness, the repetition of events. Freedman regards such movements as re-enforcing the surface action and calls his imposition of the circle only "a metaphoric convenience." Insofar as his discussion helps underscore ironic parallels and contrasts, his approach is useful, but at times his geometry seems to become its own excuse for being. Ellen Moers, in "The Finesse of Dreiser" (*American Scholar*, Winter 1963–4), a partial preview of her book, demonstrates how Dreiser shaped a style from the contrast between the daily life of his brothers and sisters and the fabricated life of popular melodrama to give "form, and even heroism, to the inarticulate." She calls attention to "rhythmic effects," the use of light and color, the contrapuntal effects of speech, and even the finesse with which Carrie's seduction is told. In analyzing this scene she refers to revisions in the manuscripts to show what mistakes Dreiser avoided.

Two other articles supplement or enlarge the analyses of both form and substance. Philip Williams, in "The Chapter Titles of *Sister Carrie*" (*American Literature*, November 1964), adds a note to the analysis of technical effects. He finds that the titles were added at the last moment, after the return of the first typescript, and although he believes that their purpose was to give the book more appeal, he discovers greater significance in their rhythmic regularity, balance, and symbolic emphasis. A more telling discussion, devoted to relating structure to philosophical assumptions, is Christopher G. Katope's "*Sister Carrie* and Spencer's *First Principles*" (*American Literature*, March 1969). Insisting that "Dreiser's art is inseparable from his views of reality," Katope shows the extent to which Spencer's formulation of the "laws" of nature provided Dreiser with a means of giving shape to experience. The "laws of evolution and dissolution formed the primary archetectonic element of the novel" (Carrie's rise and Hurstwood's decline); "the corollary concept of 'forces' helped . . . [Dreiser] solve the problem of character relationships and plot advancement"; the "laws of motion contributed to the rhythmic quality of the novel, and the laws of 'homogeneity' and 'heterogeneity' facilitated the construction of dynamic characterization." Although Katope's interpretation is schematic, it is never reductive, and, carefully documented, it succeeds in placing in accurate perspective much of the discussion of Dreiser's naturalism.

Jennie Gerhardt is the subject of no important essay. The "Trilogy of Desire" fares only slightly better. Lucy Lockwood Hazard's *The Frontier in American Literature* (New York, 1927) considers Cowperwood as a "culminating portrait of the industrial pioneer" and finds that at the end of *The Titan* the hour of triumph is also the hour of decay for the assertive individual: "The superman of industry is . . . a super-puppet. . . ." James T. Farell's review of *The Stoic*, "Greatness of Dreiser Is Attested in Final Novel" (Phila-

A Survey of Research and Criticism

delphia *Sunday Bulletin Book Review,* November 9, 1947),
argues that in "the most swiftly paced of all his novels"
Dreiser "raises the question of man's condition" and succeeds in producing a novel to rank "among the major accomplishments of American literature." Only Walter T. K.
Nugent engages in any scholarly investigation, and he
simply shows, in "Carter H. Harrison and Dreiser's 'Walden
Lucas'" (*Newberry Library Bulletin,* September 1966),
what changes Dreiser has made in the prototype of a minor
character.

The *"Genius"* was widely reviewed when it appeared, but
no reviewer provided an analysis as close as that written by
Joseph S. Auerbach as part of his oral argument before the
Appellate Division of the Supreme Court (First Division)
asking the court to determine whether suppression through
threat of arrest of the publishers should be upheld. Printed
as "Authorship and Liberty" (*North American Review,*
June 1918), it goes beyond its legal purpose to become a re-
vealing exposition of the structure and theme of the novel.
An account of Dreiser's writing of the novel, and of Floyd
Dell's editing of it, appears in Dell's *Homecoming* (New
York, 1933). And the use Dreiser made of the painter
Everett Shinn in creating Eugene Witla and describing
his work is analyzed by Joseph J. Kwiat in "Dreiser's
The 'Genius' and Everett Shinn, the 'Ash-Can' Painter"
(*PMLA,* March 1952). The only other serious analysis that
has been printed in the magazines since 1918 is Walter
Blackstock's "The Fall and Rise of Eugene Witla: Dramatic Vision of Artistic Integrity in *The 'Genius'*" (*Language Quarterly,* Fall–Winter 1966), in which Witla is presented as one who has achieved "responsible selfhood as an
artist," a thematic concern that Blackstock finds "more interesting and dramatically important than the separate
themes of either success or 'varietism.'" Blackstock reads
the novel's conclusion as a demonstration of Witla's liberation "from the bondage of immediacy and pleasure" and his
rise above self-pity to awareness.

Of the many reviews and articles that discuss the books Dreiser published between 1915 and 1925, only a few remain worth consulting: Randolph Bourne's "The Art of Theodore Dreiser" (*Dial*, June 14, 1917), for its explanation of the delight of *A Hoosier Holiday*; Howard Fast's introduction to *The Best Stories of Theodore Dreiser* (Cleveland, 1947), for its brief discussion of Dreiser's critically slighted shorter fiction; and H. L. Mencken's review of *Twelve Men* in the New York *Sun*, April 13, 1919 (reprinted in a pamphlet issued by Boni & Liveright to advertise the book), for its unique understanding that each of the twelve "was a neglected alien in a nation of the undistinguished." The source of one of these sketches—"DeMaupassant, Jr."—is discussed by Max Putzel in "Dreiser, Reedy, and DeMaupassant, Jr." *American Literature*, January 1962; embodied in Putzel's *The Man in the Mirror*, cited earlier). Putzel, in addition, in a footnote not included in his book, indicates that Dreiser's short play, "The Girl in the Coffin," is an adaptation of a story by William Marion Reedy. No other short play of Dreiser's has received any serious consideration, and *The Hand of the Potter*, the subject of impassioned controversy at the time of its production, has escaped disinterested scrutiny until recently: John J. Von Szeliski, in "Dreiser's Experiment with Tragic Drama" (*Twentieth Century Literature*, April 1966), while regarding the play as wretched, examines "Dreiser's ability to create tragedy while deifying Nature." His conclusion that the absence of ethical standards leaves an "unlikely atmosphere for tragic art" is hardly original but has the virtue of adding one more volume of Dreiser's to the discussion of Dreiser's total accomplishment.

Substantially more valuable is an article about a single one of Dreiser's short stories. Donald Pizer, in "Theodore Dreiser's 'Nigger Jeff': The Development of an Aesthetic" (*American Literature*, November 1969), compares the three existing versions of Dreiser's treatment of a lynching to show that between the mid-1890's and the publication of

Free and Other Stories Dreiser's beliefs about art and his practice as a writer evolved from "imposed sentimentality" to "moral polemicism and incipient philosophizing." Most significant is the way Pizer uses textual detail to disclose Dreiser's concern for his role as artist.

An American Tragedy is the work that not only vies with *Sister Carrie* for critical attention but also invites the greatest variety of approaches. Dreiser's use of sources—especially of the Gillette-Brown case—is the subject of Emil Greenberg's unpublished master's essay (New York University, 1936), "A Case Study in the Technique of Realism: Theodore Dreiser's *An American Tragedy*," which documents the extent of Dreiser's dependence on court records and newspaper articles and the way he substituted much of his own boyhood experience for Gillette's, and of John F. Castle's unpublished doctoral dissertation, "The Making of *An American Tragedy*" (University of Michigan, 1952), which provides a full account of what Dreiser could have drawn from the transcripts of the trial and from the press. Facts about the original case are set forth in two articles, and the story of the crime and trial is retold in a book: Edward Radin, "The Original American Tragedy" (New York *Sunday Mirror*, Magazine Section, January 26, 1947); Eleanor Waterbury Franz, "The Tragedy of the 'North Woods'" (*New York Folklore Quarterly*, Summer 1948); and Charles Samuels, *Death Was the Bridegroom* (New York, 1955). "The Ballad of Grace Brown and Chester Gillette" is printed in Harold W. Thompson, *Body, Boots, and Britches* (Philadelphia, 1940). A less direct source, but one that Dreiser mentions in his "I Find the Real American Tragedy" (*Mystery Magazine*, February 1935), is the Carlyle Harris case, originally set forth in *The Trial of Carlyle W. Harris for Poisoning His Wife, Helen Potts, at New York* (New York, 1892) and subsequently, perhaps inspired by Dreiser's allusions, recounted by Charles Boswell and Lewis Thompson in *Surrender to Love: The Carlyle Harris Case* (New York, 1955). Statements by Harris himself are

ing are inseparable, should have exchanged roles. They both, however, he insists, diminish the novelist's role, are indifferent to theme, and belittle conceptual faults. Unfortunately, there the debate stops.

A genetic approach to the evaluation of the book is undertaken by Haskell M. Block in *Naturalistic Tryptich: The Fictive and the Real in Zola, Mann, and Dreiser* (New York, 1970). Although he clearly agrees with the conclusions reached by Warren, his interest is primarily in showing how the naturalistic novelist transforms his sources and what that transformation signifies. Confining himself to a study of *L'Assomoir, Buddenbrooks,* and *An American Tragedy,* Block describes the extent to which the three writers grounded their work in material reality and at the same time imaginatively modified it. "The tensions of freedom and determinism in the naturalistic novel are," he explains, "analogous to the conflicting claims of the fictive and the real." Dreiser's efforts to be faithful to "lived experience," he feels, "offers an example that outrivals even that of Zola or Thomas Mann" and enabled his art to come "closer than that of perhaps any other major novelist of our time to breaking down the antithesis between life and art." It is precisely at that point where *An American Tragedy* transcends the documentary that it is most illuminating of the human condition.

The place of *An American Tragedy* in Western literature is partially explored in Frederick J. Hoffman's "The Scene of Violence: Dostoevsky and Dreiser" (*Modern Fiction Studies,* Summer 1960) and Strother B. Purdy's "*An American Tragedy* and *L'Étranger*" (*Comparative Literature,* Summer 1967). Hoffman proposes that in *Crime and Punishment* and *An American Tragedy* the landscape is both the reflection and the condition of violence and thus signals the increasing impersonality of violence in modern literature, and that Dreiser even more than Dostoevsky comes close to the creation of a modern hero, since Clyde is the victim of nothing specific—"a victim almost totally bound to the circumstances of the controlling scenes." Purdy sees similarities between

contained in his *Articles, Speeches, and Poems,* edited by "Carl's Mother" (Hope Ledyard [pseud.]) (New York, [1893]). An examination of Dreiser's own notes and manuscripts has not yet been made, but a preliminary chapter for the novel, one of nine rejected chapters, appears in *Esquire* (October 1958) as "Background for *An American Tragedy.*"

The early reception of the novel by reviewers, characterized more by their acclaim than by their analysis, illuminates only the state of American literary criticism, not the value of Dreiser's achievement; and although discussions of the style can be found in some of the reviews, and New Humanism becomes an issue in others, they manage merely to blow holes in the wind. More telling is the parody by Corey Ford, as the pseudonymous John Riddell, "Blue-print for Another American Tragedy," in his *Meaning No Offense* (New York, 1927).

The most careful early examination of issues posed by the novel is Albert Lévitt's prize-winning answer to the publisher's question, "Was Clyde Griffiths Guilty of Murder in the First Degree?" (mimeographed, Lexington, Ky., November 1926). Levitt's exegesis, by explaining the distinction between moral and legal questions, helps to define Dreiser's theme and point of view.

Serious consideration of the novel's thematic significance and the quality of its art has been relatively recent. F. O. Matthiessen's biography, Maxwell Geismar's essay, and the books by Ellen Moers and Richard Lehan, already cited, contain the most important discussions, but others are also valuable. Jame T. Farrell characteristically, in "*An American Tragedy*" and "Some Aspects of Dreiser's Fiction" (*New York Times Book Review,* March 6 and April 29, 1945), analyzes the book as "a tragic revelation of social ideals." He finds "the heart of the tragedy . . . in the betrayal of a youth by the ideals of his time." Historically it illustrates how in American realistic writing the theme of success replaces the themes of moral growth, self-discovery, and awareness. Sheldon Norman Grebstein, in "*An American*

Tragedy: Theme and Structure," in *The Twenties*, edited by Richard E. Langford and William E. Taylor (De Land, Fla., 1966), agrees with Farrell insofar as he sees the novel as a story of the American dream, but he emphasizes the irony and the structural devices employed to sharpen it: wordplay, parallels, and the relation of season to weather. He describes Clyde as "a metaphor of human frailty" and Clyde's career as "an arc rather than a rise and fall." Lauriat Lane, Jr., studies a single aspect of Dreiser's technique in "The Double in *An American Tragedy*" (*Modern Fiction Studies*, Summer 1966) and finds Dreiser using the anthropological, psychological, and literary tradition known as the *Doppelgänger* in a way that, though not central, makes many of the novel's central concerns dramatically and symbolically vivid. The relation of symbol to theme and of setting to psychological state is the concern of Richard Lehan's "Dreiser's *An American Tragedy*" (*College English*, December 1963; reprinted in *The Modern American Novel: Essays in Criticism*, ed. Max Westbrook, New York, 1966), which happily avoids attributing premeditation to Dreiser's writing. Less happy but still valuable is Charles L. Campbell's "*An American Tragedy*; or, Death in the Woods" (*Modern Fiction Studies*, Summer 1969), whose thesis is that Dreiser united "the nineteenth and twentieth century versions of the American myth" (the search for the western forest and the hope in the eastward quest) largely under the influence of Thoreau. Insofar as Campbell relates Dreiser's work to the tradition explored by Henry Nash Smith, R. W. B. Lewis, and Leo Marx and can note that where "Thoreau sees the Golden Age constantly being renewed Dreiser presents what is perhaps the most explicit depiction of the corrupted Garden," he contributes to the interpretation of the novel; but insofar as he treats verbal echoes as nearly deliberate transpositions and even something like a floral parade as richly symbolic, he implies that Dreiser composed with both *Walden* and some simplistic formulation of symbolic theory on the desk before him. Probably Irving Howe best summarizes the conclusions

of those who judge *An American Tragedy* to be Dreise[r's] "major achievement." In "The Stature of Theodore Dreise[r]" and "Dreiser and the Tragedy" (*New Republic*, July 25 a[nd] August 22, 1964; reprinted as an afterword in the Sign[et] Classics edition), Howe states that although this book [is] consistent with Dreiser's other work, it reflects changes th[at] are for the good: the prose is more consistent in tone, a[nd] the scope is become "enormous"—"a kind of parable of o[ur] national existence," with Clyde "a powerful representati[on] of our unacknowledged values." Dreiser has solved, How[e] states, "the problem which vexes all naturalistic novelist[s:] how to relate harmoniously a large panorama of realis[m] with a sharply-contoured form." And he analyzes the stru[c]ture and the treatment of episodes to support that jud[g]ment.

If there is any substantial disagreement about Dreiser[s] accomplishment in this novel, it is most responsibly e[x]hibited in Robert Penn Warren's "*An American Tragedy*" (*Yale Review*, October 1962) and Charles Thomas Sam[-] uels's "Mr. Trilling, Mr. Warren, and *An America[n] Tragedy*" (*Yale Review*, June 1964). Warren argues for r[e]garding style as more than words or a matter of details. I[n] *An American Tragedy* "a thousand strands run backwar[d] and forward" and "the logic of character" is transliterate[d] "into a poetry of destiny." The scenes, images, psycholog[y] rhythms, and symbols all contribute to a true and subtl[e] "tragedy of namelessness." In Samuels's opinion, though[,] Warren has simply "rewritten the book." Citing Trilling i[n] support of the argument that a writer's beliefs and his ar[t] are inseparable, he criticizes the inadequacy of Dreiser['s] language, the flatness of his scenes, the unimaginative qual[-] ity of his structure, and the "confusion and dishonesty" o[f] Clyde's moral struggle. Moreover, Dreiser even "fails t[o] particularize the social and economic worlds." Samuels find[s] it ironic that Trilling, whose defense of *Huckleberry Finn* seems to ignore the relation of form to content, and War[-] ren, whose efforts have been to show that form and mean[-]

Camus's and Dreiser's themes and events; for in both the story of Meursault and the story of Clyde there is an anomalous crime, ambiguity of guilt, and the aloneness of man in an indifferent universe, with society organized to pretend it is all untrue. In both stories the central character is passive, representative of humanity and yet isolated from it, a true twentieth-century man, a victim of his own act.

Additional light is shed on the implications of the book by articles concening its dramatization and filming. Two that have particular biographical and critical relevance are John C. Wentz's "*An American Tragedy* as Epic Theater: The Piscator Dramatization" (*Modern Drama*, February 1962) and Sergei M. Eisenstein's discussion of his adaptation of the text, in his *Essays in Film Theory*, edited by Jay Leyda (New York, 1949).

Useful articles or essays about all Dreiser's later works except *The Bulwark* are confined to Newton Arvin's review of *Dawn*, "An American Case History" (*New Republic*, August 5, 1931), relating Dreiser's life and values to his fiction; Stuart Chase's "Mr. Dreiser in a China Shop" (*New York Herald Tribune Books*, January 24, 1932) and Edmund Wilson's "Equity for Americans" (*New Republic*, March 30, 1932), disagreeing about *Tragic America* and the significance of its inaccuracies; Sulamith Ish-Kishor's introduction to Dreiser's *Moods: Philosophical and Emotional, Cadenced and Declaimed* (New York, 1935), an authorized interpretation of one of Dreiser's favorite books; and Robert Palmer Saalbach's introduction to his edition of Dreiser's *Selected Poems*, already cited, in which he demonstrates that one can find in the poetry as in the rest of Dreiser's work a merging of mechanism with a sense of wonder, to be accepted humbly and hopefully. But none of these substantially fills any corner of a critical void.

Most of the articles about *The Bulwark* relate to Dreiser's use of Quaker sources or the relation of Quaker philosophy to his own. His literary indebtednesses, most of them either directly or indirectly to Rufus M. Jones, are ably set forth in Carroll T. Brown, "Dreiser's *Bulwark* and Philadelphia Quakerism" (*Bulletin of the Friends Historical Association,* Autumn 1946); Gerhard Friedrich, "Theodore Dreiser's Debt to Woolman's Journal" (*American Quarterly,* Winter 1955), "A Major Influence on Theodore Dreiser's *The Bulwark*" (*American Literature,* May 1957), "The Dreiser-Jones Correspondence" (*Bulletin of the Friends Historical Association,* Spring 1957); and Griffith Dudding, "A Note Concerning Theodore Dreiser's Philosophy" (*Library Chronicle,* Winter 1964). The role of Quakerism in *The Bulwark,* and the relation of *The Bulwark* to Dreiser's central concerns, are analyzed in Granville Hicks, "Theodore Dreiser" (*American Mercury,* June 1946); Dustin Heuston, "Theodore Dreiser: Naturalist or Theist?" (*Brigham Young University Studies,* Winter 1961); and Sidney Richman, "Theodore Dreiser's *The Bulwark:* A Final Resolution" (*American Literature,* May 1962). Characteristics that link the novel with "the simplicity of Aeschylean tragedy and The Book of Job" are discussed in Jonas Spatz, "Dreiser's *Bulwark:* An Archaic Masterpiece," in *The Forties: Fiction, Poetry, Drama,* edited by Warren French (De Land, Fla., 1969); Spatz finds in Solon Barnes's career an encounter with reality that leads beyond disillusion to the discovery of "new meaning in the Quaker instruction to annihilate the self and to love all things." There is agreement that this novel marks the end of naturalism—or shows Dreiser's lack of connection with the literary developments of the forties—and confirmation of what Elias and Marguerite Tjader say in their books: that it is also the culmination of Dreiser's search for harmony.

Foreign

Sigmund Skard's *American Studies in Europe: Their History and Present Organization* (Philadelphia, 1958) shows that Dreiser is not either extensively or intensively studied in Western Europe and that his standing in Eastern Europe fluctuates with political conditions. Nonetheless, scholarly work has been undertaken, both in Europe and in the Orient, and although it contributes little to what has been known and accepted in the United States, it provides a new perspective for evaluating Dreiser's position in world literature. Critical surveys of some of the material available are Carl R. Anderson, *The Swedish Acceptance of American Literature* (Philadelphia, 1957); Anne M. Springer, *The American Novel in Germany: A study of the critical reception of eight American novelists between the two world wars* (Hamburg, 1960); and Deming Brown, *Soviet Attitudes Toward American Writing* (Princeton, N.J., 1962). A bibliographical guide is *Russian Studies of American Literature: A Bibliography*, edited by Clarence Gohdes, compiled by Valentina A. Libman, and translated by Robert V. Allen (Chapel Hill, N.C., 1969).

In Sweden, Anderson points out, Dreiser's work was regarded throughout the twenties as a formidable contribution to world literature, but even after the translation of *An American Tragedy* remained second to the work of Sinclair Lewis. Generally, the Swedish critics favored American authors who most sharply exposed American deficiencies. Ruben Gustafsson Berg, in *Moderna Amerikaner* (Stockholm, 1925), expresses a typical view when, after describing Dreiser's tolerance, aversion to moral codes, love of life, interest in individuals, and peasant-like qualities, he praises primarily Dreiser's portrayal of American paltriness. A more recent critic and better-known writer, Artur Lundkvist, in *Tre Amerikaner: Dreiser-Lewis-Anderson* (Stockholm, 1939), calls Dreiser "a romantic naturalist"—as distinct from Sinclair Lewis, the "realistic idealist," and Sherwood Anderson, the "romantic mystic"—but is less interested in the "romantic" than in Dreiser's opposition to moral dogma, his success in portraying the tragedy of American society, and his feeling for "reality." By comparison, what one finds in Denmark is simplistic. Frederik Schyberg, in *Moderne Amerikansk Litteratur, 1900–1930* (Copenhagen, 1930), dwells surprisingly almost entirely on Dreiser's pessimism, concern with facts, and antipuritanism. It is in Norway that there has emerged a more sensitive understanding of what Lundkvist refers to as "romantic." Nils Hellesnes, in "Theodore Dreiser" (*Syn og Syn*, March 1947), points out that there is a duality in Dreiser. There is not only insistence on lack of absolute meaning or on amorality; there is also a lyrical flight, zest, a sense of wonder. The search for beauty is as important as biological necessity.

In Germany, Mrs. Springer's book shows, Dreiser, unavailable in German until after the American success of the *Tragedy*, never equaled the appeal of Lewis or Jack London. His anticlerical and pro-Soviet views interfered with his popularity, while his naturalism seemed belated to avantgarde critics. Two full-length studies since World War II, however, signify a new interest. Karl-Heinz Wirzberger's *Die Romane Theodore Dreisers* (Berlin, 1955), reflecting orthodox East German thinking, traces Dreiser's development from individualistic critic of monopoly to Soviet sympathizer. Wolfgang Staab's *Das Deutschlandbild Theodore Dreisers* (Mainz, 1961), with a less politically motivated West German orientation, is only incidentally interested in noting Dreiser's criticism of America. Staab's subject is the development of Dreiser's view of Germany, which he finds first shaped by Dreiser's impressions of his strict father and his earliest encounters with teachers and priests, then modified by his reading of German literature and philosophy, and by his travels in Germany, and finally further modified by World War II. Staab does not limit his evidence to the few explicit statements available: he studies the events in Dreiser's life and the characters, most of them minor, in Dreiser's fiction. In interpreting Dreiser's views of Nazi Germany, Staab understands precisely how they should be related to Dreiser's view of capitalism more generally. Of more restricted value is *Das Bild New Yorks im Erzählwerk von Dreiser und Dos Passos* (Munich, 1967), by Renate Schmidt-von Bardeleben, who relates Dreiser's treatment of New York to his desire "to give a picture of conditions," a picture full of the color, wonder, and struggle that American history texts have come to label "the lure of the city." *Sister Carrie*, in juxtaposition with *Manhattan Transfer*, receives the major emphasis; but the other novels and many of the short stories, as well as Dreiser's own responses, are given seriatim consideration.

The Soviet work on Dreiser, largely journalistic but devoted, has helped perpetuate his reputation on the Continent. The party's critics have consistently valued Dreiser's exactitude in the use of physical and psychological details, his social concern, and his "growth." In the late twenties and throughout the thirties one finds with equal consistency criticisms of his petit bourgeois individualism and the limits imposed on his objectivity by his heritage and milieu. With his application for membership in the Communist party, however, his career was reviewed: his whole life was seen as one of inexorable, ideological growth, and biographers like Elias who seem to raise questions about the depth or rigidity of Dreiser's commitment were vilified as obscurantists and inverterate falsifiers. During the Stalin years any judgments resembling those of 1928 or 1929 were untenable. Dreiser's great achievements are "Ernita," *Tragic America,* and *America Is Worth Saving.* Nonetheless, the consequence was to make Dreiser's works, usually furnished with critical introductions, accessible to all who read, and in 1951 a twelve-volume edition of his collected works was oversubscribed. Some of the volumes were also made available in English, and three books about Dreiser followed: Yasen N. Zasurskiĭ and Roman Samarin, *Teodor Draĭzer v Bor'be Protiv Amerikanskogo Imperializma* (Moscow, 1952); Zasurskiĭ, *Teodor Draĭzer: Pisatel i Publitsist* (Moscow, 1957), and *Teodor Draĭzer* (Moscow, 1964). The first is wholly polemical, using quotations from Dreiser to point up the evils of capitalism and American imperialism and to represent Dreiser as one who has finally understood the basic contradictions in capitalist society. The second is less polemical in tone, and more thorough as a study of Dreiser, but it considers Dreiser's development primarily in terms of his understanding of the need to use revolutionary power against capitalism. The tone of the third book, an ambitious expansion of the second, is considerably refined, and no American biographers or critics are assailed; yet, Zasurskiĭ makes no distinction between fiction and the various categories of non-fiction. All the writings exemplify the "evolutionary development of the writer's method"; all are realistic (therefore, good); each work is an advance over its predecessor; the trip to Russia is the turning point in Dreiser's career. Yet, because in connection with *Dreiser Looks at Russia* an old criticism of Dreiser's naive contradictions and limitations reappears, one may wonder whether another general revaluation is imminent.

French critics and scholars are agreed that Dreiser is the chief American naturalist, but they differ in what is important about him. Régis Michaud, in *Le roman américain d'aujourd'hui: Critique d'une civilisation* (Paris, 1926), translated by him as *The American Novel of Today: A Social and Psychological Study* (New York, 1928), urges that the social novelist not be allowed to obscure the psychological one. Charles Le Verrier, in "Un grand romancier américain: Théodore Dreiser" (*Revue Hebdomadaire*, January 21, 1933), foresees that despite Dreiser's struggle to reconcile a profound individualism with socialism, circumstances are moving him toward communism, and therefore places his emphasis there. Pierre Brodin, *Les écrivains américains du Vingtième siècle* (Paris, 1947), and Jean Simon, *Le Roman Américain au XXe siècle* (Paris, 1950), constitute but standard summaries. Cyrille Arnavon, whose article on "Theodore Dreiser and Painting" is cited above, is finally the only one to have written a book-length study of Dreiser in French, *Théodore Dreiser: Romancier Américain* (Paris, 1956). Prepared almost entirely in 1945, it is unable to take advantage of material available at the time of its publication; nevertheless perceptive, comprehensive, and fair, it acknowledges Dreiser's gaucheries, praises his characterization, and concludes that although Dreiser may be a seeker,

412

he has remained constant as a novelist. His importance lies in his restoring attention to the American scene when James and Wharton were looking at Europe, in renewing the European tradition of documenting life, in attacking bourgeois reticence, and in making possible the postwar literature. Asselineau's article on Dreiser's transcendentalism has been already alluded to. Marianne Debouzy's "Théodore Dreiser" (*Langues Modernes,* March–April 1966) expounds a view of Dreiser's accomplishment that substantially accords with that of James T. Farrell and Robert E. Spiller.

Italian scholarship, though not prolific, has been somewhat more original. Rolando Anzilotti, in "Theodore Dreiser: Le Fonte e il Metodo de Romanziere" (*Rassegna Lucchese,* June 1966), while reviewing the kinds of literary influences that affected Dreiser's work, touches on a relationship hitherto neglected. He quotes from an unpublished part of *A Traveler at Forty* to show that Dreiser admired Henry James, and uncovers a manuscript among Dreiser's papers that testifies to Dreiser's intention at one time of drawing on *Roderick Hudson* and *The Wings of the Dove* for a description of Berenice Fleming. In "Il Viaggio di Dreiser in Italia," *Studi Americani* 12 (ed. Agostino Lombardo, Rome, 1966), Anzilotti, recounting Dreiser's visit to Italy early in 1912, makes other unpublished material available by appending thirty-four pages of what Dreiser called "the woman stuff" that was cut from *A Traveler at Forty* before publication. Offering no such new material, but centering attention on the Dreiser too often overlooked in Europe—the Dreiser interested in Thoreau, sympathetic with John Woolman, preoccupied with cosmic design—Francesco Binni, in "Dreiser oltre il Naturalismo," *Studi Americani* 11 (1965), proceeds to discuss *The Bulwark* as evidence of a fundamentally antimodern rebellion by Dreiser, and concludes that this novel stands singularly detached from the literary movement that Dreiser helped create. Although an argument that leaves one with a curiously divided author may be less than convincing, Binni's sensitivity to some of

413

Dreiser's deepest concerns is sufficiently developed to give his presentation value.

Japanese scholarship concerning Dreiser is relatively recent. A short book about him was, to be sure, published in Tokyo in 1933, *Theodore Dreiser*, by Matsuo Takagaki, but it was intended only as an introduction to Dreiser and does little more than present him as a witness of American capitalist development, with a sensitivity to social developments and a curiosity about the ultimate meaning of being. His socialism is explained as the result of his experiences and especially of his trip to the Soviet Union in 1927. Later articles are more analytic. Atsuko Takashima, in "A Study of Theodore Dreiser's Thought" (*Ei-bei Bungaku Hyoron*, Summer 1959), written in English, traces the career of Dreiser's point of view to explain how he moved from his early celebration of the earth-bound life to his later affrmation of the Inner Light. Makoto Nagahara, in "Dreiser at the Turn of the Century—*Sister Carrie*" (*Ritsumeikan Bungaku*, February 1963), examines Dreiser's early fiction to find there the beginnings of his consciousness ;of the meaning of money in society. And Shōhei Satō, in "The World of Theodore Dreiser" (*Gakuen*, April 1963), discusses the tensions between Dreiser's materialism and mysticism and how they relate to his development. Despite the dilemmas, he concludes, and despite the want of humor or a polished style, Dreiser wrote of life fairly and with sympathy, and saw the substance of Man.

In India the study of Dreiser is just beginning. R. N. Mookerjee, whose survey of the University of Pennsylvania manuscripts has already been noted, has completed a dissertation that is promised for publication in 1970 under the title *Theodore Dreiser: Social Critic*. Nothing else about Dreiser has appeared, but other dissertations are in progress. One hopes that Asian perspectives will contribute new perceptions rather than simply restate what has already been said in the United States.

Index

In this index the subheadings are arranged according to order of entry, with the minor page references last, except that Dreiser's writings are listed alphabetically after the biographical subheadings under his name.

Index

417

Index

Index

Dreiser, Theodore (*continued*)
tures, 76–8; first visit to New
York, 79–80; returns to Pittsburgh, 80; reads Tyndall, Huxley, and Spencer, 80–2; blown
to bits intellectually, 82–3; in
New York at last, on *World*,
83–7; more disillusionments,
84–5; considers writing fiction,
85–6; financial difficulties, 86;
rejects newspaper work, 87;
edits *Ev'ry Month*, 88–94; resigns from *Ev'ry Month*, 94–5;
free-lance writer for magazines,
95–102; marries Sallie White,
96; influenced by Arthur Henry,
102–9; writes first acceptable
short stories, 104–6; writes *Sister Carrie*, 106–9; publication
and failure of *Sister Carrie*,
110–16; begins *Jennie Gerhardt*, 116; discouragement,
117; visits Henry at Noank,
118–21; sells character sketches,
121; failure to write second
novel, 121–5; writes articles
about misfortune, 122, 125;
despair, 125–9; at Muldoon's,
129–30; works on New York
Central Railroad, 129, 130–1;
assistant editor of *New York
Daily News*, 131–2; writes local
color sketches, 132; editor for
Street & Smith, 133–5; edits
Hampton's *Broadway Magazine*,
135–6, 138–9; *Sister Carrie* reissued, 136–8; edits *Delineator*,
139–50; edits *Bohemian*, 146–
8; marital difficulties, 149–50;
risks of a scandal, 150; resigns
from *Delineator*, 150; completes *Jennie Gerhardt*, 151–2,
154; completes first draft of
The "Genius," 154–6; begins
The Financier, 157–9; travels
abroad, 159–62; completes *The
Financier*, 162–4; "The Lost
Phoebe," *The Bulwark*, *A Traveler at Forty*, 166–7; writes *The*

Dreiser, Theodore (*continued*)
Titan, 168–71; publishing difficulties, 174–5; revises *The
"Genius,"* 176–8, 179; writes
one-act plays, 179–81; concerned with cosmic and chemic
forces, works on *The Bulwark*
and *A History of Myself*, 181–
2; endorses other writers, 182–
3; interested in moving-picture
company, 183, 186; passive
sympathy for misfortune, 184–
5; visits childhood haunts, 185–
6; begins *A Hoosier Holiday*,
writes play and poems, 186–7;
reception of *The "Genius,"*
187–9; completes *A Hoosier
Holiday*, 189; *The "Genius"*
suppressed, 193–202; legal frustrations, 202; financial difficulties, 202–3, 207–8; criticizes
society, 203–4; *The Hand of
the Potter*, 204–7; writes "Free"
and other stories, 208–10;
Twelve Men, 210–11; *Hey,
Rub-a-Dub-Dub, A Book about
Myself, The Color of a Great
City*, etc., 211–12; interest in
science, 213–16; advocates freedom of thought, 216–17; three
years in California, 217–18; begins *The Stoic*, 218; writes *An
American Tragedy*, 218–23; financial rewards, 225–6; criticizes middle-class standards,
226–8; travels to Europe, 227;
visits U.S.S.R., 231–5; defends
Soviet experiment, 235–7; continued interest in science, 238–
41; defends U.S.S.R. against
"religionists," 242–3; tours
U.S.A., 244–5; criticizes industrialists, supports Communists,
244–6; unorthodox Marxist,
246–8; versus Hollywood (*An
American Tragedy*), 248–50;
slaps Sinclair Lewis, 250; heads
National Committee for the
Defense of Political Prisoners,

419

Dreiser, Theodore (*continued*)
"Art Work of Irving R. Wiles," 97[22]
"As a Realist Sees It," 182[13]
"As If in Old Toledo," 67[6]
"Barcelona in August," 270[4]
"Benjamin Eggleston, Painter," 96–7[21]
"Black Diva's Concert, The," 54[14]
"Bloodshed May Result," 58[24]
"Blue Sphere, The," 179–80
Book about Myself, A, 208, 212, 216[61], 218; see also *History of Myself, A* (below)
"Born Thief, The," 183
"Bowery Mission, The," 146
"Brandywine the Picturesque," 97[26]
Bulwark, The: plans for, 166; writing of, 181, 186, 189, 193, 203, 208, 269, 290–9; editing of, 299–300, 307; anachronisms in, 300; analysis, 300–2, 304; mentioned, 308
"Burned to Death," 52[9]
"Butcher Rogaum's Door," 105–6
"Carrier Pigeons in War Time," 98[29]
"Cat Became Woolly, The," 76[13]–7
"Chains," 209[34], 210
Chains, 208–10, 212[44], 226, 228[22]
"Challenge to the Creative Man," 263[77]
"Charity Teams Chosen," 58[24]
"Chicago Drainage Canal, The," 100–1[39]
"Chicago Packing Industry, The," 100–1[39]
"Child and the School, The," 259[57]
"Christmas in the Tenements," 122
"City of Crowds, The," 134–5, 135[9]

Dreiser, Theodore (*continued*)
Color of a Great City, The, 100[36], 123–4, 126[26], 132[32-7], 134–5[7], 135[9], 147–8[53], 212[51]; see also *Idylls of the Poor* (below)
"Color of Today, The," 121[6]
Concerning Dives and Larazus [*sic*], 273[20]
Concerning Our Helping England Again, 275[29]
"Concerning Us All," 141–2, 142[36], 143[40]
"Confound the Mosquito," 76[13]–7
"Convention," 212[44]
"Cosmopolitan Camp, A," 58[25]
"Country Doctor, The," 210–11
"Cradle of Tears, The," 132[34], 132[36]
Credos, 239–41, 288–9[28]
"Cripple Whose Energy Gives Inspiration, A," 121[6]
"Culhane, the Solid Man," 210–11
"Curious Shifts of the Poor," 100[35], 107, 122
Dawn, 246; see also *History of Myself, A* (below)
Dawn Is in the East, The, 273
"Descent of the Horse, The," 98[30]
"Doer of the Word, A," 121[6]
"Dream, The," 183
Dreiser Looks at Russia, 236–7, 250–1
"Dying Lips Failed," 76[13]–7
Editor & Publisher, 274[23]
"Election of Officers," 58[22]
"Equity between Nations," 270[4]
"Esther Norn," 212[45]
"Factory, The," 146
"Fakes," 41–2[8]
"Fenced off the Earth," 76[13]–7
"Fighting Now the Fad," 58[28]

Index

Index

Index

429

Index

Index

Rockefeller, John D., 190
Roosevelt, Franklin D.: promises open hearing on Kentucky indictment of TD, 257; TD supports (1936), 264; TD confers with, concerning aid to Spain, 270; TD opposes, 270–5; TD again praises, 296
Roosevelt, Theodore: and TD's child rescue campaign, 142; mentioned, 267
Rose, Chauncey, 6
Rosenfeld, Paul, 251
Rosenthal, Elias, *Theodore Dreiser's "Genius" Damned*, 200
Russell, Sol Smith, 53
Russia, *see* Union of Soviet Socialist Republics
Russian ballet, 232, 237
Russo-German pact, 272
Rykov, Alexei, 233

St. Benedict, Church of (Terre Haute): TD attends school at, 15–16; mentioned, 3
St. Boniface Cemetery, 31
St. Louis: TD's work in, ch. iii; mentioned, 122
St. Louis Globe-Democrat: TD hears about, 41; TD works for, 43–56; opinion of TD, 61
St. Louis Republic, TD works for, 44, 50–1, 56–64
San Francisco: library bans *The "Genius,"* 196; TD and Bohemian group, 217; TD aids Tom Mooney, 244
Sandison, George H., 98
Sanger, Margaret, 215
Savannah (Ga.), TD writes *A Hoosier Holiday* in, 189
Schopenhauer, Arthur, 39
Schuler, Eric, 199
Schumann-Heink, Ernestine, 147
Schwab, Charles M., 134
Science: TD's interest in, 181–2, 212–16, 237–42, 243–4, 285–90; *see also* Fort, Charles; Haeckel, Ernst; Huxley, Thom-

Science (*continued*)
as H.; Loeb, Jacques; Spencer, Herbert; Tyndall, John
Scott, Evelyn, 264, 271
Scottsboro case, 252
Scribner's Magazine, 85
Seattle Post-Intelligencer, opinion of *Sister Carrie*, 115
Sedgwick, Ellery, 201
"Serious Side of Burlesque, The," 134
Seven Arts, 203
Shay, Felix, 200
Shay, Frank, 208
Sherman, Stuart Pratt: attacks TD's naturalism, 188; praises *An American Tragedy*, 225
Shinn, Everett, 155
Simon & Schuster, 269, 290
Sinclair, Upton, 267, 275
Sing Sing prison, 220
Smart Set: TD's opinion of, 182; mentioned, 140, 158, 168, 186
Smiles, Samuel, TD's reading of *Self-Help*, 21
Smith, Alfred E., 229
Smith, Ormond G., 133
Smith, T. R., 210
Smith, William Neil, 146
Smith's Magazine: TD edits, 134–5; mentioned, 136
Sothern, E. H., 53
Soviet Russia Today, 295
Spain: TD and the outbreak of civil war, 268, 290; TD's Loyalist sympathies, 269–70; TD visits, 270; TD seeks aid for civilians, 270
Spectator, 121
Spencer, Herbert: TD's reading of *First Principles*, 80–3; cited by TD, 90; mentioned, 39, 155, 177, 185
Stalin, Joseph V., 233, 266, 296, 306
Standard, 136
Stanislavsky, Konstantin S., 232
Steffens, Lincoln, 184, 251

433

Index

434

Index